THE EVEREST HOUSE
Complete Book
of Gardening

The Everest House
Complete Book of Gardening

JACK KRAMER

Everest House Publishers
NEW YORK

LIBRARY OF CONGRESS CATALOGING IN PUBLICATION DATA:
Kramer, Jack, 1927-
   The everest house complete book of gardening.
   Includes index.
   1. Gardening. I. Title.
SB453.K717   1980   635   79-51198
ISBN: 0-89696-041-2

PUBLISHED BY EVEREST HOUSE, PUBLISHERS, NEW YORK
PUBLISHED SIMULTANEOUSLY IN CANADA BY
BEAVERBOOKS, DON MILLS, ONTARIO
MANUFACTURED IN THE UNITED STATES OF AMERICA
FIRST EDITION
RRD1082

Contents

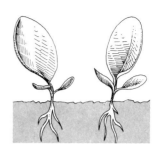

ACKNOWLEDGMENTS

I have had a great deal of help and cooperation from many people in the gardening area while doing this book and I would like especially to thank Elinor Trowbridge, Peggy Macneale, Rachel Snyder of *Flower Grower Magazine*, Charles Marson, and Charles Marden Fitch. I also want to express appreciation to the many landscape architects and homeowners who allowed us to photograph their gardens in St. Louis, Missouri; Chicago, Illinois; Richmond, Virginia; Denver, Colorado; San Francisco, California; Los Angeles, California, and New York City.

To the many agricultural experts of various counties and plant societies and the United States Department of Agriculture, an overall thank-you for your time and cooperation. To the following companies for their assistance, my grateful acknowledgment: Burpee Seed Company, California Redwood Association, George W. Park Seed Company, Wayside Gardens, and Western Wood Products.

Many people, avid gardeners, helped me by answering questions about their gardens and my thanks to them, especially Andrew Addkison who gardens on a full acre of land and to Roger Scharmer, landscape architect, who gave freely of his information on planning garden sites. To Roy Crafton, a special vote of thanks for researching plant lists and compiling difficult descriptive data for me and finally once again to Judy Smith—my sincere thanks for typing and retyping the many plant names.

In closing, I had the pleasure of working with my dear friend Helen Van Pelt Wilson who did most of the editing and helped encourage me as the book progressed. Always, my thanks to her.

Preface

IF YOU GARDEN on one acre or one square foot of land, you will at one time or another need some help. If you are the average gardener you have trees, shrubs, flowers, maybe some vegetables and herbs. If you live in the city or country you may have a patio garden, a backyard garden, a garden in the air, or only a small kitchen garden. No matter—this book covers gardening in many, many ways for beginner or experienced tiller of the soil.

A comprehensive gardening book is never done alone or in a given period of time—it is actually an accumulation of facts and first-hand doing over many years. I have written many gardening books but in this one I have tried to include all facets of gardening—an overall book for all people. I have included everything I ever wanted to know about gardening and everything I hope you'll need to know about working with the soil.

Whenever possible I have used as a reference for botanical plant names *Hortus III* but in some cases I have opted for the more common spellings one finds in suppliers' catalogs.

Because gardening is regional, there are many lists of plants with temperature requirements so that you can select those which will suit your conditions. In addition there are sections on specific regions written by experts who live in those areas. There are drawings to guide you along the garden path and photographs to stimulate you, and, I hope, good old-fashioned advice to make your plants grow-a-plenty.

In addition to dozens of garden plans there is information about plants themselves—general rather than technical but enough data to help you know plants and thus to know gardens.

In sum, this is a how-to and help-you book to assure that your garden grows and is a comfort to you and a thing of beauty. A garden has been such to me for two decades and can be for you, too.

THE EVEREST HOUSE
Complete Book of Gardening

1

A Garden for You

THE WORD *garden* means many things to many people. Some gardeners want a cutting garden, others like an ornamental garden of shrubs and trees, and many people prefer the colorful annual and perennial flower gardens for dramatic landscape effect. There are formal gardens—elegant—and there are natural gardens where wildflowers abound and native plants grow. There are water gardens and patio gardens and roof gardens. But no matter what kind of garden you have, the plants in it depend upon soil and climate. These are the key governing factors of gardening—along with, of course, care of plants.

To garden successfully, you need to know something about soil, how plants grow, and climate, and we look at these things later. Here, however, we are concerned with the kinds of gardens and what they can or cannot offer and how to determine just at the start what kind of garden your property is suitable for. The site, many times, and climate, dictate what kind of garden to have.

THE FLOWER GARDEN

This type of garden is actually a combination of flowers and ornamental plants such as sturdy shrubs and background trees. This garden is not for cutting (that is a separate garden). The flower garden, and it is a popu-lar one, is desirable because it provides color. Imagine gazing out your window at fire-red impatiens or cascading white petunias against a green backdrop. The other reward is bringing these plants to perfection.

The planning of the flower garden is not that difficult and does not necessarily require professional help (unless you have acres of land). Here we are talking about an average cultivated garden of 20 x 40 feet, or in essence about an 80-square-foot area that may be rectangular, square, or even arc-like in design. It is a garden to frame and emphasize the property and to provide visual beauty, and there are many ways of laying it out.

Sketches and Layouts

The best way to proceed is to sketch possible layouts on a piece of graph paper. You don't have to be an artist to do this. Just walk off the available area and draw the rectangle or square or whatever form you have on the paper or, to be more accurate, make rough measurements with a tape or yardstick. Next indicate some shapes—round ones for shrubs, branched drawings for trees—wiggles for flower beds. The idea is to indicate mass and balance on your sketch.

Indicate each area—trees, shrubs, annuals, perennials—with a lead pencil or colored crayon. Make one area light, another

Small but exquisitely landscaped, this garden consists of flowers, shrubs, and trees in excellent proportion to the site. (Ken Molino)

This flower garden is a perfect adjunct to the small house. The flower beds along the fence and house are resplendent with annuals, perennials, and bulbs—a handsome foil for the green lawn. One large shade tree presides. (Photo by Molly Adams)

medium dark, a third very dark, and so on. You want to visualize mass and dimension and your simple sketches will help you.

After you have a sketch that suits you, select your plants. Write in names of trees and shrubs and flowers.

The first consideration is that the garden be in sun; without sun few plants bear flowers. For beauty you want the garden some distance from the house so there is visual dimension (like looking at a painting), not close to it as you would a cutting or kitchen garden. You can, of course, just select an area, put plants in the ground, and have a flower garden, but it is far more prudent to plan it first using simple sketches. Chart the

area on paper and then fill in with groups of flowers. Make circles or oblongs for these areas. Then put in shrubs with another marking—perhaps a star—and then put in new trees (or existing ones) with another designation, perhaps an outlined little box. The idea is to achieve a balance of shapes so the garden is pleasing to the eye, and you can do this with simple rough shapes as described—you do not have to be an artist.

One of the main considerations with flower gardens (after the balance and unity elements) is how the flowers are placed in groups. Put in a large group of lupines, not just a plant or two; create drifts—concentrated areas of one plant—to create the dramatic garden. It is better to use only six or seven different types of flowers but to place them in drifts and repeat the arrangement at least once elsewhere on the plan or even three times. This gives you unity, another important part of garden planning.

Your flower garden will need a background of shrubs and trees. These plants frame the flowers so there is a definition of light and dark colors. Trees and shrubs are the backbone of any good flower garden and should be placed with thought to unity and proportion. One or two trees will only create a spotty effect and a few shrubs here and there just won't work. Again, plan your garden with shrubs in an arc or circle and with trees placed judiciously. Perhaps two or three trees at one end of the garden and a single tree at the other end. Avoid planting in pairs and rather stick to the one, three, or five plant arrangement with both shrubs and trees.

In essence, put your flowers in the front and to the sides of the area and interspace with shrubs and trees. Planning the flower garden is similar to doing a painting, and unity and balance must prevail.

THE CUTTING GARDEN

Decades ago the kitchen garden was part of the pioneer's house; it occupied a place close to the home and was a utilitarian garden with vegetables and herbs and, later, flowers. The purpose of a cutting garden is to furnish flowers for the home. Here we use the phrase *cutting garden* where you can cut flowers, harvest vegetables, and gather herbs, as opposed to an ornamental flower garden previously discussed. These gardens are gaining popularity today because they are dividends of the earth. There is nothing better than fresh vegetables and nothing more cheerful than fresh flowers in the home, or flavorful herbs for cooking. And cost is miniscule compared to what one pays today for produce and flowers.

The cutting garden has never been a large garden; its purpose is to get as much in the allotted land space as possible. I have seen cutting gardens in an area of, say, 15 x 20 feet with a single path flanking seven or eight types of flowers. A simple square or rectangular plan works well divided into grids and each grid has its specific flowers.

My garden for cut flowers happens to be near the driveway in a wedge-shaped piece of ground about 30 feet long and 20 feet wide. It is terraced for easy tending of plants: stopping and squatting is reduced to a minimum and it is easy to get to the flowers. It is a little farther from the house than I would like, but the soil is good and drainage is excellent in this area and again there is full sun.

The owner of this house wanted a cutting garden but had little land. The solution: raised brick planters, in which roses and annuals were planted. (Matthew Barr)

The cutting garden for this contemporary house is at the far right, somewhat removed but still convenient. The owner can snip fresh flowers in minutes. (M. Barr)

Plan your cutting garden by deciding what kinds of flowers you want and block out an area for each within the boundaries of the land you have. You need nothing elaborate or sophisticated; remember this is a producing garden and not a garden for show. (We discuss vegetable and herb gardens in later sections.)

THE FORMAL GARDEN

When you think of a formal garden you are apt to think of the grand gardens of Europe—they are vast and beautiful. However, it is possible to create a small formal garden which can be a handsome plan indeed. In this garden flowers are not paramount; it is the shrubs and trees that create the pattern.

Formal gardens are generally symmetrical in design; what appears at one end is duplicated at the other. It is almost a mirror-image garden where all plants are trimmed and kept in bounds to create the unified and symmetrical design. Generally, there is a lawn to create the luxurious feeling and paths to walk. The formal garden is the meditative garden where one escapes the pressures of the day and communes with nature. It is a good garden for these days of turmoil and coping with crowds and traffic. And the formal garden is indeed enjoying a renaissance.

If you are planning a formal garden, pay attention to the initial plan—box designs, rectangles, and arches are used with precision to create the garden. You can almost map your garden with a straight-edge ruler to get the formal feeling and then select appropriate plants for this design.

While the plants are certainly important in a formal garden, the paths and how they cross and relate to the garden whole are equally important. This is basically a garden where, as mentioned, one can relax with lush green nature all around.

In the beginning I said this can be a small garden but it cannot be too small like a backyard or entry garden. Space is needed—at least 50 x 100 feet to create the ultimate in the formal garden—and that space should be somewhat removed from the house. It is a garden to approach or view from a distance.

AND WHERE DOES YOUR GARDEN GROW?

Once you have decided on the kind of garden you want you must consider where to put it—backyard, front yard, side yard—where? And let us not forget the roof. Aside from the formal garden, your cutting garden or flower garden can occupy almost any area.

Cutting garden

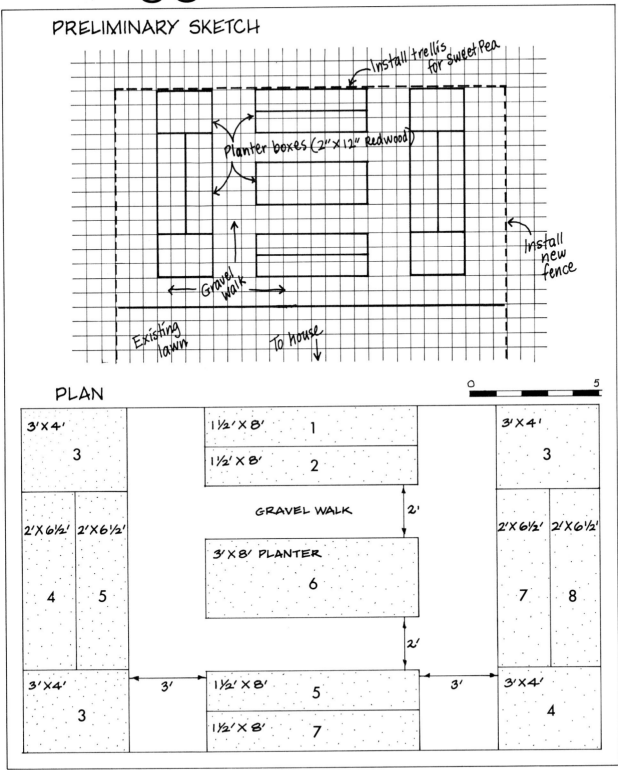

PRELIMINARY SKETCH

Install trellis for sweet Pea

Planter boxes (2"x 12" Redwood)

Install new fence

Gravel walk

Existing lawn

To house

PLAN

0   5

3' X 4' 3	1½' X 8' 1	3' X 4' 3
	1½' X 8' 2	

GRAVEL WALK   2'

2' X 6½'   2' X 6½'   4   5

3' X 8' PLANTER   6

2' X 6½'   2' X 6½'   7   8

2'

3' X 4'   3

3'   1½' X 8'   5   1½' X 8'   7   3'

3' X 4'   4

1. Lathyrus 'Spencer's Giant' Sweet Pea

2. *Dianthus barbatus* Sweet William

3. *Rudbeckia gloriosa* Gloriosa Daisy

4. Dahlia (Pompom type)

5. Tropaeolum 'Glorious Gleam' Nasturtium

6. Tagetes 'Cream Puff' Marigold

7. Salpiglossis 'Splash'

8. Chrysanthemum 'Thomas Killin' Shasta Daisy

Cutting garden

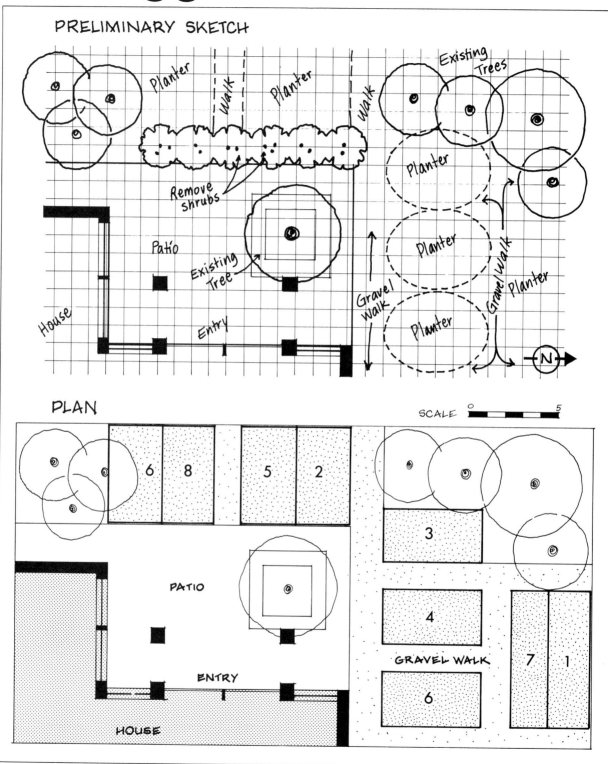

PRELIMINARY SKETCH

Planter Walk Planter Walk Existing Trees Planter

Remove shrubs

Patio

Existing Tree

House

Entry

Gravel Walk Gravel Walk Planter Planter Planter

N

PLAN

SCALE 0 5

6 8 5 2

3

PATIO

4

7 1

GRAVEL WALK

6

ENTRY

HOUSE

1. Lathyrus 'Spencer's Giant'
   Sweet Pea

2. *Dianthus barbatus*
   Sweet William

3. *Rudbeckia gloriosa*
   Gloriosa Daisy

4. Dahlia (Pompom type)

5. Tropaeolum 'Glorious Glear
   Nasturtium

6. Tagetes 'Cream Puff'
   Marigold

7. Salpiglossis 'Splash'

8. Chrysanthemum 'Thomas Killin'
   Shasta Daisy

While the house is more Colonial than formal, the garden is a handsome plan in the formal manner, with clipped hedges, sculptured trees, and a general feeling of elegance. (Thomas Brickman)

Backyard gardens are perhaps most popular because this is where there is privacy and a sense of space; these are small Edens suitable for a flower garden or a cutting garden or perhaps both. If you have larger grounds in the suburbs the flower garden with a lush planting of trees and shrubs would be handsome.

If your gardening is limited to the patio or rooftop then container gardening is the answer—you can have all kinds of plants in containers—and most any kind of garden (vegetable, herb, flower).

To help you plan your garden, let us look at the limitations of some sites.

Long Narrow Lot: In many inner cities such as Chicago the long narrow site is much in evidence. This space acts as a buffer between the houses; generally 20 to 30 feet x 30 to 40 feet long, and this is easily made into a handsome side yard garden. It can be sectioned into smaller areas and each part of the plan can be pulled together by using one common denominator—a group of small trees or shrubs, for example. Repeated plantings of perennials will do the same thing. The long paths in side gardens can sometimes be an eyesore so use circular accents of shrubs or trees to break this monotony. Large trees are not needed—they will be out of scale. Choose the smaller trees—there are many. Repeat flower beds and drifts to create a unified effect, and to screen the next yard grow handsome shrubs as hedges.

Formal garden

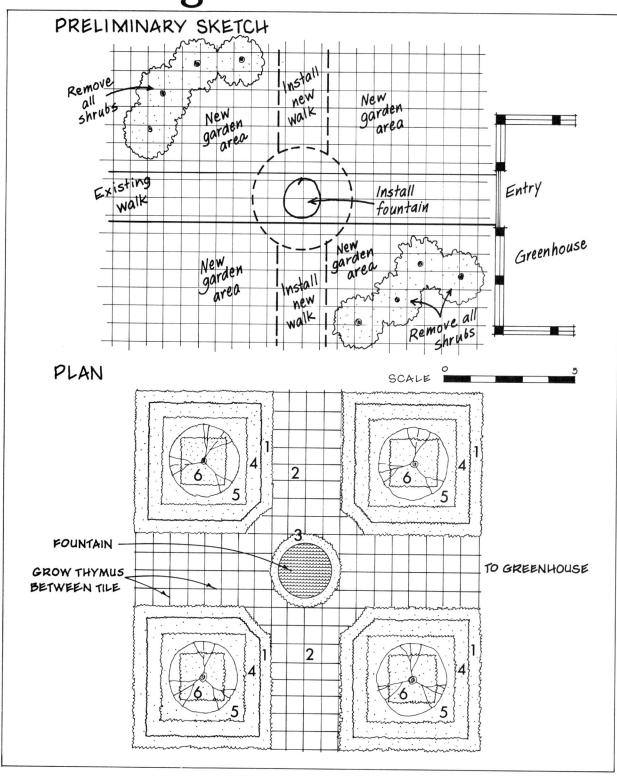

PRELIMINARY SKETCH

Remove all shrubs

New garden area

Install new walk

New garden area

Existing walk

Install fountain

Entry

Greenhouse

New garden area

Install new walk

New garden area

Remove all shrubs

PLAN

SCALE 0 ─ 5

FOUNTAIN

GROW THYMUS BETWEEN TILE

TO GREENHOUSE

1. *Teucrium chamaedrys*
   Germander

2. *Thymus serpyllum*
   Wooly Thyme

3. *Anthemis Nobilis*
   Roman Camomile

4. *Artemisia schmidtiana*
   Satiny Wormwood

5. Caladium
   'White Christmas'

6. Rosa 'Pascoli'

Formal garden

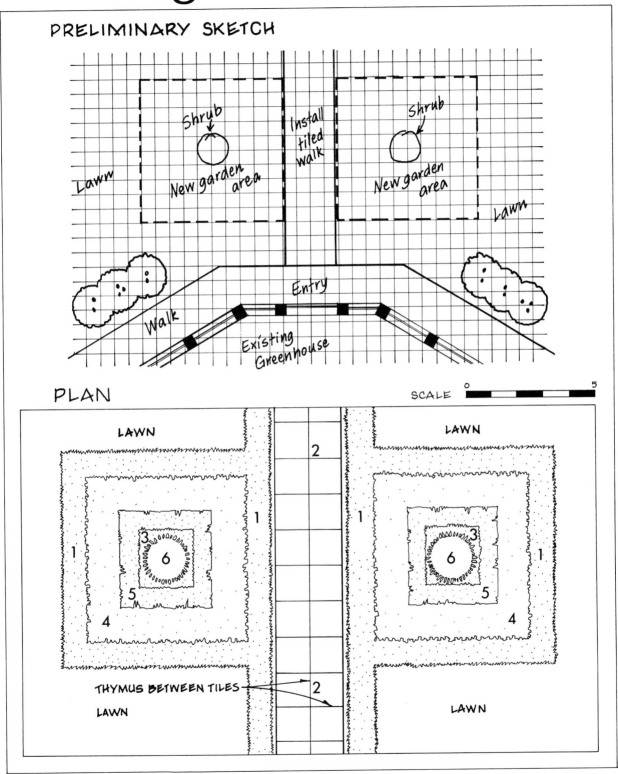

PRELIMINARY SKETCH

Shrub
Shrub
Lawn
New garden area
Install tiled walk
New garden area
Lawn
Entry
Walk
Existing Greenhouse

PLAN

SCALE 0 5

LAWN
LAWN
2
1
1
3
6
5
4
1
1
3
6
5
4
THYMUS BETWEEN TILES
2
LAWN
LAWN

1. *Teucrium chamaedrys*
   Germander

2. *Thymus serpyllum*
   Wooly Thyme

3. *Anthemis Nobilis*
   Roman Camomile

4. *Artemisia schmidtiana*
   Satiny Wormwood

5. Caladium
   'White Christmas'

6. Rosa 'Pascoli'

A patio garden in Texas. Caladiums and ferns abound, and the standard cut trees at the far right provide a vertical accent. (Designer: John Astin Perkins; photo by Max Eckert)

Rectangular Lot: This site differs from the narrow lot by generally being somewhat larger in width, say, 30 feet across. The site is an easy one to landscape handsomely and is adaptable to many plans. A conventional plan might be two or three groups of shrubs spaced in a triangle but with enough space between them for dimension. The shrubs can be a backdrop for flower beds or drifts. Paving and stepping stone areas will help give line and form to the plan and break the monotony of the rectangle.

Wedge-Shaped Lot: This site can be more desirable than it seems at first for a garden. It leaves most of the property behind the house and some interesting plantings (hedges can work wonders in the wedge plan) can be done. A central accent works well too and generally the wedge-shaped lot benefits from a single concentrated area of small trees. Flowers can be massed along the perimeter of the site—one side to add some round shapes—use flowers in drifts (arcs) and, all in all, this lot can become a handsome garden.

Large Sites: If you are fortunate to have a garden over an acre you indeed have a prize these days with land so scarce. The large garden, however, requires obviously more elaborate planning than a small narrow site or typical rectangular one. The best solution is to break up the site into several gardens rather than have one vast area where things can become a hodge-podge. Several small gardens within one site create eye interest and dimensional beauty and while each area is separate—flower garden, fern garden, terrace, lawn—the elements must all act as a total entity. There must be unity so it is best to follow a particular layout pattern for each garden so the whole flows together. Also consider having the gardens at different levels—somewhat like platforms; this type of landscaping is highly attractive because at varying heights the desired flow of materials works well.

Corner Site: The corner garden is a difficult one to plan because of the exposure to the street. Generally, walls or fences of some nature are needed for privacy or at least suitable hedges in L-shape to confine the garden. The garden itself, once the privacy barriers have been installed, follows very much the planning of a rectangular lot.

2

Climate and Plants

CLIMATE is the single most significant factor in how our plants grow—indeed in what we select to plant in the first place. Climate includes rainfall, humidity, temperature, wind, intensity of light, length of day, and soil. The effects of these elements overlap since rainfall determines the moisture content of soil, just as precipitation and temperature modify its physical nature. To garden successfully, we must garden within the climatic factors of our region.

Each area differs from every other. For example, the Plains states get less rain than other regions, and the rocky or sandy soil of the Far West is not like the rich humusy soil of the Midwest.

A number of forests in the United States are filled with deciduous plants rather than evergreens; again, this is the result of climate. And where you find trilliums and May apples, you will not find cactus. Each climatic area has its own biosphere or community of plants. Awareness of this helps to make gardening a success and a pleasure, rather than an unrewarding chore. So we must work with Mother Nature, not against her.

RAINFALL, LIGHT, AND TEMPERATURE

There are other considerations—the slope of the land and the water retention of your soil—but generally the annual rainfall of your area is a most important factor in your selection of plants. And seasonal distribution of rain is as important as the amount. Spring and summer rain does most for growth. Rainfall maps of your specific region are available from the United States Department of Agriculture to help you determine the likely amount of rain in your area.

Without light, plants cannot grow. Sun is necessary for photosynthesis, the process whereby plants use the energy of the sun to produce sugars and starches. Some plants will tolerate less light than they actually need, but they will not grow well, so it is important to select the plants suited to the light in your region. Most plants have very definite light requirements: just try growing roses in full shade and you will know what I mean.

Temperature is a strong factor in determining the effectiveness of rainfall. If your region is very hot in summer, the rate of evaporation from the soil and the rate of transpiration (plants give off water through their leaves) will be increased. For example, in Oklahoma, your garden will require twice as much rainfall because of the heat as, say, Minnesota, which is cooler, to produce a good show of flowers.

Winter injury is common in many plants that are not grown in their natural environment. Hybrid rhododendrons transported from the South are susceptible to winter kill in the New England area. On the other hand, you cannot have tulips in California, since winter cold is required if tulips are to bloom the following spring.

Actually it is the freezing and thawing that injures plants rather than constant cold, which is why mulching is important. A mulch, an organic or inorganic covering, put down after thorough watering and after the first hard frost, acts like a blanket around plants and prevents the harmful alternation of freezing and thawing. Hardiness is thus another important factor in growing plants, which is why the zone maps issued by the United States Department of Agriculture are so vital.

CLIMATE ZONES AND PLANT HARDINESS

Used by nurserymen and most publications, the Hardiness Zone Map is a universal guide of what you can or cannot grow and is prepared by the Agricultural Research Service of the United States Department of Agriculture. These maps, based on average minimal night temperatures from weather stations, separate areas of the United States into ten zones and are helpful in predicting the adaptability of plants to specific climates. The zone map is included in this chapter. Throughout this book, however, actual temperatures rather than zone numbers are given to avoid confusion and constant reference back and forth to maps.

While zone maps are helpful, they cannot show temperature differences between hill and valley or sites along bodies of water. Thermal belts and fog belts are always at work, and each small variation cannot be cited. For example, there are some zones in northern California where specific condi-

tions exist only in a five- to ten-mile radius; outside this region, temperatures may be five to ten degrees lower, winds stronger, and various other conditions prevailing.

The subject of plant hardiness is not complicated; there are only a few things you need to know. The hardiness of plants influences your choice, but it need not stop you from experimenting. My garden includes several plants—lilacs, bougainvillea, and peony—that are not supposed to survive in this region. But they do. True, they are strategically placed. Because the bougainvillea needs warmth in winter, it is purposely protected by a house wall; the lilacs are in a more exposed place where they get the cold they require.

A hardy plant survives without injury the climatic extremes of a given area. It has the ability to withstand freezing. A chemical reaction makes it possible for it to bind its moisture against low temperatures. Nonhardy plants cannot do this. Usually, the greater the cold required, the hardier the plant and the more resistant it is to freezing. The rest period or dormancy prevents growth when growth would be detrimental to the plant.

Injury from freezing comes from ice forming within the tissues. When temperature drops quickly, tissues freeze quickly, ice crystals form, and the plant dies. When temperatures fall gradually, tissues freeze slowly and can later recuperate, provided freezing does not occur too many times. Repeated freezings and thawings increase the possibility of injury.

To protect your plants against freezing, they need to make steady growth through the growing season with a gradual cessation from mid-August until the first killing frost. Fertilizer and water must be carefully applied starting in midsummer. Fluctuations in

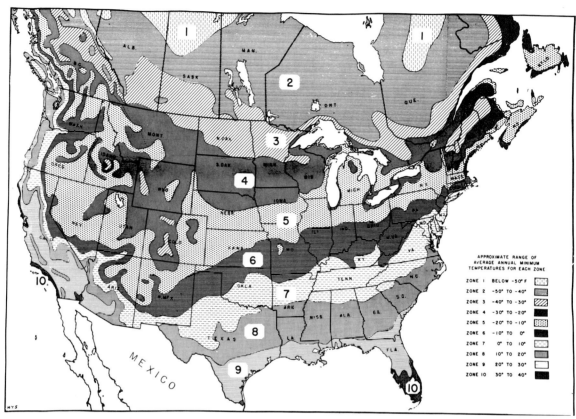

Climate map. (USDA)

growth should be avoided. Plants that lose their leaves because of insects or disease are especially vulnerable to premature freezing. Late growth can occur too and then the plant may be too immature to survive winter.

Microclimates

Certain influences within your garden create microclimates (little areas a few feet or a few hundred feet wide) that are somewhat different from the general climate of your region. For example, a fence facing south will accumulate heat; a hill away from

the protection of the house will be cooler. Warm air rises and cold air sinks, so gardens in hilly terrains have several microclimates where temperature and humidity vary.

A plant protected from western sun will experience a gradual drop in temperature; the same plant in full western sun will have a leaf temperature well above air temperature. As the sun sets, a rapid temperature drop occurs and severe damage to the plant can occur. This happens frequently with broad-leafed evergreens or with tree trunks that get scalded by sun.

Where there are windbreaks—other

houses, roofs, a line of trees—heat radiates from the buildings, and a mass of warmer air can considerably temper the existing temperatures. Yet these houses may be recent additions to the landscape, and plants formerly suggested for the area no longer will grow there.

Large bodies of water affect the climate within a zone considerably. They temper the overall climate of adjoining areas and raise the temperature as much as one full zone from inland regions. To an extent ponds and lakes can do the same thing. On the other hand, sites close to the shore and thus exposed to severe wind will have a lower hardiness zone than those of an inland region.

PLANT PARTS

Plants are living organisms and essential to our own survival. To most people, however, a plant is something to look at or to use to make a property attractive. The prudent gardener knows what a plant is and how it grows. The information included here is neither technical nor tedious but rather a story of a factory of sorts—a plant. For a plant is in essence many parts working together to support life.

Plants are composed of roots, leaves, and stems, and each of these has a purpose and a function in the development of the total plant.

Roots

Roots are the anchors of a plant; they are in contact with the soil, and most roots grow below the surface of the soil. Roots absorb water and dissolve minerals from the soil. They conduct water and minerals upward to stems and help in the manufacture of food.

The primary root of a plant grows down vertically; secondary roots develop some-what horizontally. Sometimes roots arise from stems, leaves, or other parts of the plant. These are called adventitious roots. But when we talk about the root system of a plant we mean the entire mass beneath the surface of the soil.

There are two kinds of root systems: diffuse and taproot. The diffuse root system has many roots, while the taproot is a main primary root, which is generally larger and thicker than all other roots.

Roots have two functions: they absorb water from the soil and at the same time absorb the chemicals necessary for growth. If water is not available, roots cannot function properly and the plant dies.

Roots can be powerful; they can wend their way through the soil to seek moisture. Nature has so equipped them that they can push and squeeze their way into crevices in rock and by expansion even burst it apart. The tips of roots are made of flat tough cells and these push forward from pressure below them.

The growing area of the root is just below the root tip. Here young cells multiply by dividing in two. As the plant gets bigger the roots get bigger. The main roots develop smaller roots and these develop their own roots. The older roots are the carriers of water and nutrients (or sometimes store nutrients). It can easily be seen why young plants with small root systems need more water and nutrients than older plants that have well developed roots. Delicate hairs cover the roots and it is these tiny hairs that absorb the food and water. Root hairs are sensitive to light and dryness.

Leaves

Leaves are actually chemical factories where there are cells upon cells and motion and flow everywhere. Leaves make organic

Plant structure

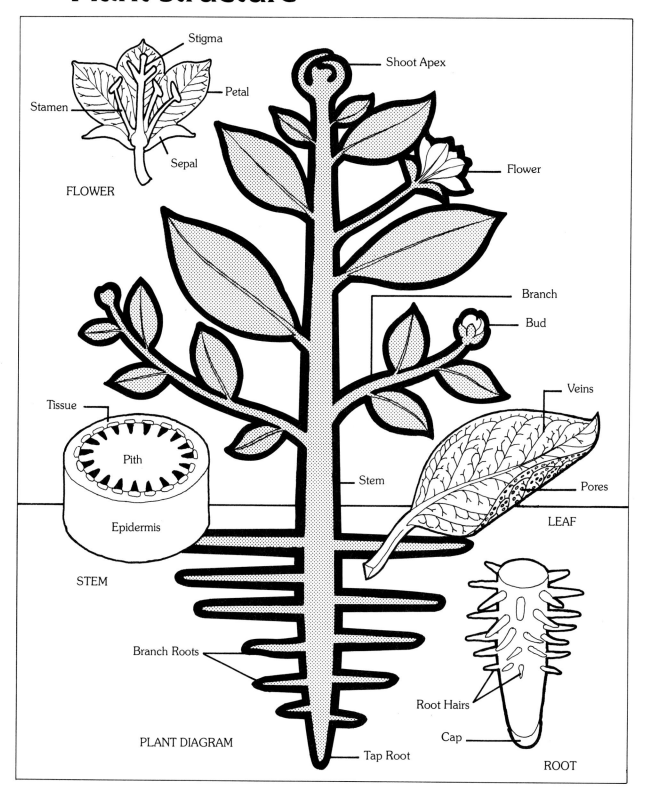

Stigma

Stamen

Petal

Sepal

FLOWER

Shoot Apex

Flower

Branch

Bud

Veins

Tissue

Pith

Stem

Pores

Epidermis

LEAF

STEM

Branch Roots

Root Hairs

Cap

PLANT DIAGRAM

Tap Root

ROOT

food out of sunlight, air, water, and soil salts. Most of the sugars needed by the plant are produced in the leaves by the process known as photosynthesis. By this process the energy of the sun is transformed into a form that is used in the life process of a plant. This process—miraculous and simple at the same time—depends upon the green material in a plant (chlorophyll) which takes carbon dioxide, water, and the sun's energy to produce the sugars and carbohydrates required by the plant.

The leaf combines gas and liquid. In one form or another it obtains oxygen, hydrogen, carbon, and nitrogen along with other elements. Water is vastly important because it brings with it hydrogen and oxygen; carbon is taken from the earth by the roots and nitrogen is used in liquid form. In leaves transpiration of water as vapor takes place. That is why when you grow many plants indoors, they supply their own humidity.

The three surfaces of the leaf are the epidermis, middle leaf, and veins. The epidermis is generally a single layer of different kinds of cells that protect the tissue within from drying out. In the middle of the leaf is the chlorophyll, and veins have elements to conduct water, inorganic salts, and food.

Stems

Stems are the essential link in plants that connects roots with leaves. But the main functions are to distribute and process the products of leaf and roots. The cells in stems must have a constant supply of moisture, food, and air. Sugar must be transformed into starch or other complicated proteins, soils, and waxes. In essence, a stem manufactures and processes as well as stores and handles distribution and transport of sugars.

The stem is the middleman of the process—carries on the functions of the roots and root hairs to transport water and nutrients to buds, leaves, and flowers. It also returns sugars manufactured in the leaves to the roots. The stem, which may be rigid or flexible, also supports the plant.

Closeup of good porous soil—crumbly and mealy, not sandy or claylike in touch or appearance. (USDA)

3 🍃

Soil

MOST SOILS lose their mineral content over the years and so must be reworked and revitalized. Topsoil may be a few inches or several inches deep. Because of its organic content it is usually a darker color than subsoil.

The subsoil, beneath the surface layer, has been there for hundreds of years; it can be a few inches below the surface or as much as twenty inches down. It varies greatly in composition (depending on where you live) and may be sandy, loamy, or claylike. A very sandy soil that retains little moisture is almost useless to plants. A clayey soil holds water too long and literally drowns plants.

Soil must be porous; that is, it must have air spaces in it so water and air can reach roots. The pores or spaces in soil make up 30 to 50 percent of soil volume. In sandy soil, which has a great deal of air space, moisture retention is slight, and water drains away quickly. If you live in an area with sandy soil, you have to add humus (organic matter) which increases water-holding capacity. Heavy soils, such as clay, have few air spaces, so the movement of water and air is slow. A clay soil can hold three to six times as much water as a sandy soil. Again, the addition of humus helps to aerate the soil and provide the air spaces needed for good plant growth.

WHAT IS GOOD SOIL?

Good soil is a basic factor of plant growth; too often soil is depleted of life-giving elements. It has often been used for decades in the growth of plants, and soil does not replenish itself with nutrients—it needs help. As the plant is a living entity, so is the soil; it contains living things, microscopic in size. It takes 500 billion bacteria to weigh a pound and in each acre of topsoil there are 30 to 40 pounds of these tiny plant microbes. The microorganisms have no green matter and cannot produce food for themselves. Some are parasitic, most are saprophytic, that is, they live by digesting dead organic matter.

Humus is the stuff soil is made of—bacteria needed for constant replenishing of soil live in decaying organic matter. As animal and vegetable materials break down they provide the necessary food for the soil bacteria which releases chemicals in the soil needed for plant growth. It is in essence nature's recycling system.

Without humus there is little bacteria. Bacteria can if necessary preserve themselves under unfavorable conditions by producing spores. The spore surrounds itself with a hard shell or cell wall so that it may retain life in adverse surroundings for years. When conditions become favorable the

Soils

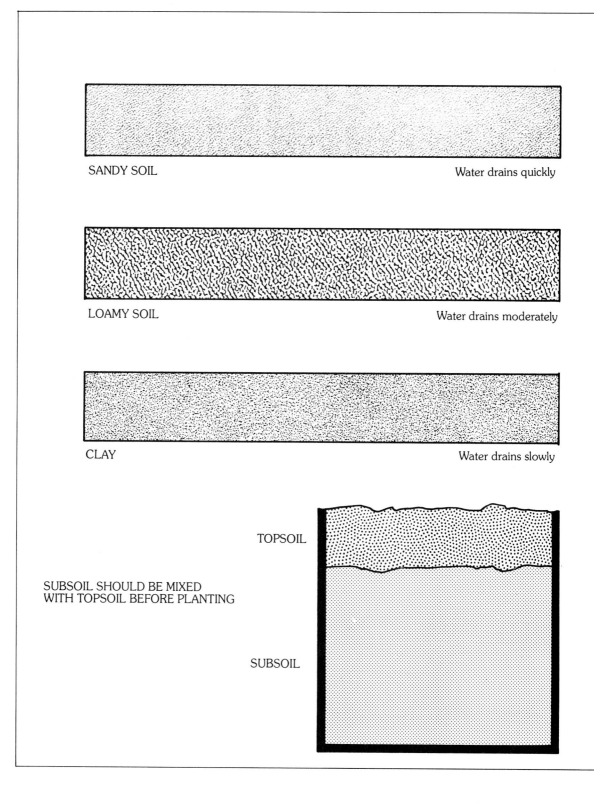

SANDY SOIL   Water drains quickly

LOAMY SOIL   Water drains moderately

CLAY   Water drains slowly

TOPSOIL

SUBSOIL SHOULD BE MIXED
WITH TOPSOIL BEFORE PLANTING

SUBSOIL

Under a cover of leaves lies good rich soil, full of life and nutrition. (USDA)

spore breaks open and the bacteria multiply in the usual manner. In winter the spores are dormant but with warm weather and rain they become active.

So for soil to do plants good, it must have excellent physical structure porosity and chemical nutrients content, both factors provided by humus. Decaying organic matter creates an open and porous soil so water and air can enter and penetrate freely and *drain freely.* Humus in soil is what makes it work.

pH SCALE

Another aspect of soil is whether it is alkaline or acid or neutral. Most plants thrive in a neutral soil. Soil acidity or alkalinity is measured by the technical pH scale. It is like a thermometer with 7 as the neutral point. Above 7 the soil becomes alkaline and below 7 it is considered acidic (in varying degrees). Soil test kits are available from suppliers or you can send a soil sample to your county agent to determine what kind of soil you

A plant being set out into the garden. Note how black and porous the soil in the hole is. (USDA)

have and then you can correct the acidity or alkalinity by adding materials to it.

To lower the pH, apply ground sulfur at the rate of one pound to 100 square feet. This lowers the pH about one point. The sulfur is spread on the soil (according to directions on package) and watered.

To raise the pH of soil, ground limestone is used at the rate of ten pounds per 150 square feet. Scatter the limestone on the soil and water. Do this in several applications over a two-month period rather than all at once. The powdered lime is fastest acting and can provide benefit if applied early in the growing season. Granular is cheaper but slower in effect; a vegetable garden, for example, would be limed in the fall.

I have never placed too much importance on soil acidity or alkalinity. I do suggest you make the initial test to first determine the pH content; make corrections if necessary. After that if you keep adding humus to your soil it will greatly decrease any possible harm to plants of too much acidity in the ground.

COMPOSTING

I have mentioned decayed vegetable and animal matter as a source of humus and composting is one way to make the material. This is done in bins or heaps in some out-of-the-way place in the garden. A place where moisture naturally collects is ideal. You can make your own compost bin from 2 x 10-inch boards nailed to four-inch posts (with a gate) or buy the metal compost containers. Either way compost is vegetable waste from household and materials from the garden like dead leaves, grass cuttings, and most dead stalks and stems. (Tomato vines are not helpful.) Egg shells, fireplace ashes, and similar materials add nutrients. (See "Chemical Elements of Soil.")

To make a compost heap: Put a few inches of manure into the compost bin; cow manure, fresh or dehydrated, sold in bags, is best; horse manure contains too much undigested grass seed. Add a layer of garden leaves, twigs, clippings, etc. Also put in vegetable wastes from the kitchen. When the

The compost bin. The organic matter is working in the soil to create a rich, nutritious humus for plants. (M. Barr)

pile is about ten inches high add a scant layer of manure and a dusting of lime. Keep the materials moistened with water but never saturated. After a few months turn the heap, bringing the sides to the top.

You can speed up the composting procedure by using a shredder (costly) or you might want to try some of the chemicals available to hasten decay.

How much humus to add to soil? It depends on the soil and the plants being grown but generally I mix in about one inch of humus to six inches of soil. I do this in early spring and again in late summer.

BUYING SOIL

Soil is not just soil—it must be alive, as we have seen, it must be porous, and it must contain essential nitrogen, phosphorus, and potassium so plants can grow (we will discuss this shortly), but for now let's look at the tricky business of buying soil. If you have a new home or an old home you will need to purchase soil. In the new home generally the topsoil has been stripped away and there is little active soil remaining. In old homes or properties the soils have been used and reused so many times that topsoil is necessary there too.

A good topsoil has in it what we have been talking about—humus, porosity, and nutrients—but there are varying grades of topsoil. My dealer has six kinds! Some is unscreened, some without humus, some sandy, and so on. What you want is porous black rich topsoil and it usually costs a good deal. Eighty-five dollars for a six-yard truckload is what it costs in my area but this will vary from place to place.

It pays to get the best topsoil you can af-

A compost pile ready for use. Note the dug-out portion where the good soil is—black and porous. (USDA)

ford but, as mentioned, buying it is tricky. You never know what's in it. I go to the dealer and look at it and run my hand through it. It should be mealy and porous and I smell it. A good rich soil has a woodsy aroma and that is what you want.

Soil is purchased by the truckload, usually six yards to a truck and delivered tailgate to your home. That means it is dumped in an appointed spot and not shoveled out for you. That's your problem, so have a suitable area where you can get to the soil easily. I generally use a wheelbarrow to transport the soil.

Soil of varying kinds is also available in large sacks three cubic feet but if you are doing any amount of gardening these sacks just don't go far and thus it is costly to buy in this way. Sacked or bagged soil comes in many trade names and again it is difficult to know what to get. Ask your neighbors; they may be a better judge than your local nurseryman.

Soils

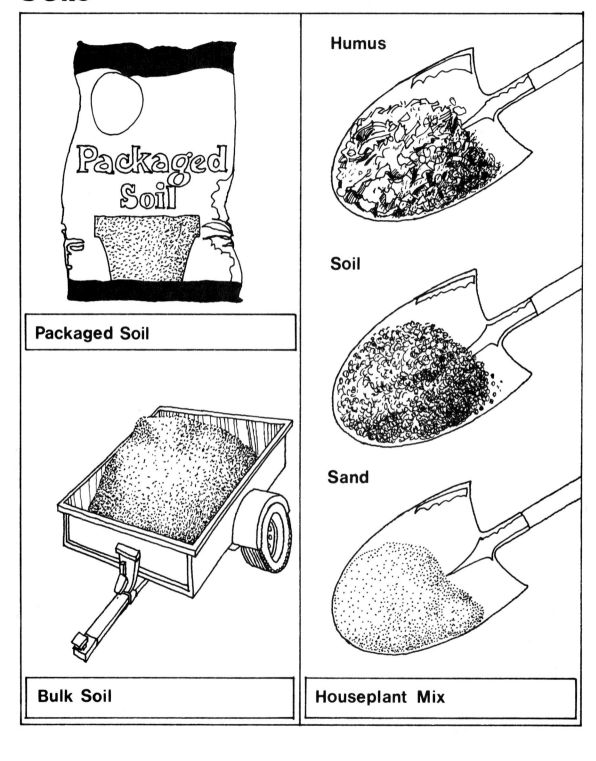

Packaged Soil

Bulk Soil

Humus

Soil

Sand

Houseplant Mix

Packaged
Soil

CHEMICAL ELEMENTS OF SOIL

Nitrogen, phosphorus, and potassium are the big three in soil; there are various trace (other) elements like manganese, boron, zinc, etc. Nitrogen is found in organic matter (already discussed) and is also available in chemicals such as ammonium nitrate and sodium nitrate. Nitrogen assures good foliage growth.

Phosphorous makes for good root growth in plants and also complements or balances the nitrogen. Superphosphate contains at least 20 percent and can be added to soils.

A wide variety of soil additives are available commercially. (M. Barr)

Potassium contributes to vigorous growth and makes for sturdy stems. If there is sufficient humus in the soil there will be ample potassium. If soil is deficient in potassium, wood ashes make a good additive.

Fertilizer Values of Common Organic Substances (percentages)

	NITRO-GEN-	PHOS-PHOROUS	POTASSIUM
Blood meal	13	—	—
Fish meals	9–14	3	—
Bone meal	3	12–24	—
Cottonseed meal	7	1.1	1.36
Meat and bone scraps	8	5	—
Dry steer and cow manure	2	—	—
Wood ashes	—	—	2.5

CHEMICAL FERTILIZERS

In addition to the organic or natural fertilizers for soil there are also man-made plant foods that contain nitrogen, phosphorous, and potassium. The contents are listed on the package or bottle marked in that order, such as "5-10-10." These fertilizers are offered in many forms:

Pelleted or granular
Concentrated liquids
Powders
Concentrated tablets

The pellets are spread on the soil and then water is applied; many pelleted or granular plant foods also contain insecticide. The liquids are the most commonly used plant food and require mixing with water and special

Making mulch for plants with a shredder, using branches and twigs. (Kemp Shredder Company)

spraying equipment (never cheap). Powdered fertilizer is used but is difficult to handle—it blows away on a windy day and may stick to foliage.

MULCHING

Mulching is a peculiar word which in essence means covering—it is basically covering the soil around the plant with a one- to two-inch layer of material. Nature uses leaves and you can too but mulches (and there are many) may be:

Leaves*
Hay and straw
Grass clippings

* Oak leaves and pine needles have acid content so use accordingly for acid-loving plants such as azaleas and rhododendrons.

Ground fir bark or wood chips
Sawdust
Peat moss (though it tends to absorb too much moisture)

Each of these materials decomposes naturally and returns to the soil. Inorganic mulches such as stones, roofing paper, black and white newspaper, plastic, or insulating fiber can also be used but will not help to improve the soil.

Mulching conserves moisture, protects plants from alternate freezing and thawing, and keeps out weeds. It is a neglected garden practice but one that offers a great help to plants. Mulches are applied after the soil has warmed up in spring and growth has started and in fall after the soil has frozen. Some gardeners keep mulches on plant areas all year.

4

Tools and Equipment

No MATTER how your garden grows or where it grows you will need some tools and equipment to keep it growing. An extensive array of power machines and such are not generally necessary but basic tools like rakes and shovels are.

You will also need some device for watering and this is more important than one may think. Using a hose for watering is just not that efficient for any size garden. Sprinklers and other devices may be in order.

HAND TOOLS

You will periodically be turning or moving soil, so shovels are a necessity. A round-pointed, long-handled shovel is fine and a square-bottomed short-handled one helps too. A spading fork comes in handy for turning soil and mixing in humus as well as breaking up clods of soil. Rakes and hoes are other garden tools you will find indispensable.

A trowel for planting bulbs and annuals is a tool you can use for dozens of jobs, or buy a special bulb-planting trowel. Today's trowels are of one piece of metal so that the head does not separate from the handle. There are several kinds: scoop, spatula, and flat edge, for example. Select a trowel that fits comfortably in your hand and is well balanced.

Weeders are important too—few gardens are without weeds. There are many types of hand weeders. I prefer the one with the iron fingers shaped like a claw. Or another good weeder is the one that has a flat blade turned at a right angle to the shaft. For deep-rooted weeds, and there are many, the fish-tail weeder does a good job.

The hoe is the oldest gardening tool and a good one. It has been modified in design but its uses are still the same: breaking up crusted soils and eliminating weeds. There is a standard hoe, a wide blade one, and other kinds. The standard hoe comes in both lightweight or heavyweight models.

A good pair of garden gloves is also essential; there is little sense in cutting or blistering your hands. Try on gloves—many come in only two sizes, large or small, and if you wear a medium size, this can cause trouble.

If you don't have pruning knives on the property you will need some (as well as clippers). A good sharp small knife for cutting flowers and opening bags of soil and fertilizer goes a long way in preventing frayed nerves when trying to open these sealed bags.

Lawn tools, both hand and power, are still another facet of garden maintenance and there are dozens—these are discussed in the chapter on Lawns.

And you might want to consider my favorite hand tool: a small miner's axe. This

Hand tools such as clippers and trowels are also necessary in the garden. (M. Barr)

short-handled tool can do a multitude of jobs in the garden, from digging plant holes to breaking up soil. One end is pointed, the other flat, and believe me this tool is worth its weight in gold. I found mine at a surplus store. I have not seen it in nurseries.

POWER TOOLS

Do you need power tools? It's up to you. They use up energy, require storage space, and always seem to need repairing. I have only a power mower on my property but if you are machine oriented by all means have some power—it does make jobs easier.

There are power tillers to break up soil—useful in some gardens but not essential in most. And there are power machines to clean up your garden—vacuum and such. There are air brooms and rakes too that blow or sweep clean a large area in one pass.

You might want a shredder—these do come in handy and, if you are looking for a birthday gift, a shredder is a good idea. Shredders make compost and mulch from leaves and twigs, and many sizes of models are available.

If you are in snow country a lightweight snow thrower may be the ticket.

Actually, there is a host of power machinery for gardening and I have only touched on the many things at suppliers. What you buy depends on your property and your pocketbook.

SPRAYERS AND DUSTERS

There are dozens of sprayers for garden use. Perhaps the most widely one used is the bottle type that attaches to a hose. Available in four- or six-gallon (or more) capacity, this mason jar attachment dispenses a fine mist to cover a plant. The sprayer can also be used to apply fertilizers.

I do not spray my garden with chemicals so I have rarely used this equipment—I prefer to battle the bugs the old-fashioned way. (See Chapter 20.) But if time is of the essence for you and quick battle against pests is necessary you will need one of these sprayers.

SPRINKLERS

A good sprinkler is hard to find—I have used various types of whirling devices and usually I get more wet than the plants; sprinklers are in my opinion water wasters. We will discuss the newer methods and conservation method of drip watering here as well.

Some sprinklers are of the oscillating type that send water from side to side; others cover a circular area and some, half circles. Some spew water to cover rectangles or squares and prices range from minimal to exorbitant. It is almost impossible to suggest any specific type of sprinkler; all I can say is that I have found over the years that the Rain Bird brand works very well for my garden needs. This is the same type of system that many highway departments use. So while sprinklers are not the final answer to watering—much water drains off to places you don't want water and they do use a lot of water—they are certainly superior to hose watering which is tedious and time consuming. It takes at least 15 minutes to penetrate a depth of 12 inches of soil in this manner.

Thorough watering is essential: wetting only the top inch or so forces roots to seek

A new way to water plants—drip system gardening—in which small amounts of water are released through the emitter over a long period of time. (USDA)

surface moistures, and subsequent dry spells or hot sun kill roots and therefore the plants.

You can also have an automatic sprinkler system; these are certainly convenient but rarely inexpensive. Pipe is generally laid underground and water heads are installed at strategic points to cover a specific area. These systems can be controlled from one outlet or may be set to work on their own with a thermostatic control. Either way this is the way to water for the busy gardener.

DRIP SYSTEMS

The drip system of gardening saves water, puts moisture exactly where it is needed (at plant roots), and all in all is the final answer for keeping plants growing big. The systems

Pruning equipment is important in any good garden. This tree pruner is especially needed for fruit trees. (Scott)

Hand pruners are worth their weight in gold for small pruning chores. (Scott)

are basically what they say: water drips slowly and continuously into the soil. Many manufacturers now offer a drip watering system and cost is not exorbitant.

Soakers are another way to water and these are essentially hoses, usually canvas, with small holes so water is fed to plant roots slowly and steadily (similar to the drip system). These are priced at average hose costs and are well worth your investigation.

HOSES

Years ago the hose was a good old-fashioned rubber type that lasted and lasted. Today, this kind of hose, although expensive, is still worth the cost. Plastic hoses of various polyurethanes are rigid, difficult to handle, freeze up occasionally, and in general are more a bother than a convenience. When it comes to hoses I do not skimp—I buy the

A good reliable pruning saw is necessary for tree work in the garden. (Scott)

best all-rubber hoses I can afford so they will last a long time.

PRUNING EQUIPMENT

No matter whether your garden is small or large some pruning and trimming of trees and shrubs will be necessary on occasion. Large shade trees are best left to the professional who can give them needed feedings, too. But you can and should prune other plants now and then to shape, promote growth, and contribute to the general good looks of the landscape. As in feeding or as in preventing pests, no extensive equipment is necessary. You will need small hand pruning shears, a pruning saw, and a good pruning knife. That's all that is really required in the average garden.

Ill-shaped shrubs and overgrown trees are easily seen in winter when leaves have fallen, and before hard frosts start. This is the time to prune away dead branches and diseased limbs. Use sharp tools and cut cleanly and then apply appropriate sealing compounds so bacteria cannot enter the plant.

You can prune low branches and small trees but for larger trees, as mentioned, consult a professional. Anything higher than a household ladder is hazardous. When pruning your trees remove the crisscrossed branches—open up the framework so light can reach the tree. Always cut branches flush with the trunk. Stubs left are unsightly. Never prune when wood is frozen or brittle. Do not butcher either—judicious surgery is in order.

Shrubs that flower on previous years' wood should be pruned after they bloom in spring or summer. You want to remove weak wood so that light and air can circulate and the plant can grow freely. Shrubs that bloom on current wood need pruning in very early spring.

Here are the rules for pruning:

Always apply a wound paint after making a cut.

Don't leave stubs, or infection might enter.

Cut away crossed branches on small trees.

Don't allow branches on any tree to rub against each other.

Remove only one branch of a main trunk—don't let it divide into a fork.

Wear gloves; use sturdy ladders and clean, sharp tools.

5

The City Garden

I HAVE written a whole book devoted to city gardens and it would be hard in this space to give complete instructions on how to plan the garden, but I would like to include a resumé of city garden planning and how it differs from other locales for plants—mainly because it is in the city where one really needs the peace and tranquility of a garden.

First, city gardens are not difficult to achieve, contrary to anything else you have read. The planning and type of plants are still basically the same with perhaps a little more emphasis on plants that can resist soot and pollution.

Again, it comes down to planning. The city garden should be of low upkeep. Generally the city dweller does not have time to give his plants daily care—it is more like weekend gardening—and for this reason the plants chosen should be more robust and resistant to pollution. (Basically, any plant if given a long enough time generally adjusts to conditions.) Easy-to-care-for plants are the answer and you will find lists at the back of the chapter. For now, let's look at the planning of a city garden.

PLANNING

In the city garden you want compactness but beauty. It is far better to have a *some-what* formal plan with reliable trees and shrubs and to plant fill-in color with seasonal annuals and perennials—easily put into the ground as prestarts at seasonal times. Make the garden plan simple with not too many plants; a jungle in the city scene may appeal to some people, but it will be a chore to care for.

An important part of city garden planning and one that is often neglected is suitable paths and walks. It is essential to get out and enjoy the garden. Walk in it and appreciate this haven in the heart of concrete. Make the garden green and lush with shrubs and trees—a retreat.

If soil is poor, and generally it is in cities, try gardening in containers. (See Chapter 6.) In a city garden try to use a center of attention—a small statue or fountain to create a focal point within the plan itself. This will give a unified effect, and do include a bench in the city garden or at least some place to sit and relax.

Again, the garden need not be large or filled with plants; the average city backyard of 25 x 25 feet works fine for an intimate and charming greenery.

I have lived in the city—in Chicago—where I had a side yard garden, about 10 x 25 feet. It was a beautiful green oasis even though it flanked an alley. I grew morning glories on the huge telephone pole that

A harmonious blend of shrubs, trees, and flowers in a city garden. The fountain is the perfect accent. (M. Adams)

stood watch over the greenery. Where I live now, some 25 miles from San Francisco, I have what is called a country garden. This garden to me is equally beautiful and always a haven at the end of the day.

But as pretty as my country garden is, I think it was the city garden amidst concrete and stone that meant the most. It was a necessity there. It seemed to be to my neighbors too, because almost every house had a garden, small though it might be. In the city you really need a garden; in the country you can walk into the fields or meadows or forests.

In the country you can create a garden quite easily—and there is usually much more space there for it than on a city lot. In urban areas, you have to plan more carefully and select plants wisely. Perseverance helps too. It is indeed more difficult to have an attractive city garden but it is well worth the extra effort.

Where?

In the city, you can plan a garden in the front of your house, at the rear (the usual place), or, lacking either space, at the side. Rooftops and terraces also make fine city gardens, and these areas can be converted into delightful settings with only a few plants.

Don't be too concerned about exposure. It is true that most flowering plants need full sun but there are some that will put on a col-

A backyard city garden. Acanthus is the background plant, and a clipped hedge provides dimension. (M. Barr)

City garden

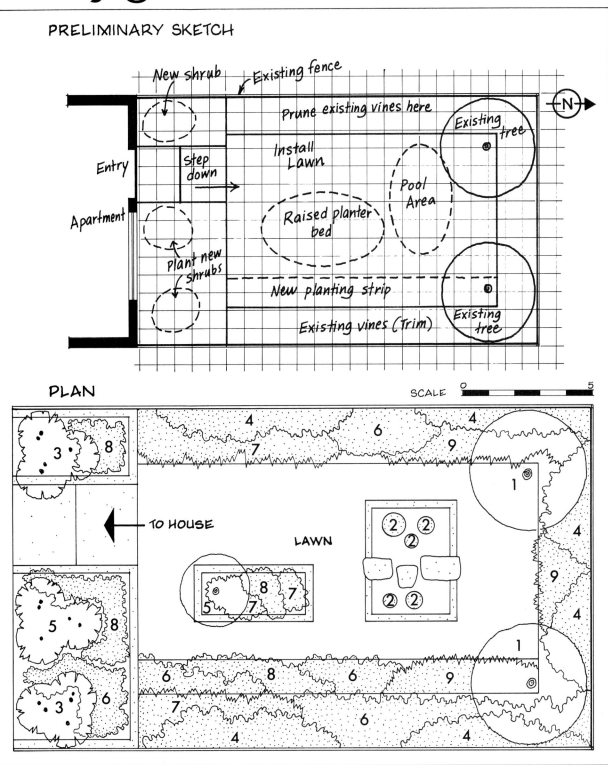

PRELIMINARY SKETCH

New shrub — Existing fence

Prune existing vines here

Existing tree

Install Lawn

Entry

step down →

Pool Area

Apartment

Raised planter bed

Plant new shrubs

New planting strip

Existing vines (Trim)

Existing tree

N

PLAN

SCALE 0 — 5

TO HOUSE

LAWN

1. *Picea pungens*
   Colorado Spruce

2. *Nymphaea odorata*
   Fragrant Water Lily

3. *Salix purpurea* 'Nana'
   Purple Osier

4. *Hedera helix*
   Ivy

5. *Betula pendula* 'Gracilis'
   Cut Leaf European Birch

6. *Hosta Lancifolia albomarginata*
   Plantain Lily

7. Petunia (Giant Double type)

8. Chrysanthemum 'Diener's Double'

9. *Convallaria majalis*
   Lily-of-the-Valley

City garden

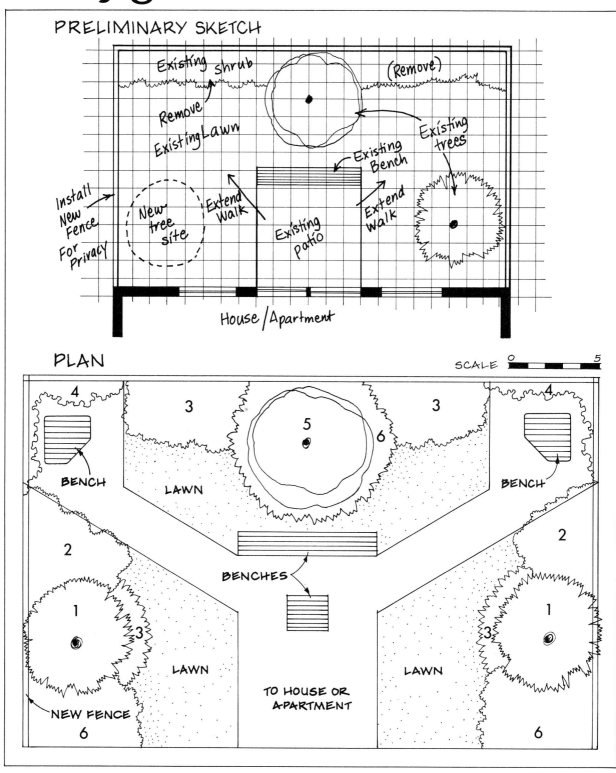

PRELIMINARY SKETCH

Existing shrub

Remove

(Remove)

Remove

Existing Lawn

Existing Bench

Existing trees

Install New Fence For Privacy

New tree site

Extend Walk

Extend Walk

Existing patio

House/Apartment

PLAN

SCALE 0 5

BENCH

BENCH

LAWN

BENCHES

LAWN

LAWN

NEW FENCE

TO HOUSE OR APARTMENT

1. *Picea pungens*
   Colorado Spruce

2. *Acer campestre*
   Hedge Maple

3. *Salix purpurea* 'Nana'
   Purple Osier

4. *Hedera helix*
   Ivy

5. *Betula pendula* 'Gracilis'
   Cut Leaf European Birch

6. *Hosta Lancifolia albomarginata*
   Plantain Lily

orful show even in north light. So, if space is a problem and exposures not good, don't give up.

And not to be overlooked in the city is the balcony garden—not my choice because it is so narrow and confining, but good effects are possible. I have seen handsome balcony gardens in New York that give the owners much pleasure.

In each case, whether you have a backyard garden or a rooftop garden, there are certain things to be considered if you want to have attractive results. But before you start thinking about plants and their care, consider possible layouts. (See page 15.)

GARDENS ON THE GROUND

Ground gardens, as I call them, to distinguish them from balcony and roof gardens, include backyard, side yard, and front gardens. In each case you will be planting into the ground and in each case you will have sun or bright light or shade depending upon the exposure you have selected (or been forced to use). Before you plant, consider the location *and the house.* See your garden as part of a unity rather than an afterthought. You want to create a total picture from within and without—that is, what you observe from inside and what you view from outside. Take your house into account and plan with it, not against it.

In any garden, you will want to have at least one tree, probably several. Select the smaller ones and those that endure city pollution; there are many. Trees will be the backbone of your garden. Start with them and place them with care. (See end of chapter and Chapter 13.)

Next consider some shrubs. These provide

mass and line, and you will need them to create the handsome picture you want. Group several shrubs of the same type. Don't place one shrub as a sentinel.

Next consider annuals and perennials. These provide color for your garden. Set out the trees and shrubs first. Then put in the prestarted plants that provide almost instant color. I have had beds of prestarted zinnias produce flowers in only two weeks. Place the flowering plants in masses, not in straight rows or they will look like soldiers. Arrange drifts or an arc of flowers to provide a dramatic rather than a spotty color effect. Your garden probably needs only three or four of these drifts to make it showy.

Whether you plan a formal or casual garden you will need a background—this means some areas of lawn or ground covers. Ground covers are easier to care for and give you a lot of green for little effort. A lawn requires time and care but there is no equal to that velvety green carpet. (See Chapter 16.)

So there you have a cursory glance at the garden on the ground—ground cover or lawn, trees, shrubs, annuals, and perennials for color (in spring perhaps some bulbs).

GARDENS IN THE AIR

If you live in the city and long for a garden but there is no space, look upwards. You can have a lovely greenery on roofs and upper terraces. And there is nothing prettier than a verdant scene tucked between concrete buildings.

Rooftop gardening is one of the oldest forms and is a unique and pleasant way to have plants in the city where space is at a premium. A small city rooftop garden properly planned is a welcome retreat. It need

Color amidst the concrete jungle of Manhattan. (M. Adams)

not be spacious nor elaborate nor a penthouse. Practically any roof can be used at any level.

Before you start climbing to your dream garden, and before you take trowel in hand and plants to bosom, know what you are doing. Rooftop gardening involves a different set of rules from the ones for gardening on the ground. And different design attitudes are necessary. Select the right plants, too; this is an important key to successful gardens in the air.

When you start your heavenly garden, consider the practical requirements. Can the roof support the weight of the soil and plants? Are there drainage facilities so excess water can escape without standing to ruin the roof? Is there an accessible water outlet nearby? No one wants to lug buckets of water upstairs for plants, and in rooftop gardening plants need plenty of water. Consider the kind of flooring for the roof garden. You can use what is there but it will rarely be attractive. Rather, set planters and tubs in place and then use pea gravel or fir bark as a flooring. These materials are easily put in place, can almost be molded into patterns with your hands, and are inexpensive. Periodically, however, they will have to be renewed.

Generally, roofs can take the extra weight of a garden and are built so water drains freely from them. Still, *check with the building owner* to be sure. Indeed, the owner may help share some of the expense since a rooftop garden will add much to the property. Also, if there are cracks or leaks in the present roof, be sure they are repaired (this is not costly). And if drainage is anything but perfect, drain tiles connected to outlets are the answer. Since you will want the rooftop garden to be an entity in itself, put up fencing or railings to define the space.

It is possible but hardly wise to dump a load of soil on a roof and start gardening. You'll have a mess. Use wooden planters, raised beds, or ornamental pots and tubs to contain soil and plants. (You can make your own wooden planters or buy them.) Fill containers with soil where they will be in the garden; moving soil-filled planters is hardly a delight. Like any other garden, the rooftop must be planned. Don't tackle a vast space all at once. Instead, try to plan boxes for one corner, and then work from there. Use redwood planter boxes at various levels rather than only on the ground. This establishes a pattern and provides eye interest. (It also makes it much easier to tend plants.)

Also provide ornamental tubs to establish contrast in shapes. Use trellises and unusual fence designs to create beauty and a place for vines to grow. Consider a partial ceiling to add a three-dimensional effect and act as an overhead screen for privacy or sun protection: Awnings and canopies are handsome; redwood lathing in trellis design is stunning.

Use the best possible soil you can get; standard outdoor soil mixes are fine and available in fifty- or hundred-pound sacks. The trick is hauling them to the roof. Recruit some good strong backs because getting the soil in place is about the toughest part of rooftop gardening. Prepare the boxes or tubs with ample drainage material; use gravel or broken pot pieces. For large tubs over 16 inches in diameter and planter boxes over 12 x 28 inches use a two-inch layer of gravel. Smaller containers will require a one-inch bed.

Wind will be a constant factor in the rooftop garden; wind increases evaporation in plants which can cause rapid desiccation and injury to soft young leaves. Install some wind protection—fencing, as mentioned—so you won't be constantly replacing plants. Do not enclose all sides with a fence or screen because then you would shut off lovely views and create a boxed-in space. Determine which is the windiest side and use buffers there. On a roof, direct sun can bake plants, so avoid this uncomfortable situation by placing overhead arbors or trellises, canopies or overhangs, to furnish shade where it is most needed.

For your arboreal garden select small shrubs to ten feet, and trees to fifteen feet, of varied leaf shape and pattern. On the roof, plants have no help from surrounding greenery because around them is either empty space or buildings. So use bold and contrasting plants to create an intimate effect.

Grow branching trees in tubs. Use round-headed shrubs in ornamental pots. At nurseries select plants for shape—vertical as well as horizontal, branching as well as round. Always avoid tall-growing weak-limbed trees; remember wind can be severe at times; instead, use small trees with sculpturesque growth habits like weeping willows and crab apple. Magnolia and gray birch are other good candidates. They need little space and have a handsome upright pattern.

Rooftop garden

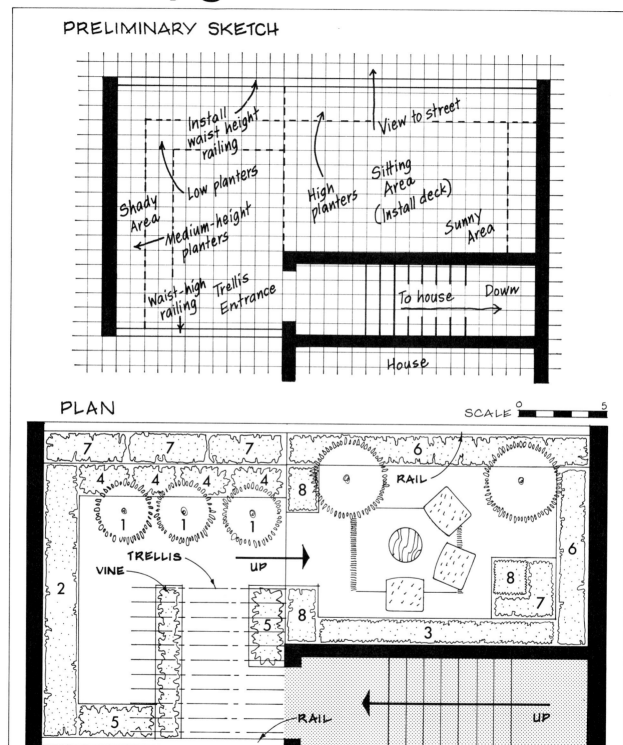

PRELIMINARY SKETCH

Install waist height railing

View to street

Low planters

Shady Area

Medium-height planters

High planters

Sitting Area (Install deck)

Sunny Area

Waist-high railing   Trellis   Entrance

To house   Down

House

PLAN

SCALE 0 — 5

RAIL

TRELLIS

VINE

UP

RAIL   UP

1. *Buddleia davidii* 'Empire Blue' Butterfly Bush

2. *Cotoneaster apiculata* Cranberry Cotoneaster

3. *Caryopteris clandonensis* 'Heavenly Blue' Bluebeard

4. Calendula 'Sunny Boy' Pot Marigold

5. *Aubrieta deltoidea* Purple Rockcress

6. *Iberis sempervirens* Evergreen Candytuft

7. Petunia (Giant Double type)

8. Chrysanthemum 'Diener's Double'

Rooftop garden

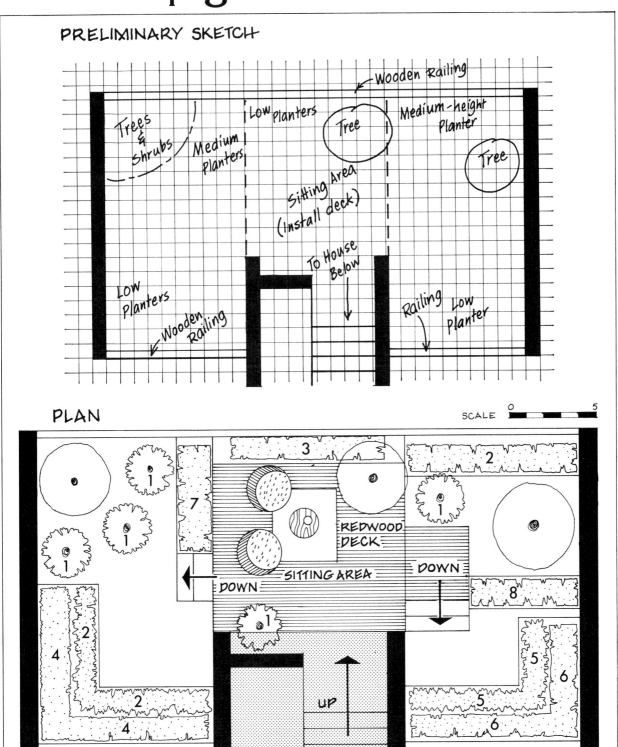

PRELIMINARY SKETCH

Wooden Railing

Trees & Shrubs

Low Planters

Medium Planters

Tree

Medium-height Planter

Tree

Sitting Area (Install deck)

To House Below

Low Planters

Wooden Railing

Railing

Low Planter

PLAN

SCALE 0 — 5

3

2

7

1

REDWOOD DECK

1

DOWN

DOWN

8

SITTING AREA

2

4

1

DOWN

UP

5

6

2

5

4

6

1. *Buddleia davidii* 'Empire Blue' Butterfly Bush

2. *Cotoneaster apiculata* Cranberry Cotoneaster

3. *Caryopteris clandonensis* 'Heavenly Blue' Bluebeard

4. Calendula 'Sunny Boy' Pot Marigold

5. *Aubrieta deltoidea* Purple Rockcress

6. *Iberis sempervirens* Evergreen Candytuft

7. Petunia (Giant Double type)

8. Chrysanthemum 'Diener's Double'

Never use a single shrub but rather mass three or four of a kind and then repeat this arrangement elsewhere in the garden to provide balance.

Along with trees and shrubs, pick your favorite annuals and perennials. Petunias do very well on rooftops because there is ample sun. You can have almost any garden flower you want, from marigolds to zinnias. If you can, select flowers by color. Have a red and blue and purple garden for dramatic display, or try a yellow and white color scheme. Remember to use vines; they are excellent for covering an unsightly wall, making a tapestry of green on a trellis, or softening the edges of square planters.

Use mulches—peat moss, fir bark—over soil in containers to prevent rapid dryout and help keep roots cool and moist. Feed plants every other watering with a 10-10-5 plant food and do water plants copiously.

Exposed to direct sun and wind, they dry out quickly. Indeed, trees and shrubs will need water every other day and perennials and annuals perhaps every day unless the weather is cloudy or rainy.

Here is a selection of plants to get you started in your rooftop garden.

TREES AND SHRUBS

Trees are the backbone of any garden, including the rooftop site. Generally, only a few trees are necessary. One medium-sized accent tree and two or three smaller trees will balance the scene and provide scale.

Flowering trees are generally small by nature, and some are ideal for rooftop gardens. Compact and colorful, they add great beauty, and with minimum care they grow well even in adverse city conditions. The flowering dogwood (*Cornus florida*) is always

A roof garden overlooking San Francisco Bay, full of tulips, azaleas, and daisies—all bordered by a delicate wall of ivy. (M. Barr)

a good choice, as is the English hawthorn (*Crataegus*) with white flowers and red berries. The fringe tree (*Chionanthus*) seldom grows more than 25 feet and is full of white flowers in spring. The sourwood (*Oxydendrum arboreum*) and some of the locusts (*Robinia*) are other fine selections. And don't forget small magnolias. The Japanese maple (*Acer palmatum*) is another beauty that does exceedingly well in a tub.

Acacia baileyana is a fine evergreen loaded with flowers in spring and it rarely grows more than 20 feet when confined to a container. The camphor tree (*Cinnamomum camphora*) with its branching habit is handsome, while loquats (*Eriobotrya japonica*) and all kinds of Eucalyptus trees are equally fine choices. The yew pine (*Podocarpus macrophyllus*) is a favorite with many people and grows almost untended. Varieties of *Taxus* are also excellent.

Once you have selected the trees you will need some shrubs for contrast and balance. Rhododendrons (including azaleas) are the most useful group. There are hundreds available. They are spectacular in bloom, yet are still attractive without flowers. Most will succeed in city rooftop conditions where there is some shade. All must be well watered in summer, for they suffer more than most plants if soil dries out. Camellias too offer a wealth of beauty for the shady rooftop where there are screens or overhangs. The Japanese holly (*Ilex crenata*), while not as showy as Rhododendrons or Camellias, is a reliable performer that tolerates soot and wind and still has fine green color. Japanese andromeda (*Pieris japonica*) is another good choice because it has handsome clusters of white flowers and does very well in various conditions. Roses and pyracantha are always sure to please.

A corner of the rooftop garden on page 58, planted with clivia and geraniums. (M. Barr)

VINES

Vines cover a multitude of sins—unsightly walls, awkward corners—and flowering vines are majestic in bloom. Vines are also excellent for fences and screens where they become living tapestries and can do much to enhance the city rooftop area. Most vines grow fast, can take sun or wind, and only need trimming and staking to make them perform at their best. Also, once established they provide privacy and are the finishing touch to fine rooftop greenery (see Chapter 12).

OTHER PLANTS

You can grow almost any kind of annual or perennial in your rooftop garden. Put plants in redwood boxes that are eight to twelve inches deep. Grow masses of one kind of plant for a real display. Keep annuals and perennials well watered and in good sun and you will have a bounty of flowers. Annuals such as petunias last only a season; perennials will bloom year after year. Plants are available at nurseries at seasonal times ready for planting. Select what you like; there is no limitation. On roofs there is usually ample sun which is the prerequisite for most flowers. Stake tall growers so wind does not break stems.

Vegetables can be grown in the air with excellent results. With ample sun they flourish. Beets, carrots, winter radishes can be planted almost any time once ground is

workable. Broccoli, Brussels sprouts, and cauliflower can be started in cool weather to have vegetables well into winter. Choose deep 12- to 20-inch planter boxes for your vegetables and have your taste of the country right in the city. (See Chapter 8.)

City Plants—Deciduous Trees

BOTANICAL AND COMMON NAME	APPROX. HEIGHT (IN FT.)	MINIMUM NIGHT TEMP.	REMARKS
Acer palmatum (Japanese maple)	20	−10 to −5F	Needs rich, well-drained soil
Albizzia julibrissin (silk tree)	20	20 to 30F	Very ornamental
Betula populifolia (gray birch)	40	−30 to −10F	Yellow color in autumn
Cornus florida (dogwood)	25	−20 to −10F	Stellar ornamental
Crataegus mollis (downy hawthorn)	30	−20 to −10F	Pear-shaped red fruit
C. Oxyacantha (English hawthorn)	20	−20 to −10F	Pink to red flowers
Ginkgo biloba (maidenhair tree)	60	−20 to −10F	Popular one
Laburnum watereri (golden chain tree)	25	−10 to −5F	Deep yellow flowers
Magnolia stellata (star magnolia)	20	−10 to −5F	Very ornamental
Malus baccata (Siberian crab apple)	45	−50 to −35F	Lovely flowers and fruit
M. floribunda (Japanese flowering crab apple)	30	−20 to −10F	Handsome foliage and flowers
Robinia pseudo-acacia (black locust)	60	−35 to −20F	Fine, late spring flowers
Salix babylonica (weeping willow)	40	−5 to 5F	Fast grower
Sorbus aucuparia (mountain ash)	45	−35 to −20F	Red autumn color
Abies concolor (white fir)	120	to −20F	Narrow pyramid shape
Acacia baileyana (Bailey acacia)	20–30	20 to 30F	Profuse yellow flowers
Bauhinia blakeana (orchid tree)	20	30 to 40F	Abundant flowers; partially deciduous
Cedrus atlantica (white cedar)	120	to −5F	Silvery light green needles
Chamaecyparis obtusa (false cypress)	100	to −20F	Broad pyramid; Glossy and green scalelike leaves; dislikes wind.
Cinnamomum camphora (camphor tree)	40	20 to 30F	Dense branching habit
Eriobotrya japonica (loquat)	20	5 to 10F	Needs well-drained soil
Eucalyptus gunnii (cider gum)	40–75	20 to 30F	Shade or screen tree

City Plants—Deciduous Trees (continued)

BOTANICAL AND COMMON NAME	APPROX. HEIGHT (IN FT.)	MINIMUM NIGHT TEMP.	REMARKS
Juniperus virginiana (Eastern red cedar)	90	to −50F	Scalelike foliage
Picea abies (*excelsa*) (Norway spruce)	75	−50 to −35F	Not for small areas
Podocarpus macrophylla (yew pine)	60	20 to 30F	Grows untended
Taxus cuspidata 'capitata' (Japanese yew)	50	−20 to −10F	Good sturdy tree
Thuja occidentalis (American arbor-vitae)	60	to −50F	Columnar; green to yellow-green needles
Tsuga canadensis (hemlock)	90	to −35F	Dark green needles; slender form

City Plants—Shrubs

BOTANICAL AND COMMON NAME	APPROX. HEIGHT (IN FT.)	MINIMUM NIGHT TEMP.	REMARKS
Abelia grandiflora (glossy abelia)	5	−10 to −5F	Free flowering
Chaenomeles speciosa (flowering quince)	6	10 to −20F	Lovely flowers
Euonymus alatus (winged euonymus)	9	−35 to −20F	Sturdy; easily grown
E. japonicus (evergreen euonymus)	15	10 to 20F	Splendid foliage
Forsythia intermedia (border forsythia)	2–9	−20 to −5F	Deep yellow flowers
F. ovata (early forsythia)	8	−20 to −10F	Earliest to bloom and hardiest
Ilex cornuta (Chinese holly)	9	5 to 10F	Bright berries; lustrous foliage
Ligustrum amurense (Amur privet)	6–30	−35 to −20F	Small spikes of white flowers
Photinia serrulata (Chinese photinia)	36	5 to 10F	Bright red berries
Pieris japonica (Japanese andromeda)	9	−10 to −5F	Splendid color
Pyracantha coccinea (scarlet firethorn)	8–10	−5 to 5F	Many varieties; valued for bright berries
Rhododendron	8–15	5 to −10F	Lovely flowers, evergreen leaves
Rosa (rose)	8–15	−5 to −10F	Many fine varieties
Salix caprea (French pussy willow)	25	−20 to −10F	Vigorous grower

The author works in his container garden, where 2"-x-10" redwood was used to create large planter bed/boxes. (M. Barr)

Gardening in Containers

CONTAINER gardening offers many advantages. With containers you can make an instant garden in the course of a weekend. You can mix and match plants, grouping and regrouping pots and boxes to get attractive effects.

Almost any small tree or shrub will be suitable, annuals and perennials, many vines, and various bulbs as well. There really are no specific container plants, although some accept the confined life better than others.

Basically, there are three types of containers: (1) tubs and boxes for individual tree, shrubs, and flowers, (2) long planters (windowbox type) for combinations, and (3) conventional clay or plastic pots for seasonal specimens. And of course dozens of decorative containers. If you wish, you can buy planters and boxes but they are expensive and bought ones do not always fit a given area. If you can, do make your own. Just consider that five sections of wood will make a box: four pieces for the sides and a bottom. It really isn't that difficult.

CONSTRUCTING BOXES

A wooden box for a plant may be of elaborate or simple design; it may be plain or have outside detailing. The design can vary. It may have overlapped corners or crossed timbers.

Plant boxes are popular and easy and cheap to make. They can be large or small, square or rectangular, circular or part-circular—the size and shape depending on your preference. As I have mentioned, the simplest box has four sides and a bottom with drainage holes. You can merely nail a box together, but a combination of glue and screws makes a box last longer. Use brass screws and good quality glue or epoxy. For small boxes, one-inch lumber is fine; for larger boxes, use two-inch stock.

A standard rectangular box you can buy is 16 x 20 inches and five inches deep. It is made of redwood. It is suitable for annuals, bulbs, almost any plants of limited size. Nail small pieces of wood under each corner of the box to elevate it slightly (to prevent rotting of wood on bottom). Air can thus circulate and a hiding place for insects is eliminated.

The cube, another type of box, is also simple to make. For a 12-inch cube, use 1 x 12-inch strips of redwood. Screw and glue together the four sides and bottom, and then—to give the box character—fasten some wooden two-by-two-inch moldings at the top and along the edges. Run the edge moldings vertically to define the box.

You can add other refinements to boxes: Try spacing the slats ½ inch apart, tacking trellis-work onto the face, or scoring the box

Making boxes is not all that difficult; with five pieces of wood you can do the job quickly. Note that planters are elevated on small blocks of wood. (M. Barr)

The completed container garden—boxes of color that transform an empty pool deck. (M. Barr)

Even small flats or boxes filled with annuals can make a striking garden setting. These are placed strategically on a patio to provide that necessary touch of color. (California Redwood Association)

These planter boxes feature attractive detailing and provide a handsome setting for the daisies. The espalier on the fence was added for vertical green accent. (California Redwood Association)

with a simple decorative design. You can also taper the box and bevel (angle-cut) the corners, and add a plywood base to give a finished appearance. There are various ways to make a box more than just a box.

BUILDING PLANTERS

Planters are wooden containers that are longer and narrower than boxes, often of window-box shape. Small planters coordinate with small plants; large planters with big plants.

Outdoors, elevate your planters with two-inch blocks under each corner.

Outdoor planters are easy to make and can be built from construction-grade redwood. They need not be painted, and, if they are made of redwood, they will eventually turn a pleasant silvery shade. Make outdoor planters from 2 x 4- or 1 x 12- or 2 x 12-inch lumber; a good size is 12 inches wide, 10 inches deep, and 36 inches long. Of course you can alter the size to your needs and the plants you want to grow. Large plants will, by necessity, need large planters; most small

Simple redwood boxes always look good and can easily create a garden where none existed. Here, a profusion of jade plants whose careful tending has enabled them to flourish. (California Redwood Association)

plants can be accommodated in a 12- or 16-inch planter. For finishing touches, apply moldings at the top.

Handsome square modular planters can be used outdoors in varying plans to create a total container garden—stacked, lined up, and so forth. A practical size is 20 x 20 inches.

WINDOW BOXES

Window boxes are popular in Europe, but here, unfortunately, they are not used nearly as much as they could be. The window box is actually a very effective way of growing and having some flowers or tiny vegetables even if you live in an apartment. The drawbacks are that in winter the box must be covered and it looks bleak. However, it can be decorated with evergreen branches inserted in the soil. Also, a window box may not be permitted in your apartment building. But window-box greenery does a lot to make some gardening possible in the city, so check with your landlord if you are a cliff dweller, and make sure the window box is properly fastened, for fatal accidents have occurred when objects slip and fall from window ledges.

Nurseries sell plastic or wooden window boxes, but these don't look like much and are usually not the right size. You are better off making your own. Use redwood or cedar, at least one inch thick, and a ¾-inch base of plywood. Regardless of the design you want, make the window box at least ten inches wide and ten inches deep to allow enough root room for plants. Drill drainage holes in the bottom of the box at eight-inch intervals.

The window box can be a simple rectangle with straight sides, or, if you live where winters are severe, consider a box with sides that slope outward. This type lets soil expand when it is frozen—without damage to the box.

Attaching the box to the window is more difficult than actually making the box. Use metal L-shaped brackets for support underneath; to secure a box to the house wall, use screws, lag bolts, or toggle bolts.

POTTING CONTAINER PLANTS

A good soil is important for all plants, more so for plants in containers that spend their life in a confined space. Here are some basic soil mixes I use:

For most plants
  2 parts garden loam
  1 part sand
  1 part leafmold
  1 teaspoon bonemeal for each eight-inch pot

For Begonias and Ferns
  2 parts garden loam
  2 parts sand
  2 parts leafmold

For Bulbs
  2 parts garden loam
  1 part sand
  1 part leafmold

For Cacti and Succulents
  2 parts garden loam
  2 parts sand
  1 part leafmold
  Handful of limestone

For successful potting, place enough drainage material in the bottom of the container so that excess water can drain off freely. Use broken pot pieces or some small or crushed stones. Then put in a mound of soil.

Remove the plant from its nursery container. First moisten the soil so the root ball can come out intact. Center the plant on the mound of soil in the new pot. Put soil in and around the roots, pressing it down to eliminate air pockets. Add more soil until the tub is filled to a proper level.

Tubs and boxes when filled with soil can be extremely heavy so position the box where you want it and then fill with soil and plant. However, even if you have planned the garden with containers in specific places there will come a time when you might want to move them. This is probably the only disadvantage of gardening in containers. Moving takes muscle and time. A small tree in a 24-inch tub can weigh as much as 600 pounds—quite a weight.

To move large shrubs and trees in boxes use a dolly or handtruck or you will kill yourself (or your back at least).

Repotting and Topdressing

Eventually, soil in containers becomes depleted of nutrients and new soil must be added so plants grow vigorously. Repotting a large planter box or a 20-inch tub takes some time and doing. You must first remove all old soil and start again and the procedure is the same as potting a new plant. However, since most plants in large boxes can go two to three years without repotting, a good way to add some soil to a planter is to top dress a plant. This merely means digging out the top two to eight inches of soil and filling in with new soil.

Instead of repotting the plant into a larger container as you do with houseplants, with boxed and tubbed plants generally you plant back into that same container. Here is how

to remove soil from a large box: First, dig around the perimeter of the soil with a hand trowel to loosen soil and break it up; punch down as deep as you can. Now gently take the plant in hand and wiggle it—move it left and right, back and forth to get the roots loose. Do not pull it or jerk it loose because this will harm the plant. Loosen the plant slowly and gently. Scoop out the old top soil you have broken up with the trowel and discard it. Dig down deeper now and loosen more soil around the root ball. Repeat this procedure until you can grasp the plant and remove it without undue pulling on the plant.

When the plant is out of the container crumble off soil from the root ball—do not remove all soil, just the soil that will loosen with your hand efforts. If you can, turn the box on the side now and remove remaining soil—generally this can be done with a shovel or spade or perhaps the hand trowel again. The idea is to discard the old soil. When this is accomplished fill with pot shards for drainage again and then use the standard potting methods as described earlier.

After potting always water plants thoroughly.

POSITIONING PLANTERS

Any planter or tub or box set directly on soil, on a deck, or on patio paving should have small cleats underneath it—wooden blocks. This is an important aspect of container gardening because as we noted earlier the space beneath the container and the paving or ground allows air to enter the container and eliminates a hiding place for insects as well.

The size of the cleats will depend on the

Container garden

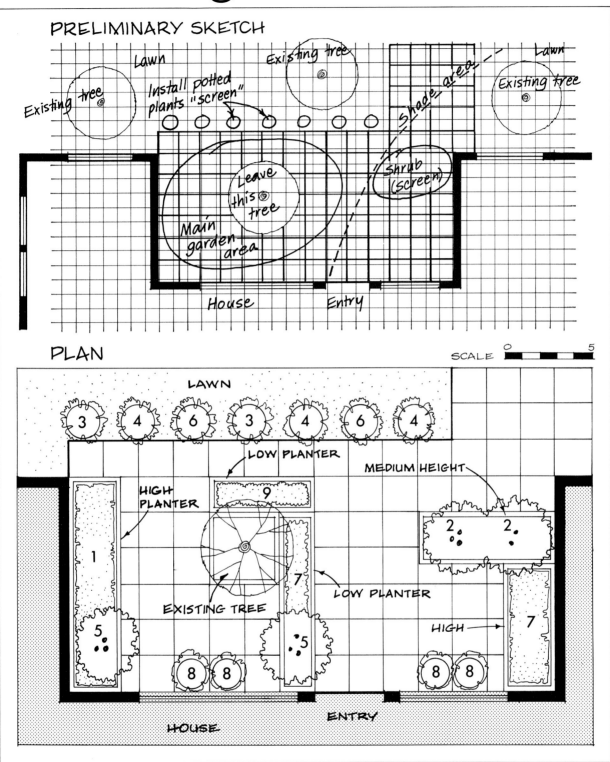

PRELIMINARY SKETCH

Lawn

Existing tree

Existing tree

Install potted plants "screen"

Shade area

Lawn

Existing tree

Leave this tree

Shrub (Screen)

Main garden area

House

Entry

PLAN

SCALE 0 5

LAWN

LOW PLANTER

MEDIUM HEIGHT

HIGH PLANTER

EXISTING TREE

LOW PLANTER

HIGH

HIGH

HOUSE

ENTRY

1. *Viburnum opulus* 'Nanum' European Cranberry Bush

2. *Hydrangea macrophylla* 'Mariesii'

3. Iris 'Ochroleuca Gigantea'

4. Tulipa 'Inga Hume'

5. *Paeonia moutan* Peony

6. Narcissus 'Jeanne d'Arc' Butterfly Narcissus

7. Iris 'Lemon Flare'

8. Hyacinthus 'Lady Derby'

9. *Convallaria majalis* Lily-of-the-Valley

Container garden

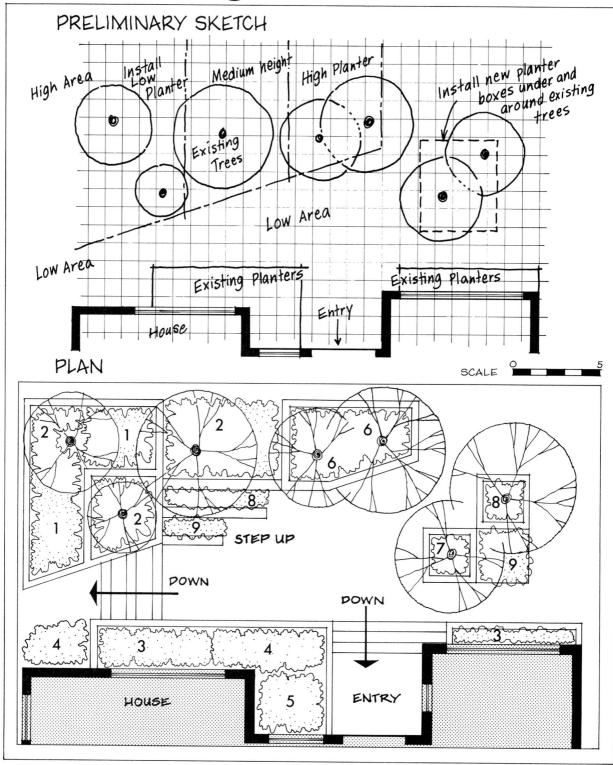

PRELIMINARY SKETCH

High Area

Install Low Planter

Medium height

High Planter

Install new planter boxes under and around existing trees

Existing Trees

Low Area

Low Area

House

Existing Planters

Entry

Existing Planters

PLAN

SCALE 0 ___ 5

STEP UP

DOWN

DOWN

HOUSE

ENTRY

1. *Viburnum opulus* 'Nanum'
   European Cranberry Bush

2. *Hydrangea macrophylla*
   'Mariesii'

3. Iris
   'Ochroleuca Gigantea'

4. Tulipa 'Inga Hume'

5. *Paeonia moutan*
   Peony

6. Narcissus 'Jeanne d'Arc'
   Butterfly Narcissus

7. Iris 'Lemon Flare'

8. Hyacinthus 'Lady Derby'

9. *Convallaria majalis*
   Lily-of-the-Valley

size of the box: Planter boxes should have several cleats spaced equidistant from each other while a 24-inch box needs only four cleats—one at each corner. The cleats can be nailed to the box when you make it or they can be set in place and the planter put directly on them. The weight of the soil in the container will keep the cleats in place. I use pieces of 2 x 4 inch boards for cleats, usually about 6 to 8 inches long.

WATERING/FEEDING

Container plants exposed to the elements dry out quicker than plants in the ground. How much and how often to water depends on various conditions—the size of the container (large ones dry out more slowly than small ones), the amount of rainfall, the type of box or tub. Glazed pots without drainage holes—urns, jugs, and so on—need careful watering to avoid a stagnant condition. Wooden tubs, boxes, and planters dry out slowly and soil in metal containers stays wet for days.

When you water plants, be sure the stream is not so strong that it washes away soil. Be sure to soak plants. Sparse watering results in pockets of soil becoming wet, eventually waterlogged. Water should run out of the drainage holes. A good rule is to water plants thoroughly and then allow them to dry out a little before watering them again. The feel of the top soil is a good guide.

Apply a commercial soluble fertilizer, 10-10-5 (contents marked on the bottle) mixed weaker than the directions indicate, but use it more often. Avoid set rules for fertilizing. In general, feed plants in large containers, 18 to 26 inches in diameter, about four times in summer; those in smaller boxes, about once a month.

There is no end to the kind of plants that can be grown in a tub or box. Small trees are desirable for patios, shrubs are almost essential to make a setting attractive, and vines and colorful bulbs in boxes brighten any area. Standards—plants grown to tree form—and espaliers—shaped and trained plants—are the extra touch that make an outdoor area unique.

Shrubs for Container Gardening

BOTANICAL AND COMMON NAME	DESCRIPTION	TEMP.	REMARKS
Abutilon (flowering maple)	Bell-shaped flowers of paper-thin texture	40F	Give plenty of water and sun
Azalea (see Rhododendron)	Brilliant flowers, lush growth, many varieties	Check with nursery	Great for portable gardens
Camellia japonica	Handsome flowers in many colors	5 to 10F	Excellent container plant
Camellia sasanqua	Mostly small white flowers	5 to 10F	Many varieties
Cotoneaster (many varieties)	Glossy leaves, colorful berries	Check with nursery	Small and large ones

Shrubs for Container Gardening (continued)

BOTANICAL AND COMMON NAME	DESCRIPTION	TEMP.	REMARKS
Fatsia japonica (aralia)	Foliage plant, fanlike leaves on tall stems	Tender	Makes bold appearance
Gardenia jasminoides	Dark green leaves, fragrant white blooms	10 to 30F	New varieties available
Hibiscus rosa-sinensis (Chinese hibiscus)	Dark glossy green foliage, large flowers	20 to 30F	Good performer in tubs or boxes
Ilex crenata (holly)	Glossy leaves, bright berries	−5 to 5F	Many good varieties
Juniperus communis depressa (prostrate juniper)	Blue green foliage	−50 to 35F	Forms dense mass
Juniperus chinensis 'Pfitzeriana' (pfitzer juniper)	Blue green foliage	−20 to −10F	Good screen plant
Ixora	Small red to white flowers	Tender	Splendid color in white tubs
Nerium oleander (oleander)	Dark green leaves, bright flowers	10 to 20F	Needs large container and lots of water. Dangerously poisonous juice
Osmanthus ilicifolius (holly olive)	Glossy leaves on upright stems	−5 to 5F	Grows fast in tubs. May be used as hedge
Pittosporum tobira	Arching branches	10F to 20F	Can be trained to shape
Plumbago capensis (blue phlox)	Small leaves, blue flowers	20 to 30F	Robust grower
Podocarpus macrophylla	Bright green leaves	Tender	Attractive in tubs
Rhododendron	Many varieties	Check with nursery	Excellent container plants
Rosa (many)	All kinds and colors	Check with nursery	Does very well in containers
Thuja occidentalis (arborvitae)	Evergreen	−50 to −35F	Tough plants for untoward conditions
Viburnum (many)	Attractive leaves, pretty flowers and berries	Check with nursery	Many varieties
Yucca filamentosa (Spanish bayonet)	Blue green, sword-shaped leaves	−20 to 10F	Dramatic in tubs

Trees for Container Gardening

BOTANICAL AND COMMON NAME	DESCRIPTION	TEMP.	REMARKS
Acer palmatum (Japanese maple)	Lovely lacy leaves	−10 to 0F	Handsome in soy tub or round container
Araucaria excelsa (Norfolk Island pine)	Pyramid shape	Tender	Good vertical accent in Spanish flare-lip pot

Trees for Container Gardening (continued)

BOTANICAL AND COMMON NAME	DESCRIPTION	TEMP.	REMARKS
Betula populifolia (gray birch)	Deciduous, irregular in shape	−30 to −10F	Fine tree for patio or along house wall
Cedrus atlantica glauca (blue atlas cedar)	Needle evergreen with sprawling habit	−30 to −10F	Fine accent in large tubs near house corners
Citrus (orange, lemon, lime)	Dark green leaves, nice branching effect	30 to 40F	Excellent trees, indoors or out
Eriobotrya japonica (loquat)	Round headed with dark green leaves	20 to 30F	Good for tubs and boxes
Ficus benjamina (weeping fig)	Tiny dark green leaves, branching habit	Tender	Good special effect in garden or indoors in tubs
Ginkgo biloba (ginkgo)	Deciduous, lovely foliage	−30 to −10F	Handsome in containers, nice accent near house walls
Laburnum watereri (goldenchain tree)	Deciduous, columnar shape	−20 to −10F	Good patio tub plant. Seeds poisonous if eaten
Lagerstroemia indica (crape myrtle)	Deciduous with pink flowers	−20 to −10F	Showy for patio
Magnolia soulangeana (saucer magnolia)	Deciduous with round form, lovely flowers	−20 to −10F	Good near fence or wall
Malus sargentii (sargent crabapple)	Dwarf, round topped form	−30 to −20F	Perimeter decoration for paved area
Phellodendron amurense (cork tree)	Deciduous, attractive branching tree	−40 to −30F	For a special place
Phoenix loureirii (date palm)	Lovely, arching fronds	Tender	An indoor-outdoor favorite
Pinus mugo mughus (mugho pine)	Irregular outline, broad and sprawling	−40 to −30F	To decorate paths, walks, and patios
Pinus parviflora glauca (Japanese white pine)	Needle evergreen with horizontal growth	−10 to 0F	Nice feature in and around garden
Pinus thunbergi (Japanese black pine)	Good spreading habit	−20 to −10F	Excellent container plant
Podocarpus gracilior	Graceful willowy branches	Tender	Good doorway plant
Rhapis excelsa (lady palm)	Dark green fanshaped leaves	Tender	A stellar container plant
Salix matsudana 'Tortuosa' (contorted Hankow willow)	Lovely sweeping branches	−20 to −10F	For a special place
Schefflera actinophylla (Australian umbrella tree)	Graceful stems tipped with fronds of leaves	Tender	Handsome in terra-cotta Spanish pot

Latticed walls are the special feature of this patio garden. (M. Eckert)

7 ❧

The Patio Garden

THE PATIO we know today exists because many houses in the 1950s were built with slabs of concrete at the back primarily for barbecueing and outdoor parties. Through the years the patio evolved into a garden, for with limited land it was often the only place for it. But where do you plant when you have a solid slab of concrete or other paving material with perhaps a little growing space around it? Basically, you don't plant—you garden in containers and arrange the boxes or tubs on the patio to create a colorful design. And around the patio for background you plant a small tree or two and some shrubs.

To accomplish your patio garden, do use containers such as lovely pots, tubs, and urns on the patio but use them in groups—three pots to a corner perhaps, and a long planter box on one side.

Draw a sketch of the patio and make shapes for potted plants, for boxes, and for planters—a planter is a long box similar to a window box—and place these elements so there is some balance and unity. Plan judicious use of trees and shrubs but do use some to pull the whole plan together.

The patio or terrace garden involves more construction than gardening and involves careful planning as to location and size. Consider too that when you are working with a paved garden you may be extending your home, later enclosing your patio to give additional living space.

But whether small or large, for growing plants, for dining or lounging, patios are special and need special planning. But before we consider the method of construction let's assess location and size.

SELECTING THE SITE

Your individual climate is to be considered in locating your patio garden. An area

A patio garden does not have to be large; this small brick patio works very well as a tiny retreat from the world. Fuchsias and other pot plants make the setting. (Roger Scharmer)

Patio garden

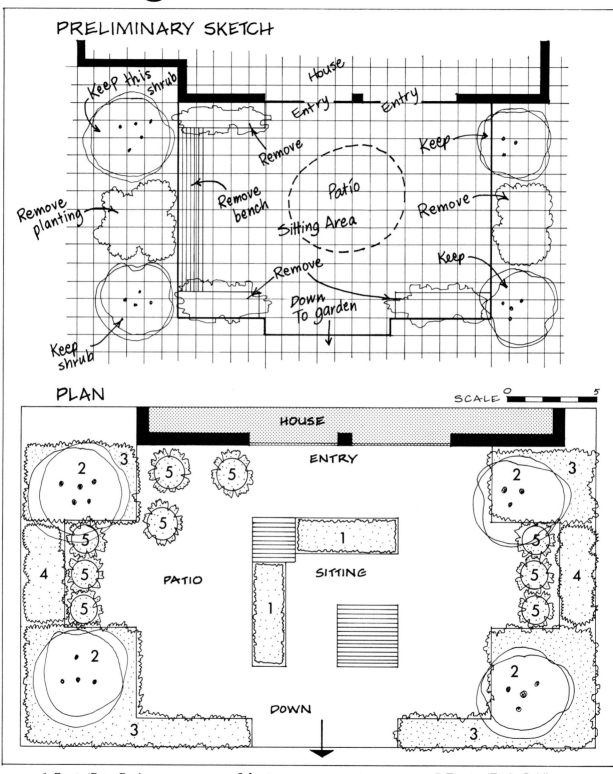

PRELIMINARY SKETCH

Keep this shrub

House

Entry   Entry

Keep

Remove

Remove planting

Remove bench

Patio
Sitting Area

Remove

Keep

Remove

Down
To garden

Keep shrub

PLAN

SCALE 0   5

HOUSE

ENTRY

3   5   5

2   5   2   3

5   5

4   5   4
          5   5
5   5

PATIO   1

SITTING

1

2   2

3

DOWN

3   3

1. Zinnia 'Peter Pan'

2. *Rhamnus frangula*
   'Columnaris'
   Alder Buckthorn

3. Lantana nana compacta

4. Rosa 'Don Juan'

5. Tagetes 'Triple Gold'
   Marigold

6. Salvia 'St. John's Fire'
   Scarlet Sage

Patio garden

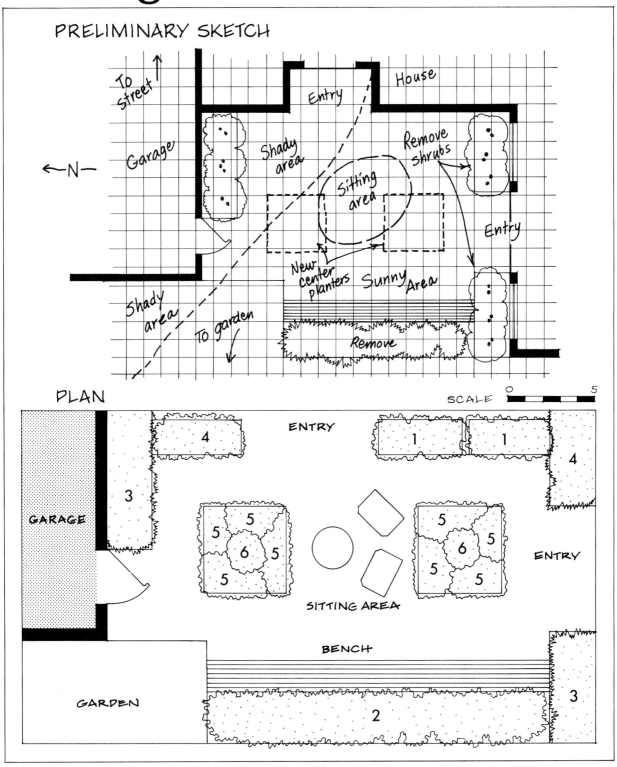

PRELIMINARY SKETCH

To street ↑

House

Entry

← N →

Garage

Shady area

Remove shrubs

Sitting area

Entry

New center Planters

Sunny Area

Shady area

To garden

Remove

PLAN

SCALE 0 — 5

ENTRY

4

1

1

4

3

GARAGE

5

5

5

5

6

5

5

5

6

5

5

5

SITTING AREA

ENTRY

BENCH

GARDEN

2

3

1. Zinnia 'Peter Pan'

2. *Rhamnus frangula* 'Columnaris' Alder Buckthorn

3. Lantana nana compacta

4. Rosa 'Don Juan'

5. Tagetes 'Triple Gold' Marigold

6. Salvia 'St. John's Fire' Scarlet Sage

that bakes in the sun most of the day precludes daytime use and a windy site is not comfortable. In cold climates a south patio that basks in the sun can be a blessing. West is ideal for morning and evening use, and an east-facing patio offers morning sun but afternoon shade, an ideal condition. Northern exposures need not be overlooked since many plants thrive in shade.

Patios are usually placed in the rear of a property because privacy and space are there; however, patios beside the house are lovely too. I had one of these in Northfield, Illinois; it was a fine flagstone terrace that ran the length of the yard and in time I developed an attractive garden there.

No matter what the material of your patio or its location, don't make it too large in relation to your house. A *general* guide to size of this outdoor room is about half the size of your living room unless this is very large.

If the property is vast (how fortunate you are) segment the area into several small ones. Keep each a sensible size and you will create a balanced attractive picture with lawns linking the paved areas together.

Most patios are rectangular or square but they can be circular or elliptical in shape; these can be effective and do not automatically place the patio at the rear next to the living room where most patios are. There is nothing wrong and everything right with a patio off a bedroom or even next to the kitchen.

PATIO PAVINGS

The floor of the patio is the main consideration and do approach it wisely. I still regret the time I was talked into an aggregate concrete floor that forever caught dirt and plant debris and never looked clean even when I

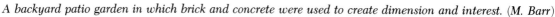

A backyard patio garden in which brick and concrete were used to create dimension and interest. (M. Barr)

A small, somewhat formal patio garden that relies on brick for its beauty and interest. Note the ground cover growing between the bricks—an added plus. (M. Barr)

This handsome patio features a wooden floor, a stone planter, and a lush canopy of foliage. (M. Barr)

A patio garden elegantly landscaped with agapantus and flowering trees. (Ken Molino)

spent much labor and money on sheen-type coatings to make it something it never could be. And the slick concrete floor is not that good either. It looks like a playground. Opt for a concrete floor (if that is what you are using) that has some texture but not too much.

Brick seems to make the most handsome patio; certainly it is expensive but bear in mind it will be in place for decades and will enhance the beauty and value of your home. With brick you can do almost anything to create handsome patterns and a beautiful patio. More on the shapes and colors available later.

Before you select your patio flooring, consider:

Will the floor be easy to maintain?
Will it withstand weather and wear?
Will it be pleasant to walk on?
Will water sink through or flow off in sheets, making it slippery?
What color should the paving be? (Light colors reflect heat, causing glare. Dark paving stores up heat.)

Concrete is a durable low-cost paving but in large areas it looks drab. However, it is long-lasting, easy to clean, and generally inexpensive. To make it attractive use a grid system of wood to separate the concrete—four-foot square blocks work nicely. Be wary of a heavy aggregate floor (I warn you again) because while it does look good it requires constant maintenance if there are plants about.

Similar to concrete are concrete blocks and pavers which you can install yourself. These are offered in many styles and colors—some textured, some colored, and in several sizes with the 16-inch square perhaps the most popular. If you install the blocks without wood spacing—2 x 4 rails or such—they look like a checkerboard which is hardly attractive. Use them but properly installed with dividers.

Tile, of course, is elegant but very expensive. But it is almost impossible to stain, easier than any paved surfaces to maintain, and has a lovely finished look when properly installed. There are many shapes and sizes of tile but outdoors the surfaced type of rough

A patio of concrete aggregate, with board fencing for privacy. (Western Wood Products)

tiles ¾-inch thick is generally used. Of all the tiles, quarry tile makes the most dramatic floor; this is heavy-duty ceramic material that comes in squares or rectangles in many special shapes and sizes. Colors run from off-white to blue-green with brilliant red or rust tones.

Brick is certainly my choice. It is difficult to go wrong with it, and brick comes in a variety of earthy colors that look good outdoors and give a pleasing contrast in texture. There are rough- and smooth-surfaced brick, and glazed or unglazed. A really beautiful world of materials. Hexagon and octagon shapes are handsome. But generally, standard house brick laid in patterns, as herringbone, is very attractive.

The best bricks for patios are smooth-surfaced or rough-surfaced housebricks—preferably used ones, which afford more "character"—a mellowed look. Select hard-burned brick rather than green brick. It should be dark red rather than a salmon color, which indicates an under-burned process and less durability. If you live in a severe winter climate ask for SW (severe weathering) brick.

Fieldstone, slate, and flagstone are other paving materials. Each has its values, and all make beautiful patio floors but all are expensive and all are difficult to lay.

INSTALLATION

You can probably put down your own brick floor or a concrete aggregate floor but it is hardly a joy, and, if people tell you you can lay brick on sand without mortar, tell them to go do it. It never looks right and is rarely satisfactory. In other words, if you are going to spend the money on brick, you might as well have it installed properly by a professional. You will be sure to thank yourself for the decision.

See Chapters 5 and 6 for list of plants for patios.

8 🌿

The Kitchen Garden

THE OLD TERM *kitchen garden* is still used for the vegetable garden that supplies food for the kitchen, and in these days this garden has had a renaissance because of many things. (The colonial dooryard or kitchen garden included herbs but today herbs are so popular we include a special chapter for them later.) It provides you with food that tastes as it should—flavorful and straight from nature without any middlemen and delay of getting the food from fields to packers to markets to you. It saves money and the risk of eating sprayed produce (most commercial crops are sprayed).

Even the apartment gardener can have some vegetables—midget kinds in window boxes—and the owner of the suburban home with little space can have some home-grown produce. It only takes a space 5 x 10 feet to grow fresh food and I have extolled upon that subject in a book called *The Five by Five Garden.* Let's look at all the ways you can have fresh food for your tables—easier than you think.

WHERE?

For convenience, if at all possible, place the kitchen garden near the house—to one side if possible where you can get to the plants easily. You will be more apt to water and care for the plants if they are close by and in one section.

Find your place for the garden and map it out—put beans here, beets there, carrots some other place. Use walls and fences for those vining crops like squash and peas—no formal plans or painstakingly mapped out areas—just get a general idea and then start. How do you start? With soil. Any existing soil generally has had the nutrients drained from it and vegetables really need good nutritional soil and plenty of water. You can get away with starved soil for some flowers but not with vegetables. Dig down at least a foot and crumble the soil. Simply take the hoe or shovel and break up clods and big pieces. Rototilling would be nice but not necessary unless you can afford it. The main prerequisite of good vegetable gardens is good porous soil, soil that drains readily and is full of good old-fashioned humus—decayed vegetable matter.

Once you have the site properly prepared, spread top soil—at least two to six inches, and eight inches is better. When this is done, and this takes work hauling soil to and fro, it is time to make your rows and put in seeds or prestarted plants. Making a row is just what it says and always remember to leave paths so you can get to and from the vegetables. How important paths are and how often they are forgotten!

Put seeds in at seasonal times. Seasonal times mean when it is safe for you to plant in your area, and the information on the seed

This small kitchen garden is 10' x 10'—sufficient space for growing many vegetables. (M. Barr)

Two types of lettuce, Boston and curly, grow with herbs and nasturtium (whose strong smell repels insects) in a kitchen garden.

Kitchen garden

PRELIMINARY SKETCH

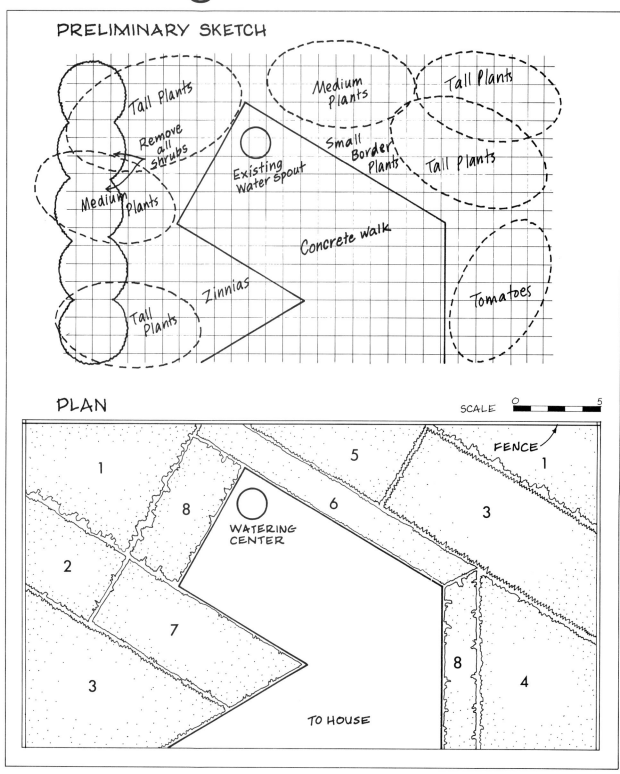

Tall Plants

Medium Plants

Tall Plants

Remove all shrubs

Small Border Plants

Tall Plants

Existing Water Spout

Medium Plants

Concrete walk

Tall Plants

Zinnias

Tomatoes

PLAN

SCALE 0   5

FENCE

1

5

1

8

6

3

WATERING CENTER

2

7

8

4

3

TO HOUSE

1. Helianthus 'Piccolo' Sunflower
2. *Anethum graveolens* Dill
3. Corn 'Golden Cross Bantam'
4. Tomato 'Patio'
5. Tagetes 'First Lady' Marigold
6. Radish 'Tendersweet'
7. Zinnia (Paint Brush type)
8. Tropaeolum 'Jewel' Nasturtium

Kitchen garden

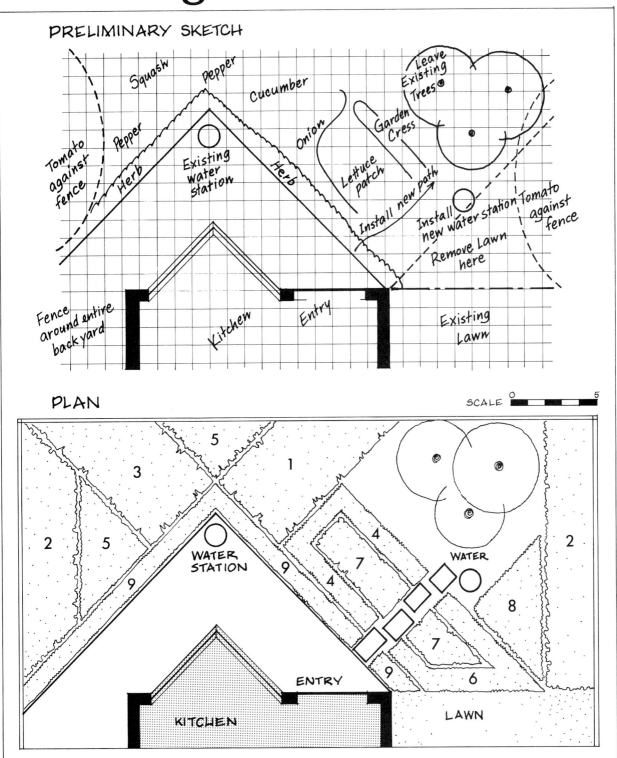

PRELIMINARY SKETCH

Squash

Pepper

Cucumber

Tomato against fence

Pepper

Herb

Existing water station

Onion

Herb

Leave Existing Trees

Garden Cress

Lettuce patch

Install new path

Install new water station

Remove Lawn here

Tomato against fence

Fence around entire back yard

Kitchen

Entry

Existing Lawn

PLAN

SCALE 0   5

5

3

1

2

5

9

WATER STATION

9

4

7

4

WATER

2

8

7

9

6

ENTRY

KITCHEN

LAWN

1. Cucumber 'Patio Pik'
2. Tomato 'Sugar Lump'
3. Squash 'Aristocrat'
4. Garden Cress 'Curlycress'
5. Sweet Pepper 'Yolo Wonder'
6. Onion 'Beltsville Bunching'
7. Lettuce 'Oakleaf'
8. Radish 'Scarlet Globe'
9. *Ocimum basilicum* Sweet Basil

package tells you this. Start cool-growing crops like spinach and cabbage in early spring as soon as it seems likely that the last frost has gone; USDA maps will indicate the possible time in your locality (you can write for these maps). Get your first planting in early and, if seeds are too much trouble or your area has a short frost-free growing season and you can't sow them in early spring, then pick up prestarted plants at a nursery and get them in the ground when appropriate. Before selecting any seed—or prestart—check the days to maturity information; you may not have sufficient time before frost of next fall to grow and harvest certain vegetables. Remember, however, some crops, like kale, are best picked *after* the first frost.

SEEDS AND PRESTARTS

What is the difference between sowing seed and buying prestarted plants? Well, it is claimed you get better plants from seeds, but this is hardly true. I used to start all my vegetables and flowers from seed, but when prestarts came in, I decided to try them and found that they saved a lot of work. It's also easier to see prestarted plants in your garden; you may mistake a sprouting plant for a weed and remove potential crops in hoeing. The difference is cost. Prestarts cost more than seeds.

SOWING SEED

Once the soil is prepared, you can sow seed—and this is usually done in rows. Space vegetable seed according to the table at the end of this chapter. Label each row so you know what you are growing. Even the experienced gardener is apt to forget what is where. It is easy to space large seeds, such as radish and spinach, but small seeds can be tedious.

The row method gives you space to walk between plants, so you can tend them easily. Row planting also helps you differentiate between weeds and the early seedlings. (And there will always be weeds.) The distance between rows is also indicated in the vegetable chart.

Before you sow, be sure the soil is moist. The shallow trenches between rows indicate when you have watered enough, for signs of moisture show there. Keep the seed bed evenly moist but never soggy during the crucial time of germination. And do remove any weeds that appear for they take the nourishment from the soil that your plants need.

When the seedlings are two to four inches high, thin them so there will be ample space for them to grow. This means pulling up smaller seedlings and discarding them or you can use them for fill-ins in other areas. Also friends are usually delighted to receive your extras.

Indoors

Let us look at the various ways to start seeds indoors. You can start seed in clay pots or household containers like cottage cheese cartons or aluminum trays frozen rolls come in. Be sure to punch drainage holes in the bottom of all seed containers. To start seed you need a sterile medium free from disease-causing organisms; vermiculite is the most widely acceptable medium. This light-weight expanded mica product is in packages at nurseries. You can also start seeds in any sterile soil mix or a packaged "starter" mix sold at nurseries.

When you sow seed indoors you get a head start in spring; also, you can sow specific varieties of plants you might want rather than what is generally available at nurseries at seasonal times.

To sow seed in vermiculite or starter

mixes, use a tray or container at least 3 inches deep. Fill the container to within ½ inch from the top with mix. Now insert seed about ¼ inch into the vermiculite. Water the vermiculite lightly, and cover the container with a plastic Baggie or similar material to ensure good humidity. Place the seed container in a warm and bright but not sunny place (most seeds germinate at 75 to 78F). Remove plastic cover when the first true leaves come up. When the seedling has four leaves transplant it into soil in larger containers. Then put each container in a warm, bright window but not in direct sun, making sure the plants have enough space to grow. Always keep the growing medium moist, never wet or dry.

You can also start seed indoors in more expensive special containers like Jiffy-7 pellets. These pellets are compressed peat disks that contain fertilizer. When the pellets are placed in water, they expand; you put seed inside the expanded disk. Kys Kubes are ready-to-use fiber cubes that contain fertilizer. Water the cube and immediately place the seed directly into the cube. (Fiber pots, trays, and tapes are other ways of starting seeds.) Once seedlings are in cubes or Jiffy pellets, grow them the same way you would seeds in a container. The advantage of the seed pellet and cubes is that there is less shock at transplanting time because the entire block or pellet goes directly into the soil.

Many gardeners start seed indoors under artificial light. If you want to try this method, use Gro-Lux lamps—two tubes to a fixture—and two eight-watt incandescent lamps. Start seeds in trays in starter mix as already prescribed; give plants twelve to sixteen hours of artificial light daily. When the first true leaves appear, transplant them.

No matter which method of starting seed you use, remember that young plants should not go directly from indoors to outdoors. Gradually accustom seeds to outdoor conditions by placing them outside part of the day and bringing them in at night for about three or four nights. In other words, gradually expose seeds to more light and warmth in stages rather than in one swift change.

When you thin plants—no matter how carefully—you are likely to disturb those left in the ground and they may suffer somewhat. Water freely before and after thinning. Not all seeds will come up; some may be sterile, others may not germinate, because of improper conditions. But no matter, you will probably have enough seedlings from a standard package to supply your wants.

Vegetables: Seed Spacing and Depth, Germination Temperatures and Times

COMMON NAME	DISTANCE BETWEEN PLANTS (INCHES)	DISTANCE BETWEEN ROWS (INCHES)	DEPTH TO PLANT SEED (INCHES)	GERMINATION TEMPERATURE (F.)	GERMINATION (IN DAYS)
Artichoke	60	72	½	68–86	7–21
Asparagus	18	36	1½	68–86	7–21
Beans:					
Garden	6–8	18–20	1½–2	68–86	5–8
Lima	6–8	24–30	1½–2	68–86	5–9

Vegetables: (continued)

COMMON NAME	DISTANCE BETWEEN PLANTS (INCHES)	DISTANCE BETWEEN ROWS (INCHES)	DEPTH TO PLANT SEED (INCHES)	GERMINATION TEMPERATURE (F.)	GERMINATION (IN DAYS)
Beans:					
Runner	6–8	Grow vertically	$1\frac{1}{2}$–2	68–86	5–9
Beet	2	12–14	1	68–86	3–14
Broccoli	12–14	24–30	$\frac{1}{2}$	68–86	3–10
Brussels Sprouts	12–18	24–30	$\frac{1}{2}$	68–86	3–10
Cabbage	16–20	24–30	$\frac{1}{2}$	68–86	3–10
Cabbage, Chinese	12–18	20–24	$\frac{1}{2}$	68–86	3–7
Carrot	1–2	12–18	$\frac{1}{4}$	68–86	6–21
Cauliflower	8–10	30–34	$\frac{1}{2}$	68–86	3–10
Celery	8–12	24–30	$\frac{1}{8}$	50–68	10–21
Chard, Swiss	4–8	18–24	1	68–86	3–14
Corn, Sweet	4–6	30–36	2	68–86	4–7
Cress, Garden	10–12	12–16	$\frac{1}{4}$	68	4–10
Cucumber	10	40–50	1	68–86	3–7
Eggplant	12–16	30–36	$\frac{1}{2}$	68–86	7–14
Endive	9–12	12–24	$\frac{1}{2}$	68–86	5–14
Kale	8–12	18–24	$\frac{1}{2}$	68–86	3–10
Kohlrabi	3–4	18–24	$\frac{1}{2}$	68–86	3–10
Leek	2–4	12–18	$\frac{1}{2}$–1	68	6–14
Lettuce	12–14	18–20	$\frac{1}{4}$–$\frac{1}{2}$	68	7
Muskmelon (including Cantaloupe)	12–16	48–72	1	68–86	4–10
Mustard	2–6	12–18	$\frac{1}{2}$–1	68–86	3–7
Okra	15–18	28–30	1	68–86	4–14
Onion	2–3	12–14	$\frac{1}{2}$	68	6–10
Parsnip	3–4	16–20	$\frac{1}{2}$	68–86	6–28
Pea	2–3	Grow vertically	2	68	5–8
Pepper	16–18	24–30	$\frac{1}{4}$	68–86	6–14
Potato	12–14	24–36	4	68	
Potato, Sweet	12–18	36–48	(Plants)	77	
Pumpkin	30	72–100	$1\frac{1}{2}$–2	68–86	4–7
Radish	1–2	6–12	$\frac{1}{2}$	68	4–5
Rhubarb	30–36	60	Up to crown	68–86	7–21
Rutabaga	8–12	18–20	$\frac{1}{2}$	68–86	3–14
Spinach	2–4	12–14	$\frac{1}{2}$	59	7–21

Vegetables: (continued)

COMMON NAME	DISTANCE BETWEEN PLANTS (INCHES)	DISTANCE BETWEEN ROWS (INCHES)	DEPTH TO PLANT SEED (INCHES)	GERMI- NATION TEMPERA- TURE (F.)	GERMI- NATION (IN DAYS)
Spinach, New Zea- land	16–18	20	2	50–86	5–28
Squash	20–24	Grow vertically	1	68–86	4–7
Tomato	18–30	30–48	½	68–86	5–14
Turnip	1–3	15–18	½	68–86	3–7
Watermelon	14–18	50	1	68–86	4–14

BEETS

When indoor or outdoor seeds are about two inches high, thin the plants so they are about three inches apart. When the plants reach eight or nine inches, thin them again by removing every other plant, leaving three-inch spaces between plants.

Beets like a cool temperature, so put them in a shady, somewhat cool location. If plants heave out of the soil, add some fresh soil. Keep plants evenly moist. Like most vegetables, beets thrive on plenty of water.

HINTS: Grow beets quickly; pick them when they are young, otherwise they will lose their flavor. Give beets buckets of water when they are showing good growth. Try Spinel and Ruby Queen. Takes 55 to 80 days to harvest time.

Carrots

Carrots need a very porous soil and rapid growth. (If carrots grow slowly, they are pithy.) Frequently feed and water plant. Use a food marked 10-10-5.

Sow carrot seed in spring or fall. Germination may take as long as four weeks. Outdoors plant two rows of carrots, and thin

them when they are about two inches tall. Again thin the plants in one month. Most varieties of carrots take about 75 days to mature.

HINTS: Carrots are slow to germinate, so do not panic if you do not see green for a while. Once carrots are starting up, thin them or the crop will be sparse. Try:

	MATURITY
Sucram	50 to 70 days
Baby Finger Nantes	45 to 50 days
Midget	55 to 65 days
Little Finger	55 to 65 days
Short n' Sweet	68 days

Cucumbers

Cucumbers make good houseplants because they have pretty scalloped leaves. There are many cucumber varieties: smooth, warty, tiny, or huge. Cucumbers love heat and even moisture at the roots. Grow the plants on trellises.

Pick cucumbers as soon as they are ready or they will not yield further growth. Fertilize plants with rotted manure and occasional applications of fish emulsion.

Good salad cucumbers are:

	MATURITY
Baby	55 days
Mincu	55 days
Mini	55 days
Tiny Dill Cuke	55 days
Patio Pik	57 days
Cherokee	60 days

Eggplant

Eggplant needs daytime temperatures of 80F, and 70F at night. Plant prestarts when the weather is settled. (Seeds take weeks to germinate.) Give plants even moisture at the roots and good sun.

Pick the fruits when they are young, about two-thirds their mature size, and when the skins are still glossy. Cut off the fruits with pruning shears. Good varieties are:

	MATURITY
Black Beauty (standard and small sizes)	80 days
Burpee Hybrid (standard and small sizes)	70 days
Early Beauty Hybrid (standard and small sizes)	62 days
Modern Midget	65 days
Golden Yellow	75 days

Lettuce

Growing your own lettuce is so simple. The loose-head (leafy) types are excellent for growing in containers and are ready for plucking within 45 days. Protect plants against heat. Give plants light, but sun is not necessary to guarantee a crop. Use a vegetable fertilizer, and give lettuce lots of water once it is growing. Although average maturity time is 45 days, in about one month you can eat the excellent "thinnings." These are seedlings you remove to make growing space for the stronger plants. When lettuce is mature, cut off a few outer and inner leaves. Wash and eat the leaves.

HINTS: If you want good lettuce yield, cool weather is the secret. Keep picking lettuce to get more. Try these recommended butterhead, looseleaf, and romaine varieties:

Butterhead	MATURITY
Butter King	70 days
Buttercrunch	65 days
Summer Bibb	77 days
Big Boston	75 days
Loose Leaf	
Oakleaf	45 days
Salad Bowl	50 days
Prizehead	45 days
Romaine	
Paris Island Cos	76 days
Dark Green Cos	76 days

Peas

Peas will bear profusely with minimal care. Peas like cool moisture in the soil. Grow peas vertically on pole or trellises. Water plants frequently; never let the soil get dry. Plant seeds in sunny areas because peas like brightness. Lightly feed plants with fish emulsion. Pinch back the growing tips of stems to thin out the vine and to encourage a large harvest.

You must pick peas as soon as they are mature. They will become pithy and lose their succulent, sweet taste if left on the vine too long.

The common green peas are called English peas and are grown for their seed. The edible pea pods, known as Chinese pea pods, sugar peas, or snow peas, are grown for eating. Try these varieties:

Green peas (vine type)	MATURITY
Little Marvel	62 days
Tiny Time	60 days
Mighty Midget	60 days
Pea pods	
Burpee's Sweet Pod (standard size)	70 days
Dwarf Gray Sugar	65 days
Sweetgreen	60 days

Peppers

Peppers, besides tasting good, are charming foliage plants. Peppers flourish in hot weather, above 60 degrees. But if it gets too hot, say 90 degrees, peppers will not set fruit. Buy prestarted plants, and plant them 12 inches apart. You can grow peppers vertically if you tie stems to trellises or strings.

Give peppers lots of moisture. Feed the plants with fish emulsion when the first blossoms open. To encourage more fruit, keep picking peppers as they mature (when they are firm and crisp). You can pick peppers when they are green, or let them turn red on the plant. Pick hot peppers only when they are completely ripe.

Try these varieties:

	MATURITY
Pinocchio	60 days
Nosegary	60 days
Tokyo Bell	58 days
Vinedale	60 days
Sweet Cherry (standard size)	70 days
Yolo Wonder (standard size)	70 days

Radishes

Radishes will grow no matter how inexperienced you are. Radishes do not like hot weather, so start seeds early in spring. Water plants very thoroughly so the radishes will be crisp and tender. Fertilize plants when first young leaves appear.

HINT: The easiest vegetable to grow. Try:

	MATURITY
Cherry Belle	23 days
French Breakfast	23 days
All Seasons	45 days

Spinach

Spinach rarely grows in heat, so plant seeds or transplants in the coolest, shadiest location in the garden. Spinach is not easy to grow because it flowers quickly. The flowering stops foliage production, and the foliage is what you eat. But it is worth a try.

Spinach needs plenty of water. Most varieties mature in about 50 days. Buy blight-resistant varieties of spinach seed, and keep plants thinned to three inches apart.

HINTS: Start spinach in very early spring or late fall because of its preference for coolness. Keep picking spinach; never let plants go to seed.

Try Winter Bloomsdale—40 days for maturity.

Tomatoes

Tomatoes (really fruits, not vegetables) need lots of sunlight and water. If you use prestarted plants, put them 16 inches from the base of a stake. (Tomatoes need stakes because they grow upward.) You can grow tomatoes in trench method, on trellises, or even in mounds of soil. Nighttime temperatures must be between 60 and 70F. Tomatoes do get their share of disease, so try to grow disease-resistant varieties.

Tomatoes do not need feeding. In fact, too much fertilizer can produce lots of leaves but few fruits. Good varieties are:

	MATURITY
New Yorker (standard size)	64 days
Better Boy (standard size)	72 days
Burpee's VF Tomato (standard size)	72 days
Small Fry	52 days
Tiny Tim	50 days
Patio Hybrid	65 days
Fireball	65 days
Burpee's Pixie	52 days
Window Box	50 days
Presto	50 days

VEGETABLE INSECTS

The following chart lists insects that might like your vegetables as much as you do. Once these insects get a foothold in the garden they can ruin a crop, so you have to get rid of the critters. Some people hand pick them, but you may have to resort to natural chemicals.

If you take good care of your plants, you probably will never have an army of insects. If you see a few pests in the garden, hose them off with a strong spray of water, or hand pick them off and kill them. But should insects get a foothold, use some of the natural insecticides like pyrethrum or rotenone. Follow the directions on the package carefully, and keep the insecticides in a safe place so little children or pets cannot get at them.

See Chapter 20 for complete information on pests and diseases.

Insects

INSECT	DESCRIPTION	VEGETABLES ATTACKED	DAMAGE
Aphids	Soft-bodies green, red, or black insects	All vegetables	Eat stems and leaves
Bean leaf beetles	Reddish with black spots	Beans	Make circular holes in leaves
Cucumber beetles	Spotted or striped	Cucumbers	Eat leaves
Mexican bean beetles	Copper-colored, with many spots	Beans	Eat leaves, leaving them almost skeletonized
Rust flies	White maggots	Carrots	Eat crown and roots
Slugs and snails	Easily recognizable	All vegetables	Eat leaves and fruit
Striped or spotted cucumber beetles	Brown	Cucumbers	Eat plants
Tomato hookworms	Green	Tomatoes	Eat leaves
Tomato cutworms	Dark colored	Tomatoes	Eat stems, fruit

VEGETABLE DISEASES

If blights or bacteria hit your vegetables, be prepared to cope with the problems.

Once you have diagnosed the disease from the following chart, get the appropriate remedies, which are called fungicides.

When using any fungicide, check the label

to determine when to stop using the product before harvesting (generally it is two to three weeks). Benomyl and Zineb are the two fungicides most recommended by nurseries for fighting vegetable disease problems.

Vegetable Diseases

VEGETABLE	DISEASE	SYMPTOMS
Beans	Bacterial blight	Water-soaked spots on leaves
Carrots	Leaf blight	Leaves turn yellow, then brown
Peas	Bacterial wilt,	Vines rapidly wither
	Blight	Colored dark streaks on stems, round dark spots on leaves
Tomato	Powdery mildew	Grayish powdery coating
Pepper	Blight (early, late)	Brown to black spots on leaves, water-soaked areas
Eggplant	Bacterial spot	Greasy spots, yellow margins on leaves

9 🖎

The Orchard Garden

IF YOU have space and want some more good bounty from the earth you might try having some berry bushes. And fruit trees need no introduction—even a few apple and peach trees can make the ordinary garden a veritable orchard. Then if there is some space still left on your property, why not try a few nut trees—not to everyone's liking, I know, but favored by many. A few nut trees can increase the bounty, and the trees are lovely and not that difficult to grow.

BERRIES

Too often berries are overlooked because most gardeners believe they take up acres of space. Actually, they need not. Bushes can be set against fences or trellises and pruned narrow. They don't have to take over a garden if you keep them in bounds.

Select the varieties best suited to your area. Blueberries do best in cool northern sections. You can grow strawberries in almost any part of the country.

A Good Start

You can count on a fine yield of berries for the bushes are tolerant and easy to care for. Prepare the soil properly to ensure healthy, productive plants. Spade the ground, turn the soil, and work in organic matter, usually compost. Avoid fresh manure; manure for berries must be well rotted and thoroughly composted.

The sooner you get the bushes into the ground the better chance they have of surviving. If you obtain your stock by mail order, soak the roots (except strawberry plants) in a pail of water for about two hours, and keep the roots away from direct sun and air.

Set each bush one inch deeper than it grew in the nursery. Make a small well around it—water it well—and water copiously.

Blackberries

Blackberries have long had the reputation of being a pest in the garden. The bushes certainly can be because they are invasive, but the berries are also wonderful as jams and jellies, so I can put up with them. (After all, if they get too rampant, you can always cut them back.) Besides their take-over quality, most blackberries have strong thorns, but now some thornless varieties have been developed.

To keep the bushes in hand, grow them vertically on trellises. A well-grown plant can yield a lot of berries in one season, so you need only a few plants to ensure plenty

Berries of all types, such as these elderberries, can be grown in your garden. Select an out-of-the-way space for them, and with reasonable care you will have a fine harvest. (USDA)

of good eating. The canes bear fruit the year after they sprout. When they die, cut them off, and new ones will spring up to replace them. An established blackberry patch may go on bearing for ten years.

Blackberries grow best in mild climates and in the South. The bush is shallow-rooted, requiring ample moisture, good drainage, and protection from drying winds. The common varieties are hardy, semihardy, or tender; select the type that is known to grow best where you live. Plant in spring in the North and in fall or early winter in the South.

When plants arrive, trim away long roots and cut back canes to about six inches. Dig deep holes, spread the roots out fanwise, and fill the hole with drainage material and soil.

Pack the soil rather tightly around the collar of the plant, and, depending on variety, space plants three to five feet apart.

There are bush- and vine-type blackberries. Space the bush types five feet apart. When the new summer shoots reach 36 inches, cut off the stem tips to force the growth of side branches. The next spring, after flower buds appear, remove weak canes and thin others to stand about ten inches apart. Next reduce the side branches to 18 inches; the buds on the remaining side branches will produce white flowers followed by midsummer fruits. While the fruit is being produced, new growth is starting for the next year's crop. Cut off the tips of these canes, and then late in summer, after fruiting is over, cut away and destroy all canes that have borne fruit.

Vine blackberries need slightly different pruning. In the first season let the vines creep along the ground until they are eight feet long; then cut off the tips to encourage side branching. During summer, or early in spring, install supports (trellis or posts) at ten-foot intervals, lift the canes, and train them up on the supports. When the fruiting season ends, cut back the bearing canes to 12 inches, and remove the old canes entirely.

Harvest blackberries in midsummer when they are ripe enough to drop at the slightest touch. Then propagate bush-type plants by digging up and replanting the suckers. Propagate vine types by tip-layering: bend down the canes and cover the tips with two inches of soil in midsummer. (See Chapter 18.)

PROBLEMS: Since blackberries are vigorous plants, they have few problems. Pests and diseases are likely to be the same as those for raspberries. Buy mosaic- and leaf-curl-resistant varieties. Red spiders may attack, but are easily hosed off. Eliminate white grubs with Malathion, and use rotenone dust to take care of any berry fruitworms.

Blueberries

Blueberries like an acid soil, so be sure the soil has a pH of about 4.2 to 5.0. To make your soil acid, add peat moss, partially decayed oak leaves, or acid plant food. Do not add manure, which tends to make soil alkaline.

Blueberries are largely self-sterile, so you have to grow a few different varieties for plants to bear. Three good varieties are Highbush, Lowbush, and Rabbit-eye. The Highbush does well in North Carolina, New Jersey, Massachusetts, and Michigan, and grows to about eight feet. The Lowbush berry is a small plant to three feet, fine for the New England states. Rabbit-eye grows best in the southeastern United States and is a useful plant because it adapts to various soil conditions.

Set out plants in spring or fall. Prepare the soil carefully, mixing in sandy loam and some sulfur and sawdust. Dig holes twice the size of the root balls, and set plants six to eight feet apart, high in the ground, the crowns two inches *above* the soil line. Do not fertilize at planting time; wait at least until bushes leaf out and are fully mature. In any case feed sparingly; (use genuine fruit fertilizers); over-fed bushes tend to be all leaves and no fruit. Because their roots are fine, blueberries tolerate little feeding. It is wise to fertilize only if plants indicate a deficiency (pale leaf color is one sign). Then apply a handful of cottonseed meal; this is a slow-release type and non-burning.

When you transplant, cut plants back about halfway. Then mulch with wood chips

Above: A St. Louis cutting garden that is well planned and produces abundantly. (R. Scharmer)
Below: A natural-looking garden of cosmos and lilies. (M. Barr)

Right: Random stones were used to create a focal point. Their natural color blends with the drifts of flowers. (M. Barr) Below: A kitchen cutting garden with an emphasis on abundance and usefulness. (M. Barr) · Bottom: A backyard flower-cutting garden. (M. Barr)

Left: A garden adds needed color to a Chicago backyard. (M. Barr) Below: A New York City townhouse garden built on two levels: low-growing ground cover and shrubs above, a patio sitting area below. (M. Barr) Bottom: A long, narrow yard enhanced with low plantings. (M. Barr)

Right: The author's own box garden filled
with bulbs and azaleas. The varying
levels add extra interest. (M. Barr)
Below: A patio container garden in Phoenix,
featuring several cacti. (M. Barr)

Left: One large fuchsia is the accent in a walled patio garden. (M. Barr)
Below: Container gardening on a shady portico in Los Angeles. (M. Barr)

*Right: A fine clump of azaleas
and a flowering vine frame a patio
outside a California home. (M. Barr)
Below: A quiet place for sitting,
on a patio in St. Louis. (R. Scharmer)
Bottom: A patio garden
framed by greenery. (M. Barr)*

Left: Containers of flowers and shrubs on a tile patio in Pasadena. (M. Barr) Below: Roses complement the muted color of cobblestones in a patio courtyard garden. (Roger Scharmer)

A small patio garden in Arizona. The deep green of the plantings contrasts strikingly with the white stone walls. (Photo by Matthew Barr)

or sawdust. Prune bushes when they are dormant in winter or early spring. Remove weak growth and old wood (the largest fruit is borne on new canes). Cut back cane tips so only four to six flower buds remain on each twig; otherwise plants tend to bloom themselves to death. Pick off all blossoms the first two years, but allow a small crop to mature in the third year. Crops will increase naturally year after year.

Let fruits remain on the plants at least a week after they turn blue. To determine if they are ripe, twist them gently: They should fall off. Avoid pulling or ripping berries from the plants.

PROBLEMS: If grown properly, blueberries are incredibly free of insects and disease. Neglecting to gather fruit when it is ripe will encourage an entourage of fruit flies, so keep berries picked, and clean up all trimmings promptly. If insects do attack, dust plants with rotenone. Birds love blueberries as much as people do, so plant enough for everyone!

Grapes

European grapes are cultivated in California, but American varieties will probably thrive anywhere in the country. From the family Vitis, *V. labrusca* is an eastern variety—the Concord is an example. *V. rotundifolia* is a southern grape—this includes the wonderful scuppernong and muscadines—and *V. vinifera* is our western grape.

Most people shy away from grapes because they have read something about the complex job of pruning and training. But for our purposes grape growing can be made simple. Unless there are grapes already on your property, you will be starting fresh, which is usually the best way. Buy one-year-

old stock from local suppliers, who will have the type that grows in your area. The one-year-old vine with a good root system is easier to establish than, say, the two-year-old transplant. When selecting grapes, look for a bushy and solid root system, the key to a healthy plant.

In vineyards grapes are usually grown on a southern hill, where they get lots of sun and good air circulation. For home growing, you can actually start grapes in any area that has *some* sun (at least five hours a day) and good air circulation (but not high winds). Remember that grapes are vining plants and so will need some support. You do not have to install supports the first year, but by the second year grapes must have a trellis or arbor to climb. Use twine to tie your vines loosely and firmly to the support.

Plant grapes in a well-drained fertile soil; dig up the soil and crumble it with a rake and hoe, and use a lot of humus to get the plant growing well. (The soil should be mixed and ready for the vines when you get them.) Grapes grow best in a neutral soil, one with a pH of 6 or 7. Space grape plants about eight feet apart, always keeping in mind that once grapes start growing, they really grow and take up more space than you think. In other words, do not overplant grapes.

Some initial pruning will be necessary to encourage the important development of feeder roots. Vines have a double set of roots, one set aboveground, the other set, which spreads out, belowground. The feeder roots are the roots aboveground. To prune the vine, cut back all canes but two. Leave two or three buds on each cane. Spread out the roots on a layer of topsoil in a large hole 24 inches in diameter and at least 24 inches deep. Fill in the hole with soil so the new plant sits a little lower in the ground than it did in the original container. Make a saucer around the plant to facilitate watering. Water the soil thoroughly and deeply.

Once plants are growing, keep them well watered so they are heavy and thriving. The rooted vines should be heavy and well grown—water does the trick. Keep the ground around the vines level and well tilled; that is, soil should be broken up, not caked. Break up soil gingerly with a rake so as not to injure roots. If the soil is very poor, apply a 5-10-5 fertilizer before spring to help plants along. Grapes do not have stringent requirements, but they will need your help if they are in very poor soil, so tend them regularly as you would other plants.

Do not get involved in the hundreds of different ways to prune grape vines. Just remember that in the second winter pruning is really important, to shape the plant. Prune in the late winter, after the leafy growth has come out, and leave a little more wood than the previous year. Leave about ten buds on each of the main canes. Cut off all laterals but one from each cane; these remaining laterals become the main canes in the following year. The laterals must be kept growing horizontally (on the support), so training is absolutely necessary. In spring the new growth can be trained to grow vertically.

If well grown, grapes can thwart most insects, although a common disease problem is a fungus called black rot. The grapes rot from the inside out; if you see this, immediately remove the grapes so the disease does not spread. Chemicals will not help this disease—you can only minimize this disease, not really cure it. Thrips may occasionally attack grapes, but they can be eliminated with a commercial spray. If the grape berry moth invades your grapes, consult your local agricultural department for necessary remedies.

Grapes are ready for harvest when stems begin to dry slightly. Harvest your grapes in the morning. Use scissors, and do not twist the stems. Set the grapes in a cool shady place.

All grape plants take at least three years to bear, so do not expect an immediate vinery.

Raspberries

Raspberries may produce for as long as ten years. The types offered are red, black, purple, and yellow, in early, midseason, and late varieties. Select the kinds best adapted to your areas and make every effort to secure one-year-old, virus-free plants.

Raspberries must have moisture to produce a really bumper crop; they also require good drainage. Plant red raspberries in early spring in northern sections, in the fall in the South. Black raspberries are less hardy than red and so should be planted in spring once weather is settled. Avoid letting plants dry out completely or they will die.

Plant red or yellow raspberries two to three inches deeper than they grew in the nursery, three feet apart in rows eight feet apart. After planting, cut back red raspberries to eight to 12 inches. (Do not plant black and purple raspberries as deep as red ones. Also, space them six feet apart, rather than the three feet for red raspberries.)

When the shoots of black or purple raspberries are two to three feet high, start pruning the tip of new canes in midsummer to encourage the lateral branching that will bear the following year. By late summer or early fall, fruit buds develop; they will stay dormant through winter. In spring, cut back the laterals to five or six fruit buds.

Let summer-fruiting red and yellow raspberries grow undisturbed until the second spring. Then when buds show green tips, remove all but three healthy canes per row of shoots to initiate lateral branches that will bear fruit in midseason. Cut back everbearing red and yellow types to the ground late in fall rather than in spring or early summer so they can grow through summer to produce a heavy fall crop.

When berries are fully ripe, pick them every two or three days, preferably in late afternoon. Remember berries are perishable, so don't crush them in your gathering baskets; handle judiciously. Indoors, keep berries where it is shady and cool.

Red and yellow raspberries propagate themselves by runners under the soil. With black and red raspberries, tip-layer them by arching over the tips and covering them with two inches of soil; a new plant will pop up in spring. Cut off the tip, dig up the plant, discard it, or replant it elsewhere.

PROBLEMS: Pests and diseases are likely to be the same as those for blackberries.

Strawberries

Strawberries are an amenable crop that everyone can grow. The plants, which can be cultivated in most parts of the United States, are perennials that live for several years while blossoming and bearing fruit each season. The best crops are produced the first two years; after that plants must be replaced. Strawberries are usually called everbearing, but they are better considered early, midseason, and late bearers. Even a dozen plants will yield a harvest, sparse the first year, prolific the second.

When you are ready to set out your plants, trim back roots to four or five inches, dig holes wide enough to accommodate them, and set plants in place so that the crowns are at ground level. If crowns are placed too deep in the holes, growth will be retarded; if they are set too high, plants will die. Strawberries need a rich moist soil and plenty of sun to do their best. The ideal is a sandy loam, but even in lesser soils, plants prosper if there is good drainage. In the North, set out in spring; in the South, fall is fine.

The strawberry, a member of the rose family, bears lovely, white, scented blossoms that look like small wild roses. Plants hug the ground, the leaves produced on short woody stems. Most gardeners pinch off the first blossoms. Then the strength of the plant is not depleted by setting fruit too early and the resultant crop, when the plant matures, is heavy. I pinch off some, not all, of the first blossoms and do get a fine crop. But not every flower produces fruit since cross-pollination is necessary. This is naturally accomplished by insects or wind and every blossom may not be reached. Do not fertilize strawberries the first year; wait until the second, when plants are mature.

There are so many ways to grow strawberries that it can be confusing. If space is limited, strawberry jars are fine. Plants can also be grown in matted or mulched rows with the mother plant setting runners at will until a solid bed is produced. Strawberries may also be spaced 12 inches apart and grown by the hill system. Raised beds are another way of producing bushels of berries;

strawberry rings or pyramids can be accommodated in six-foot areas.

PROBLEMS: The best way to avoid insects and disease is to obtain virus-free plants at the start. The most damaging insect is the strawberry weevil, a sucking insect that can ruin a crop. The crown borer is another pest. Suitable preventatives are sold at nurseries. Verticillium wilt and gray mold are the most prevalent diseases; these are carried by soil-borne fungi that infect roots and kill plants. Control for disease can be accomplished by using appropriate remedies (obtained at nurseries). I cannot really recommend specific remedies or controls because I do not use them; my strawberries are rarely bothered by pests or diseases. Your plants will be healthy too if you grow virus-free varieties.

Spray Schedule for Berries

PLANT	WHEN TO SPRAY	PEST/DISEASE	PREVENTATIVE
Blueberries	When blossoms have fallen; repeat twice at seven-day intervals	Flea beetles, fruitworms, spittlebugs, botrytis rot	Combination spray: Malathion, Carbaryl* (Sevin)
Blackberries and Raspberries	When leaves have fully emerged	Aphids, fruit worms, leaf chewers	Combination spray* (as for blueberries)
Strawberries	When leaves have fully emerged	Aphids, leaf rollers, strawberry weevils, mites	Combination spray* (as for blueberries)
	Before blossoms appear	Same as above	Same as above

* Available ready-mixed at suppliers.

FRUIT TREES

Fruit trees have lovely blossoms and fresh green leaves in spring, and nothing equals the taste of fruit fresh from the tree and the dividends of preserves made from your own crops. If you already have fruit trees on your property you are fortunate; if you do not, I urge you to set some out. Once planted and growing, fruit trees need some care; they do not require acres of land—you can have them even in a small garden. For example, in an area 150 feet long and 50 feet wide I have cherry, peach, apricot, and apple trees.

At the Start

If you are selecting trees, you will want to know how long each takes to bear. Bearing time is determined by the kind of fruit and also the variety. I have five varieties of apples; each bears at a different time—the first in May, the last in October or November. Generally apple and pear trees require from four to six years to produce; peach, plum, and cherry take three to four years. Miniature varieties vary somewhat. This information is generally available in catalogs, or your local nurseryman can give you the information.

Fruit trees

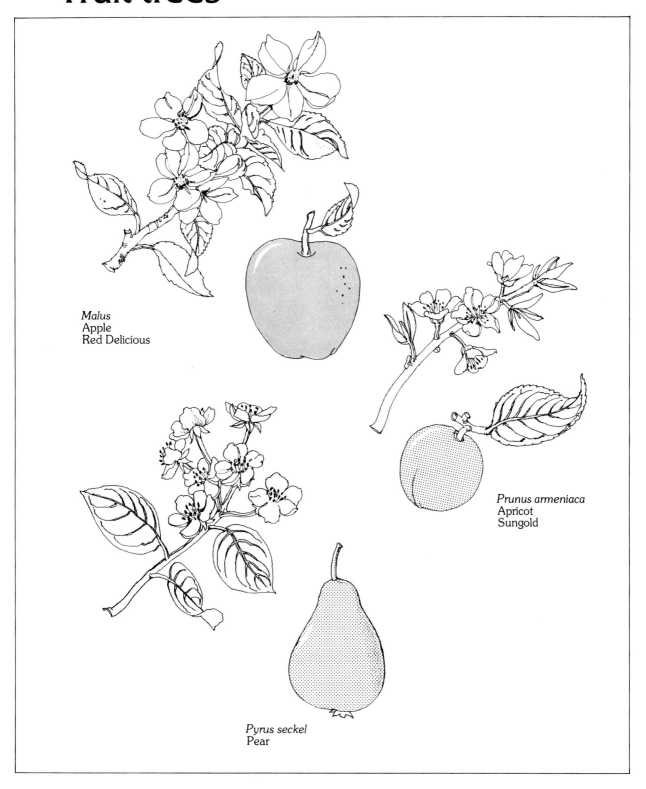

Malus
Apple
Red Delicious

Prunus armeniaca
Apricot
Sungold

Pyrus seckel
Pear

Local climate dictates what fruits you can grow; it is only good sense to plant those that will flourish in your area. They must be hardy enough to stand your coldest winters and hottest summers. Northern types belong in the North, southern types in the South. Your local nursery is probably the best source of information as well as the place to buy your stock. Select your varieties with care; some apples are excellent for eating, others for cooking or preserving. And some, like the McIntosh, are good for every purpose. A few trees of each type would be nice if you have the room for them. With apples and pears you will also have to determine whether you want early, midseason, or late crops.

Another point, many varieties of fruit trees are self-sterile, which means that they will not set crops unless other trees that blossom at the same time to furnish pollen grow nearby. Make sure such cross-pollination is provided or that the variety you are buying is self-fruiting.

Buying Trees

Dormant trees from your local nursery will almost always survive if they are properly planted. If you plan to buy from a mail-order house, first find out the tree's season and its hardiness for North or South, whether it is meant for eating or cooking, and, most important, its resistance to diseases and insects. In other words, don't buy any old tree because it is a fruit tree—be discriminating, just as you are with your other purchases.

Ideally one- or two-year-old trees are best. Most stone fruits are sold when one year old; apples and pears are generally sold when they are about two years old. Select trees that are stocky and branching rather than spindly and compact. Let your nurseryman guide you to a certain extent, and then use your eyes to determine a well-proportioned tree.

Whether you buy from a local source or by mail, plant trees at once, if possible. If there must be a delay, "heel in" the trees. This is temporary planting: dig a trench wide and deep enough to hold the roots, lay the plants on their sides, cover the roots with soil, and water them. Keep the new trees out of hot sun and strong wind.

Planting Trees

Even a half-dozen trees can be grouped as ornamentals on a property no larger than a quarter acre, so do not worry about limiting the number of trees you plant. Also do not brood over spacing. Experts usually advise 30 to 40 feet between trees, but my apples, pears, and peaches are only 15 to 20 feet apart and they are prospering and bearing fruit.

The placement of your trees is not very important. I have set ten fruit trees in an arc at the front of the house, some 12 trees at the back, and four more in another area. I have a good supply of apples, peaches, apricots, pears, plums, and cherries—what else could one want?

Prepare the ground with care. You want a friable, workable soil, one with many tiny air pockets. Dry sandy soil will not hold water, and clayey soil will not drain properly. To have a friable soil that drains, you usually have to work in lots of organic matter—your own compost or purchased sacks of it. Work the organic matter well into the soil. Add a little at a time until the soil is crumbly and rich. This may seem like a lot of work, but it pays in the quality of your fruit.

Plant your trees in fall or spring when the

land is warm and mellow, and hope for good showers and sun to get the plants going. Dig holes deep enough to set your trees at the level they stood at the nursery. Make holes wide enough to hold the roots without crowding. As you dig, pile the surface soil on one side, the subsoil on the other so the richer topsoil can be put back directly around the roots. Pack the soil firmly, but don't tramp it—you want the soil somewhat loose to prevent fast evaporation. Water thoroughly, but don't feed your trees yet; apply fertilizers sparingly, if at all, in the first year for your trees are not yet ready for it.

Some experts advise pruning fruit trees; others say not to. Usually sparse pruning is all that is necessary. Only peach trees seem to benefit from severe pruning. Give your fruit trees careful attention the first year: Make sure they are growing straight (stake them if necessary); note the foliage color, which indicates what is going on. Any change from luxuriant green to yellow means something is awry—the chlorophyll, the green element, in the foliage is not functioning well. Small leaves or just a few are other signs of something wrong.

Keeping Trees Growing

Home fruit trees require some attention to sun, water, feeding, pruning, and insect protection. You cannot do much about the sun, but in a normal year there will probably be plenty of sunlight. If there is adequate rain, you will not have to water much; if it is a dry year, you will. Established, actively growing trees need feeding about twice a year with a standard 10-10-5 plant food or one specifically made for fruit trees. Pruning and spraying are the most important. Proper pruning increases vigor. Leaves and shoots need a constant supply of nutrients, so when you decrease the size of the plant top, the remaining parts grow more vigorously. A good rule of pruning is to maintain a slender habit of growth. Don't let trees droop or spread too much; prune lightly but judiciously. Peaches and apples can take more pruning than pears or cherries. The stone fruits, especially the peach, bear fruit on the previous year's growth. If you do not prune, the new crop will be borne farther and farther from the trunk. Enough pruning keeps the bearing wood near the trunk. Apple and pear trees bear fruit on spurs on wood two or more years old, so extensive pruning is not necessary for them.

Fruit trees are subject to pests and occasionally to disease so apply a dormant oil spray in early spring. The prepared sprays are sold at nurseries. Because conditions vary greatly from one state to another, ask your Agricultural Extension Service for a spraying schedule and also a list of recommended preventatives. In general, apply a dormant oil spray when leaves are about a quarter-inch long. Then use an all-purpose fruit spray when blossoms show color, again when the last petals are falling, and every ten days thereafter until two weeks before harvest. (See the spray schedule for insects at the end of this chapter.)

Apple

Apples, the hardiest of fruit trees, can be grown in every state but Florida. They tolerate a wide range of climates; some will even tolerate −20F. The ideal climate is somewhat cool, with plenty of sun and abundant rainfall. Apple trees grow best in well-drained, almost neutral soil, with a pH of 6.5 to 7.0.

Varieties that thrive in the North Atlantic

states may not grow in the South. There are so many varieties of apples that it is hazardous to suggest the best for each area, but the hardiest trees for really cold climates and short seasons are probably Wealthy, Yellow Transparent, and Alexander. The next hardiest group are McIntosh and Milton. In the cold Northeast, Baldwin, Gravenstein, and Jonathan excel; for milder climates, such as regions south of New York, Delicious and Winesap are always good.

Standard apple trees still get my vote, but if your space is limited, grow the dwarfs or semidwarfs. Set dwarf varieties about ten feet apart, standards about 30 feet. Good robust two-year-old trees are the best buy. Plant with only light pruning, a branch here or there.

Once trees are established, by the second year, feed lightly three or four times in the warm seasons. Too much fertilizer can promote leaf growth but may reduce the size of the crop. Apple trees may bear so heavily that branches can't support the fruit, so thin them out sometime in June.

Insects that may attack apple trees include aphids, leaf rollers, apple maggots, and scale; possible diseases are apple scab and fire blight.

Apricot

Most apricots will bear fruit if planted alone, but some, such as Sungold, need two trees for cross-pollination. The best way to find out is to ask your nurseryman. Grow apricots in neutral soil. They thrive almost

Always welcome in the small orchard are apricots—handsome trees, beautiful fruit. (USDA)

everywhere except in areas of severe winters where temperatures go below −30F. Space standard-sized trees ten to 15 feet apart, dwarfs about six feet. Prune the trees lightly when you set them out and remove deadwood and crowded branches every year. I prune somewhat more severely because the apricot can be shaped into a handsome specimen, and I value it as an ornamental in the landscape.

Apricots need some feeding once trees are established; 10-10-10 is a satisfactory food. The trees are easy to grow; just make sure you start them off properly. They live about thirty years, never get tall enough to be overpowering, and look fine on your property.

Apricot trees may be infested by red mites and scale if you do not give them proper care.

Cherry

Cherries—sweet and sour—are a most delightful crop. The Sweet cherries—Bing and Queen Anne—are delicious for out-of-hand eating; sour cherries are the ones to preserve for jams and pies; they are much hardier and easier to grow than the sweet ones. Generally cherries do well under the same climatic conditions as apples. Sour cherry trees bear in the fourth or fifth year; sweet cherry trees a few years later. Bush-type cherries grow six to eight feet high (I have never grown these), the standard trees to 25 feet.

Make sure that the cherry trees you buy

Cherry trees are always popular in the garden—lovely flowers in the spring and, later, succulent cherries. (USDA)

are "double-bearing," otherwise pollination will be difficult to manage. Check with your local nurseryman.

Cherries require good light, so prune trees every year so that five or six limbs of a young tree can become the main bearing limbs. Let a single limb grow straight up as a leader; trim other branches so they are shorter than the leader. You want your tree to have plenty of open space and a good vertical form.

Cherries more than other fruit trees are intolerant of a wet soil, so good drainage is of the utmost importance. The pH should be above neutral, about 8.0. When you plant the tree, remove all but four of the strongest branches. The trees will tolerate a light feeding now and then through the summer (10-10-10) but in general they do not need much additional food.

The trees attract birds who devour the cherries. Netting is one ugly solution. Of course you can hope that the birds arrive after the cherries form or that the cherries develop before the birds find them. But the best decoy, if you have the time and fortitude, is to plant a mulberry tree nearby—birds like mulberries even better than cherries.

Cherry trees are prone to attacks by aphids, scale, and mites. Brown rot is the most likely disease.

Peach

Peach trees offer not only a genuine taste treat but also a genuine patience problem. Peaches grow almost everywhere in this country, but they are temperamental, often bearing heavily one year, little the next. Peaches need both cold (below 40F) and warmth. However, one late cold snap can wipe out a crop, and fruit is sparse without summer warmth! But peach trees are worth every effort because they supply fruit that is immeasurably good and unlike any you can buy at a market.

Select from the many varieties those that will tolerate your climate. Most are self-pollinating, but to be sure of fruit, plant two or three peach trees. They will bear in about four years. I don't encourage pruning most fruit trees at planting time, but peaches need some pruning because they do not take well to transplanting. You have to prune the top to stimulate root development so the tree will get a good start. Cut back the leader, the center branch, a little and the other branches to about four inches. Trees seem to react favorably to feeding, so apply a 10-10-10 plant food at every other watering.

The dwarf peach Bonanza is a popular tub plant, but don't expect too much from it; mine had fruit for a few years and then gave out. Other gardeners have told me that the same thing happened to theirs.

Peach trees are subject to leaf curl and brown rot, aphids, moths, scale, and mites. Keep the area around the trunk of the tree (where bacterial diseases may start) free of debris.

Pear

Pear trees need a good winter chill to be at their best; they grow in the same regions as apples and peaches. Pears flower earlier than apples, so late frost may cause a disappointment. Pears do fairly well even in poor soil if there is good drainage. Select pears in different varieties to ensure pollination (although trees are mostly self-fertile). Pears need almost no pruning.

Pear trees come standard-size or dwarf. Standards bear in their fifth year, dwarfs in

*If you don't have space
for standard-size fruit
trees, consider dwarf trees,
such as these peaches.*

*A closeup of the author's
pear tree—one of many
fruit trees in his garden.
(M. Barr)*

the third. Cut back young standard trees to three feet at planting time. Train the trees as they grow; once the skeleton is established, pruning is no longer necessary.

Pears do well in a somewhat heavier soil than most fruit trees. Feeding is not necessary if soil is good; watch the leaves for any signs of starvation: If leaves are pale or yellow-green, apply a weak fertilizer.

Don't let the pears ripen on the tree or they will develop brown centers and soft flesh. Pick the fruit when it is slightly green.

Fire blight is the nemesis of pears and it can scorch all parts of a tree. Cut out any blighted area as soon as you see it. Don't wait. The worst time for blight is from bloom to fruit, so watch plants closely during that period.

Plum

Plum trees need some cold weather to bear profusely; they can be grown in those parts of the United States where temperatures do not drop below −20F. Select a locally adapted variety. Plums preserve well and can supply you with lots of prunes. "Prune plums" are best for this purpose, although regular plums are sometimes used too.

Most plum trees are self-fertile, so you will need only one variety. Fall planting is better where winters are mild, but spring planting is satisfactory, too. Prune trees so they are wide open and spreading. As with cherries, birds are the main problem rather than diseases or insects, so net your trees or plant mulberries nearby.

Spray Schedule for Fruit Trees

TREE	WHEN TO SPRAY	PESTS	PREVENTATIVES
Apple	1. Green-tip stage: When blossom buds are opening	Aphids, scale, mites, redbugs	Superior oil, 60 to 70 viscosity
	2. Petal-fall stage: After petals fall	Codling moth, curculio, leaf roller, canker worm, mites, tent caterpillar, scab	Malathion/Captan°
	3. Second application ten days after petals fall	Same as above	Same as above
	4. Third application two weeks after second application	Same as above	Same as above
Cherry	1. Delayed dormant: When the leaves at the blossom ends unfold ¼ inch	Black cherry aphids, European red mites, scale	Superior oil, as for apples
	2. First application: When buds begin to show color	Aphids, mites, brown rot	Malathion/Captan°

Spray Schedule for Fruit Trees (continued)

TREE	WHEN TO SPRAY	PESTS	PREVENTATIVES
	3. Second application: When last petals are falling	Aphids, mites, curculio, brown rot	Same as above
Peach	1. Before buds show any green at the tip	Leaf curl disease	Ferbam
	2. Before fruit buds develop	Aphids, red mites, cottony peach scale	Superior oil
	3. Petal-fall	Curculio, mites, fruit moths, brown rot, scab	Malathion/Captan*
Pear	1. Green-tip stage	Psylla and leaf blister mites	Superior oil, as for apples
	2. When petals fall	Psylla, blister mite, scab	Malathion/Captan*
	3. Another application two weeks after petal-fall	Same as above	Same as above
Plum and Apricot	1. Green tip stage: When blossom buds are opening	European red mites, European fruit lecanium, San Jose scale	Superior oil, as for apples
	2. When last petals fall	Same as peach	Malathion/Captan*

* Do not use insecticides on any fruit tree during flowering period. Combination sprays for fruits come ready-mixed at nurseries.

NUT TREES

Nut trees make excellent shade trees for gardens and are easier to grow, than, say, fruit trees. However, it does take them a long time to mature and bear but in the meantime you have a pretty tree to look at. There are nut trees for all parts of the country, although soft-shelled almonds do not bear in very cold climates, hard-shelled almonds do.

Nut trees, like fruit trees, need good drainage and plenty of water through the years. A northern or eastern slope is the best site for most of these. Many varieties are hardy throughout the United States, although, as with fruit trees, some are best planted in specific regions. The pecan, for example, is primarily a southern tree. Check with your local nurseryman for the best varieties for your region.

Most nut trees need light pruning yearly, but if pruning is neglected, trees will still grow well once they are established. A dormant oil spray will help keep down insects,

Walnut trees are handsome and large, and provide a good crop as well. Worth the time to cultivate. (USDA)

although established nut trees are rarely bothered by insects.

Nut trees will, if necessary, grow in almost any soil, but ideally well-drained loose subsoils are best because these trees are mostly deep-rooted and a soil that contains organic matter helps to retain moisture between rains. Neutral or slightly acid soils are best for almonds, filberts, and hickories; butternuts, pecans, and black and English walnuts like slightly alkaline soil.

The roots of nut trees are easily damaged by sun and wind, so try to keep them moist until planting, and never expose them to sun or wind. At planting time, remove one third to one half of the tops because in planting some roots are destroyed and so cannot support the entire top growth at first. After the roots establish themselves, new growth will develop rapidly on the pruned branches.

Set trees in planting holes slightly deeper than they were at the nursery (you can usually see the soil line on the bark). Put about six inches of soil in the hole and spread out the roots carefully. Tamp down the soil with your foot. Next pour water into the hole to fill air pockets. Let the water seep into the soil; then fill the rest of the hole with soil; pack down again and thoroughly soak again. If this sounds like a lot of water, it is, but it is necessary to ensure a good start for the young tree. Leave a slight saucer-like depression around the tree to catch rainwater.

Most nut trees come balled and burlapped, but some come bare-rooted (without protection) because it is cheaper to ship trees this way. Bare-root trees need to be planted as soon as possible after arrival. If you buy bare-root trees that are exceptionally dry, before planting soak them with their entire length in water for several hours or overnight.

A tree that has been transplanted experiences a shock, so the first year give the tree more than usual attention. Spread a mulch of peat, straw, or even lawn clippings around the tree in a 30-foot diameter to keep roots cool in summer and conserve moisture. Be sure the tree has ample water; the soil should never become dried out, but do not drown the tree—keep soil evenly moist. You might also want to put some burlap or aluminum foil around the tree trunk to protect it from sun scald. I have never done it and my trees are fine; still, it might be a wise precaution in areas with very severe hot weather. Also, remove any wire tags because as the tree grows, the wire can split the bark and provide an opening for the entrance of fungus.

Pollination

The male flowers of nut trees appear in the form of a catkin that sheds pollen in spring. The female flowers are at the end of a small nutlet that must open at the same time the pollen is available in order to be fertilized. On many trees the flower forms open at the same time, but if pollen sheds at the wrong time, other trees of the same kind must be close enough for wind to aid in pollination. Spring frosts can damage catkins, and sometimes trees will produce catkins for a few years before they produce nutlets.

Almond

This member of the rose family is a valuable and pretty tree, which is its problem: The white and pink blooms open so early that they are susceptible to frost injury—thus you get no harvest. The variety Nonpareil is the best one for California. In northern states select Hall's Hardy, which blooms late and does not require cross-pollination. Almond trees will grow wherever peach trees thrive.

Plant them in any well-drained location. Rich soil is not necessary; these trees grow well even in poor soils. Set them somewhat high because they settle a great deal after planting. In other words, don't dig the hole any deeper than necessary, and plant with the upper roots just below the soil surface. Never plant the trees deeper than they grew in the nursery. Watch for sunburn on bark; wrap trees in burlap if sunburn occurs.

Fertilize almonds only very lightly with a high nitrogen fertilizer; if rains are regular, no additional watering is necessary (almond trees do not like wet feet). Prune lightly when you plant, and prune a little again in summer.

Almond trees are not seriously bothered by pests and can fare for themselves without chemical intervention. To produce nuts, they all require pollen from another variety. Honey bees are the pollinators.

Chestnut

The American chestnut tree is almost extinct, but the much smaller Chinese chestnut is available. This tree yields well. As with most early-blooming trees, the Chinese chestnut should be grown on a northern slope to delay flowering so chill does not ruin the blooms. You will need to plant several trees, about 20 feet apart, to ensure pollination. Nuts generally appear in the fourth or fifth year, and from then on you should have high yields.

The chestnut tree is a beautiful, spreading, round-headed tree as cold-hardy as the peach; it grows in a wide range of climates and soils. It will withstand −20F when fully dormant and lives a long time. The tree bears young and may even produce a crop the second year after planting.

Grow chestnuts in rather sandy soil with plenty of organic matter. Pruning and culture are about the same as for apples or peaches.

The chestnut tree is rarely troubled by insects or disease.

Filbert and Hazelnut

Filbert and hazelnut trees bear large crops. The filbert, which has the better of the two nuts, was imported from Europe; the hazelnut tree is American—both nuts are similar in appearance and eating quality. In general, the filbert is grown in areas of mild winters, the hazelnut serves for cross-pollination.

The best time to plant is in early spring. Select an eastern or northern location. Remove the root suckers. The filbert is good because it has no special requirements. It has no long taproots so transplanting is easy. A moderate nitrogen fertilizer is best. At planting time, prune to two feet above the ground, leaving four to six branches. Prune lightly every year thereafter until the tree is bearing.

Filbert and hazelnut trees are rarely bothered by disease or insects.

Hickory

Hickory trees are cousins of pecans. The common hickories are the shagbark, shellbark, and mockernut or pignut (the pignut is of little or no value). The hickory has an extremely long taproot, so it is a tough tree to transplant properly. The hole for the tree must be deep enough to accommodate a root of, say, ten feet. Fill the hole gradually with soil, watering as you go along, and keep the area around the tree well weeded and mulched with fir bark, peanut hulls, or any organic matter that trees use for food.

Prune to get rid of weak branches; you want a strong framework. Start pruning when the tree is young.

Hickories are tough trees rarely bothered by insects or disease.

Pecan

The pecan is generally considered a southern tree that needs a long and hot growing season to produce a harvest. But some varieties can survive winters of −10F and still produce. Stuart and Schley are probably the most widely grown. Some varieties mature late, others early, some are disease-resistant, some are known for their ability to produce heavily. In other words, there is a pecan tree to suit every purpose.

Unlike most nut trees, pecans require a rich soil and ready drainage. Plant in a deep, really deep, hole to accommodate the long taproots. Plant in early spring in the South, later farther north. Getting transplants to live through the summer is a tough job but not impossible.

Most varieties are self-fruiting, but sometimes catkins come in before nutlets, or something goes wrong, so it's best to plant more than one variety. Also consider that wet weather during pollination can severely check distribution of pollen.

The major insects that attack pecans are pecan nut case-bearers, pecan weevils, and sebworms. Spray for the case-bearers in May; for pecan weevils, in August or September. Contact your local agricultural agent for specifics since conditions vary in different parts of the country.

To keep trees free of insects, apply dormant oil spray in late winter before leaf buds appear. This is when insects that hatch from eggs laid the previous fall are coming out. The insecticides most used are Malathion and Sevin, which can be mixed with fungicides. The most serious disease of pecan trees is scab, a fungus that damages developing nuts and foliage in spring.

Walnut

This favorite tree is a beauty. For eating you will want a Carpathian, the hardy English tree, which is cold-resistant, yielding lots of high-quality, thin-shelled nuts. Walnut trees need a well-drained but not necessarily rich soil. The true black walnut takes about one hundred years to bear, but the Carpathians usually yield in six to seven years after planting, which is not too long when you consider the beauty and fine taste of walnuts from your tree. (Recent reports indicate that black walnuts are toxic to other plants, like apples and tomatoes. The toxicity may be in the roots or leaves.)

Plant trees in deep holes with adequate drainage and in good soil; walnut trees do not fare well in poor, gravelly soils. Most nut trees do not need extensive feeding, but the walnut does; a 10-10-5 fertilizer applied three times a year is necessary to help trees bear.

Avoid letting water settle around the trunks because these are susceptible to crown rot, a fungus that attacks bark just below the soil line. Keep a three- to four-foot area around the tree free of other plants that require watering. If you suspect rot, dig up the soil around the trunk and expose the crown, letting it dry out. This usually checks further infection. Or you can cut away rotted bark and apply Bordeaux mixture (from a supplier). My walnut trees have large stones around the base to prevent crown rot. Air can enter between the stones.

Walnut blight sometimes attacks, but this disease destroys only the nuts, not the trees. Spray with a fungicide early in the year, at the prepollen stage. Walnut aphids and caterpillars suck sap from a tree; control these insects with Malathion. Also use Malathion in repeated applications for walnut husk flies. Control scale by spraying trees with a dormant oil spray in February (follow instructions on the bottle).

Nut Trees

NUTS	FROST DAMAGE	SOIL	LIFE SPAN	INSECT DAMAGE	CROSS-POLLINA-TION NEEDED	REMARKS
Almond (*Prunus amygdalus*)	Occasion- ally	Neutral	Medium long	Usually not troubled	Yes	Grows well wherever peaches thrive
Chestnut (*Castanea*) Chinese (*C. mollissima*)	Very rarely	Acid	Medium long	Weevils	Yes	Seedlings preferred in north
Japanese (*C. crenata*)	Very rarely	Acid	Medium long	Weevils	Yes	Quality poor
Hazelnut or Filbert (*Corylus*) Filbert (*C. avellana*)	Occasion- ally	Neutral	Short	Filbert worm	Yes	Mites in some areas
American (*C. americana*)	Rarely	Neutral	Short	—	Yes	Very hardy
Hickory (*Carya*) Shagbark (*C. ovata*)	Rarely	Neutral	Medium long	Usually not trouble- some	Yes	Needs extra care
Shellbark (*C. laciniosa*)	Rarely	Neutral	Medium long	Some	Yes	Nuts thick-shelled
Pecan (*C. pecan*)	Rarely	Neutral	Long	Some	Some varieties	Needs long growing season
Hybrids	Rarely	Neutral	Long	Some	Uncertain	Attractive
Peanut (shrub) (*Arachi hypogaea*)	Rarely	Neutral	Matures in 4 months	Leaf hoppers, soil pests	Yes	Needs long season of heat

Nut Trees (continued)

NUTS	FROST DAMAGE	SOIL	LIFE SPAN	INSECT DAMAGE	CROSS-POLLINA-TION NEEDED	REMARKS
Walnut *(Juglans)*						
Black *(J. nigra)*	Rarely	Neutral	Very long	Many pests	No	Differs in hardiness and pest resistance
Butternut *(J. cinerea)*	Very rarely	Neutral or slightly acid	Short	Fair	No	Very hardy
Japanese *(J. sieboldiana)*	Rarely	Neutral	Long	Fair	No	Fast-growing

Even one clump of annuals—here, daisies—can create a happy color spot in a garden, as shown in this small townhouse yard. (M. Barr)

10

Annuals

ANNUALS provide instant color in the garden and are indeed indispensable. They are inexpensive, easy to grow, and offer rich colors; with annuals you can create a glowing garden in a short time. Prestarted plants of petunias are resplendent in a few weeks—so are zinnias, or impatiens, for shady spots. You can also grow plants from seed, which is easy, but it takes more time.

Plant annuals in various places to give color—between shrubs perhaps or among perennials. They also can provide bright corner or background color. Or you can mass them for a fast concentration of color. Because annuals are so important, learn how to use them effectively; they make even a first year garden look good.

THE PLANTS

Annuals are plants whose life cycle lasts but one season. In that time, they grow and bloom and die. Some annuals, like dianthus, bloom in early spring, others in late spring, like iberis; some in summer like cosmos, and there are those like zinnias, for fall as well. There are indeed hundreds of annuals to grow. Because of the popularity of annuals, hybridizers have produced a great many different kinds—enough to boggle the mind. Some of the most popular kinds—marigolds, zinnias, and petunias, for example—are available in many different sizes and colors.

As a rule annuals are easy to grow. Once in the ground all they need is good moisture and plenty of sunshine (except the shade-lovers, of course) and they are on their way. Let's now explore both ways of growing these indispensables—from seed or from prestarts.

SOWING SEED—OUTDOORS OR IN

The secret of successful outdoor seed sowing is not so much how, but when. If the weather is too cold and soil too wet, seeds

Impatiens and mums thrive in this handmade wooden box. (Western Wood Products)

rot and that's that. Germination—seed sprouting—requires a combination of proper temperature, moisture, and light. The trick is to balance these elements at the right time, and that time is after frost, usually mid-April or early May in most parts of the country. In mild climates seed can be sown outdoors as early as February.

Some gardeners start seed indoors to get a head start on spring, and this is fine. It is more time and trouble but if you are an enthusiast that's the way to do it. Seed is sown indoors in flats or pots containing a sterile starting mixture, which you can buy. We will look more closely at sowing indoors in the following pages. Seedlings are then transplanted to roomier quarters and finally to gardens after a hardening–off period. Hardening off is just a matter of acclimatizing plants gradually to outdoor conditions— on the porch or patio or other protected areas before you plant them outside in soil.

Whether you sow seed outside or in, the

Annuals of all kinds fill this colorful garden. Kept in beds, they are easy to tend, provide handsome viewing, and are an excellent frame for the lawn.

Clumps of annuals provide handsome color in front of these roses and the vine-grown fence. (M. Barr)

soil for seedlings should be well prepared, for good soil with moisture is the basis of good culture. You can't just throw seed on the ground and have it sprout like popcorn. The soil must be porous and rich in humus. A porous soil is one that is full of air and has good tilth (porosity). Humus, as we have seen, is the decayed organic matter that makes good soil.

Even if you break up soil with a rototiller or with hoe and spade, it is not enough. You still need to add humus to make it fertile. You can buy humus. It is available as leaf-mold and rotted manure, and it also comes in packages at nurseries (this is expensive), or you can develop your own compost pile.

You will need two to three inches of humus worked into the soil and mixed to a depth of eight to 12 inches. Break all clods and large sections of soil with the back of a shovel; then rake and level. If you have heavy clay soil, you had better add some gypsum or dolomite (lime); about ten to 15 pounds per 100 square feet. If the soil is sandy, add good top soil. In either case, humus is still necessary.

Once the soil is prepared, and it does take work, that's it. But it doesn't take much effort to keep it in good tilth for successive plantings.

There are several ways of sowing seed. Some gardeners opt for row sowing; others simply throw the seed about (broadcasting). No matter how you handle seeds, cover them with ⅛ to ¼ inch of soil or peat moss. Then soak the seed bed—but with a "mister," not a hose, or you will dislodge the seeds and they will float to other areas where you probably don't want them. The idea is to keep the seed bed *uniformly* moist and this means frequent misting rather than heavier sporadic watering. And let me stress that a

Annuals in containers make this elegant garden sing with color. (M. Barr)

few days without water will kill your seeds. So be prepared to tend to beds for a week or two until your seeds have germinated. After that you can be less vigilant.

Most seeds germinate in about two weeks, and once seedlings are popping up and growing, the process known as thinning out must take place—and it is an important process. Seeds are considered to have germinated when two to four leaves show. Thinning out is important because plants have to have space to grow. Crowded, they may not die but they will not grow into healthy plants that bloom well. So getting rid of weak plants to make room for the strong is necessary.

Instead of sowing seeds in the open ground, you can sow in flats or in cold frames. In this way you can control the soil mix and can easily move the flats around so as to give plants the right amount of light. Watering is easier, too. You can set the flats

Planting From Flats

① CUT OUT PLANTS IN SQUARES WITH KNIFE OR TROWEL.

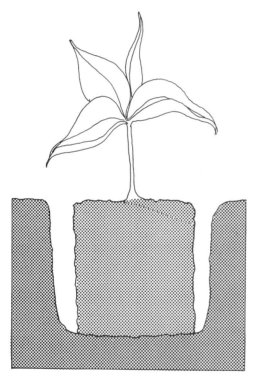

② GENTLY PLACE IN HOLE (DON'T FORCE IN).

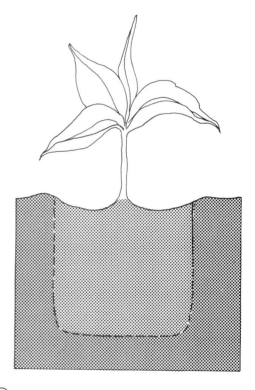

③ FIRM SOIL & MAKE DEPRESSION FOR WATER.

in a greenhouse, or at a house or basement window, or on a heated porch.

It takes three to four months to get bloom from most annuals so it is a good idea to get seeds started as soon as possible.

SOWING SEED IN FLATS

Flats are simply wooden boxes approximately 16 x 20 inches and four inches deep that are available from nurseries or hardware stores. Today, plastic has more or less replaced the wooden box, but I still prefer wood because plastic holds water longer and this sometimes results in the rotting of seeds. You can also use large shallow clay pots or any container with drainage holes. (You can, of course, make boxes.) It all depends on the number of seeds you plan to sow.

Fill the container half an inch from the top with one of the sterile seed mixes. (These come in packages from suppliers.) Firm the soil, mark off rows with a piece of lath or a ruler, and then press larger seeds about an eighth-inch deep into the mix. Sow fine seeds on top of the mix; do not bury them.

Now water carefully with a mister—I use a spray bottle I bought for 50 cents at a supermarket. Place the container in a warm place (about 78 degrees) but out of direct sun. Light is fine but no sun yet. Keep the seed bed uniformly moist, never soggy (or damping off may result) and never bone dry (or seeds may die). You may want to spread a piece of plastic over the container to assure good humidity; if so, punch a few holes in the plastic for air circulation. You can make a plastic tent over the container by inserting a stick in each corner of the box to support the plastic above the soil.

When seeds have germinated, remove all coverings and place the seeds in a brighter place (still no sun). Again, keep the seedlings just barely moist. When the first leaves appear, transplant the seedlings to containers with more space so they can develop. And now use a soil mixture. A good mix is two parts garden loam to one part sand to one part humus. Space seedlings about two inches apart and water. Keep them watered and gradually expose them to more sun. In four to five weeks, or when the plants touch each other, move them outside to their permanent places, provided all danger of frost is past.

Transplant seedlings when they are ready but do it carefully. Take as much of the root ball as possible and insert them in small holes in their permanent locations. The soil should be porous and rich as for sowing seed in ground. (Seed sowing for perennials follows the same procedure as for annuals.)

PRESTARTED PLANTS

The prestarted plants available seasonally in nurseries and various shops in your region are just what they say they are—prestarted. Sowing of seed and germination are over with and the plants are ready for the ground.

Remove them from the flats with a cake server or a knife and handle them gently. Again, the idea is to get as large an intact root ball as possible. Dig holes in the ground for the plants and set them in place. Firm the soil and water well.

As with all plants the soil should be carefully prepared—porous and rich.

Ways to Prolong Bloom

Select the annuals that will grow well in your region.

Keep faded blooms picked.

Start feeding as soon as plants are in the

ground. Feed every two weeks with a 10-10-5 plant food.

Mulch to conserve moisture and keep down weeds. Control insects with natural methods (see Chapter 20).

SOME RELIABLE ANNUALS

Ageratum houstonianum. Blue, white, and pink varieties, 6 to 18 inches high. Forms compact mounds of foliage. Needs well-drained soil and somewhat heavy watering.

Althaea rosea (hollyhock). Neglected in recent years, hollyhocks are making a reappearance in gardens; I recommend them because they are so colorful and survive in practically any situation. They grow to 6 feet, with large flowers in a spectrum of color: pink, rose, yellow, red, and white. (Generally classed as a biennial, but it is best to start them fresh every year.)

Antirrhinum majus (snapdragon). Lovely with beguiling flowers in most colors except blue. Snapdragons come in many heights, 6 inches to 3 feet, and make excellent vertical accents in the garden. Will tolerate some shade, but basically prefer sun. To increase bloom, cut flowers frequently and remove faded blossoms. Many varieties in many sizes.

Calendula officinalis (pot-marigold). Bright, round flowers, single or double, in orange, cream, or gold colors, on 2-feet-high plants. Open from summer to frost. They are hard to beat and grow with little care. A workhorse of the garden.

Callistephus chinensis (China aster). These 1- to 2-foot plants have wiry stems and beautiful white and pink, to deep red flowers. Some varieties bloom early, others in midseason, and some provide late color. One of the best flowers for cutting.

Centaurea cyanus (bachelor button, cornflower). Growing from 1 to 2½ feet, these reliable plants bear pink, white, wine, or blue flowers from June to September. The gray-green foliage makes a pleasing display. To bloom profusely, plants need regular pinching out.

Coleus blumei (coleus). A 3-foot foliage plant that comes in a tapestry of colors—red, green, yellow, variegated. Toothed leaves are effective and plants can be potted in fall for indoors. Pinch growing tips to get compact growth. Good background plant.

Iberis umbellata (globe candytuft). Masses of pink, salmon, or white flowers make this a good choice for the beginning gardener. Plants mound to 12 to 15 inches, and in late spring and early summer bloom their heads off. Good for cutting or garden display.

Impatiens balsamina (garden balsam). These have many virtues in the garden. They grow to 30 inches and bloom profusely, white, red, or yellow. They like some sun but also succeed in shade.

Lobularia maritima (alyssum). Available in white, violet, and pinkish tones, this is low-growing to 1 foot; excellent as an edging plant. Has many other uses in the

Annuals

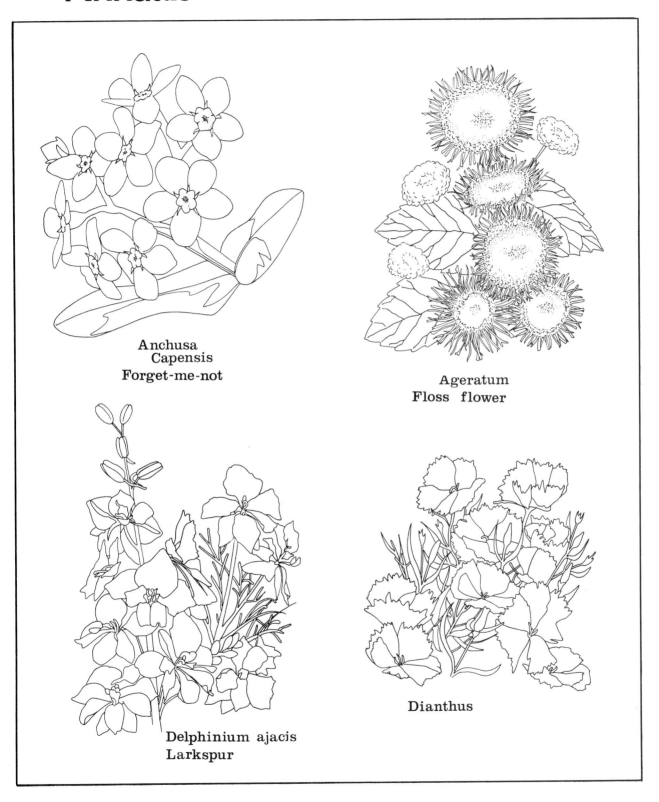

Anchusa
Capensis
Forget-me-not

Ageratum
Floss flower

Delphinium ajacis
Larkspur

Dianthus

Annuals

Cleome spinosa
Cleome

Gaillardia puchella
Rose-ring gaillardia

Godetia amoena
Farewell-to-Spring

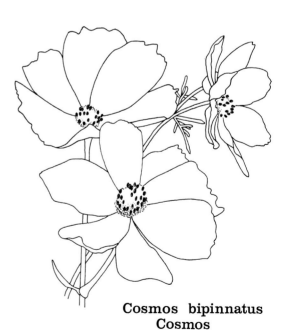

Cosmos bipinnatus
Cosmos

Annuals

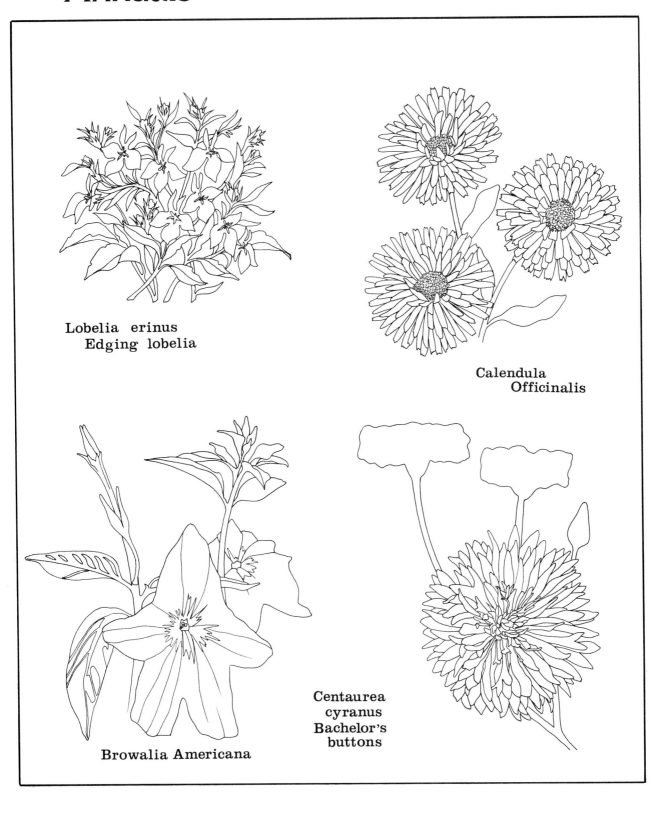

Lobelia erinus
Edging lobelia

Calendula
Officinalis

Browalia Americana

Centaurea
cyranus
Bachelor's
buttons

garden when combined with other plants or used as a filler around perennials. Will grow in hot, dry situations if necessary.

Phlox drummondi (phlox).   Growing to 16 inches, this bears lovely clusters of 1-inch flowers, in rose, crimson, salmon, white, scarlet, and violet, often with contrasting eyes. Bloom is abundant, and plants are seldom bothered by insects. Grow in sun with plenty of water.

Senecio cruentus (cineraria).   A florist's annual that blooms in shade. The daisylike flowers come in light or dark shades of blue, purple, and magenta. Plants grow to 18 inches and have handsome foliage. Keep them shaded and moist in a well-drained place.

Tagetes erecta (marigold).   These all-time favorites can be the backbone of a garden. The 6- to 40-inch plants grow quickly and bloom constantly from summer to fall, in shades of yellow, orange, dark red, and maroon. They can be used alone for lovely accents or with other plantings. Types include French dwarf to 18 inches in a fine array of color; African dwarf to 16 inches, and some new varieties. Most need an evenly moist soil in a sunny place.

Tropaeolum majus (nasturtium).   This can bring a wealth of color to your first garden, and easier plants to grow can't be found. Nasturtiums bloom from early summer until frost, and come in single, semidouble, or double forms in shades of yellow, orange, crimson, pink, maroon, and multicolors. Dwarf plants can be used for borders, taller varieties for spot color. Most nasturtiums crowd out weeds and grow rapidly with little care.

Zinnia elegans (zinnia).   This popular annual comes in many sizes and forms, in heights 1 to 3 feet, and colors of orange, yellow, pink, red, lavender, white, and some bicolors. Zinnias have many uses in the garden and are fast growers that need little care but plenty of moisture.

General List of Annuals
(PD = Planting Distance in inches)

BOTANICAL AND COMMON NAME	APPROX. HEIGHT IN INCHES	RANGE OF COLORS	PEAK BLOOM SEASON	SUN OR SHADE
Ageratum houstonianum (floss flower)	4 to 22 PD 12	Blue, pink, white	Summer, fall	Sun or shade
Amaranthus caudatus (love-lies-bleeding)	36 to 84 PD 18	Red tassellike flower spikes	Summer	Sun

General List of Annuals (continued)

BOTANICAL AND COMMON NAME	APPROX. HEIGHT IN INCHES	RANGE OF COLORS	PEAK BLOOM SEASON	SUN OR SHADE
A. tricolor (Joseph's coat)	12 to 48 PD 18	Bronzy-green crown; foliage marked cream and red	Summer	Sun
Anchusa capensis (summer forget-me-not)	12 to 18 PD 6 to 9	Blue with white throat	Summer	Light shade, sun
Antirrhinum majus (snapdragon)	10 to 48 PD 10 to 18	Large choice of color	Late spring and fall; summer where cool	Sun
Arctotis stoechadifolia grandis (African daisy)	16 to 24 PD 10	Yellow, rust, pink, white	Early spring	Sun
Begonia semperflorens (wax begonia)	6 to 18 PD 6 to 8	White, pink, deep-rose; single, double	All summer; perennial in temperate climate	Sun or shade
Browallia americana	12 to 24 PD 6 to 9	Violet, blue, white	Summer	Sun
Calendula officinalis (calendula or pot marigold)	12 to 24 PD 12 to 15	Cream, yellow, orange, apricot	Winter where mild; late spring elsewhere	Sun
Callistephus chinensis (aster or China aster)	12 to 36 PD 10	Lavender-blue, white, pink, rose, crimson	Late spring where mild; late summer elsewhere	Sun
Catharanthus roseus (*Vinca rosea*) (Madagascar periwinkle)	6 to 24 PD 12	White, pink, some with contrasting eye	Summer until early fall	Sun or light shade
Celosia Plumosa (plume cockscomb)	12 to 36 PD 6 to 12	Pink, red-gold, yellow	Summer through fall except where very hot	Sun or light shade

General List of Annuals (continued)

BOTANICAL AND COMMON NAME	APPROX. HEIGHT IN INCHES	RANGE OF COLORS	PEAK BLOOM SEASON	SUN OR SHADE
Centaurea cyanus (bachelor button or cornflower)	12 to 30 PD 12	Blue, pink, wine, white	Spring where mild; summer elsewhere	Sun
Clarkia amoena (godetia) (farewell-to-spring)	18 to 30 PD 9	Mostly mixed colors; white, pink, salmon, lavender	Late spring; summer where cold	Sun or shade
C. unguiculata (mountain garland)	12 to 48 PD 9	White, pink, rose, crimson, purple, salmon	Late spring to summer	Sun
Cleome spinosa (spider flower)	48 to 60 PD 14 to 16	Whitish-pink	Spring, summer	Sun
Coleus blumei (coleus)	12 to 30 PD 9 to 12	Grown for its variegated leaves	Midsummer through early fall	Partial shade
Coreopsis tinctoria (calliopsis)	8 to 30 PD 18 to 24	Yellow, orange, maroon, and splashed bicolors	Late spring to summer; late summer where cool	Sun
Cosmos bipinnatus (cosmos)	48 to 72 PD 12 to 15	White, pink, lavender, rose, purple	All summer	Sun
Delphinium ajacis (larkspur)	18 to 60 PD 9	Blue, pink, lavender, rose, salmon, carmine, white	Late spring to early summer	Sun
Dianthus species (pinks)	6 to 30 PD 4 to 6	Mostly bicolors of white, pink, lavender, purple	Spring, fall; winters where mild	Sun
Dimorphotheca pluvialis S. sinuata (African daisy, Cape marigold)	4 to 16 PD 12 to 18	White, yellow, orange, salmon	Winter where mild; summer elsewhere	Sun
Eschscholtzia californica (California poppy)	12 to 24 PD 9	Gold, yellow, orange;	Winter and spring in mild	Sun

General List of Annuals (continued)

BOTANICAL AND COMMON NAME	APPROX. HEIGHT IN INCHES	RANGE OF COLORS	PEAK BLOOM SEASON	SUN OR SHADE
		Mission Bell varieties include pink, rose	climates	
Gaillardia pulchella (rose-ring Gaillardia)	12 to 24 PD 9	Zoned patterns in warm shades; wine, maroon	All summer	Sun
Godetia amoena (see *Clarkia amoena*)				
Gomphrena globosa (globe-amaranth)	9 to 36 PD 12	White, crimson, violet, pink	All summer; heat resistant	Sun
Gypsophila elegans (baby's breath)	12 to 30 PD 6	White, rose, pink	Early summer to fall, but of short duration	Sun
Helianthus annuus (sunflower)	36 to 120 PD 3	Yellow, orange, mahogany, or yellow with black centers	Summer	Sun
Helichrysum bracteatum (strawflower)	24 to 48 PD 9 to 12	Mixed warm shades; yellow, bronze, orange, pink, white	Late summer; fall	Sun
Iberis amara (rocket candytuft)	12 to 15 PD 12	White	Late spring	Sun
I. umbellata (globe candytuft)	12 to 18 PD 16	Pastel pink, lavender, rose, lilac, salmon, white	Late spring	Sun
Impatiens balsamina (garden balsam)	8 to 30 PD 9	White, pink, rose, red	Summer to fall	Light shade, sun where cool
I. walleriana (impatiens)	6 to 24 PD 9	Scarlet, mauve, coral, magenta, purple, pink, white	Summer through early fall	Light shade

General List of Annuals (continued)

BOTANICAL AND COMMON NAME	APPROX. HEIGHT IN INCHES	RANGE OF COLORS	PEAK BLOOM SEASON	SUN OR SHADE
Lathyrus odoratus (sweet pea, winter flowering)	36 to 72 PD 6	Mixed or separate colors; all except yellow, orange, and green	Late winter where mild. Not heat resistant	Sun
L. odoratus (sweet pea, summer)	Same (new low-growing bedding varieties are available) PD 6	Same	Spring, where mild; early summer elsewhere. Somewhat heat resistant	Sun
Limonium bonduelii L. sinuatum (statice, sea-lavender)	18 to 30 PD 15	Blue, rose, lavender, yellow, bicolors with white	Summer	Sun
Linum grandiflorum Rubrum (scarlet flax)	12 to 18 PD 9	Scarlet to deep red, rose	Late spring and fall	Sun
Lobelia erinus (lobelia)	2 to 6 PD 6 to 8	Blue, violet, pink, white	Summer	Sun, light shade
Lobularia maritima (alyssum, sweet)	4 to 12 PD 12	White, purple, lavender, rosy-pink	Year-round where mild; spring to fall elsewhere	Sun, light shade
Lupinus hartwegi (lupine, annual)	18 to 36 PD 12 to 18	Blue, white	Early summer	Sun, light shade
Mathiola incana (stock)	12 to 36 PD 9 to 12	White, cream, yellow, pink, rose, crimson-red, purple	Winter where mild; late spring elsewhere	Sun
Mirabilis jalapa (four-o'clock)	36 to 48 PD 12	Red, yellow, pink, white;	All summer	Light shade or full sun

General List of Annuals (continued)

BOTANICAL AND COMMON NAME	APPROX. HEIGHT IN INCHES	RANGE OF COLORS	PEAK BLOOM SEASON	SUN OR SHADE
		some with markings		
Molucella laevis (bells of Ireland)	18 to 30 PD 9 to 12	Green, bell-like bracts resembling flowers	Summer	Sun
Myosotis sylvatica (forget-me-not)	6 to 12 PD 6 to 9	Blue with white eye	Spring, late fall	Light shade or dappled
Nemesia strumosa (nemesia)	10 to 18 PD 9	All colors except green	Spring where mild; early summer elsewhere	Sun
Nicotiana alata N. sanderae (flowering tobacco)	18 to 48 PD 12	Greenish-white, crimson, magenta	Summer	Light shade or sun
Nigella damascena (love-in-a-mist)	12 to 30 PD 9	Blue, white, rose-pink	Spring	Sun
Papaver rhoeas (Shirley poppy)	24 to 60 PD 12	Red, pink, white, scarlet, salmon, bicolors	Late spring	Sun
Petunia hybrids	12 to 24 PD 6 to 12	All colors except true blue, yellow, and orange	Summer and fall	Sun
Phlox drummondii (annual phlox)	6 to 18 PD 6 to 9	Numerous bicolors. All shades except blue, gold	Late spring to fall	Sun, light shade
Physalis alkekengi (Chinese lantern)	12 to 24 PD 6 to 12	White flowers; orange bracts	Late summer	Sun or shade
Portulaca grandiflora (rose moss)	4 to 8 PD 6	Satiny red-purple, cerise, rose-pink, white, orange, yellow	Summer	Sun

General List of Annuals (continued)

BOTANICAL AND COMMON NAME	APPROX. HEIGHT IN INCHES	RANGE OF COLORS	PEAK BLOOM SEASON	SUN OR SHADE
Reseda odorata (mignonette)	8 to 18 PD 12	Greenish-brown clusters	Late spring to fall	Sun
Salpiglossis sinuata (painted tongue)	18 to 36 PD 9	Bizarre patterns of red, orange, yellow, pink, purple	Early summer	Sun, light
Salvia splendens (scarlet sage)	10 to 36 PD 18	Bright-red, rose, lavender-pink	Summer and fall	Sun
Scabiosa atropurpurea (pincushion flower)	24 to 36 PD 12	Purple, blue, mahogany, white, rose	Summer	Sun
Schizanthus pinnatus (butterfly flower)	10 to 18 PD 9 to 12	White, rose, purple-spotted	Spring	Light shade
Tagetes erecta (hybrids and species) (African or American marigold)	10 to 48 PD 12 to 18	Mostly yellow, tangerine, and gold	Generally, all summer	Sun
T. patula (hybrids and species) (French marigold)	6 to 18 PD 9	Same as African types; and also russet, mahogany, and bicolors	Early summer	Sun
T. tenuifolia signata (signet marigold)	10 to 24 PD 9 to 12	Small; yellow, orange	Generally, all summer	Sun
Tithonia rotundifolia (Mexican sunflower)	72 to 100 PD 30	Orange	Summer	Sun
Trachymene caerulea (blue lace flower)	18 to 24 PD 9	Blue to violet-blue	Late spring, early summer	Sun
Tropaeolum majus (nasturtium)	12 to 18 Some spread vigorously PD 12 to 15	White, pink, crimson, orange, maroon, yellow	Spring and fall; summer	Sun or shade
Verbena hybrida (hortensis) (garden verbena)	6 to 12 PD 9 to 12	Bright pink, scarlet, blue, purple, some bicolors	Summer	Sun

General List of Annuals (continued)

BOTANICAL AND COMMON NAME	APPROX. HEIGHT IN INCHES	RANGE OF COLORS	PEAK BLOOM SEASON	SUN OR SHADE
Viola tricolor hortensis (pansy)	6 to 8 PD 9	"Faces" in white, yellow, purple, rose, mahogany, violet, apricot	Spring and fall; winter where mild	Sun, light shade
Zinnia angustifolia (Mexican zinnia)	12 to 18 PD 6 to 9	Yellow, orange, white, maroon, mahogany	Summer	Sun
Z. elegans (small-flowered zinnia)	8 to 36 PD 9	Red, orange, yellow, purple, lavender, pink, white	Summer	Sun
Z. elegans (giant-flowered zinnia)	12 to 36 PD 12	Same colors as small-flowered zinnia	Summer	Sun

A garden largely of evergreens, with bright perennials for variation in color. (K. Molino)

11 ✍

Perennials

PERENNIALS are plants that provide masses of color in the garden from April to November and their value, aside from their flowers, is that they come up year after year. (We will consider bulbs in Chapter 14.) Plants grow well and multiply without too much work. In fact, the majority of perennials are easy to grow once they are established.

The world of perennials is vast: Plants such as columbines and daisies, chrysanthemums and asters are magnificent, eager to create garlands of bloom in your garden. The same plants bloom year after year, and some can go three to four years without division and resetting. These herbaceous plants (with fleshy stems) usually die down before winter. But the roots stay alive ready to send up new growth next spring.

Perennials constitute the backbone of your garden for they can be grown in many areas for many purposes. Whether it is accent planting or a whole terrace garden, along borders or to frame trees, perennials have dozens of uses and, like annuals, there is an infinite variety of them. There are many hybrids and a wide choice of flowers for color and form.

You can start perennials from seed in the same way as annuals, or you can buy prestarted plants at seasonal times in nurseries. Most gardeners opt for purchased small plants when it comes to perennials, and these are available in flats—12 to a container or three or six to a box. With prestarts, get them in the ground as soon as possible; if you let plants go a few days or a week without planting, they have a harder time getting started.

PLANNING THE PERENNIAL GARDEN

Annuals are used for spot color or seasonal display and once they bloom are discarded, but perennials can be with you for years. It is wise to plan your garden with this longevity in mind. I like perennials in terraced beds—this way it is easy to tend plants and the terrace plan always looks good. At levels, plants are easy to see and there is a dimensional effect.

The terrace or raised garden also assures good drainage; each level of soil drains readily and plants grow well, almost to perfection if drainage is good. However, not everyone wants to do the construction necessary for terraces and many prefer to put perennials into the ground without additional work. Of course this is fine, but again be sure that the soil drains quickly. Waterlogged soil kills plants. Good drainage is achieved by making sure soil is porous and mealy—never caked or sandy.

Perennials make up most of this garden in town; planted in raised boxes, they are easy to tend and provide necessary color. (M. Barr)

So, once again the success of plants depends upon the preparation of the soil.

SOIL

Perennials will be part of your garden for years and where you put them is probably where they will stay for a long time. Preparing the soil properly is paramount, even more so than with annuals which bloom but once. And keeping the soil full of nutrition is equally important because most perennials do not reach their peak for two to three years.

Dig down at least six to eight inches and break up the old soil—you don't want to pulverize the soil but certainly it should be loose and mealy like a baked potato. When you have turned and broken up the soil, be sure to add some good top soil. A layer of two inches is fine and four inches is even better. Work the top soil into the existing soil. If the top soil does not have sufficient organic matter in it, and you can tell—it should smell woodsy and have a crumbly feeling in your hand—it is a good idea to add some humus as compost, decayed cow manure, or leaf mold. All of these are available in tidy sacks these days. I also add some bonemeal to the soil. How much? It all depends,

Perennials are grown almost exclusively in the author's terraced garden. (M. Barr)

Gazinias are the predominant plant in this garden, with perennials echoing the color along the fence.
(K. Molino)

but generally a bushel to a 25-square foot area is satisfactory. Generally, I throw out two small bags of bonemeal in my garden, which is 20 x 40 feet. The bags are at nurseries—each one cubic foot.

Every spring I replenish some soil that has been washed away for soil loses nutrients—plants consume it. Humus or organic matter is again the stuff good soil is made of, and I add perhaps an inch or two to the existing soil and work it in. Always I try to keep the soil loose—never caked.

Even the smallest front yard garden has room for perennials here and there. (M. Barr)

WATERING AND FEEDING

If all conditions are good, as to drainage and sunlight, plants can consume pails of water, especially such flowering plants as perennials. Often it does not rain for weeks. Then I water at least three times a week through spring and summer (twice a week in fall), and watering means just that—a thorough wetting of the soil with moisture seeping down at least 20 inches so roots can reach for it. This means watering for at least two to three hours at a stretch, and handwatering just cannot be managed for so long.

Therefore I use sprinklers or drip watering to send a gentle shower of water over the soil.

Of course watering depends on rainfall and, if it rains heavily in your area, you must temper your watering schedule accordingly. Remember that perennials can sop it up and this means in spring, in summer, and in fall. In winter when it is cold and in regions where it snows, watering is stopped, of course.

CARE OF PLANTS

If you have a rich, well-drained, and porous soil and you water routinely and feed plants, the rest is easy. You can sit back and enjoy their beauty. Here are some of the general practices I follow with perennials (annuals, too).

I water the soil whenever the surface looks dry and in warm weather this may mean every second day (depending on rainfall). I apply water slowly but for a long time—it takes six hours to soak 16 inches of soil.

I always weed—if you allow weeds to enter the flower bed they sap moisture and nutrition from the plants. I weed by hand every few days rather than leaving it all for one time—then it takes too much strength and too much time. To prevent weeds from getting a foothold (if I am on vacation or off on assignment), I cover the ground between the plants with perforated black plastic (available at lumber yards). This prevents weeds from cropping up. I never use chemical preventatives—they are much too strong; they do kill weeds but usually your plants as well.

I label all plants so I can remember what I am growing; labels only need to be tiny metal plates stuck somewhere in the vicinity where the plants are growing. After a few years you are otherwise apt to forget what you are growing where.

Such tall perennials as delphiniums are easily knocked over by wind unless they are staked—that is, tied to staking sticks (available at nurseries). Time-consuming to do I admit, but necessary.

I disbud plants to encourage bushy new growth and so I get more flower stalks.

And I always take the necessary precautions to keep pests out of the garden (controls are discussed in Chapter 20).

SOME FAVORITE PERENNIALS

Alyssum saxatile (basket-of-gold). Splashes of golden flowers make this a most desirable 12-inch plant. Foliage is gray, an interesting contrast in the garden. (Don't confuse this plant with the annual sweet alyssum, which is *Lobularia*.)

Anchusa azurea (bugloss). Clusters of bright true–blue blossoms make this outstanding. Plants grow to 5 feet and require staking. Some excellent new varieties are now available, such as the deep blue Dropmore and pale blue Opal.

Aster frikartii (aster); *A. novae-angliae* (New England aster). Their dramatic blue and purple flowers make these two fine perennials outstanding. The daisy flowers, which are produced in abundance, are bright and showy. Plants come in several heights and make fine displays in large drifts. Both like lots of sun and water.

Perennials

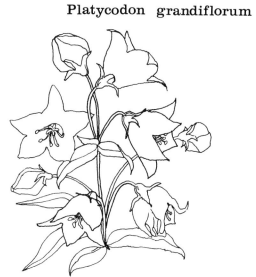

Balloonflower
Platycodon grandiflorum

Chinese peony
Paeonia lactiflora

Primula polyantha
Polyanthus primrose

Pincushion flower
Scabiosa caucasica

Perennials

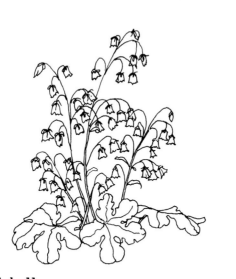

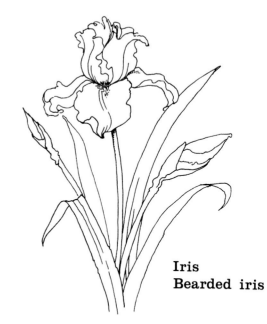

Iris
Bearded iris

Coral-bells
Heuchera sanguinea

Purple loosetrife
Lythrum salicaria
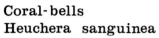

Four-o'clock
Mirabilis jalapa

Perennials

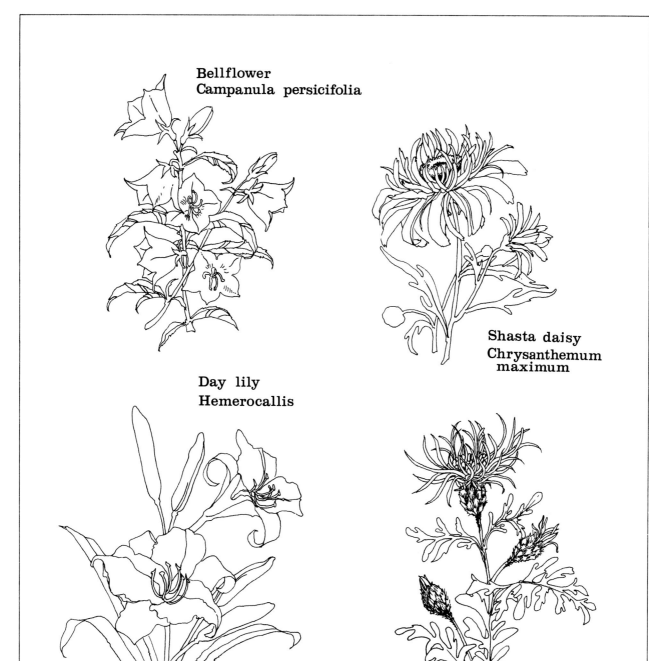

Bellflower
Campanula persicifolia

Shasta daisy
Chrysanthemum
maximum

Day lily
Hemerocallis

Dusty miller
Centaurea
rutifolia

Perennials

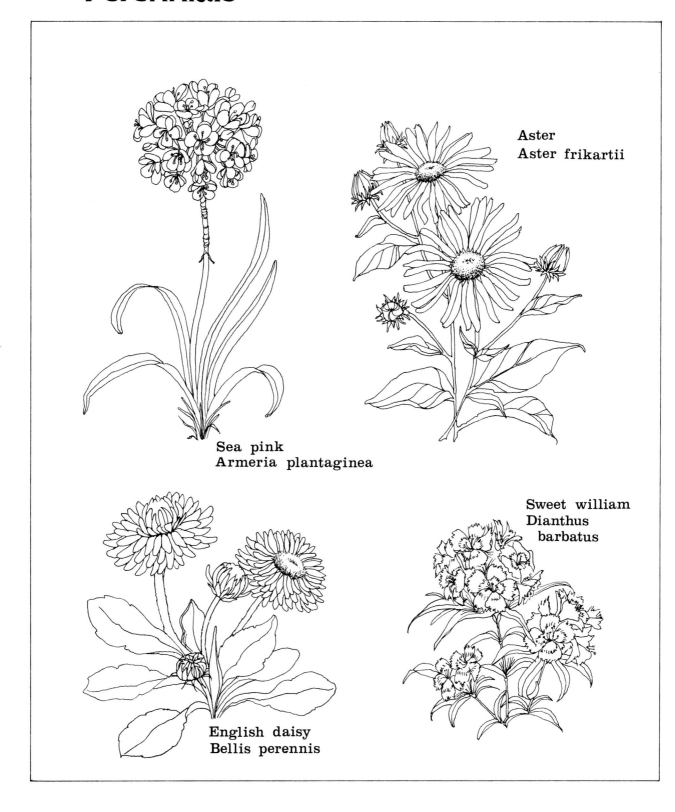

Sea pink
Armeria plantaginea

Aster
Aster frikartii

English daisy
Bellis perennis

Sweet william
Dianthus
barbatus

Astilbe japonica (false spirea). A perennial for shady places, with white, pink, or red flowers on wiry stems. The bronze-green leaves are attractive; the bloom season is summer. Ideal for mixing with shrubs, plants grow from 18 inches to 3 feet. Moist soil is essential.

Campanula persicifolia (peach-leaved bell-flower). Bellflowers should be grown more often because they offer so much color. With their white or violet flowers in June and July, they form mounds of color and grow to 2 feet. Give plants full sun or light shade, and be sure they are in well-drained soil.

Chrysanthemum maximum (Shasta daisy); *C. morifolium* (garden chrysanthemum). These are available in a wide range of shapes—spoon, cushion, pompon, and button—and colors from white to yellow, gold, orange, pink, everything but blue. Heights vary from 2 to 5 feet, and there are chrysanthemums for all kinds of uses in the garden. They will tolerate dry soils and still flourish.

Delphinium elatum (delphinium, larkspur). Handsome plants growing to 6 feet with spires of flowers, they are excellent for background plantings in a perennial border. Colors range from white to pink to superb blues. Rich, well-drained soil and sun are essential. *D. grandiflorum*, the Chinese delphinium, is also handsome, a feathery, bushy grower to 2 feet.

Gaillardia aristata (blanket-flower). Gaillardias produce showy flowers from June to November. The blooms are daisylike and generally bright yellow, although bronzy scarlet types have been introduced too. Undemanding, they do best in a slightly sandy soil with full sun.

Gypsophila paniculata (baby's breath). Dainty, lacy plants that grow rapidly to 2–3 feet and produce clouds of small, rounded white flowers. (There are also pink-and-white varieties.) Blooms last for more than a month, and plants make excellent garden fillers. Do best when not thinned out.

Hemerocallis (daylily). These large effective plants in many varieties produce fountains of grassy foliage and yellow, pink, cream, orange, and bronze flowers. Some kinds start blooming in May, some bloom in fall, but mainly these are summer flowers. Heights vary from 18 inches to 4 feet. Plants need space and bloom in full sun or light shade.

Papaver orientale (oriental poppy). These are coming into popularity again, and it is difficult to find more dramatic flowers than these in bold orange, red, pink, or white. Once established, they bloom profusely. Plants are 2 to 4 feet high, with 6- to 8-inch flowers. They need well-drained soil and some sun, but not direct, intense sun.

Phlox subulata (ground pink, moss pink, creeping phlox). Three- to five-foot plants bear a wealth of large pink-tone flowers. Phlox are compatible with most garden flowers and make splendid accents. They do, however, need a deep fertile soil and sun to prosper.

General List of Perennials

(* = Biennial; † = Many varieties)

BOTANICAL AND COMMON NAME	APPROX. HEIGHT IN INCHES	RANGE OF COLORS	PEAK BLOOM SEASON	SUN OR SHADE
Acanthus mollis (Grecian urn)	to 60	White, lilac	Summer	Sun or shade
Achillea ptarmica (yarrow sneezewort)	to 18	White	Summer, fall	Sun
Aconitum anthora (monkshood)	36	Pale yellow	Summer	Sun or shade
Althaea rosea* (hollyhock)	60 to 108	Most colors except true blue and green	Summer	Sun
Alyssum saxatile (alyssum) (basket of gold)	8 to 12	Golden-yellow, tinged with chartreuse	Early spring	Sun
Anchusa capensis (summer forget-me-not)	12 to 18	Pure, bright blue	Early summer	Sun or light shade
Anemone coronaria (poppy-flowered anemone)	to 18	Red, blue, white	Spring	Sun
Anemone hupehensis japonica† (Japanese anemone)	25 to 48	White, pink, rose	Fall	Sun or light shade
A. pulsatilla (prairie windflower) (pasque flower)	9 to 15	Lavender to violet	Spring	Sun or light shade
Anthemis tinctoria (gloden marguerite)	24 to 36	Yellow	Summer, fall	Sun
Aquilegia alpina (dwarf columbine)	to 12	Blue	Early summer	Sun or light shade
Arabis caucasica (wall rock cress)	4 to 10	White	Early spring	Sun or light shade
Armeria plataginea (sea-pink or thrift)	to 12	White, dark red, pink	Spring, summer	Sun
Artemisia albula (wormwood or Silver King Artemisia)	24 to 48	Silvery-gray	Summer, fall	Sun
A. frigida† (fringed wormwood or wildsage)	12 to 18	Silvery-white (foliage)	Summer, fall	Sun

General List of Perennials (continued)

BOTANICAL AND COMMON NAME	APPROX. HEIGHT IN INCHES	RANGE OF COLORS	PEAK BLOOM SEASON	SUN OR SHADE
Asclepias tuberosa (butterfly weed)	24 to 36	Orange	Summer	Sun
Aster, dwarf type†	8 to 15	Red, blue, purple	Late summer	Sun
Aster, English hardy† (Michaelmas daisy)	30 to 48	Blue, violet, pink, white	Fall	Sun
A. frikartii	30 to 36	Blue, lavender	Summer, fall	Sun
Aubrieta deltoidea† (common aubrieta or purple rock cress)	2 to 4	Blue	Spring	Sun or shade
Bellis perennis (English daisy)	3 to 6	White, pink, rose	Spring, winter in mild climates	Sun
Bergenia cordifolia (heartleaf bergenia)	12 to 18	Rose	Early summer	Sun or light shade
Campanula carpatica (bellflower)	8 to 10	Blue, white	Summer	Sun
C. persicifolia (peach-leafed bellflower)	24 to 36	White, blue, pink	Summer	Sun
Centaurea gymnocarpa (dusty miller)	18 to 24	Velvety-white leaves; purple flowers	Summer	Sun
Chrysanthemum coccineum (Pyrethrum) (painted daisy)	24 to 36	White, pink, red	Early summer	Sun
C. maximum (Shasta daisy)†	24 to 48	White	Summer, fall	Sun or shade
C. morifolium† (florists' chrysanthemum)	18 to 30	Most colors except blue	Late summer, fall	Sun
Convallaria majalis (lily-of-the-valley)	9 to 12	White, pink	Spring, early summer	Light to medium shade
Coreopsis grandiflora (tickseed)	24 to 36	Golden yellow	Summer	Sun
Delphinium hybrid† (Connecticut Yankee)	24 to 36	Blue, violet, white	Early summer	Sun

General List of Perennials (continued)

BOTANICAL AND COMMON NAME	APPROX. HEIGHT IN INCHES	RANGE OF COLORS	PEAK BLOOM SEASON	SUN OR SHADE
D. hybrid† (Pacific Giant)	48 to 96	Blue, white	Early summer	Sun
Dianthus barbatus° (sweet William)	10 to 30	White, pink, red; zoned and edged	Early summer	Sun or light shade
D. deltoides† (maiden pink)	8 to 12	Rose, purple white	Early summer	Sun
Dicentra spectabilis (bleeding heart)	24 to 36	Pink, rose, white	Spring	Light shade
Dictamnus albus (gas plant)	36	White, pink, purple	Summer	Sun or light shade
Digitalis purpurea° (foxglove)	18 to 48	Mixed colors, marked and spotted	Early summer	Partial shade or sun
Echinops exalatus (globe thistle)	36 to 48	Steel-blue	Late summer	Sun
Epimedium grandiflorum (Bishop's hat)	12	Red, violet, white	Summer	Light shade
Erysimum asperum (Siberian wallflower)	12 to 18	Golden-orange	Spring	Sun
Felicia amelloides (blue marguerite)	20 to 24	Blue	Spring, summer	Sun
Gaillardia grandiflora (blanket flower)	24 to 48	Yellow or bicolor	Summer, fall	Sun
Gazania hybrids†	10 to 12	Yellow and brown bicolors	Summer; fall; and spring where mild	Sun
Gentiana asclepiadea (willow gentian)	20 to 24	Blue to violet	Late summer	Light
Geranium grandiflorum (cranesbill)	10 to 12	Blue marked red	Summer	Light shade
Geum chiloense (*coccineum*) (geum)	20 to 24	Yellow, red-orange	Early summer	Light shade
Gypsophila paniculata† (baby's breath)	24 to 36	White	Early summer and summer	Sun
Helenium (various) (Helen's flower)	24 to 48	Orange, yellow, rusty shades	Summer, fall	Sun

General List of Perennials (continued)

BOTANICAL AND COMMON NAME	APPROX. HEIGHT IN INCHES	RANGE OF COLORS	PEAK BLOOM SEASON	SUN OR SHADE
Helianthus decapetalus multiflorus (sunflower)	40 to 60	Yellow	Summer	Sun
Hemerocallis (various)† (daylily)	12 to 72	Most colors except blue, green, violet	Midsummer	Sun or light shade
Hesperis matronalis° (sweet rocket)	24 to 36	White, lavender	Early summer	Sun or light shade
Heuchera sanguinea† (coral bells)	12 to 24	Red, pink, white	Early summer	Sun or light shade
Hosta plantaginea (plantain lily)	24 to 30	White flowers; yellow-green leaves	Late summer	Light shade
Iberis sempervirens (evergreen candytuft)	8 to 12	White	Early summer	Sun or light shade
Iris (various)	3 to 10 (dwarf)	Many colors	Spring, early summer	Sun
Iris (bearded)	15 to 28 (intermediate) 24 to 48 (tall)	Many colors	Spring, early summer	Sun
I. cristata (crested iris)	6 to 8	Lavender, light blue	Spring	Light shade
I. dichotoma (vesper iris)	30 to 36	Pale lavender marked purple	Summer	Sun
I. kaempferi (Japanese iris)	40 to 48	Purple, violet, pink, rose, red, white	Spring, early summer	Sun or light shade
Kniphofia (various) (torch lily)	24 to 72	Cream, white, yellow, orange	Early summer	Sun
Liatris pycnostachya (gayfeather)	60 to 72	Rose-purple	Summer	Sun or light shade
Limonium latifolium (statice, sea lavender)	24 to 36	Blue, white, pink	Summer, fall	Sun
Linum perenne (blue flax)	20 to 24	Sky-blue	Summer	Sun
Lithodora diffusa	6 to 12	Blue	Summer	Sun

General List of Perennials (continued)

BOTANICAL AND COMMON NAME	APPROX. HEIGHT IN INCHES	RANGE OF COLORS	PEAK BLOOM SEASON	SUN OR SHADE
Lobelia cardinalis	24 to 36	Red	Late summer	Sun, light shade
Lupinus polyphyllus	24 to 48	Red	Summer	Sun or shade
Lythrum (various)	50 to 60	Rose to purple	Summer, fall	Sun or light shade
Mertensia virginica (Virginia bluebell)	16 to 24	Bicolor blue	Early spring	Light shade
Monarda didyma (bee balm)	30 to 36	Scarlet-red, pink	Summer and fall	Sun, light shade
Oenothera (various) (evening primrose)	20 to 72	Yellow, pink	Summer	Sun
Paeonia (various)† (peony)	18 to 48	White, pink, crimson, lavender, cream	Early summer	Light shade
Papaver orientale† (Oriental poppy)	24 to 48	Pink, white, scarlet, salmon, orange	Early summer	Sun
Pelargonium domesticum (Lady Washington geranium)	18 to 48	Many bicolors; white, pink, red, purple	Summer, fall	Sun
Penstemon (various)† (beard tongue)	18 to 36	Blue, pink, crimson; mostly bicolors	Summer, fall	Sun
Phlox divaricata† (sweet William phlox)	10 to 12	Blue, white, pink, rose	Early spring	Sun or light shade
P. paniculata† (summer phlox)	36 to 60	Pink, purple, rose, white, orange, red	Late summer, fall	Sun
Physostegia virginiana (false dragonhead)	36 to 48	White and rose bicolors	Midsummer to later summer	Sun
Platycodon grandiflorum (balloonflower)	18 to 42	Pink, white, purple, blue	Midsummer to late summer	Sun or shade
Polygonatum multiflorum (Solomon's seal)	10 to 12	White	Spring	Sun or shade

General List of Perennials (continued)

BOTANICAL AND COMMON NAME	APPROX. HEIGHT IN INCHES	RANGE OF COLORS	PEAK BLOOM SEASON	SUN OR SHADE
Potentilla atrosanguinea (cinquefoil)	10 to 12	Red	Summer	Sun
Primula (various)†	10 to 14	Bicolors, blue, red, yellow, orange, pink	Late spring, summer	Sun or shade
Pyrethrum (various)† (See *Chrysanthemum coccineum*) (painted daisy)				
Rudbeckia hirta (coneflower)	36 to 48	Yellow, pink, orange, white	Summer	Sun
Salvia patens (blue salvia or meadow sage)	24 to 36	Dark blue	Summer, fall	Sun
Scabiosa caucasica (pincushion flower)	24 to 30	White, blue, purple	Summer, fall	Sun
Sedum sieboldii	6 to 8	Pink, coppery foliage in fall	Late summer, fall	Sun or shade
Solidago (various) (goldenrod)	20 to 36	Yellow	Summer	Sun or light shade
Tithonia rotundifolia (see annuals)				
Veronica (various)† (speedwell)	24 to 36	Blue, pink, white	Midsummer	Light shade
Viola cornuta† (tufted viola)	6 to 8	Purple; newer varieties in many colors	Spring, fall	Light shade
Yucca filamentosa (Adam's needle)	36 to 72	White	Late summer	Sun

Vines are lovely in gardens. Here the popular wisteria, in full bloom, decorates a small house and garden to charming effect. (M. Barr)

12

Dependable Shrubs and Vines

SHRUBS form the background of the landscape. They offer beautiful bloom for spring and summer, colorful fruits in fall and winter, and also a variety of foliages. Used as a hedge, shrubs can frame a property or the taller ones can form a screen. Shrubs also make fine accents in a garden, and, of course, they associate beautifully with perennials.

Like trees, most shrubs are long-lived and once planted need little care except for some judicious pruning now and then. But, unlike trees, they come into peak of beauty sooner; generally in four or five years shrubs are at their zenith of form and color, and continue to grow in beauty for many more years. While most shrubs can tolerate untoward conditions and still thrive, most do much better with good treatment.

The majority of shrubs bloom in spring or early summer, and some bring color into autumn even up to the first frost. The vivid fruits of many of them offer handsome accents when other plants are waning. Colorful foliage is desirable too, so in many ways shrubs offer more than many other plants.

SELECTING SHRUBS

Because there are so many excellent shrubs, the beginning gardener often finds it difficult to select wisely. It does indeed pay to take time and know what you are putting into the ground. Try to determine just what your site offers as to exposure and soil and those shrubs most likely to prosper in the individual situations. Of course you will want to select some shrubs for flowers and foliage you like and then modify existing conditions to suit them. This usually means working in top soil before planting and also fertilizing.

Here are some hints for buying your shrubs:

Don't select a sun-loving shrub like hibiscus for a shady place or a shade-loving one like hydrangeas for a sunny spot, although the plant may survive.

Check ultimate size and necessary spacing. The small shrub you see in the nursery is not the size it will become—it will grow, so allow appropriate space for it.

Be sure you select shrubs that are hardy in your climate. Catalogs usually describe a shrub as "hardy," but hardy where—in 20F or 20F below? It makes a difference. (See lists.)

Shrubs are usually sold B & B, that is, balled and burlapped or in cans; either way is fine. Try to avoid shrubs offered bare root or those enclosed in plastic wrappers. Without soil, roots may be damaged if planting time is delayed; furthermore, you have no idea how long plants have been out of the ground at the nursery. Shrubs in containers

Lush shrubs planted on multilevel rock terraces lend an air of privacy to this handsome backyard deck. (Western Wood Products)

are fine if they have been container-grown and not taken from the fields and stuffed into containers for display. To distinguish between a field-grown container plant and one originally container grown, notice if roots are sticking out above the soil and over the rim of the container. If so, the plant was probably field grown.

WHEN TO PLANT AND HOW

Spring is usually the recommended planting season, but I find that fall is better. In spring, soil can be so wet, even muddy, that it is difficult to work it; in fall soil conditions seem just right. And set out early in fall; a shrub makes roots during growing weather and is ready to burst into leaf in spring. Spring planting I think loses time.

Set shrubs so they will have space to grow. A mistake I have made in my own garden is to plant too close and so I have had a tangle of plants. I know better, of course, but in my rush to get a garden growing, I have crowded plants. I do hate to see bare ground.

Masses of rhododendrons are the mainstay of this country garden. Planting in groups like these creates an abundance of color. (M. Barr)

All that is needed is a few shrubs and trees to make a green accent area in a garden. (Western Wood Products)

You can probably dig holes and set shrubs in the existing soil but I have found through the years that preparing the soil—digging it up and working in some top soil—takes little time and avoids much work later. Planted properly in fertile soil, a shrub will grow almost on its own.

To give roots growing room, dig holes at least six inches wider on all sides than the root ball of the plant. And holes should be deep—deep enough to allow the shrub to grow at the same level as in the nursery. Shrubs sunk too low look bad, and set too high, suffer from dryness because water never really penetrates the root zone but rolls off. I always, and I strongly urge this, set out a new shrub with a slight bowl depression above the surface roots; the basin then catches all available water.

SOIL

I have already had much to say about soil preparation for other plants; for shrubs a proper soil is just as important. It should be porous with a good content of humus. Humus is leaf mold or compost, an organic material essential to the soil activation. Organic matter opens up nonporous soils to admit the air necessary for good growth. In porous soils leaf mold is also needed to retain moisture that otherwise drains away in sandy soils. Allow one part organic matter to two parts soil and mix it well into the subsoil that you have excavated from the hole. You could also add a dusting of bonemeal to the soil—always good for plants.

For acid-loving shrubs, such as azaleas and rhododendrons, use a fertilizer like cottonseed meal—about two handfuls for a standard shrub.

CARE/CONDITIONING

Shrubs properly planted and watered will grow with little help from you—an occasional feeding is usually all that is necessary. However, they will, after a time, need some pruning. For shapeliness, remove all dead wood after flowering, and to promote bloom next year, remove faded flowers, especially from lilacs and mock orange. Pruning—a little here and there—a few times a year will do wonders for shrubs.

Pruning is usually done in early spring but you can do it in late fall before winter sets in. If a shrub becomes overgrown, you can rejuvenate it by cutting it back to within five inches off the ground. Do this in early spring and let it get started again.

I prune in early spring and again a little in summer. I like shrubs to be shapely and never errant in growth. Exceptions would be hedges that require more pruning than standard shrubs.

As a rule, it is not necessary to prune shrubs at planting time. Some gardeners do trim bareroot specimens; they claim that trimming makes them grow more vigorously. I have never observed any difference in the rate of growth between an unpruned and a pruned shrub.

SHRUBS FOR HEDGES

Used effectively hedges can be a beautiful part of the landscape design. Hedges can be tall or short, evergreen or deciduous, prostrate or rigid, clipped or left natural. They can also be effective for tall screenings. Some, like barberry and taxus, take to trimming better than others; many do not respond and simply appear shaggy. The best shrub for you is the one of desired ultimate

Transplanting a shrub

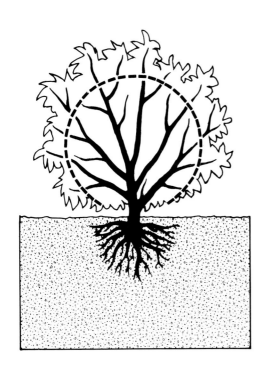
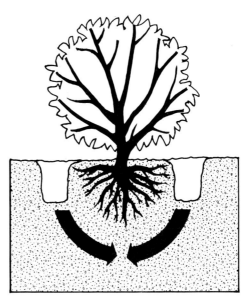
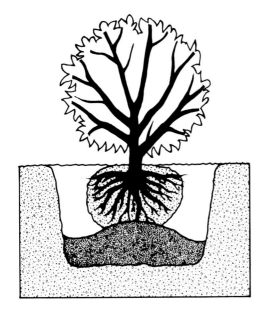
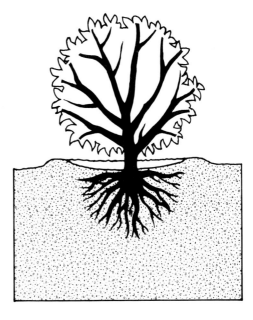

Pruning shrubs

height and width. Some shrubs are more suitable for hedges than others. They are naturally compact and easily pruned into desired shapes; most are inexpensive. In California, ligustrum is widely used as a hedge.

Since an attractive hedge depends upon good proportion, plant it with care. Stretch a string along the planting area and mark this line on the ground. Dig the first hole at the end of the line and then decide how far apart to place the plants. Privet is usually set 12 inches apart, barberry 12 to 16 inches, and large deciduous and evergreen shrubs about 24 to 36 inches, but this depends on individual size at maturity.

Evergreen hedges can be planted in fall or spring; deciduous ones in spring.

Trim hedges wider at the base than at the top to provide sufficient light for the lowest branches and so avoid die-back there. The pyramidal shape is most popular, although other shapes are frequently seen. Evergreens, such as yew and arborvitae, are sheared either before growth starts in spring, in very early summer, or after the new growth has had a chance to harden.

Don't fertilize hedges unless you are prepared to trim them more frequently than is usually necessary.

SOME FAVORITE SHRUBS

In the following discussion we look at the more commonly grown shrubs for gardens such as camellias and cotoneaster and so forth. A more general list of plants follows this section.

Berberis (barberry)

A group of dense, thorny shrubs, deciduous and evergreen, with small, bright flowers in spring. Plants are effective as barriers

Hedges

SIDE VIEW	END VIEW
Berberis Wilsoniae (Barberry)	To 4 feet (trimmed)
Spiraea prunifolia plena (Bridal Wreath)	To 6 feet (untrimmed)
Prunus laurocerasus (Cherry Laurel)	To 12 feet plus (trimmed)

Shrubs at right and left balance the predominance of trees in this deck garden. (Brickman)

or as landscape specimens; many species have an attractive branching habit. Small bright red or purple-black berries appear in autumn. These shrubs grow in almost any kind of soil, in sun or in light shade. A very useful group.

B. buxifolia (Magellan barberry). Hardy to −10F; upright growth to 6 feet, with small leathery leaves. Orange-yellow flowers and dark-purple berries. Evergreen.

B. koreana (Korean barberry). Hardy to −10F; grows to 6 feet. Deep-red foliage color in fall and winter; yellow flowers in May.

B. mentorensis (mentor barberry). Hybrid; hardy to −10F; evergreen in some regions, deciduous in others. Dark-red berries and yellow flowers.

B. thunbergi (Japanese barberry). Hardy to −5F; graceful growth with arching stems. Deep-green foliage and fiery-red berries in fall. Deciduous. Many varieties.

B. verruculosa (warty barberry). Hardy to −10F; neat habit, grows to about 4 feet. Glossy, dark-green leaves and golden-yellow flowers.

Camellia

Evergreen shrubs that bear handsome flowers from January to May; more than

Masses of brilliant portulacas decorate a small side yard garden. (R. Scharmer)

Opposite page: Above: Bignonia is a popular vine that can become rampant. Here its orange flowers decorate a window in August. (R. Scharmer) Below left: Anemones, favorite perennials, add striking color to a brick-bordered garden. (M. Barr) Below right: Clumps of pale-colored perennials lend old-fashioned charm to this stone pool behind a cottage in the country. (R. Scharmer)

Right: Natural stone is an effective foil for the flowers' brightness. (R. Scharmer) Below: A small kitchen cutting garden that provides produce for a family of four. (R. Scharmer) Bottom left: Paths provide access to vegetables and flowers in a kitchen garden. (R. Scharmer) Bottom right: A stone ornament adds interest to a kitchen cutting garden in Mississippi. (M. Barr)

Above: Shrubs and trees arranged informally in a Southern garden. (M. Barr)
Below: The entrance to an old house is planted with shrubs in an arc design.
Note the gradation of shrubbery from small to large,
leading the eye to the house. (R. Scharmer)

Right: A terrace garden of lush ground cover and low shrubbery creates an inviting entrance to a house. (R. Scharmer)
Below left: Hedges and brick are used to define a garden. (M. Barr)
Bottom right: Ground covers, shrubs, perennials, and annuals combined harmoniously in a St. Louis terraced garden. (M. Barr)

Masses of annuals and perennials in a herbaceous border complementing an old brick wall. (R. Scharmer)

Above: A rich green lawn framed by flower borders. Note the use of brick to separate lawn from garden. (R. Scharmer)
Below: Effective use of simple flower borders to accent a healthy lawn. (J. Werner)

The herbaceous border. Artistic use of flowers and plants of varying heights make this garden especially pleasing to the eye. (M. Barr)

Shrubs are the mainstay of this city garden, providing both easy-maintenance gardening and a lush green background. (M. Adams)

3,000 named varieties that vary in color, size, and form. Japonica hybrids are perhaps the most popular, with flowers from pure white to dark red and many shades in between. Sasanqua hybrids are desirable too; these bear smaller, generally single flowers that open before the japonicas.

Camellias require a well-drained, rich soil with coolness at the roots. Avoid planting them with the base of the trunk below the soil line. Keep soil moist, but never wet; fertilize with a commercial acid plant food. Prune immediately after blooming or in fall. Watch for aphids, scale, and mites and apply remedies as needed. Scorched or yellow leaves are due to sun-scald; yellow leaves

SHRUBS

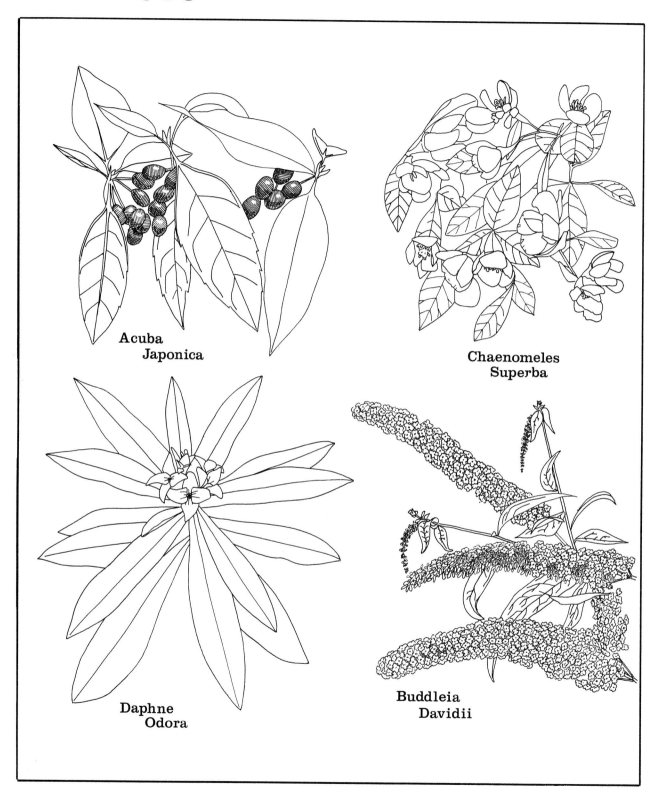

Acuba
Japonica

Chaenomeles
Superba

Daphne
Odora

Buddleia
Davidii

SHRUBS

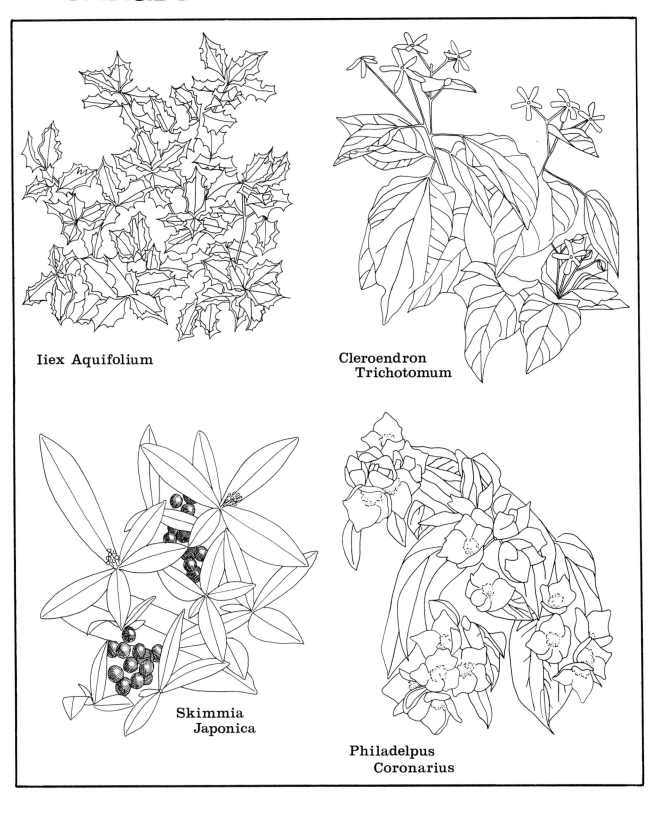

Iiex Aquifolium

Cleroendron
Trichotomum

Skimmia
Japonica

Philadelpus
Coronarius

SHRUBS

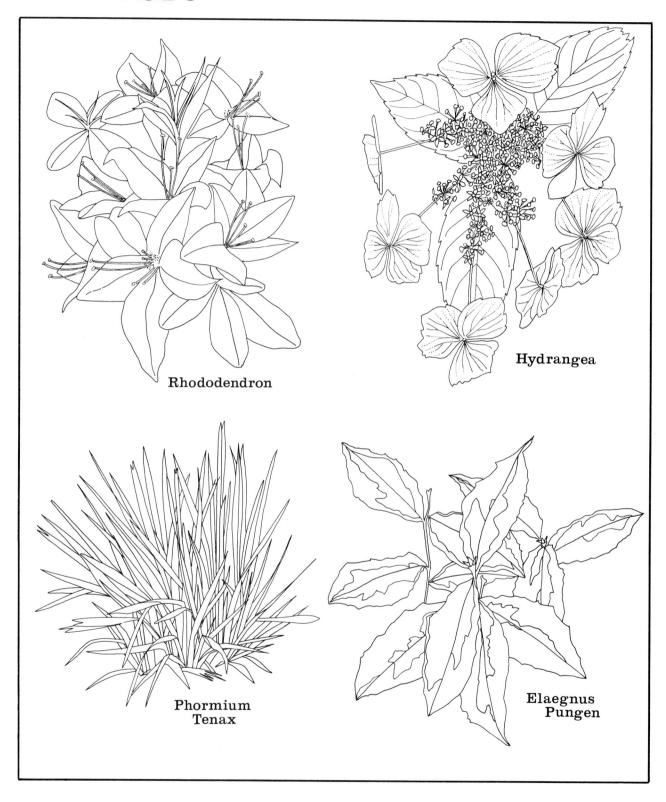

Rhododendron

Hydrangea

Phormium
Tenax

Elaegnus
Pungen

Shrubs

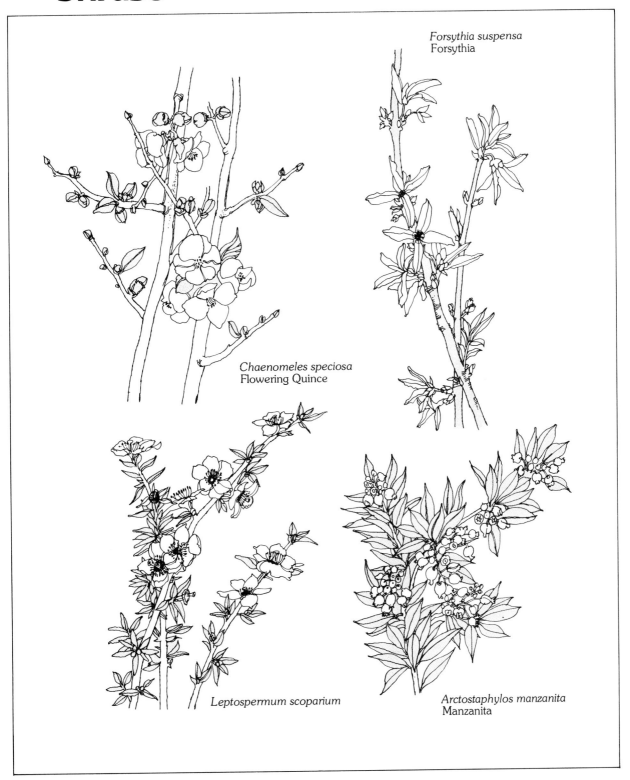

Forsythia suspensa
Forsythia

Chaenomeles speciosa
Flowering Quince

Leptospermum scoparium

Arctostaphylos manzanita
Manzanita

with green veins indicate the need for more iron in the soil. (Iron chelate is available at nurseries.) If flower buds drop, don't panic; it is probably from drought, overwatering, or it may be a natural tendency of the variety.

C. japonica (common camellia). Hardy to 5F; large shrub variable in habit and flower color.

Adolph Audusson	Prince Eugene Napoleon
Aunt Jetty	Purity
C. M. Hovey	Reg Ragland
Finlandia	Tiffany
Herme	White Nun
Lady Clare	

C. sasanqua (sasanqua camellia). Hardy to 5F; varies in habit from upright and dense to vinelike and spreading. Dark-green, shiny leaves; bloom time, early autumn; very floriferous.

Blanchette	Sparkling Burgundy
Briar Rose	Tanya
Cleopatra	White Frills
Jean May	

Chaenomeles (flowering quince)

Bright-colored flowers appear in early spring before the leaves. The plants have been hybridized, resulting in a range of stunning flower colors—white, shades of pink, red, and orange. Some flowers are single, others semidouble or double; fruits are green, turning yellow at maturity. Several varieties are thorny. The majority grow to about 6 feet, so they are ideal for small gardens.

C. japonica (Japanese quince). Hardy to −20F; reaches to 3 feet. Red flowers in early May. Deciduous. Alpina—seldom grows beyond 1 foot. Dense growth, with orange flowers.

C. speciosa (flowering quince). Hardy to −20F; grows to 6 feet. Dark-green, glossy leaves, and red, pink, or white flowers.

Nivalis—white
Cameo—pink
Crimson Beauty—red

Cotoneaster

These shrubs flourish under untoward conditions, but they do not tolerate full shade. The bright-red berries are handsome, and the white or pink flowers a charming asset to the garden. Many species have interesting habits, making them good landscape subjects. Some cotoneasters are deciduous; others, semideciduous; and still others, evergreen. In dry, hot weather the plants are susceptible to red spider or lace bug attacks which must be kept under control or the shrubs may die.

C. apiculata (cranberry cotoneaster). Hardy to −20F; grows to 4 feet. Bright-green leaves, pink-white flowers, and red fruit. Deciduous.

C. conspicua (wintergreen cotoneaster). Hardy to −5F; arching branches; grows to 6 feet. Narrow, oval, dark-green leaves and white flowers. Bright-red fruit. Evergreen.

C. dammeri (barberry cotoneaster). Hardy to −10F; prostrate trailing habit. Oval, bright-green leaves, white flowers, red fruit. Beautiful cascading plant; evergreen.

C. divaricata (spreading cotoneaster). Hardy to −10F; stiff branches. Grows to 6 feet, with dark-green leaves, pink flowers followed by red fruit. Good hedge or screen. Deciduous.

C. horizontails (rock-spray cotoneaster). Hardy to −10F; low-growing to 3 feet, but spreading, with stiff branches. Small, glossy, bright-green leaves, white flowers, and red fruit. Good bank cover or espalier subject. Deciduous.

C. microphylla (small-leaf cotoneaster). Hardy to −10F; somewhat of a trailer, to 3 feet tall. Small green leaves and white flowers followed by large red fruit. Good ground cover. Evergreen.

Deutzia

These are dense shrubs, growing from 3 to 8 feet. It is their spring flowers that make them so desirable. Prune the plants annually in spring to keep them handsome. Select species for bloom time; some flower in May, others later. Deutzias grow in any decent soil; prefer full sun but will withstand light shade. Usually free from insects and disease.

D. gracilis (slender deutzia). Hardy to −20F; slender, graceful shrub, to 3 feet. Bright-green leaves, and snow-white flowers. Deciduous.

D. grandiflora (early deutzia). Hardy to −10F; grows to 6 feet, with white flowers. Early blooming. Deciduous.

D. lemoinei. Hybrid; hardy to −20F. Compact grower to about 7 feet. Toothed leaves and clusters of white flowers.

Compacta—Dwarf form

D. scabra. Hardy to −10F; tall species to 10 feet. Dull-green leaves, with clusters of white flowers. Several varieties. Deciduous.

Candidissima—Double white flowers

Euonymus

While flowers are insignificant, the autumn color, spectacular. Plants grow vigorously in any good garden soil but are susceptible to scale and must be sprayed regularly. Some in this group are vines, others shrubs. Most are excellent landscape subjects.

E. alata (winged euonymus). Hardy to −35F; horizontal and branching habit. Grows to 10 feet, with dark-green leaves that turn red in fall. Deciduous.

Compacta—excellent dwarf to 4 feet

E. bungeanus semipersistens (midwinter euonymus). Hardy to −20F; vigorous, to 15 feet. Light green leaves and yellow to whitish-pink flowers. Good hedge plant. Deciduous.

E. fortunei. Hardy to −10F; vine or shrub to 15 feet. Dark-green leaves. Good one. Evergreen.

Berryhill—upright grower
Sarcoxie—upright, to 4 feet

E. japonica (evergreen euonymus). Hardy to 10F; upright to 10 feet. Lustrous green leaves; pinkish-orange fruit.

Albo-Marginata—green leaves edged white
Grandifolia—large dark-green leaves

E. latifola (broadleaf euonymus). Hardy to −10F; leaves reddish underneath. Red to orange fruit. Deciduous. Grows to 20 feet.

Forsythia

Popular in many regions, their bright flowers, harbingers of spring when all else is bleak. In the North, flowers open on leafless stems in March or April, and then the plants are outstanding. While the flowers are the chief asset, many forsythias have a graceful habit. Forsythias bloom on the previous years' growth, so they are pruned *after* they flower, not before. There are several types—dwarf and compact, or upright and spreading.

F. intermedia (border forsythia). Hardy to −10F; long, arching branches. Pale to deep-yellow flowers. Deciduous. Grows to 10 feet.

Densiflora—upright growth; pale-yellow blooms
Nana—dwarf form
Spectabilis—large, bright-yellow flowers

F. ovata (early forsythia). Hardy to −20F; early yellow flowers. Deciduous. Grows to 8 feet.

F. suspensa (weeping forsythia). Hardy to −10F; grows to 10 feet, with vinelike branches. Golden-yellow flowers. Deciduous.

Fortunei—more upright than the species

Ilex (holly)

The hollies, evergreen or deciduous, are very popular because they are amenable plants. The bright-red or black berries are desirable for landscape color. Hollies (with few exceptions) have separate sexes, so both must be present in the area to ensure fertilization of flowers. (Chinese holly can produce fruit without the pollen of other hollies.) Most plants are easily grown in a good garden soil but they do need good drainage; they are relatively free of pest and diseases.

I. aquifolium (English holly). Hardy to −5F; grows to 15 feet. Variable in leaf, shape, and color. Many varieties. Evergreen.

I. cornuta (Chinese holly). Hardy to 5F; dense or open growth to 10 feet. Glossy, leathery leaves; bright red berries. Evergreen.

Burfordii—spineless leaves
Dazzler—compact; many berries
Giant Beauty—upright and large
Jungle Gardens—yellow fruit

I. crenata (Japanese holly). Hardy to −5F; dense and erect; sometimes to 20 feet. Finely toothed leaves and black berries. Evergreen.

Compacta—densely branched
Green Island—low and spreading
Microphylla—tiny leaves

I. glabra (inkberry). Hardy to −35F; grows to 9 feet. Black berries. Evergreen.

I. verticillata (winterberry). Hardy to −35F; grows to 10 feet. Bright-red berries. Deciduous.

Ligustrum (privet)

These are popular hedge plants. The leaves may be evergreen in the South or deciduous in the North. Vigorous and fast-growing, with small white flowers followed by blue or black berries, privets also make good specimen plants against a fence or wall. Grow in almost any kind of soil. There are many privets, one hardly distinguishable from another until they are mature, so ask your nurseryman about them before you buy.

L. amurense (Amur privet). Hardy to −35F; deciduous in the North, evergreen in the South. Grows to 15 feet, with small spikes of white flowers. Small black berries. Similar to California privet, but hardier.

L. japonicum (Japanese privet). Hardy to 5F; dense grower to 12 feet. Clusters of small white flowers. Evergreen.

Lusterleaf (texanum)—very large leaves

L. lucidum (glossy privet). Hardy to 5F; round-headed shrub that can reach 30 feet. Small white flowers, black berries. Evergreen.

L. ovalifolium (California privet). Hardy to −10F; creamy-white flowers. Black berries, but not in the North. Semideciduous. Grows to 15 feet.

Aureum (golden privet)—leaves with yellow edges

L. vulgare (common privet). Hardy to −20F; grows to 15 feet. Clusters of white flowers, black berries. Deciduous.

Pyramidale—excellent hedge plant

Lonicera (Honeysuckle)

Vigorous shrubs or vines, popular although they have no autumn color. Some turn brown in winter. Most are trailing or climbing; only a few are upright growers. The plants thrive in full sun, some tolerate light shade. Plants need little care, and have no special problems.

L. fragrantissima (winter honeysuckle). Hardy to −10F; grows to 6 feet. Stiff, leathery leaves and very early fragrant, white flowers. Deciduous, but evergreen in mild climates.

L. henryi. Hardy to −20F; vine with dark-green leaves and yellow to purple flowers, followed by black fruit. Good bank cover. Evergreen or semi-evergreen.

L. maacki (Amur honeysuckle). Hardy to −50F; grows to 15 feet. White, fragrant flowers, and dark-red berries. Good fall color.

L. nitida (box honeysuckle). Hardy to 5F; seldom grows beyond 6 feet. Creamy-white flowers, and blue-purple berries. Deciduous in the North, evergreen in the South.

L. tatarica (Tatarian honeysuckle). Hardy to −35F; twiggy branches, big, to 10 feet. Oval blue-green leaves, and pink flowers. Deciduous.

Alba—pure white
Rosea—rose-pink flowers
Sibirica—deep-pink blooms

Philadelphus (mock orange)

Grown for the white flowers with heady fragrance. Plants are vigorous and bloom when young. There are low and tall growers, and most can take heavy pruning. The plants take hold in almost any kind of soil. There is great variation in shape; many are sculptural and very handsome.

P. coronarius (sweek mock orange). Hardy to −20F; robust, to 10 feet. Oval leaves and very fragrant white flowers. Deciduous.

P. grandiflorus (scentless mock orange). Hardy to −20F; grows to 10 feet, no fragrance. Deciduous.

P. lemoinei. Hybrid; hardy to −10F. Grows to about 6 feet with white single or double flowers. Deciduous.

Avalanche—arching branches; very fragrant flowers
Girandole—double flowers

P. virginalis. Hybrid; hardy to −10F. Single or double white flowers.

Glacier—double blooms
Minnesota Snowflake—double fragrant flowers
Virginal—fast grower

Rhododendrons

This large group of ornamental woody plants includes rhododendrons with broad evergreen leaves and azaleas with small leaves, evergreen, semievergreen, or deciduous. The flowers of both types of plants are well known, and in bloom plants offer a striking display. Both kinds of plants thrive in acid soil and need plenty of water. The rhododendrons dislike hot summers and drying winds and require a partially shaded place with only a little sun. The azaleas can take more sun; the deciduous types require cooler winters than the evergreen azaleas.

Plant rhododendrons in early spring while they are blooming; plant azaleas (deciduous) when dormant unless they are in cans. The evergreens can be put into the ground any time of year except late spring and summer when buds for the following year are developing.

Rhododendrons and azaleas are shallow-rooted, so dry conditions injure them. Keep the soil moist, especially in early summer when new growth is forming. Use an acid-type fertilizer as specified on the container. (There are many of them.) Always remove faded blooms from rhododendrons so that seed does not develop.

Azaleas are generally listed as:

Kurume azalea. Hardy to 10F; somewhat small flowers and leaves; dense growth.

Apple Blossom
Christmas Cheer
Salmon Beauty

Ghent azaleas. Very hardy. Flower color ranges from pure yellow to white to combinations of pink and red. Usually double form.

Altaclarense
Coccinea Speciosa
Fanny
Nancy Waterer

Mollis azaleas. Deciduous; some hardy in New England. Clusters of flowers in shades of yellow or orange; a few red.

Adrian Koster
Christopher Wren
Dr. Jacobi

Knaphill exbury azaleas. Deciduous; large flowers sometimes ruffled in colors from pink to orange to red and rose, often with contrasting blotches. Fragrant.

Berryrose
Cecile
Toucan

Southern indica. Evergreen; for sunny places. Outstanding vigor.

Rhododendrons are generally classified as:

Catawba hybrids: extremely hardy and dependable.
Griffithianum hybrids: largest flowered species, but not hardy in northeastern United States.
Fortune hybrids: quite hardy, thriving as far north as Cape Cod.

WHITE RHODODENDRONS	HARDY TO:
Countess of Haddington	20F
Dora Amateis	−15F
Great Lakes	−25F
Sappho	− 5F
White Pearl	5F

PINK RHODODENDRONS	HARDY TO:
Alice	− 5F
Cadis	−15F
Countess of Derby	− 5F
Kate Waterer	−10F
Pink Pearl	− 5F
Scintillation	−10F

RED RHODODENDRONS	HARDY TO:
America	−25F
Brittannia	− 5F
Caractacus	−25F
Holden	−15F
Lady Bligh	0F
Mars	−10F

BLUE AND PURPLE RHODODENDRONS	HARDY TO:
Barto Blue	5F
Blue Ensign	−10F
Blue Jay	− 5F
Lee's Dark Purple	− 5F
Sapphire	0F

YELLOW SHADES OF RHODODENDRONS	HARDY TO:
Butterfly	0F
Crest	− 5F
Devonshire Cream	0F
King of Shrubs	5F
Unique	5F

Rosa (rose)

Roses are the most popular garden flower, with thousands of hybrids—teas, floribundas, grandifloras. All require a definite program of maintenance to keep them at their best. The native or wild roses are easier to grow, and do not have as many problems as the hybrids. Single or double flowers in a range of colors, pure white to pale yellow to pink and the reddest purple. Plants vary greatly in size, will grow in a poor soil if necessary, and do not need a great deal of attention. While the hybrids certainly have their place in the garden, the wild or shrub roses have great interest, too, and should be grown more.

R. banksiae (Banks rose). Hardy to 5F; climber to 20 feet. Glossy, leathery leaves, and small yellow or white flowers. Evergreen.

Alba plena—double white fragrant flowers
Lutea—double yellow flowers; no scent

R. centifolia (cabbage rose). Hardy to −10F; grows to 6 feet with prickly stems; double pink flowers. Deciduous.

Muscosa (moss rose)—stalks and bases have mossy texture

R. chinensis (China rose). Hardy to 5F; prickly or smooth stems. Glossy, green leaves and single flowers. Deciduous.

Minima (fairy rose)—single or double rose-red bloom; grows to 10 inches

R. damascena (damask rose). Hardy to −20F; grows to 6 feet. Pale-green leaves and fragrant double flowers. Deciduous.

Trigintipetala—semidouble red flowers

R. gallica (French rose). Hardy to −10F; grows to 4 feet. Smooth, green leaves; red or purple flowers. Deciduous.

R. hugonis (Father Hugo rose). Hardy to −10F; grows to 8 feet. Deep-green leaves; yellow flowers. Deciduous.

R. multiflora (Japanese rose). Hardy to −10F; grows to 10 feet. Flowers usually white. Floriferous and vigorous. Deciduous.

R. odorata (tea rose). Hardy to 5F; grows to about 12 feet. Pink double flowers. Evergreen or semievergreen.

R. rugosa (rugosa rose). Hardy to −35F; vigorous grower to 8 feet. Glossy, green leaves. Single or double flowers in a wide range of colors. Deciduous. Also see Chapter 18.

Spiraea (spiraea)

Spiraeas have red or white flowers that add color outdoors. Two groups; spring blooming and summer blooming. Some spiraeas have a pleasing branching habit and are small; others reach 15 feet. Most are vigorous, not particular about soil conditions, nor demanding about light. They grow in sun or light shade; in general they need little pruning, nor are they bothered by insects.

S. billardii. Hybrid; hardy to −20F. Arching branches, to 6 feet, and tiny pale-pink flowers. Deciduous.

S. bullata. Hardy to −5F; dense grower to 2 feet. Round leaves and pink flowers; good rock garden plant. Deciduous.

S. bumalda. Hardy to −10F; grows to 3 feet. Narrow, oval leaves and pale-pink blooms. Deciduous.

Anthony Waterer (dwarf red spiraea)—bright-carmine flowers

S. prunifolia plena (bridalwreath spiraea). Hardy to −20F; leaves turn orange in fall. Double white flowers. Deciduous. Grows to 6–9 feet.

S. thunbergii (Thunberg spiraea). Hardy to −20F; grows to 5 feet. Leathery branchlets and single white flowers. Deciduous.

Syringa (lilac)

Every homeowner has a spot in his heart and in his garden for fragrant lilacs. There are at least 250 named varieties offered today. These are vigorous upright shrubs easily grown in almost any kind of soil, but have a slight preference for a lime-type soil. (And while some lilacs do have insect trouble, there are many new ones that are resistant to pest and disease.) Pruning is important to keep plants healthy. Flowers become less numerous and smaller if suckers take away plant strength. For best results prune lilacs this way: take out one-third of the old stems of mature plants one year; another third, the next year; and the remaining, the third year. Then plants will always appear handsome.

S. chinensis (Chinese lilac). Hybrid; hardy to −10F; grows to 15 feet. Fine-textured foliage, and fragrant rose-purple flowers. Deciduous.

S. josikaea (Hungarian lilac). Hardy to −50F; dense, upright grower to 12 feet. Gloss, green leaves; lilac flowers. Deciduous.

S. lacinata (cut-leaf lilac). Hardy to −10F; open growth to 6 feet. Rich green foliage, and fragrant pale-lilac flowers. Deciduous.

S. microphylla (littleleaf lilac). Hardy to −10F; grows to 6 feet. Pale-lilac flowers. Deciduous.

S. villosa (late lilac). Hardy to −50F; dense, upright grower to 10 feet. Rosy-lilac to white flowers. Deciduous.

S. vulgaris (common lilac). Hardy to −35F; bulky shrub to 20 feet. Fragrant lilac flowers. Deciduous.

Edith Cavell—French lilac; white
Cavour—French lilac; single violet
Ellen Willmott—French lilac; double white
Clarke's Giant—French lilac; single blue

Viburnum (viburnum)

For every season of the year there is a viburnum for the garden. Many are valued for their spring flowers, others for their beautiful glossy, green summer foliage and several have lovely fall colors. Almost all viburnums grow with little care, and are tolerant of practically any soil; many grow in light shade. Several have vivid autumn color, and a few hold berries all through winter. The leaves are deciduous or evergreen. Viburnums are rarely attacked by insects.

V. carlcephalum (fragrant snowball). Hardy to −10F; grows to 7 feet. Dull, grayish green leaves, and fragrant white flowers. Deciduous.

V. davidii. Hardy to 5F; grows to 3 feet. Dark green, veined leaves, and white flowers. Evergreen.

V. dentatum (arrowwood). Hardy to −50F; grows to 15 feet. Creamy white flowers, and red autumn color. Deciduous.

V. dilatatum (linden viburnum). Hardy to −10F; tall and broad. Gray-green leaves and creamy white flowers. Deciduous.

V. japonicum (Japanese viburnum). Hardy to 5F; grows to 20 feet. Glossy, dark-green leaves, and fragrant white flowers. Evergreen.

V. lantana (wayfaring tree). Hardy to −35F; grows to 15 feet. Oval leaves turn red in fall; tiny white flowers. Deciduous.

V. opulus (European cranberry bush). Hardy to −35F; grows to 20 feet. Maple-shaped leaves turn red in fall; clusters of white flowers. Deciduous.
Nana—dwarf

V. trilobum (American cranberry bush). Hardy to −50F; grows to 15 feet. Similar to **V. opulus,** but not so susceptible to aphid damage. Deciduous.

Weigela (weigela)

These have brilliant flowers and are vigorous growers, but they do not have autumn color. Some varieties start blooming in May with flowers until June. A few weigelas are valued for their bronze or variegated leaves.

W. middendorfiana. Hardy to −10F; dense and broad shrubs to 4 feet. Dark-green, wrinkled leaves, and yellow flowers. Deciduous.

General List of Shrubs

SE = semievergreen; D = deciduous; E = evergreen; GC = ground cover

BOTANICAL AND COMMON NAME	SE D E	APPROX. HEIGHT IN FEET	AVERAGE TEMP.	REMARKS
Abelia grandiflora (glossy abelia)	SE	5	−10 to − 5F	Free-flowering
Abeliophyllum deistichum (Korean white forsythia)	D	3 to 4	−10 to − 5F	Prune after bloom
Amelanchier canadensis (shadblow service berry)	D	30	−20 to −10F	Slow grower
Amelanchier grandiflora	D	25	−20 to −10F	Large flowers
Andromeda polifolia (bog rosemary)	E	1 to 2	−50 to −35F	Likes moist locations
Arbutus unedo (strawberry tree)	E	10 to 20	10 to 20F	Does not like alkaline soil
Arctostaphylos uva-ursi (barberry)	E	GC	−50 to −35F	Grows in any soil
Arctostaphylos manzanita	E	6 to 20	5 to 10F	Branching habit
Aucuba japonica (aucuba)	E	15	5 to 10F	Good for shady places
Berberis koreana (Korean barberry)	D/E	2 to 10	−10 to − 5F	Good outstanding colors; red berries
Berberis thunbergi (Japanese barberry)	D/E	7	−10 to 5F	Grows in any soil
Buddleia alternifolia (fountain buddleia)	D	12	−10 to − 5F	Graceful; branching
Buddleia davidii (butterfly bush)	D/SE	15	−10 to − 5F	Many varieties
Buxus microphylla japonica (Japanese boxwood)	E	4	−10 to − 5F	Low and compact
Buxus microphylla koreana (Korean boxwood)	E	6 to 10	−20 to −10F	Hardiest; foliage turns brown in winter

General List of Shrubs (continued)

BOTANICAL AND COMMON NAME	SE D E	APPROX. HEIGHT IN FEET	AVERAGE TEMP.	REMARKS
Buxus sempervirens (common boxwood)	E	20	−10 to − 5F	Many varieties
Callistemon citrinus (bottlebrush)	E	25	20 to 30F	Lovely flowers
Calluna vulgaris (heather)	E	15	−20 to −10F	Bright color and foliage
Carissa grandiflora (natal plum)	E	15	20 to 30F	Spiny, branching one
Carpenteria californica (California mock orange)	E	8	5 to 20F	Showy shrub
Ceanothus americanus (New Jersey tea)	E	3	−20 to −10F	For poor soil
Ceanothus ovatus	E	3	−20 to −10F	Upright grower
Ceanothus thyrsiflorus (blue blossom)	E	30	−20 to −10F	Grows in sandy soil
Chaenomeles speciosa (flowering quince)	D	6	−20 to −10F	Lovely flowers
C. superba	D	6	−20 to −10F	Fine hybrid
Clerodendrum trichotomum	E	10	20 to 30F	White flowers
Clethra alnifolia (summer sweet)	D	9	−35 to −20F	Fragrant summer bloom
Cornus alba Sibirica (Siberian dogwood)	D	10	−50 to −35F	Spectacular autumn color
Cornus mas (cornelian cherry)	D	Up to 18	−20 to − 5F	Early blooming
Daphne odora (fragrant daphne)	D/E	4 to 6	5 to 10F	Fragrant
Elaeagnus angustifolia (Russian olive)	D	20	−50 to −35F	Fragrant flowers
Elaeagnus multiflora (cherry elaeagnus)	D/E	9	−20 to −10F	Bright-red fruit
Elaeagnus pungens (silverberry)	D/E	12	5 to 10F	Vigorous grower
Enkianthus campanulatus (redvein enkianthus)	D	30	−20 to −10F	Red autumn color
Enkianthus perulatus	D	6	−10 to − 5F	Red autumn color
Erica canaliculata (heather)	E	6	20 to 30F	Pink, purple flower
Eugenia uniflora (Surinam cherry)	E	10 to 15	20 to 30F	White, fragrant flowers

General List of Shrubs (continued)

BOTANICAL AND COMMON NAME	SE D E	APPROX. HEIGHT IN FEET	AVERAGE TEMP.	REMARKS
Euonymus alata (winged euonymus)	D	9	−35 to −20F	Sturdy; easily grown
Euonymus japonica (evergreen euonymus)	E	15	10 to 20F	Splendid foliage
Euonymus latifolius	D	20	−10 to − 5F	Vigorous grower
Euonymus sanguineus	D	20	−10 to − 5F	Best deciduous one
Fatsia japonica (Japanese aralia)	E	15	5 to 10F	Handsome foliage
Forsythia intermedia (border forsythia)	D	2 to 9	−20 to − 5F	Deep-yellow flowers
Forsythia ovata (early forsythia)	D	8	−20 to −10F	Earliest to bloom and hardiest
Fothergilla major (large fothergilla)	D	9	−10 to − 5F	Good flowers and autumn color
Fuchsia magellanica (Magellan fuchsia)	D	3	−10 to 5F	Floriferous
Gardenia jasminoides (Cape jasmine)	E	4 to 6	10 to 30F	Fragrant
Gaultheria shallon (salal)	E	5	−10 to − 5F	Sun or shade
Gaultheria veitchiana (veitch wintergreen)	E	3	5 to 10F	White or pink, bell-shaped flowers
Hamamelis mollis (Chinese witch hazel)	D	30	−10 to − 5F	Very fragrant flowers
Hamamelis vernalis (spring witch hazel)	D	10	−10 to − 5F	Early spring blooms
Hibiscus rosa-sinensis (Chinese hibiscus)	E	30	20 to 30F	Stellar flower
Hibiscus syriacus (shrub althaea)	D	15	−10 to − 5F	Many varieties
Hydrangea arborescens Grandiflora (hills-of-snow)	D	3	−20 to −10F	Easy culture
Hypericum densiflorum	D/SE	6	−10 to − 5F	Fine-textured foliage
Hypericum prolificum	D/SE	3	−20 to −10F	Very shrubby
Ilex cornuta (Chinese holly)	E	9	5 to 10F	Bright berries; lustrous foliage

General List of Shrubs (continued)

BOTANICAL AND COMMON NAME	SE D E	APPROX. HEIGHT IN FEET	AVERAGE TEMP.	REMARKS
Ilex crenata (Japanese holly)	E	20	− 5 to 5F	Another good holly
Jasminum grandiflorum (Spanish jasmine)	SE/D	10 to 15	20 to 30F	Blooms all summer
Jasminum nudiflorum (winter jasmine)	D	15	−10 to − 5F	Viny shrub; not fragrant
Jasminum officinale (common white jasmine)	SE/D	30	5 to 10F	Tall-growing
Juniperus chinensis Pfitzeriana (Pfitzer juniper)	E	10	−20 to −10F	Popular juniper
Juniperus communis (common juniper)	E	30	−50 to −35F	Many varieties
Kalmia angustifolia (sheep laurel)	E	3	−50 to −35F	Needs acid soil
Kalmia latifolia (mountain laurel)	E	30	−20 to −10F	Amenable grower
Kerria japonica	D	4 to 6	−20 to −10F	Bright-yellow flowers
Kolkwitzia amabilis (beauty bush)	D	10	−20 to −10F	Has many uses
Lagerstroemia indica (crape myrtle)	D	20	5 to 10F	Popular summer bloom
Laurus nobilis (sweet bay)	E	30	− 5 to 5F	Tough plant
Leptospermum scoparium	E	6 to 20	20 to 30F	Ground cover and shrubs
Ligustrum amurense (Amur privet)	D/E	6 to 30	−35 to −20F	Small spikes of white flowers
Lonicera fragrantissima (winter honeysuckle)	D/E	3 to 15	−10 to − 5F	Early fragrant flowers
Lonicera maackii (Amur honeysuckle)	D	15	−50 to −35F	Holds leaves late into fall
Lonicera tatarica (Tatarian honeysuckle)	D	10	−35 to −20F	Small pink flowers in late spring
Mahonia aquifolium (Oregon grape)	SE/E	3 to 5	−10 to − 5F	Handsome foliage
Mahonia repens (creeping mahonia)	SE/E	1	−10 to − 5F	Small; good ground cover
Nandina domestica (heavenly bamboo)	SE/E	8	5 to 10F	Red berries in winter

General List of Shrubs (continued)

BOTANICAL AND COMMON NAME	SE D E	APPROX. HEIGHT IN FEET	AVERAGE TEMP.	REMARKS
Nerium oleander (oleander)	E	15	5 to 20F	Popular flowering shrub; dangerously poisonous juice
Osmanthus heterophyllus (holly osmanthus)	E	18	− 5 to 5F	Sun or shade
Phormium tenax (New Zealand flax)	E	15	10 to 20F	Many hybrids
Photinia serrulata (Chinese photinia)	E	30 to 40	5 to 10F	Bright-red berries
Pieris floribunda (mountain andromeda)	E	5	−20 to −10F	Does well in dry soil
Pieris japonica (Japanese andromeda)	E	9	−10 to − 5F	Splendid color
Pittosporum tobira (Japanese pittosporum)	E	10	10 to 20F	Fragrant, white flowers
Poncirus trifoliata (hardy orange)	D	30	− 5 to 5F	Dense growth; attractive foliage
Potentilla fruitcosa (cinquefoil)	D	2 to 5	−50 to −35F	Many varieties
Prunus laurocerasus (cherry laurel)	E	5	10 to 20F	Many varieties
Pyracantha coccinea (scarlet firethorn)	E	8 to 10	− 5 to 5F	Many varieties; valued for bright berries
Raphiolepis umbellata (yeddo hawthorn)	E	6	5 to 10F	Sun or partial shade
Ribes sanguineum (flowering currant)	D	4 to 12	−10 to − 5F	Deep-red flowers; March to June
Salix caprea (French pussy willow)	D	25	−20 to −10F	Vigorous grower
Salix repens (creeping willow)	D	3	−20 to −10F	Good low willow for poor soil
Sarcococca ruscifolia	E	6	5 to 10F	Takes shade
Skimmia japonica (Japanese skimmia)	E	4	5 to 10F	For shade
Spiraea arguta	D	6	−20 to −10F	Free-flowering
Spiraea prunifolia (bridal wreath spiraea)	D	9	−20 to −10F	Turns orange in fall

General List of Shrubs (continued)

BOTANICAL AND COMMON NAME	SE D E	APPROX. HEIGHT IN FEET	AVERAGE TEMP.	REMARKS
Spiraea thunbergi (thunberg spiraea)	D	5	−20 to −10F	Arching branches
Spiraea veitchii	D	12	−10 to − 5F	Good background; graceful one
Syringa henryi Lutece	D	10	−50 to −35F	Early June bloom
Syringa villosa (late lilac)	D	9	−50 to −35F	Dense, upright habit
Syringa vulgaris (common lilac)	D	20	−35 to −20F	Many varieties
Tamarix aphylla (Athel tree)	E	30 to 50	5 to 10F	Good wide-spread tree
Tamarix parviflora Pink Cascade, Summer Glow	D	15	−20 to −10F	Prune immediately after bloom
Taxus canadensis (Canada yew)	E	3 to 6	−50 to −35F	Will tolerate shade
Viburnum davidi	E	3	5 to 10F	Handsome leaves
Viburnum dentatum (arrowwood)	D	15	−50 to −35F	Red fall color
Viburnum dilatatum (linden viburnum)	D	9	−10 to − 5F	Colorful red fruit
Viburnum lantana (wayfaring tree)	D	15	−35 to −20F	Grows in dry soil
Viburnum lentago (nannyberry)	D	30	−50 to −35F	Good background or screen plant
Viburnum opulus (European cranberry bush)	D	12	−35 to −20F	Many varieties
Viburnum prunifolium (black haw)	D	15	−35 to −20F	Good specimen plant
Viburnum sieboldi	D	30	−20 to −10F	Stellar performer
Viburnum trilobum (cranberry bush)	D	12	−50 to −35F	Effective in winter
Vitex agnus-castus (chaste tree)	D	9	− 5 to 10F	Lilac flowers
Weigela Bristol Ruby	D	7	−10 to − 5F	Complex hybrid
Weigela Bristol Snowflake	D	7	−10 to − 5F	Complex hybrid
Weigela florida	D	9	−10 to − 5F	Many available
Weigela middendorfiana	D	1	−20 to −10F	Dense, broad shrubs

VINES

I compare vines to frosting on a cake and if you have ever seen an unfrosted cake you will know that vines are the finishing touch to the garden. These fine plants can make a bare wall beautiful, a fence a thing of beauty, and can, with careful placement, hide unsightly and ugly areas that seem to crop up even in the most carefully planned garden. Most important, perhaps, vines provide that needed vertical accent in a way that trees cannot.

There is a wonderful world of vines—some for foliage such as Akebia, creeping fig (*Ficus pumila*) and English ivy (*Hedera helix*). And there are vines for flowers such as the wonderful clematis and Clystoma. There are small-leaved vines and large-leaved ones like Dutchman's pipe (*Aristolochia durior*). And aside from their decorative value, vines are an interesting group of plants that should be used more. I would not be without my fine morning glory that blooms on a trellis near my doorway. It is a welcoming sight.

Vines are climbing plants and the majority need support in the form of a trellis or wire framework. The plants climb by means of tendrils or discs; some have twining stems that grasp any surface. In the first few weeks with you, vines do need attention; you must get them to start properly—that is, you attach them to the support with vine hangers or other devices (sold at hardware stores). However, in a few months vines grow by themselves and require only occasional care. That includes pruning and that is why I believe most gardeners do not give vines more attention. Vines do not need constant pruning but they do need it periodically to keep them handsome and, while it is true that some vines can become a tangled mess, most grow beautifully.

Planting

Vines require a deep planting hole—about three to four feet—because most of them have spreading, rambling roots that require space to grow. Use good top soil and prepare the planting area as you would for annuals or perennials—plenty of rich soil and add some humus. When the plant is in the hole, tamp the earth gently around the collar of the plant—you want to eliminate air pockets. Water thoroughly and deeply. Put vines in the ground at the same level at which they were growing in the nursery and keep the rootball intact—no whacking or cutting of the roots which can retard the growth of the plant.

Once vines are in place put in suitable supports such as a trellis or wires they may climb; do it now, not later. Once started without support vines are a chore to place on supports. You can buy trellises or make your own from wood lath. Use tie-ons or nylon string to anchor vines to wood grids. If on a fence use standard vine hangers.

Care

Vines can take more water than one might think if planted properly and if they have good drainage. They are greedy plants and most of them grow rapidly—morning glory and bougainvillea to name a few. Soil should be uniformly moist at all times and feeding is necessary once plants are established—in about six weeks. Feed every other watering with a 10-10-5 plant food.

Pruning as previously mentioned is necessary, and in the lists that follow you will find directions for keeping plants in form. Remember that vines must be pruned now and then.

List of Vines

The following vines are ones I have used through the years. Choose the ones that suit the conditions you can give them—sun or shade—and the plants you like for flower or foliage. And last, consider just what job each will do for the garden—screen an unsightly place, provide a colorful covering, or simply afford beautiful decoration.

Vines

BOTANICAL AND COMMON NAME	MIN. NIGHT TEMP.	GENERAL DESCRIPTION	SUN OR SHADE	REMARKS
Akebia quinata (five-leaf akebia)	−20 to −10F	Vigorous twiner; fragrant, small flowers	Sun or partial shade	Needs support; prune in fall/early spring
Allamanda cathartica	Tender	Dense with heavy stems, lovely tubular flowers	Sun	Prune annually in spring
Ampelopsis breviped-unculata (porcelain ampelopsis) (blueberry climber)	−20 to −10F	Strong grower with dense leaves	Sun or shade	Prune in early spring
Antigonon leptopus (coral vine)	Tender	Excellent as screen	Sun	Needs light support; prune hard after bloom
Aristolochia durior (Dutchman's pipe)	−20 to −10F	Big twiner, mammoth leaves	Sun or shade	Needs sturdy support; prune in spring or summer
Clytostoma *Bignonia capreolata* (cross vine) (trumpet vine)	−5 to 5F	Orange flowers	Sun or shade	Thin out weak branches in spring; clings by discs
Celastrus scandens (American bittersweet)	−50 to −35F	Light-green leaves, red berries	Sun or shade	Prune in early spring before growth starts

VINES

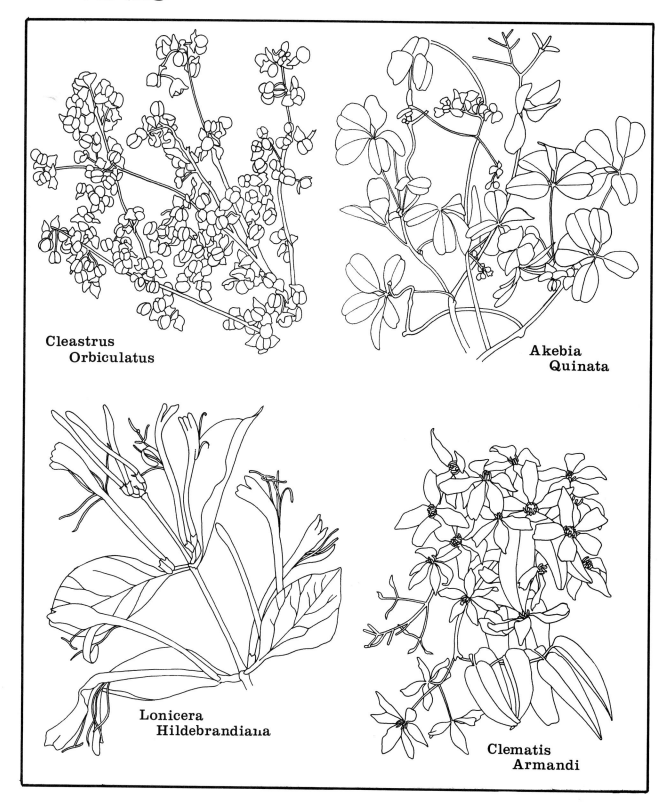

Cleastrus
Orbiculatus

Akebia
Quinata

Lonicera
Hildebrandiana

Clematis
Armandi

Vines (continued)

BOTANICAL AND COMMON NAME	MIN. NIGHT TEMP.	GENERAL DESCRIPTION	SUN OR SHADE	REMARKS
Clematis armandi (evergreen clematis)	5 to 10F	Lovely flowers and foliage; many colors	Sun	Needs support; prune lightly after bloom
Doxantha unguis-cati	10 to 20F	Dark green leaves; yellow blooms	Sun	Needs no support; prune hard after bloom
Euonymus fortunei (wintercreeper)	−35 to −20F	Shiny leathery leaves; orange berries in fall	Sun or shade	Needs support; prune in early spring
Fatshedera lizei	20 to 30F	Grown for handsome foliage	Shade	No pruning needed
Ficus pumila (repens) (creeping fig)	20 to 30F	Small heart-shaped leaves	Partial shade	Thin plant in late fall or early spring
Gelsemium sempervirens (Carolina jasmine)	Tender	Fragrant yellow flowers	Sun or partial shade	Needs support, thin plant immediately after bloom
Hedera helix (English ivy)	−10 to −5F	Scalloped neat leaves; many varieties	Shade	Prune and thin in early spring
Hydrangea petiolaris (climbing hydrangea)	−20 to −10F	Heads of snowy flowers	Sun or partial shade	Thin and prune in winter or early spring
Ipomoea purpurea (Convolvulus) (morning glory)	Tender	Flowers are white, blue, purple, pink, or red	Sun	Bloom until frost
Jasminum nudiflorum (winter jasmine)	−10 to −5F	Yellow flowers	Sun or shade	Needs strong support, thin and shape annually after bloom

Vines (continued)

BOTANICAL AND COMMON NAME	MIN. NIGHT TEMP.	GENERAL DESCRIPTION	SUN OR SHADE	REMARKS
Jasminum officinale (white jasmine)	5 to 10F	Showy dark green leaves and white flowers	Sun or shade	Provide strong support, thin and shape after bloom
Kadsura japonica (scarlet kadsura)	5 to 10F	Bright red berries in fall	Sun	Needs support prune annually in early spring
Lonicera caprifolium (sweet honeysuckle)	−10 to −5F	White or yellow trumpet flowers	Sun	Prune in fall or spring
Lonicera hildebrandiana (Burmese honeysuckle)	20 to 30F	Shiny dark green leaves	Sun or partial shade	Needs support; prune in late fall
Lonicera japonica Halliana (Hall's honeysuckle)	−20 to −10F	Deep-green leaves, bronze in fall	Sun or shade	Provide support, prune annually in fall and spring
Mandevilla suaveolens (Chilean jasmine)	20 to 30F	Heart-shaped leaves and flowers	Sun	Trim and cut back lightly in fall; remove seed pods as they form
Parthenocissus quinquefolia (Virginia creeper)	−35 to −20F	Scarlet leaves in fall	Sun or shade	Prune in early spring
Passiflora caerulea (passion flower)	5 to 10F	Spectacular flowers	Sun	Needs support; prune hard annually in fall or early spring
Phaseolus coccineus (scarlet runner bean)	Tender	Bright red flowers	Sun	Renew each spring
Plumbago capensis (plumbago)	20 to 30F	Blue flowers	Sun	Prune somewhat in spring
Pueraria thunbergiana (Kudsu vine)	−5 to 5F	Purple flowers	Sun or partial shade	Provide sturdy support; cut back hard annually in fall

Vines (continued)

BOTANICAL AND COMMON NAME	MIN. NIGHT TEMP.	GENERAL DESCRIPTION	SUN OR SHADE	REMARKS
Rosa (rambler rose)	−10 to −5F	Many varieties	Sun	Needs support; prune out dead wood, shorten long shoots, and cut laterals back to 2 nodes in spring or early summer after bloom
Smilax rotundifolia (horse brier)	−20 to −10F	Good green foliage	Sun or shade	Prune hard annually any time; needs no support
Trachelospermum jasminoides (star jasmine)	20 to 30F	Dark-green leaves and small white flowers	Partial shade	Provide heavy support; prune very lightly in fall
Vitis coignetiae (glory grape)	−10 to 5F	Colorful autumn leaves	Sun or partial shade	Needs sturdy support; prune annually in fall or spring
Wistaria floribunda (Japanese wisteria)	−20 to −10F	Violet-blue flowers	Sun	Provide support and prune annually once mature to shorten long branches after bloom or in winter; pinch back branches first year

13

Trees–The Framework

TREES should be the first concern in the planting of a property, for trees are the focal points, the essential elements of the design. There are many types of trees—deciduous, evergreen, flowering, and fruiting. There are shade trees and decorative trees, trees with many different values. Basically, think of trees as the skeleton of a *good garden*—and also think of them for specific purposes such as shading an area or lending autumn color to the overall *landscape* plan.

Your property—its size and shape—will dictate the number of trees you need, and usually there will already be some trees on the site. Whenever possible, keep what is there; a good tree—that is, a healthy one—is worth money. Furthermore, even if it is a tree you do not particularly like, removing it will be expensive so it is best to hold onto what you have. But if the site is bare, then, of course, the privilege of selection is yours.

GETTING ACQUAINTED WITH TREES

Basically, there are two groups of trees—the deciduous that drop their leaves in fall and the evergreen. Within these two groups there are others. The deciduous trees include flowering types, and the evergreens, which we usually think of as pine and spruce, include many fine broadleaves. Some trees grow to 120 feet—the beech, for example—while others, like the magnolias, usually stay within a 35-foot range. Some trees like the Norway maple grow quickly, others like the oak grow slowly. Some trees will grow in almost any climate; others cannot tolerate extreme cold.

Hardiness and height are the best guide in selection. When you buy a tree, keep in mind that the three-foot specimen you are taking home may in time reach 100 feet. This may be good or bad—good, if you have a large property that can accommodate it; bad if such a giant will be out of scale on your restricted lot. (So, before you purchase, check the heights of trees on the lists at the end of this chapter.)

Think next about the role your tree will play—if deciduous, is it to provide shade? If evergreen, is it to be an important year-round accent, windbreak, or screen? Then make selections. Don't be too concerned about culture, the soil you have, or the need for moisture. Most established trees can cope with a variety of conditions—eventually nature will take over. So selection depends mainly on climate and your purpose.

BUYING TREES

It is not easy to select trees. In the nursery trees look much alike as to height and shape, and the shape of a young tree hardly indi-

Even one small flowering tree—in this case an old apple—can bring beauty to a small garden. (M. Adams)

cates what it will look like in two or three years. Nursery trees are offered "bare root" (that is, without wrappings), "B and B" (balled-and-burlapped), and in cans.

Bare root trees: From fall through winter many deciduous trees are sold without root covering. Trees so offered are those that tolerate uprooting while dormant. The roots are covered with sawdust or a similar material at the nursery so they will not get broken.

Balled-and-burlapped: Needle-leaved trees and broadleaf evergreens are generally sold B and B. The tree is dug with a gener-

ous rootball of soil and then wrapped in burlap.

Container-grown trees: In spring and summer nurseries offer trees in five- or ten-gallon cans. These container-grown trees are safer for nurserymen to carry over until they are sold.

Now let's look at planting methods.

Bare root trees: Dig a deep, wide hole—at least two feet across and two feet deep. Pile the soil you remove at the side of the hole; mix it with some leaf mold or other humus and make it porous by breaking it up into small particles with a spade or hoe. Until

Tree shapes

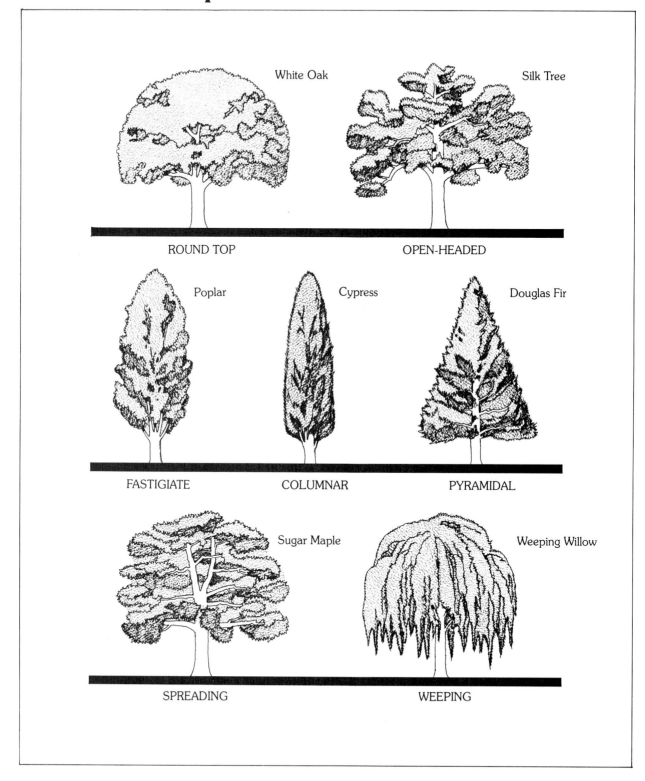

White Oak

Silk Tree

ROUND TOP

OPEN-HEADED

Poplar

Cypress

Douglas Fir

FASTIGIATE

COLUMNAR

PYRAMIDAL

Sugar Maple

Weeping Willow

SPREADING

WEEPING

Planting Trees

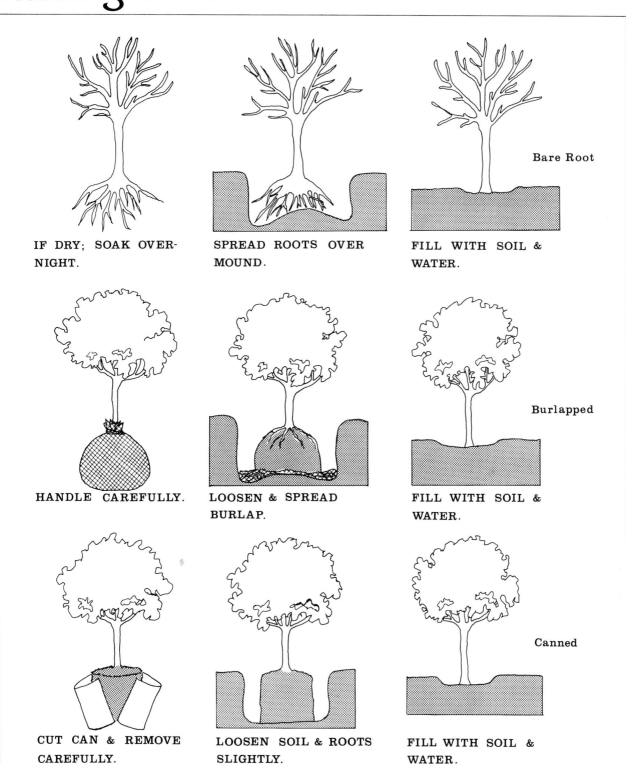

IF DRY; SOAK OVER-NIGHT.

SPREAD ROOTS OVER MOUND.

FILL WITH SOIL & WATER.

Bare Root

HANDLE CAREFULLY.

LOOSEN & SPREAD BURLAP.

FILL WITH SOIL & WATER.

Burlapped

CUT CAN & REMOVE CAREFULLY.

LOOSEN SOIL & ROOTS SLIGHTLY.

FILL WITH SOIL & WATER.

Canned

you plant the tree keep the roots in a pail of water or cover them with moist burlap or wet newspapers. Never expose bare-root trees to the air. Next put some of the prepared soil in the hole so as to form a mound and place the tree on it, spreading out the roots. Set the tree at the same depth it has been growing before; your guide will be the color change on the bark just above the point where the roots grow. Position the tree in the hole so that this point is about two inches above the soil surface. With the tree in place, fill the hole halfway with soil and water it thoroughly. Then add more soil to fill the hole and allow enough to build a ring of earth around the rim to form a basin. Now water again slowly and thoroughly.

Balled-and-burlapped: Prepare the hole in the same manner—wide and deep. After the tree is positioned untie the string that holds the burlap but do not remove the burlap. Just fill in around it with soil. In time the burlap disintegrates. However, if the rootball is wrapped in plastic type material, then do remove it. Some nurseries are doing this.

Container-grown trees: If you are planting within a day or two, have the nurseryman cut the container, making a slit on each side. Then when you plant you can tug it loose from the can. If you are not going to plant soon, you will have to cut the can yourself—not difficult if you have a proper cutter.

TREES IN THE LANDSCAPE

When I moved into my California house—an old house—I accepted what trees were on the property and let it go at that— what a mistake! The eucalyptus trees near the deck that were only five to six feet high then now tower 50 feet and pose a threat to anyone on the deck in a high wind. The pine—that small pretty tree in the center of the flower bed—grew, it seemed to me, overnight into a 30-foot demon that now dominates the garden, and the bay trees became mammoth overnight—actually in ten years. Trees in such wrong places should have been removed at the start.

In my suburban Illinois home the situation was different—the grounds had been well landscaped and the existing trees became part of the picture through the years as well they should—small birches skirted the terrace and two large shade trees close to each other created a pleasant canopy of green in summer at the edge (not in the center) of the lawn area. Smaller trees framed the house itself and in the background beyond the lawn and far back were deciduous trees of all kinds and a lovely wildflower garden. Someone who had known trees had lived there, I imagined, and I reaped the rewards.

Anyway, be wise regarding trees already on your property and leave them if you can but, if they are going to get in the way of your landscape plan, get rid of them at the start. How do you decide? That's the reason for this chapter. Know your trees as to height and purpose while they are still small. Trees, it seems, grow overnight or maybe it's just that time passes so fast. And don't think you won't live to see that little tree become a big one: It will—and before you know it.

How can I tell you how to landscape with trees? I do it simply—perhaps that is the best course, so let me outline how I help friends who have new houses and new sites. First, I draw a plot plan of the property. This is not a great piece of art, merely a freehand drawing (that you can do). I then sketch in what exists on the site. With a pencil I indicate forms shaded light gray,

Evergreen trees provide windbreak and a necessary green accent in this unusual deck arrangement. (Western Wood Products)

This large garden property relies on trees for definition and privacy. (M. Adams)

One giant flowering tree provides a dramatic canopy for a bonsai garden that makes excellent use of varying levels, and textures of wood and stone. (California Redwood Association)

dark gray, black, and so forth. I indicate flower beds or other plantings friends seem to want, and then last, I select the trees. These I mark with black pencil. I try to balance the landscape so there is continuity and the trees appear natural rather than exclamation points on the plan.

Then, and most important, I draw an elevation of the site where there are trees—an elevation in laymen's terms is simply a side view, and I draw a straight line to the assumed height of the tree. This side view can tell you much. I suppose by rote I select trees for flowering or for shade without

much thinking. I have done so many tree lists in my day that the little remarks in my lists happily come to mind as I design and sketch. You will have to check out the lists to see which trees are best for your purposes.

I never worry about what tree will grow in what soil or whether it should be on the south side of the property or the north. Perhaps this is unorthodox and I suppose any landscape architect will tell you so but through the years and with few exceptions, I can say that trees will virtually grow in any soil in any situation as long as they are established properly, and this means some ob-

Pruning trees

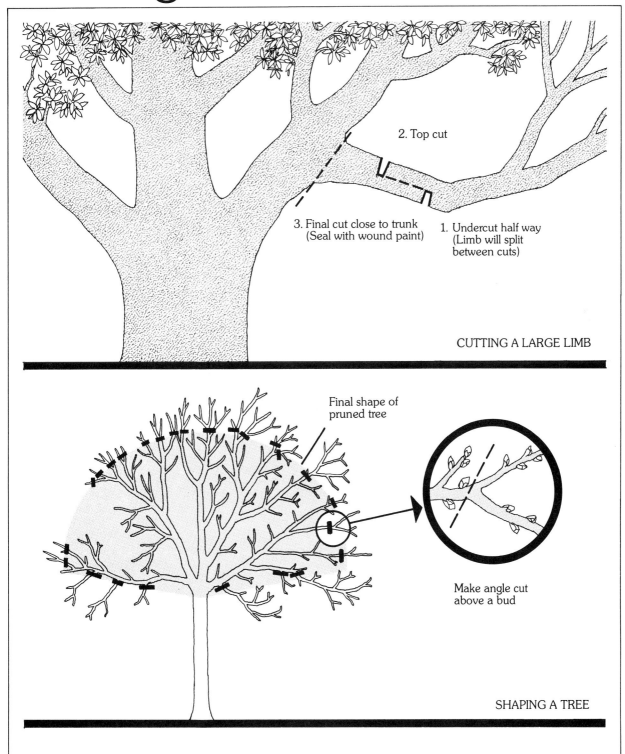

2. Top cut

3. Final cut close to trunk
(Seal with wound paint)

1. Undercut half way
(Limb will split
between cuts)

CUTTING A LARGE LIMB

Final shape of
pruned tree

Make angle cut
above a bud

SHAPING A TREE

servation and care in the first year or so. After that nature does it with an occasional help from you in the guise of pruning.

SOME POPULAR TREES

Abies (fir)

On the whole these evergreens are pyramidal with rigid horizontal branches, making them a decisive accent in the landscape. Use them sparingly. Needles will last for about five years before they fall; cones are ornamental, but do not appear every year. Trees have few insect or disease problems, but as they mature the lower branches become unsightly and, once removed, they do not grow back so that a mature specimen lacks symmetry. They need a cool, moist climate to grow well; in heat they deteriorate rapidly. Firs are Christmas favorites.

A. concolor (white fir). Hardy to −20F; narrow, pyramidal in shape to 120 feet. Bluish-green needles; rapid grower.

A. koreana (Korean fir). Hardy to −10F. Pyramidal to 50 feet; horizontal branching habit. Dark green needles.

A. magnifica (red fir). Hardy to −10F. Stiff pyramid to 200 feet; dense.

A. veitchi (veitch fir). Hardy to −35F. Pyramidal in shape, rather stiff, to 75 feet. Dark green needles, whitish underneath.

Acacia

Evergreen shrubs and trees for temperate areas; they differ widely in foliage and habit. Some have feathery divided leaves, others have wide flattened leaves. Acacias are short-lived (to about 25 years), yet they are useful and lovely in the garden, especially in February and March when they are covered with clouds of yellow flowers.

A. armata (kangaroo thorn). Hardy to 30F; light green, waxy leaves on thorny branches; grows to 15 feet. Single yellow flowers.

A. baileyana (Bailey acacia). Hardy to 30F; grows to 30 feet. Feathery, fine-cut, blue-gray leaves and clusters of yellow blooms.

A. decurrens (green wattle). Hardy to 30F; can grow to 50 feet. Feathery, dark green foliage and yellow blooms.

A. longifolia floribunda (Sydney golden wattle). Hardy to 30F; spreading habit to 20 feet. Dense-leaved.

A. pendula (weeping acacia). Hardy to 30F; blue-gray leaves on weeping branches. Yellow flowers.

Acer (maple)

Maples are popular deciduous shade trees, and there are many kinds for many uses. Varied in habit and rate of growth, size, and leaf shape, some of them (Japanese maple) are low and spreading; others (Norway maple) are rounded at the top and quite tall. Smaller varieties are ideal for landscaping in limited spaces. While some maples have interesting colorful bark, it is the autumn color of the foliage—brilliant reds and yellows—that makes them popular. Maples grow in any good garden soil, and are generally not bothered by pest or disease.

Evergreen trees

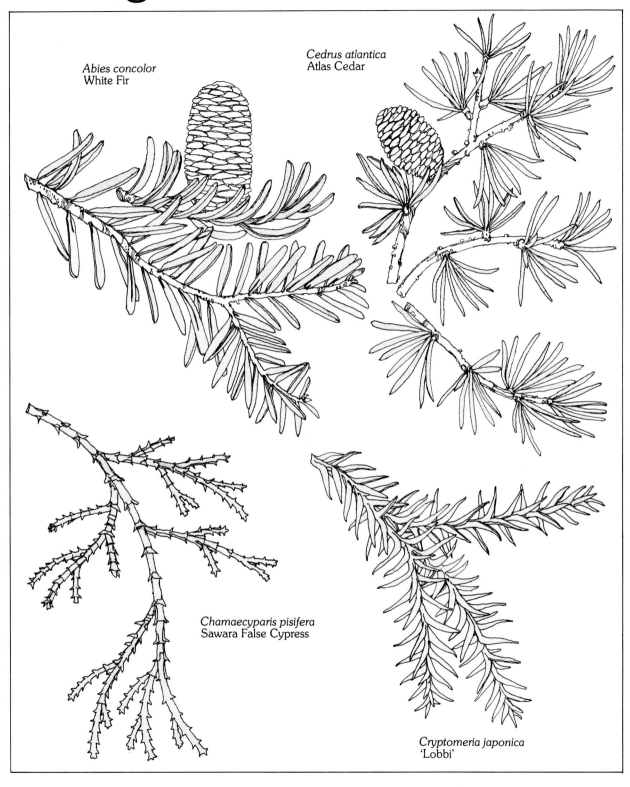

Abies concolor
White Fir

Cedrus atlantica
Atlas Cedar

Chamaecyparis pisifera
Sawara False Cypress

Cryptomeria japonica
'Lobbi'

Trees

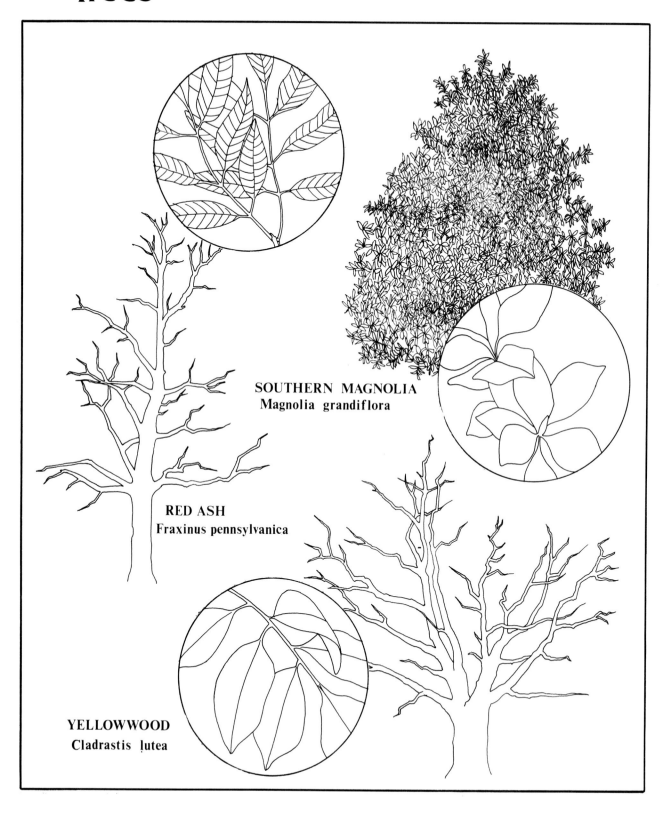

SOUTHERN MAGNOLIA
Magnolia grandiflora

RED ASH
Fraxinus pennsylvanica

YELLOWWOOD
Cladrastis lutea

Trees

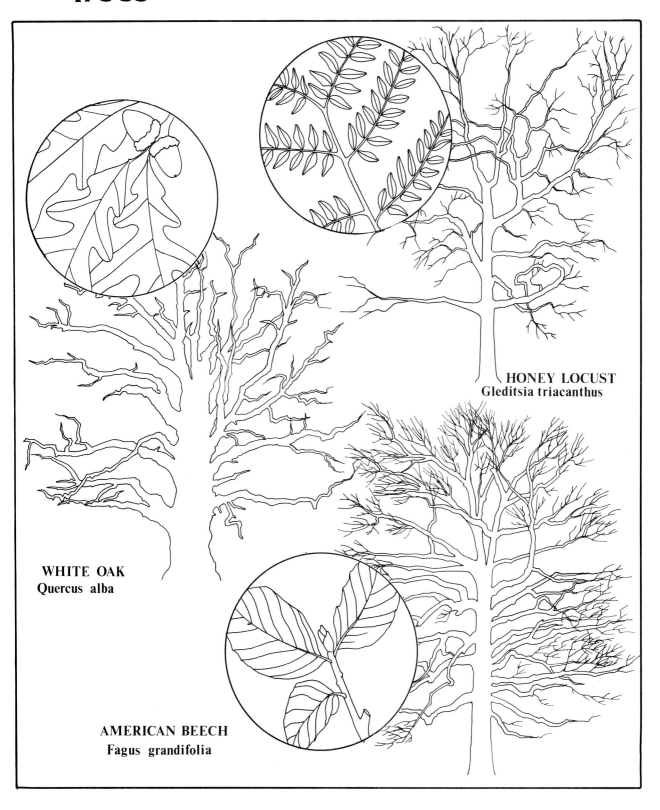

HONEY LOCUST
Gleditsia triacanthus

WHITE OAK
Quercus alba

AMERICAN BEECH
Fagus grandifolia

Trees

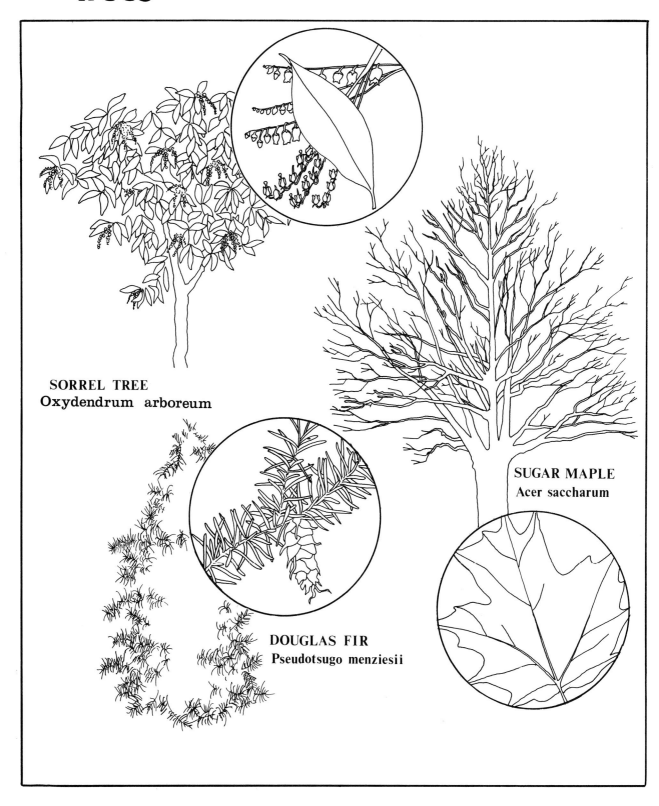

SORREL TREE
Oxydendrum arboreum

DOUGLAS FIR
Pseudotsugo menziesii

SUGAR MAPLE
Acer saccharum

A. buergerianum (trident maple). Hardy to −5F. Rounded habit; grows to 20 feet. Foliage is brilliant red in fall. Deciduous.

A. ginnala (Amur maple). Hardy to −50F; grows to about 20 feet, with striking red autumn color. Deciduous.

A. japonicum (full-moon maple). Hardy to −10F. Can reach 30 feet, lobed leaves. Good fall color.

Aconitifolium (fernleaf maple)—leaves deeply lobed
Aureum (golden maple)—handsome yellow foliage

A. macrophyllum (big-leaf maple). Hardy to −5F. Grows to 90 feet. Lobed leaves turn yellow in fall.

A. palmatum (Japanese maple). Hardy to −10F; rounded habit to 20 feet. Dense, handsome tree.

Atropurpureum—bronze leaves
Burgundy Lace—finely cut leaves; red
Dissectum (laceleaf maple)—leaves cut into threadlike segments
Versicolor—leaves green with white, pink, and light green variation

A. platanoides (Norway maple). Hardy to −35F; broad-crowned to 60 feet. Leaves turn yellow in fall; greenish-yellow spring flowers.

Columnare (pyramidal Norway maple)—slow grower
Faasen's Black—pyramidal with dark purple leaves

A. rubrum (red maple). Hardy to −35F; fast-growing to 100 feet. Red twigs and buds.

A. saacharum (sugar maple). Hardy to −35F; fast grower to 100 feet. Silver-gray bark; orange and red fall color.

Albizzia (silk tree)

An overlooked fine, small tree with delicate fernlike foliage and charming summer flowers. With arching stems and compact growth, it is an outstanding landscape subject. It likes sun and a good garden loam somewhat on the sandy side. In the North it is likely to die down to the ground in winter; remove dead stems early in spring to encourage new growth.

A. distachya (plume albizzia). Hardy to 20F; fast-growing to 20 feet. Dark green, velvety foliage and greenish-yellow flowers in spring.

A. julibrissin (silk tree). Hardy to 5F; rapid grower to 40 feet. Pink fluffy flowers in spring and ferny-leaved branches.

Betula (birch)

Birches are favorite ornamental deciduous trees of graceful appearance; the most popular ones have handsome white bark. Somewhat short-lived, the trees are difficult to transplant unless they are balled and burlapped. Most important, move them in spring. Once established, most birches are easy to grow and will thrive in wet or dry soil. The bright yellow autumn color is certainly desirable in the landscape. All in all birches are well worth planting.

B. albo-sinensis (Chinese paper birch). Hardy to −10F; rounded habit to 90 feet.

Handsome yellow color in autumn and orange-red bark.

B. papyrifera (canoe birch). Hardy to −50F; grows to 90 feet. White bark peels off in thin sheets.

B. populifolia (gray birch). Hardy to −20F; reaches 30 feet, with several trunks to a clump. Bark is white with black markings.

B. verrucosa (*pendula*) (European white birch). Hardy to −50F; pyramidal. Grows to 60 feet; white bark.

Fastigiata—upright grower
Purpurea—rich purple color
Youngi—pendulous branches

Carya (hickory)

Robust deciduous trees, once established they become giants. While they are free of insects and disease, they are difficult to transplant and should not be moved unless it is necessary. In general, hickories are excellent ornamentals with golden autumn foliage; they make superior accents on a property that has space for them. Some are broad in habit; others, narrow and upright.

C. illinoinensis (pecan). Hardy to −10F; a giant spreading tree to 150 feet. Dense-leaved, with striking yellow autumn color.

C. ovata (shagbark hickory). Hardy to −20F; upright, irregular growth to 120 feet. Golden brown autumn color, and bark that flakes off in large pieces.

Cedrus (cedar)

Big evergreens that need plenty of space; their sculptural growth is desirable in the landscape. They require a somewhat rich soil, and are relatively trouble-free. Some species are stiff in appearance; others are more graceful, having pendent branches.

C. atlantica (atlas cedar). Hardy to −5F; widely pyramidal to 120 feet. Silvery to light green needles in bunches.

Glauca (blue Atlas cedar)—silvery blue needles
Pendula—lovely pendent branches; graceful

C. deodara (deodar cedar). Hardy to 0F; narrow pyramidal growth to 150 feet with pendulous branches. Needles in dense bunches.

C. libani (cedar of Lebanon). Hardy to −10F; pyramidal growth to 120 feet, with stiff horizontal branches.

Cercis (redbud)

Small deciduous trees rarely over 25 feet with lovely heart-shaped leaves and clusters of small magenta-pink blossoms in spring. The flowers are long lasting; foliage turns bright yellow in fall. The redbuds will grow in full sun or light shade, and are not particular about soil.

C. canadensis (eastern redbud). Hardy to −20F; flat-topped tree to 35 feet. Small purplish-pink blooms and yellow leaves in fall.

C. chinensis (Chinese redbud). Hardy to −5F; often shrublike to 40 feet. Dense, feathery, rosy-purple flowers.

C. siliquastrum (Judas tree). Hardy to −5F; flat-topped tree to 30 feet. Profuse bright purplish-rose flowers.

Chamaecyparis (false cypress)

Favorite evergreens, with many color forms and varieties. The Japanese species withstand a drier atmosphere than do others in the group. Generally dense and pyramidal in shape, these trees are free of insects and disease. They are popular additions to the landscape, and need little care.

C. lawsoniana (Lawson false cypress). Hardy to −10F; slender tree to 120 feet. Usually with blue-green foliage; shredding bark.

Allumii (scarab Lawson cypress)—grows to 30 feet
Compacta—to 6 feet; gray-green foliage
Fletcheri—to 10 feet; blue-gray; purplish or brown in winter
Stewartii—golden-yellow foliage, usually turning green

C. obtusa (Hinoki false cypress). Hardy to −20F; broad pyramid to 120 feet. Glossy, green scalelike leaves.

Aurea (golden Hinoki cypress)—to 40 feet, golden-green leaves
Filiciodes (fernspray cypress)—to 15 feet; medium-green dense foliage
Nana (dwarf Hinoki cypress)—small form

C. pisifera (Sawara false cypress). Hardy to −35F; pyramidal to 150 feet, with horizontal branching habit. Open foliage.

Filifera (thread Sawara cypress)—dark green foliage
Plumosa Aurea—soft, feathery, golden-yellow foliage
Squarrosa Minima—dwarf; several forms under this name

Cornus (dogwood)

Dogwoods are just about the best small deciduous trees you can find; they grow rapidly and have splendid color in bloom and are showy again in autumn with brilliant red foliage. There is a dogwood for almost any part of the United States. Some are wide and spreading with horizontal branches; others are narrow and upright. There are many varieties of *C. florida* offered; but not all of them are good ones, so choose with care.

C. alba (Tartarian dogwood). Hardy to −35F; upright growth to 10 feet. Branches densely clothed with leaves; red twigs in winter.

C. florida (flowering dogwood). Hardy to −20F; horizontal branching habit; grows to 40 feet. Red color in autumn.

Cherokee Chief—rich red leaves
Pendula—stiff, pendulous branches
Rubra—pink or rose flower bracts

C. kousa (Japanese dogwood). Hardy to −10F; horizontal branching habit. Grows to 20 feet; red color in autumn.

Milky Way—profuse bloomer.

C. mas (cornelian cherry). Hardy to −20F; round, dense shrub type, to 20 feet. Small yellow flowers before leaves. Red autumn color.

C. nuttalli (Pacific dogwood). Hardy to 5F; pyramidal, with dense foliage. Grows to 75 feet; large flowers, spectacular in bloom.

Goldspot—leaves splashed with yellow.

Crataegus (hawthorn)

A widely distributed group of deciduous trees, hawthorns are dense, twiggy, dependable, and loaded with flowers in May. Of slow growth, they are desirable because they are compact and beautiful in the landscape. It is the picturesque shapes that make them so popular and, too, the bright red fruit in fall. Hawthorns will grow in poor soil; some of them hold fruit all winter.

C. arnoldiana (Arnold hawthorn). Hardy to −20F; round habit to 30 feet. Dense branching, with red fruit in early autumn.

C. monogyna (single-seed hawthorn). Hardy to −20F; round-headed, with pendulous branches. Red color in autumn. 30 feet.

Stricta—upright grower.

C. oxyacantha (English hawthorn). Hardy to −20F; round-headed to 15 feet. Dense branching.

Paul's Scarlet—popular; double red to rose flowers.
Doublewhite—lovely white form.

C. phaenopyrum (Washington hawthorn). Hardy to −20F; broadly columnar to 30 feet. Red fall color.

Fagus (beech)

Elegant, the deciduous beech is beautiful all year, but especially in fall when it blazes with golden color. Usually it is a large tree with a stout trunk and smooth bark. When you plant a beech, consider that very little can be grown underneath because of the dense shade.

F. sylvatica (European beech). Hardy to −20F; pyramidal to 90 feet. Glossy, dark green foliage; dense. Bronze autumn color.

Atropunicea (copper beech)—reddish or purple leaves

Fastigiata—narrow form
Laciniata (cutleaf beech)—narrow green leaves
Pendula (weeping beech)—spreading form, green leaves
Purpureo-pendula (weeping copper beech)—purple-leaved weeping form
Tricolor (tricolor beech)—green leaves marked with white and pink

Fraxinus (ash)

The deciduous ash is a rapid grower; brilliant yellow to purple color in fall. It is large; some grow to 100 feet and need lots of space; hardly suitable for a small property. Trees grow without much attention in any reasonably good soil.

F. americana (white ash). Hardy to −35F; straight trunk, oval crown. Grows to 100 feet, with dense foliage.

F. excelsior (European ash). Hardy to −35F; grows to 120 feet. Round-headed, with open branches.

Nana—low, globe-shaped
Pendula (weeping European ash)—spreading umbrella-shaped tree

F. pennsylvanica (lanceolata) (green-ash). Hardy to −50F; dense round-headed tree to 60 feet. Yellow autumn color.

Marchall's seedless ash—selected male form

F. velutina (Arizona ash). Hardy to −10F; round-headed tree. Grows to 45 feet.

Juniperus (juniper)

These evergreens are valued for their colorful berries in fall and winter. Both male and female plants have to be grown near each other to ensure fruiting. The junipers are tall and dense in habit, and prefer a somewhat alkaline soil.

J. chinensis (Chinese juniper). Hardy to −20F; pyramidal habit. Grows to 60 feet; scalelike leaves.

Columnaris—columnar, silvery green foliage
Keteleeri—stiff trunk; loose, green foliage
Mountbatten—gray green, narrow growth
Pyramidalis—blue gray needle foliage

J. scopulorum (Rocky Mountain juniper). Hardy to −10F; narrow and upright to 35 feet. Green to light blue foliage.

Blue Haven—narrow gray blue pyramid
Emerald Green—compact, bright green foliage
Pathfinder—gray blue, upright grower

J. virginiana (red cedar). Hardy to −50F; dense pyramid to 90 feet. Foliage varies, but usually scalelike.

Burkii—steel blue foliage
Cupressifolia—dark green
Glauca—silvery blue

Magnolia

A popular group with spectacular flowers, many blooming in early spring before the leaves appear. In a wide range of colors—white, pink, red, reddish-purple. Many are wide-spreading trees and tall (to 90 feet); others grow to 30 feet. Some are deciduous; others are evergreen. Many have early flowers, and some bloom in summer. All like a good well-drained soil and lots of water in summer. Any pruning should be done immediately after flowering. There is a magnolia for almost every garden; as a flowering tree, it is tough to beat.

M. denudata (yulan magnolia). Hardy to −5F; round habit. Grows to 35 feet. White tulip-shaped, fragrant flowers. Deciduous.

M. grandiflora (southern magnolia). Hardy to 5F; usually dense pyramidal form. Pure white flowers; evergreen. 90 feet.

Exoniensis—white flowers
Majestic Beauty—immense 12-inch blooms
St. Mary—full flowers on small tree
Samuel Sommer—very large flowers

M. kobus (kobus magnolia). Hardy to −5F; good, sturdy tree to 30 feet. White 4-inch flowers. Deciduous.

M. soulangeana (saucer magnolia). Hybrid; hardy to −10F; white to pink or purplish-red flowers. Variable in size and form. Deciduous.

Alba—flowers with purple markings
Alexandrina—deep pink and white blooms
Brozzoni—huge whitish-pink flowers
Burgundy—deep purple and pink blooms
Lilliputian—small pink and white flowers
San Jose—large rosy-purple flowers

M. stellata (star magnolia). Very early white fragrant flowers before leaves. Hardy to −10F; to 20 feet but likely to be more shrub than tree. Deciduous.

M. veitchii. Hybrid; hardy to 5F; open habit. Grows to 40 feet; pink flowers. Deciduous.

M. virginiana (*glauca*) (sweet bay). Hardy to −10F; globular shape. Creamy-white flowers. Evergreen. Grows to 40–60 feet.

Malus (crab apple)

Good ornamental, deciduous flowering trees in vivid color in May; some varieties have single blooms; others, semidouble or double flowers in color range from pure white to purple-red. Many are fragrant. The fruit of some hold color well into winter, making the trees of four-season value. Most crab apples are small, to about 30 feet, although a few reach to 50 feet. Several have pendent branches, but actually shapes run the gamut from columnar to round-headed. Crab apples need sun, and when young require some additional feeding. A regular schedule of spraying is necessary because these have the same problems—fire blight, scale, and borers—as the common apple.

M. arnoldiana (Arnold crab apple). Hardy to −20F; broad and spreading. Fragrant pink flowers.

M. atrosanguinea (carmine crab apple). Hardy to −20F; upright branches. Grows to about 20 feet, with dark green leaves. Fragrant crimson to rose-purple flowers.

M. baccata mandshurica. Hardy to −50F; bushy and dense to 40 feet. Dark green foliage; fragrant white flowers.

Columnaris—white, fragrant 1-inch flowers
Dorothea—hybrid; double pink blooms
Hopa—hybrid; fragrant, single rose-red flowers
Katherine—hybrid; double pink flowers
Red Jade—hybrid; floriferous; small white flowers

Red Silver—hybrid; deep wine-red flowers

M. sargenti (Sargent crab apple). Hardy to −20F; rounded and low branching. Grows to 8 feet, with pure white, fragrant flowers.

Picea (spruce)

Young evergreen spruce trees make a pretty picture in the landscape, but mature ones generally lose their lower branches and become unsightly. Because most spruces grow to about 100 feet, they are not for the small property. Still, there are some good evergreens in the group.

P. abies (Norway spruce). Hardy to −50F; pyramidal growth to 150 feet. Dark green needles.

Columnaris—narrow and columnar

P. glauca (white spruce). Hardy to −50F; pyramidal and grows to 90 feet. Bluish-green needles.

Conica—compact dwarf

P. pungens (Colorado blue spruce). Hardy to −50F; stiff horizontal branches. Grows to 100 feet.

Argentea—silvery-white foliage
Pendens—Bluish-white foliage

Pinus (pine)

Many good evergreens; some better than others for ornamental use. Needles vary in length on each tree, but are usually from 2 to 12 inches long. Some pines are dwarf and very picturesque; others rounded. Many appear graceful in the landscape; a few are quite stiff and hardly desirable. Make selections carefully.

P. aristata (bristlecone pine). Hardy to −10F; dense and bushy to 40 feet. Dark green needles, whitish underneath.

P. banksiana (jack pine). Hardy to −50F; open and broad-headed tree, often shrubby. Bright green needles. Grows to 70 feet.

P. contorta (beach pine). Hardy to 10F; round top, dense-headed tree to 30 feet. Dense, dark green needles.

P. densiflora (Japanese red pine). Hardy to −20F; horizontal branching tree to 100 feet. Bright bluish-green needles.

P. mugo (Swiss mountain pine). Hardy to 10F; low pyramidal growth. Dark green, stout needles.

P. strobus (eastern white pine). Hardy to −35F; rounded or pyramidal growth to 150 feet. Blue-green, soft needles.

Fastigiata—narrow and upright
Nana—grows to only 7 feet

P. sylvestris (Scotch pine). Hardy to −50F; pyramidal when young, round-topped when mature. Blue-green, stiff needles. Grows to 75 feet.

P. thunbergiana (thunbergi) (Japanese black pine). Hardy to −10F; dense spreading habit. Bright green, stiff needles. Grows to 90 feet.

Quercus (oak)

Sturdy trees valued for their autumn color; the majority of them reach large size.

The wood is strong, does not easily split, and the tree is long lived. Only the North American species have autumn color; European ones do not. The oaks are fine shade trees for large properties, but they can have their problems—borers, oak gall, various leaf diseases—and must have routine spraying.

Q. agrifolia (California live oak). Hardy to 20F; round-headed to 90 feet, with spreading habit. Evergreen, hollylike leaves.

Q. alba (white oak). Hardy to −20F; broad, open-crowned tree to 90 feet. Bright green leaves turning purple in fall. Deciduous.

Q. coccinea (scarlet oak). Hardy to −20F; open-branching habit that can reach 80 feet. Leaves turn brilliant red in autumn. Deciduous.

Q. palustris (pin oak). Hardy to −20F; pyramidal in shape, with drooping branches. Red leaves in autumn. Deciduous. Grows to 75 feet.

Q. robur (English oak). Hardy to −10F; broadheaded tree, with open habit. No autumn color. Deciduous. Grows to 75–150 feet.

Salix (willow)

Willows like water and moist conditions. Although the weeping willow is certainly graceful and lovely, remember that in many regions willows are troubled with insects and disease and have weak wood that cracks easily. Deciduous trees.

S. alba (white willow). Hardy to −50F; spreading branches, loose and open. Yellow leaves in autumn. Grows to 80 feet.

Tristis (golden weeping willow)—graceful and lovely

S. babylonica (weeping willow). Hardy to −5F; long, pendulous branches. Fine-textured foliage; best of the willows. Grows to 30–50 feet.

S. caprea (French pussy willow). Hardy to −20F; small tree, to 25 feet. Dark green, broad branches.

S. matsudana (Hankow willow). Hardy to −20F; upright pyramidal growth to 50 feet. Bright green, narrow leaves.
Navajo (glove willow)—round-topped spreading habit
Tortuosa (corkscrew willow)—twisted branches

Taxus (yew)

Dark green, evergreen trees that thrive in many different kinds of soil; tough ones to kill. Some yews make excellent hedges and screens, and they bear bright-red fruit in fall. Most are slow growing.

T. baccata (English yew). Hardy to −5F; dense branching; grows to about 60 feet. Dark green needles.
Aurea—golden yellow leaves
Erecta—erect and formal in appearance
Repandens—spreading type
Stricta (Irish yew)—dark green columnar growth

T. cuspidata (Japanese yew). Hardy to −20F; grows to 50 feet. Dark green needles.
Capitata—upright pyramidal form
Densiformis—very branched
Nana—slow grower; small

T. media (hybrid). Columnar to pyramidal. Hardy to −20F.
Hatfieldii—broad columnar
Hickssi—narrow upright
Hills—narrow upright

Thuja (arborvitae)

Generally with flat, scalelike leaves, the evergreen arborvitaes are quite shrubby and somewhat pyramidal in shape. None of them tolerates dry conditions, but rather prefers moisture at the roots and in the air too. A few of them are unsatisfactory because their leaves turn brown in winter. For the most part, this group is slow growing and has its problems.

T. occidentalis (American arborvitae). Hardy to −50F; columnar growth to 60 feet. Bright green to yellow-green needles.
Douglas Pyramidal—vigorous green pyramid
Fastigata—narrow, tall type to 25 feet

T. plicata (giant arborvitae). Hardy to −10F; narrow form to 180 feet. Scalelike foliage that does not turn brown in winter.

Tilia (linden)

Some excellent deciduous trees, possibly the best ones for shade. They have handsome heart-shaped leaves and lovely sweet-scented pendulous flowers in early summer. As a group, the lindens have much to offer, and require very little attention.

T. americana (American linden). Hardy to −50F; grows to 60 feet. Dull, dark green leaves.

T. cordata (little-leaf linden). Hardy to −35F; densely pyramidal. Dark green leaves, silvery underneath. Grows to 50–90 feet.

Greenspire—upright form
Rancho—conical shape

T. tomentosa (silver linden). Hardy to −20F; broad and dense. Light green leaves, silvery underneath. Grows to 90 feet.

Tsuga (hemlock)

Narrow-leaved evergreens, the hemlocks are beautiful, but they need buckets of water. All of them withstand shade, but will grow better with some sun. The Japanese hemlock is possibly the best in the group. All hemlocks bear small cones, but not every year. There are many varieties offered.

T. canadensis (Canadian hemlock). Hardy to −35F; long, slender horizontal branches. Dark green needles. Grows to 90 feet.

Dawsoniana—slow growing, dark green
Globosa—dense and rounded

T. heterophylla (western hemlock). Hardy to −5F; short, drooping branches. Fine-textured, dark green to yellowish-green foliage. Grows to 125–200 feet.

The Evergreen Trees

BOTANICAL AND COMMON NAME	APPROX. HEIGHT IN FEET	MINIMUM NIGHT TEMP.	REMARKS
Abies balsamea (balsam fir)	70	−35 to −20F	Handsome ornamental
A. concolor (white fir)	100	−20 to −10F	Good landscape tree
Acacia baileyana (Bailey acacia)	20 to 30	30 to 40F	Profuse yellow flowers
Bauhinia blakeana (orchid tree)	20	30 to 40F	Abundant flowers; partially deciduous
Cedrus atlantica (atlas cedar)	100	− 5 to 5F	Nice pyramid
Chamaecyparis obtusa (Hinoki false cypress)	130	−20 to −10F	Broadly pyramidal
C. pisifera (sewara false cypress)	100	−35 to −20F	Many varieties
Cinnamomum camphora (camphor tree)	40	20 to 30F	Dense branching habit
Cryptomeria japonica Lobbi	30 to 50	− 5 to 5F	Pyramidal shape
Eriobotrya japonica (loquat)	20	5 to 10F	Needs well-drained soil
Eucalyptus camaldulensis (red gum)	80 to 100	20 to 30F	Fine landscape tree
E. globulus (blue gum)	200	20 to 30F	Good windbreak
E. gunnii (cider gum)	40 to 75	0 to 10F	Shade or screen tree
E. polyanthemos (silver dollar gum)	20 to 60	10 to 20F	Fine landscape tree
Juniperus virginiana (eastern red cedar)	30 to 50	−50 to −35F	Slow growing
Picea abies (excelsa) (Norway spruce)	75	−50 to −35F	Not for small grounds

The Evergreen Trees (continued)

BOTANICAL AND COMMON NAME	APPROX. HEIGHT IN FEET	MINIMUM NIGHT TEMP.	REMARKS
Pinus bungeana (lacebark pine)	75	−20 to −10F	Slow-growing tree
P. densiflora (Japanese red pine)	80	−20 to −10F	Flat-top habit
P. nigra (Austrian pine)	90	−20 to −10F	Fast-growing tree
P. parviflora (Japanese white pine)	90	−10 to − 5F	Handsome ornamental
P. ponderosa (ponderosa pine)	150	−10 to − 5F	Rapid growth
P. thunbergana (Japanese black pine)	90	−20 to −10F	Dense spreading tree
Podocarpus gracilior (fern pine)	60	30 to 40F	Robust grower
P. macrophyllus (yew pine)	60	5 to 10F	Grows untended
Taxus baccata (English yew)	60	− 5 to 5F	Best among yews
T. cuspidata Capitata (Japanese yew)	50	−20 to −10F	Good landscape tree
Thuja occidentalis (American arborvitae)	65	−50 to −35F	Sometimes needles turn brown in winter
Tsuga canadensis (hemlock)	75	−35 to −20F	Many uses; hedges, screens, landscape
T. caroliniana (Carolina hemlock)	75	−20 to −10F	Fine all-purpose evergreen
T. diversifolia (Japanese hemlock)	90	−10 to − 5F	Smaller than most hemlocks
Umbellularia californica (California laurel)	75	5 to 10F	Favorite West Coast tree

The Deciduous Trees

BOTANICAL AND COMMON NAME	APPROX. HEIGHT IN FEET	MINIMUM NIGHT TEMP.	REMARKS
Acer circinatum (vine maple)	25	−10 to − 5F	Small, compact size
A. ginnala (Amur maple)	20	−50 to −35F	Red fall color
A. palmatum (Japanese maple)	20	−10 to 0F	Needs rich, well-drained soil
A. platanoides (Norway maple)	90	−35 to −20F	Grows rapidly
A. rubrum (red maple)	120	−35 to −20F	Best show in late spring
A. saccharum (sugar maple)	120	−35 to −20F	Several varieties
A. spicatum (mountain maple)	25	−50 to −35F	Grows in shade
A. tataricum (Tatarian maple)	30	−20 to −10F	Good small tree
Aesculus carnea (red horse chestnut)	60	−35 to −20F	No autumn color

The Deciduous Trees (continued)

BOTANICAL AND COMMON NAME	APPROX. HEIGHT IN FEET	MINIMUM NIGHT TEMP.	REMARKS
A. glabra (Ohio Buckeye)	30	−35 to −20F	Good autumn color
Ailanthus altissima (tree-of-heaven)	60	−20 to −10F	Very adaptable
Albizzia julibrissin (silk tree)	20	5 to 10F	Very ornamental
Alnus glutinosa (black alder)	70	−35 to −20F	Tolerates wet soil
A. incana (common alder)	60	−50 to −35F	Round-headed habit
Betula papyrifera (canoe birch)	90	−50 to −35F	Stellar ornamental
B. pendula (European birch)	60	−40 to −30F	Graceful, but short-lived
B. populifolia (gray birch)	40	−20 to −10F	Yellow color in autumn
Carya glabra (pignut)	120	−20 to −10F	Slow grower
C. ovata (shagbark hickory)	130	−30 to −10F	Narrow upright habit
Castanea mollissimia (Chinese chestnut)	60	−20 to −10F	Round-headed, dense tree
Catalpa speciosa (western catalpa)	50	−20 to −10F	Large white flowers
Celtis occidentalis (hackberry)	75	−50 to −35F	Good shade tree
Cercis canadensis (eastern redbud)	25	−20 to −10F	Lovely flowers
Chionanthus virginica (fringe tree)	20	−20 to −10F	Bountiful flowers
Cornus florida (dogwood)	25	−30 to −10F	Stellar ornamental
C. kousa (Japanese dogwood)	20	−10 to − 5F	Lovely flowers in June
Cotinus americanus (smoke-tree)	25	−10 to − 5F	Outstanding fall color
Crataegus mollis (downy hawthorn)	30	−20 to −10F	Pear-shaped red fruit
C. oxyacantha (English hawthorn)	20	−20 to −10F	Pink to red flowers
C. phaenopyrum (Washington hawthorn)	30	−20 to −10F	Profuse flowers, brilliant autumn color
Diospyros virginiana (persimmon)	40	−10 to − 5F	Round-headed habit
Elaeagnus angustifolia (Russian olive)	20	−50 to −35F	Vigorous; any soil
Fagus grandifolia (American beech)	120	−35 to −20F	Stellar tree
F. sylvatica (European beech)	100	−20 to −10F	Several varieties
Franklinia alatamaha	30	−10 to 0F	Large white flowers; red foliage in autumn
Fraxinus americana (white ash)	120	−35 to −20F	Grows in almost any soil
F. holotricha	35	−10 to − 5F	Fast low-growing shade tree

The Deciduous Trees (continued)

BOTANICAL AND COMMON NAME	APPROX. HEIGHT IN FEET	MINIMUM NIGHT TEMP.	REMARKS
F. ornus (flowering ash)	35	−10 to 0F	Dense foliage; pretty flowers
Ginkgo biloba (maidenhair tree)	120	−20 to −10F	Popular one
Gleditsia aquatica (water locust)	60	− 5 to 5F	Wants moist place
G. triacanthos (sweet honey locust)	100	−20 to −10F	Several varieties
Jacaranda acutifolia	50	30 to 40F	Blue flowers in summer
Koelreuteria paniculata (golden-rain tree)	30	−10 to − 5F	Magnificent summer bloom
Laburnum watereri (golden chain tree)	25	−10 to − 5F	Deep yellow flowers
Liquidambar styraciflua (sweet gum)	90	−10 to − 5F	Beautiful symmetry
Liriodendron tulipifera (tulip tree)	100	−20 to −10F	Robust grower
Magnolia soulangiana (saucer magnolia)	25	−10 to − 5F	Many varieties; also evergreens, shrubs
M. stellata (star magnolia)	20	−10 to − 5F	Very ornamental
Malus baccata (Siberian crab apple)	45	−50 to −35F	Lovely flowers and fruit
M. floribunda (Japanese flowering crab apple)	30	−20 to −10F	Handsome foliage; and flowers
Phellodendron amurense (cork tree)	50	−35 to −20F	Massive branches; wide open habit
Platanus acerifolia (plane tree)	100	−10 to − 5F	Popular street tree
P. occidentalis (buttonwood)	100+	−20 to −10F	Heavy frame
Populus alba (white poplar)	90	−35 to −20F	Wide-spreading tree
P. canadensis Eugenei (Carolina poplar)	100	−20 to −10F	Vagrant roots
Prunus amygdalus (almond)	25	− 5 to 5F	Handsome pink flowers
P. serotina (black cherry)	100	−20 to −10F	Handsome foliage; many varieties; some evergreen
P. serrulata (Japanese cherry)	25	−10 to 0F	Low grower; many kinds, some evergreen
P. triloba (flowering almond)	10	−10 to − 5F	One of the best; sometimes classed as shrub
Quercus alba (white oak)	80	−20 to −10F	Needs room to grow
Q. coccinea (scarlet oak)	80	−20 to −10F	Brilliant autumn color
Q. palustris (pin oak)	120	−20 to −10F	Beautiful pyramid

The Deciduous Trees (continued)

BOTANICAL AND COMMON NAME	APPROX. HEIGHT IN FEET	MINIMUM NIGHT TEMP.	REMARKS
Q. rubra (red oak)	80	−35 to −20F	Oval round top tree
Robinia pseudoacacia (black locust)	80	−35 to −20F	Fine, late spring flowers
Salix alba (white willow)	40	−50 to −35F	Good upright willow
S. babylonica (weeping willow)	40	−10 to − 5F	Fast grower
Sophora japonica (Japanese pagoda tree)	60	−20 to −10F	Good shade tree
Sorbus aucuparia (mountain ash)	45	−35 to −20F	Red autumn color
Tilia americana (American linden)	90	−50 to −35F	Fragrant white flowers in July
T. cordata (small-leaved linden)	60	−35 to −20F	Dense habit
T. tomentosa (silver linden)	80	−20 to −10F	Beautiful specimen tree
Ulmus americana (American elm)	100	−50 to −35F	Most popular shade tree

14

Bulbs for Three Seasons

AFFODILS, tulips, and hyacinths are the glory of the spring garden, and we can hardly plant enough of them. They grow from bulbs, as do many other lovely plants like the lilies that bloom in summer. Then there are the related plants, the spring crocus and summer-into-fall gladiolas that come from corms; the tuberous-rooted plants like dahlias for summer and early autumn; and the cannas with their thickened underground stems, the bloom stalks so familiar in park beds in summer. In general, gardeners are likely to think of them all as growing from bulbs.

Perhaps my favorite plants are bulbs—I enjoy them everywhere in the garden. They offer guaranteed color at the edge of beds, in masses, or in corners where nothing will grow. They are also at home in containers placed on patios for color. And, important, some bulbs will bloom the first year anyway, regardless of soil conditions. They are tough plants to make your gardening easier.

TYPES OF BULBOUS PLANTS

Bulbs have a self-serving mechanism within themselves. They contain nutrients that assure bloom the first year after planting. In the broad category of bulbs are the "true" bulbs, the corms, the tubers, and the rhizome-type plants. The tulip and narcissus are true bulbs. The crocus and gladiolus grow from corms that have a somewhat different shape and size from bulbs but also contain a solid mass of storage tissue. Dahlias depend on swollen food-storage roots; the canna is nourished by a thickened underground stem, or rhizome.

So "bulbs" have various forms but all have one common denominator—a storehouse of underground food. They can survive even untoward environments and still bear flowers. Put a crocus on a shelf in a dry place and it will still bloom, such is the tenacity of a bulbous plant.

Most bulbous plants will bloom the first time around; it is in the next year that they require care. Leaves must be given time to

Tulips are always a handsome addition to a garden. Planted in groups, they have a stellar effect, and provide masses of color.

An iris garden in a small space—handsome planter boxes are the accent. (*California Redwood Association*)

replenish the underground food supply for the coming year. Foliage must not be cut until it has turned yellow; even after it has been removed, bulbs continue to work underground—some even after they are dug up—storing food for next year. Miracle plants you ask? Maybe so. Possibly nature at her most magical.

Some Technical Notes

True bulbs are shaped like medium-sized onions and have a scaly coating. Daffodils, lilies, hyacinths, tulips.

Corms have no fleshy scales, are smaller than bulbs and generally more flattened at the base. Gladiolus, crocus.

Tubers are flattened bulbs with a tough skin; they hardly resemble true bulbs. Caladiums, tuberous begonias, anemones.

Tuberous roots have various shapes with those of dahlias looking like small sweet potatoes.

Rhizomes, enlarged roots (rootstocks), are actually thickened stems. Calla lilies, cannas.

WHERE TO BUY

I suppose bulbs are often passed up at nurseries because dried bulbs in packages hardly tempt the amateur who cannot imagine what beautiful flowers are waiting inside for the proper temperature and moisture to bring them forth. Also, selecting good quality bulbs is hardly easy—it's like buying a blind product. You never know what you are getting until it is too late. That is why it is important to buy your bulbs from reputable dealers. This is one case where I urge you to deal only with mail-order houses that specialize in bulbs. They cannot ship you poor ones or they will not stay in business.

There is so much that can go wrong with bulbs—from field to you—that it is important for you to know your source well. Bulbs may be improperly cured and they can be overheated in transit. You will see bulbs in packages, plastic sacks, mesh sacks, boxes at nurseries. Buy here if you are sure of reliability, but it is usually safer to locate a top-grade mail-order house. If you are selecting bulbs in person, try to get one out of the

Bulbs, corms and tubers

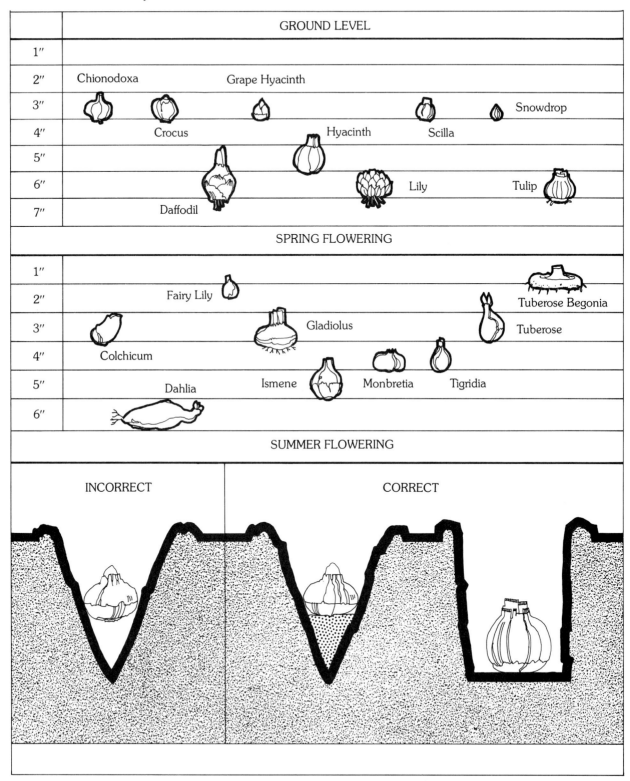

package to feel it. It should be firm without spots or bruises; buy it as you would an onion, looking for blemishes or soft spots.

PLANTING

In general, spring-flowering bulbs and those that are winter hardy and bloom in summer are put into the ground in fall. Summer-and-fall flowering bulbs are planted in spring. Make a hole six to eight inches deep for each one. Take care to break up the soil so it will be porous. If there is a basic requirement for bulbs, it is the need for good drainage. They will quickly succumb in a clay or poorly drained soil. You may find a bulb-planting tool—a small scooplike device—convenient to use in planting.

Which end of the bulb is the bottom can be a puzzle. The drawings can help you with this. Keep in mind that a recommended three-inch depth means that the *top*, not the bottom, of the bulb is to be set three inches below the ground level. In most cases this top is the pointed end or the one showing growth. Make sure the holes are concave, not pointed, and so leave an air pocket beneath the bulb.

It is not necessary to fertilize bulbs at the start but after bloom, while plants are still growing, a mild fertilizer is beneficial for the bulbs that are to stay in the ground all year, as most spring-flowering and some summer-flowering types. The best fertilizer is a 10-10-5—neither too strong nor too weak.

The earlier you can plant the spring-flowering bulbs in fall the better chance for a good crop of flowers. There is still a stretch of good growing weather before severe cold, and the more time bulbs have to put out roots before the freezing, the stronger the plants will be.

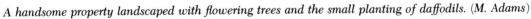

A handsome property landscaped with flowering trees and the small planting of daffodils. (M. Adams)

After planting, spring bulbs do not need protection against frost. However, in severe climates freezing and thawing can heave bulbs out of the ground and so damage roots. Where this is likely, a one- to two-inch layer of mulch applied after the soil has frozen at least two inches deep may be advisable. Pine needles, wood shavings, or bark chips make good mulches.

After spring bulbs have bloomed, leave them in the ground while they build up energy for the next year's cycle. Only when the leaves have yellowed can you safely cut them off. While spring bulbs can remain in the ground, some gardeners prefer to lift tulips and hyacinths. They claim this guarantees better flowers, but when I lived in Illinois I left tulip bulbs in the ground for several years and always had a good supply of blooms. I should add that they were planted very deep, some 12 inches down.

You can extend the bloom of spring-flowering bulbs by staggering the schedule and selecting different varieties; for example, there are early, mid-season, and late-spring tulips.

MULTIPLYING BULBS

Most gardeners plant bulbs and let them be for years, and this is fine. But it is possible to lift them, separate them, and so get more from an original planting at no cost. You can also start bulbs from seed but I find this time-consuming and a great chore. Rather, since most bulbs develop two or more offsets each year, these offer a logical way to add stock to your garden. Corms of crocus and gladiolus shrivel and produce one or more new corms by the end of a season, and these may be separately planted. Bulblets also may appear at stem junctures as with lilies.

Such bulbous plants as caladiums and tuberous begonias have eyes or incipient buds like a sweet potato. You can cut up these roots, making sure each piece has an eye, and so get more plants than you started with. Dahlias do not have eyes on the tubers; with them you must include a section of the original stem in each cut piece.

Rhizomes of cannas and callas with their thickened stems can be easily divided with a knife; each piece must contain an eye.

When is the best time to dig up bulbs to get more plants? There are no specific time tables; as I said, I left tulips in the ground in Illinois for three years and had good results. In the fourth year, I dug them up, separated them, and replanted. I think timing is a matter of personal convenience. Some people simply let bulbs be and buy new ones after several years.

CULTURE FOR SIX NOTABLE BULBOUS PLANTS

Begonia tuberhybrida (tuberous begonia)

For sheer drama and summer color, these plants are stars. Tuberous begonias today have been bred to near-perfection in flower form, size, and color. The choice is vast, each prettier than another: Camelliaeflora, Ruffled, Cristata, Fimbriata, Marginata in two forms (Crispa Marginata with frilled single flowers; and Double Marginata with petals lined and edges with a contrasting color). Other forms include: Narcissiflora, Picotee, and Rose.

In March, select large tubers and put them in a wooden flat or other suitable container. Spread with a two-inch layer of peat moss and sand in a one-to-two ratio. Set the

Planting tuberous begonias

1. Dig up after leaves wilt. Cut off leaves

2. Store loosely in cool, dry place

3. Start inside in damp peat moss. Transplant when four leaves sprout

4. Or, plant directly in loamy soil in semishade

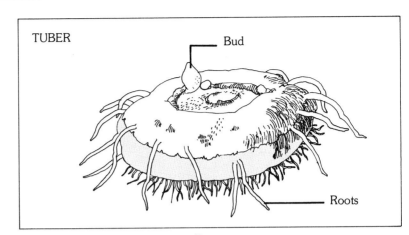

TUBER

Bud

Roots

STARTING IN FLATS

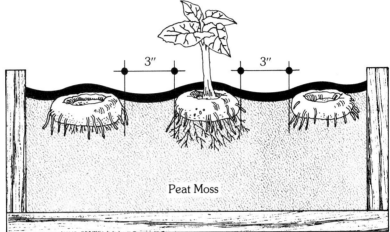

3″   3″

Peat Moss

PLANTING IN GROUND

10″ - 12″

1″

2″

3″

Loamy Soil

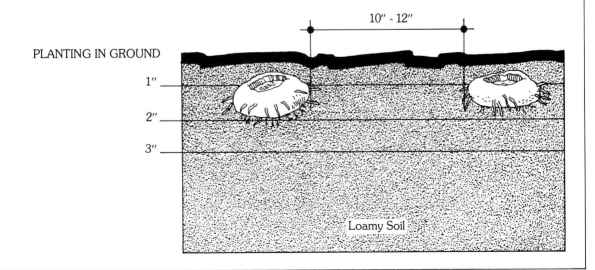

tubers two inches apart and ½ inch deep, the dented side up. Cover with ¼ inch of the starting medium. Set the container in good light in a 60 to 70 degree temperature, and keep the tubers barely moist. Too much water causes rot, but not enough curtails growth. When sprouts are two inches high (in about two weeks) shift the plants to the garden (after danger of frost is past).

If plants develop too fast and get too big before they are to go outside, they can be held back by cool temperatures. If they are not growing fast enough, more warmth will accelerate growth. Set the plants in scattered sunshine. They will survive some heat during the day, but they need nights of 55 to 60 degrees. Water the plants heavily in bright weather, but not so much when it is cloudy. When they are actively growing, apply a 5-10-5 commercial liquid fertilizer mixed half-strength every second week.

After the begonias bloom, when leaves begin to turn dry and yellow, water sparingly but let growth continue for as long as possible. When foliage is completely yellow, dig up the tubers, wash off the soil, remove stems, and place the plants in an airy, sunny place for a few days. Then store them in paper sacks in a cool, frostfree location until time to start them again in spring.

Dahlia

Dahlias have been bred extensively. Before you select, consider the possibilities: giant formal, cactus, sweetheart, dwarf, miniature, pompom, and single-bedding types. The color range is extensive.

The plants have tuberous roots, and rest between seasons. The next year's flower is produced by a fleshy extension of the old stem. For best results, grow dahlias in a sandy soil in full sun with bone meal worked into the soil.

Make plantings early but not so early that there is danger of chilling. First soak the tubers for a day; then set them horizontally in three- to four-inch predug holes. Inset a stake beside each plant because most dahlias need support. Soak the plants when you water.

As soon as tops are killed by frost in fall, cut the plants back to about four inches above the crown and then dig them up a few days later. Dry them in a well-ventilated place for a day before storing them in a basket of peat moss or vermiculite in a cool, but not freezing, area. In spring, divide the tubers, allowing one eye or bud to each root, and replant.

Gladiolus

Popular garden plants that grow in almost any soil and with little attention provided they have sun. Plants develop quickly, blooming in ten to 12 weeks. There are tall varieties and charming small ones in a wide selection of colors. When freezing weather is safely past, set the corms four to six inches deep and about six inches apart in a well-cultivated bed that is at least 15 inches deep. Keep the soil moist; the gladiolus needs a lot of water. When buds show between the leaves, apply a complete fertilizer. In fall, dig up and store the corms if you are in a cold climate; in mild climates they can remain in the ground. When foliage turns brown, cut off the tops, then dry the bulbs in an airy, shaded place for a few weeks. You will notice new corms on top of the dried withered ones; store the new ones in paper bags in a dark place at about 45 to 50 degrees until spring planting time.

Storing & Planting Gladiolus

① DIG UP WHEN LEAVES
START TO TURN BROWN,
DO NOT CUT OFF.

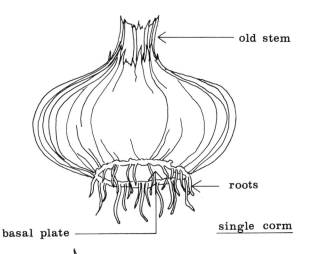

old stem

roots

basal plate

single corm

② STORE IN COOL AIRY
PLACE FOR 8 WEEKS
UNTIL DRY.

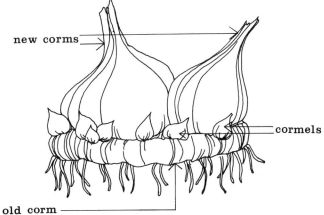

new corms

cormels

③ CUT OLD STEMS, DUST
CORMS & STORE IN DRY
PEAT MOSS, SAND, ETC.

old corm

④ PLANT AS SHOWN IN
WELL-DRAINED SOIL,
6" APART.

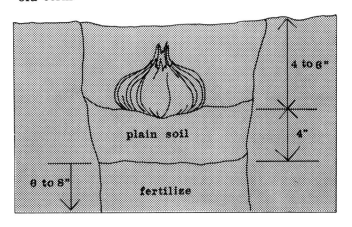

4 to 6"

4"

plain soil

6 to 8"

fertilize

planting depth

G. colvillei. Baby gladiolus; white, pink, red, or lilac. Loose spikes on 18-inch stems.

G. hybrida. Common type in a wide color range; many varieties.

G. primulinus. Tropical African species with yellow flowers.

G. tristis. Small with 2- to 3-inch yellow flowers, purple-veined, called evening flower gladiolus.

Iris

The bulbous irises produce lovely cut flowers and their color and form are highly desirable in the garden. The most popular kinds are the Spanish, English, and Dutch types.

Spanish iris (*I. xiphium*) with narrow grassy leaves grows to about 12 inches. The flower comes in various shades of blue with a characteristic yellow blotch on the falls. Bloom time starts in May and ends in early June. Plants need good drainage, full sun, and shelter from wind.

English iris (*I. xiphiodes*) blooms after the Spanish with larger leaves and showy flowers in several colors, with blue predominating. Plants need a moist, acid soil and coolness; they do not prosper in heat or drought.

Dutch iris are hybrids that resemble the Spanish but are more robust and floriferous with colors ranging from white to yellow to blue. Plants need good drainage, sun, and a light soil. They put on their colorful display in March and April.

Plant these bulbous irises four inches deep and about four inches apart. In regions where freezing occurs provide a winter mulch. After foliage ripens, plants can be dug up, dried, and stored in a cool place. Or they can be safely left in the ground.

Iris reticulata is another lovely type that blooms early in spring. Plant bulbs in September or October in semishade, spacing them four to six inches apart. The flowers resemble the Spanish and Dutch iris, but are smaller; plants rarely grow above six inches.

Lilium (lily)

Lilies bring grace and beauty to the garden and in recent years hybridists have given us some spectacular plants. Easy to grow, lilies may be left undisturbed for years while they increase. As soon as you get bulbs—and do buy the best—plant them, whether it is spring or fall. Give them a rich neutral soil—neither too acid nor too alkaline—that drains readily. Sun is necessary for bountiful flowering, and thorough soakings bring lilies to perfection. Plant bulbs at a depth three times the length of the bulb; place three to five bulbs in each group, with tall varieties at the back, low-growers in the center and front. Don't be concerned if plants bloom very little the first year; they are at their best the second and third years. Eventually, the bulbs must be lifted and divided; do this about four weeks after they bloom and then replant. Before or during the blooming period give a light feeding of 5-10-5 or a similar commercial fertilizer. While lilies sometimes may have problems of pests and disease, it is nothing drastic, but a regular spraying or dusting program may be necessary. Of more concern are mice. They love the bulbs, so if rodents are prevalent in your area, protect the bulbs with hardware cloth or grow them in pots.

The easiest way to increase your supply of lilies is to divide well-developed bulbs. Or use the scale method; that is, remove four or five thick outside scales of old bulbs at re-planting time. Then put the scales in four-inch deep trenches and cover them with sand.

L. auratum (goldband lily). Flowers waxy white and fragrant, with spots and golden bands on each segment. August or September bloom.

L. candidum (madonna lily). Beautiful white, fragrant blooms; plants die down after flowering but make new growth in autumn.

L. longifolium (Easter lily). Fragrant, trumpet-shaped flowers on short stems. Several varieties. Not for severe climates.

Aurelian Hybrids. Colors from white to yellow with many orange shades; 3 to 6 feet tall. June and July flowering.

Bellingham Hybrids. Yellow or orange or orange-red flowers spotted reddish-brown. June and July bloom.

Fiesta Hybrids. A vigorous group of sun loving lilies that open nodding flowers in July. Colors range from mahogany and amber to red, to burgundy, to lemon-yellow.

Harlequin Hybrids. Wide open flowers from ivory-white through lilac to violet and purple. Plants grow to 5 feet and bloom in July.

Martagon Hybrids. Many flowers to a stem; yellow, orange, lilac, tangerine, purple, and mahogany.

Olympic Hybrids. Trumpet-shaped flowers, white, cream, yellow, pink, shaded on the outside with greenish brown. July and August bloom; grows to 6 feet.

Oriental Hybrids. Mammoth flowers with segments in white or red, often banded with gold or red and spotted deep-red. Sweet scent; August and September flowers.

Tulipa (tulip)

If you are only familiar with tulips as they were even a few years ago, you are in for a surprise. There are so many new varieties. The tulip has indeed progressed from an ordinary to an extraordinary flower. There are parrot, fringed, tall, small, cottage type, Darwin, Mendel, and so on. Such is the beautiful world of tulips today.

Because there are so many, you can choose the ones that appeal specially to you—small ones for a woodsy planting, the tall regal type for borders, or perhaps the lily-shaped ones if this form is a favorite of yours. If you select early and late varieties, you can enjoy bloom for months rather than weeks. Give plants a sunny place where they are protected from strong winds. Provide a light, well-drained soil; tulips will not prosper in very sandy or clayey soil.

In general, it is best to plant tulips deep, say, with tops ten to 12 inches below the surface; then there is less danger of botrytis blight. With deep planting, it is possible to plant annuals in the same place after the tulips have bloomed. Set early types four inches, Darwins about six inches apart. If you are planting large areas, it is a good idea to spade up the entire space and then set the bulbs, instead of planting them one at a time. From October to mid-November is the best time.

After blooming, bulbs can be left in the ground or lifted to give space for other plantings. In this case, lift them with roots and leaves attached and keep them in shade to ripen. When the foliage has turned brown, store them in a cool, dry place until planting time in the fall. Tulips need cold weather; in an all-year temperate climate, select precooled bulbs or store regular bulbs in the refrigerator for six weeks before planting.

Tulips are classed as:

Early single: old favorites; easy to grow.
Early double: large, wide-open flowers; long lasting.

Mendel (mid-season): lovely shapes and beautiful colors.
Triumph (mid-season): robust; good range of colors.
Darwin (May-flowering): most popular; globular in shape. Average size.
Darwin Hybrids (mid-season): giants with stiff stems.
Lily-shaped: beautiful reflexed and pointed petals.
Cottage: flowers large and almost egg-shaped.
Variegated: dramatic; lovely.
Parrot: fringed and scalloped flowers.
Late double: peony-type.
Fosteriana: dainty; many unusual hybrids.
Kaufmanniana: large flowers, early blooming.

Spring Flowering Bulbs

BOTANICAL AND COMMON NAME	WHEN TO PLANT	DEPTH IN INCHES	SUN OR SHADE	REMARKS
Allium (flowering onion)	Fall	3	Sun	Prettier than you think
Crocus	Fall	3	Sun	Dependable for years
Chionodoxa (glory of snow)	Fall	3	Sun	Do not disturb for several years
Daffodil (jonquil, narcissus)	Fall	6	Sun	The name daffodil is used for all members
Eranthis (winter aconite)	Early fall	3	Shade	Very early bloom
Erythronium (dogtooth violet)	Early fall	6	Shade	Good for naturalizing
Fritillaria	Fall	4	Shade	Overlooked but lovely
Galanthus (snowdrop)	Fall	3	Shade	Blooms while snow is on ground
Hyacinthus (hyacinth)	Fall	6 to 8	Sun	Protect from wind and mice
Leucojum (snowflake)	Fall	3	Shade	Flowers last a long time
Muscari (grape hyacinth)	Early fall	3	Sun	Easy to grow
Scilla	Fall	2	Sun or light shade	Once established, blooms for years

Bulbs

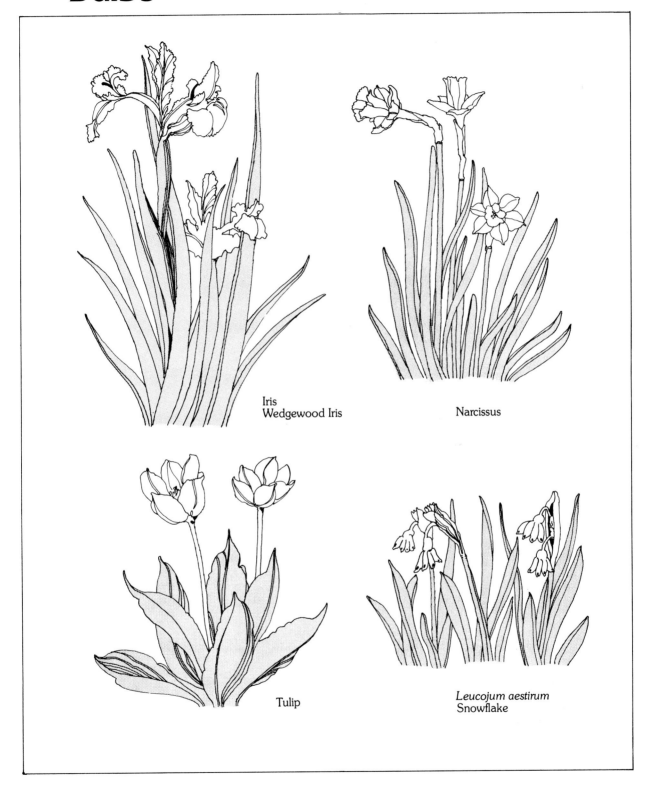

Iris
Wedgewood Iris

Narcissus

Tulip

Leucojum aestirum
Snowflake

Bulbs

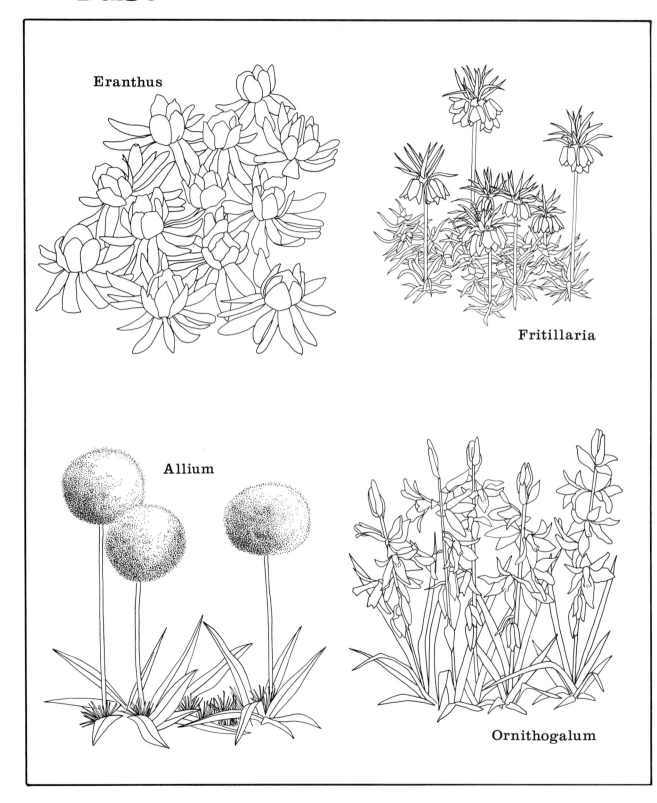

Eranthus

Fritillaria

Allium

Ornithogalum

Above: A townhouse courtyard garden achieves stark elegance with few plants and one accent cactus. (M. Barr) Left: Irregularly shaped wedges of stone form an attractive retaining wall for this garden of ground cover and low shrubs. (M. Barr)

Above left: White callas and other bulbous plants grow above and below an informal stone wall that gives a rock-garden effect. (M. Barr) Above right: A simple rock sculpture adds new texture to this lush garden spot. Scilla grows in the left foreground. (M. Barr)
Below: A flower border above a wall provides the perfect frame for lawn and trees. (M. Barr)

A small step garden of rough stone, enhanced with clumps of plants and flowers. (R. Scharmer)

Above: An old fountain is the focal point of a lush backyard garden. (M. Barr) Below: A hot tub set off by a border of cobblestone paving and masses of white pansies within neat hedges. (J. Werner)

*The textures of brick, wood, and stone are a perfect foil
for a few carefully selected plants on this patio in Phoenix. (M. Barr)*

Opposite page: In California, roses are frequently a favorite part of the garden plan, as in this backyard spot in Palo Verde. (M. Barr)

Left: Lush shrubs are the backdrop for a symmetrical garden plan featuring white petunias in this old-fashioned country setting. (R. Scharmer) Below: Symmetrical walkways through rich lawn, with a prized sculpture as elegant focal point. (R. Scharmer)

Above: The white garden, a charming old-fashioned tradition. (R. Scharmer)
Below: Low-lying red-and-white flower beds combine with aggregate paving and stone to create a pleasing entrance to a California home. (J. Werner)

Bulbs

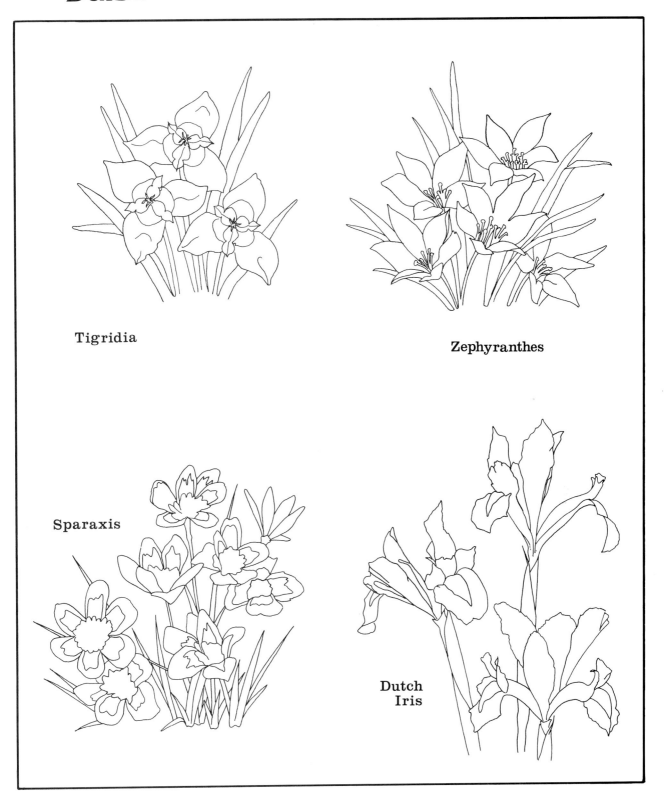

Tigridia

Zephyranthes

Sparaxis

Dutch
Iris

Summer and Fall Flowering Bulbs

BOTANICAL AND COMMON NAME	DEPTH IN INCHES	SUN OR SHADE	REMARKS
Agapanthus (flower-of-the-Nile)	1	Sun	New dwarf varieties available
Alstroemeria	4	Sun	Good cut flowers
Canna	2	Sun	Showy flowers; lift after frost kills tops
Galtonia candicans (summer hyacinth)	6	Sun	Buy new bulbs yearly
Polianthes tuberosa (tuberose)	1	Sun	Plant after danger of frost
Sprekelia formosissima (Jacobean lily)	3	Sun	Good in pots
Ranunculus (buttercup)	1	Sun	Lovely colorful flowers
Tigridia (tiger flower)	2 to 3	Sun	Plant in early May
Tritonia (montbretia)	2 to 3	Sun	Plant in early May
Zephyranthes (zephyr lily)	1	Sun or light shade	Plant after danger of frost

15 🌿

Herbs for Flavor and Fragrance

OH, THOSE flavorful herbs we pay so much for in stores and those fragrant ones we all love should be grown more. There is immense pleasure in growing these plants and immense savings if you are a gourmet cook. Food prepared with fresh herbs is the epitome of good taste (store-bought herbs simply do not have that flavor!).

And herbs are also excellent for fragrance—for making potpourri and sachets—old-fashioned trinkets I must admit, but there is nothing wrong with a little nostalgia these days. And basically herbs are easy to grow and need not occupy a large area of the garden or, on the other hand, for you herb aficionados, you might just have a delightful little herb garden.

You can have little places for herbs or look to the grandeur of yesterday when the lovely formal herb garden was in vogue—good then and fine now. So, no matter how much space you have you can have fresh herbs for flavoring cookery, for salads (incredibly good), for fragrance, and even for teas whether you class these as medicinal or otherwise. Let's look at all the possibilities of the wonderful herbs.

Formal herb gardens are a delight and you always see them at flower shows; they are enjoying a renaissance now so I thought I would include information on them.

The knot garden of yesterday is probably the most popular plan for the formal herb arrangement but the sun dial garden with easy access to plants is also very attractive.

Plan your formal herb garden on paper first—just make sketches of size and location—remember that most herbs like sunlight. Once you have the space and place for the garden, decide which herbs you want to grow. Then start planning: You can use planting beds shaped like triangles, rectangles, or semi-circles with a few herbs planted in each sector and others between them. Or you can plant a number of different herbs in each bed. Remember that herbs have different tones and shades of green so plan for texture as well. Prepare planting beds as for standard garden herb growing but with one exception: Here you want dividers to keep things neat; boards sunk into the ground will define the areas for you. Now establish paths—paths generally converge at a central place on the plan.

INFORMAL

Herbs can become a passion, occupying a great deal of space, with carefully planned geometric gardens reminiscent of long ago, or simply be in a small space near the kitchen. You can even grow a few in pots if you prefer.

Herb garden

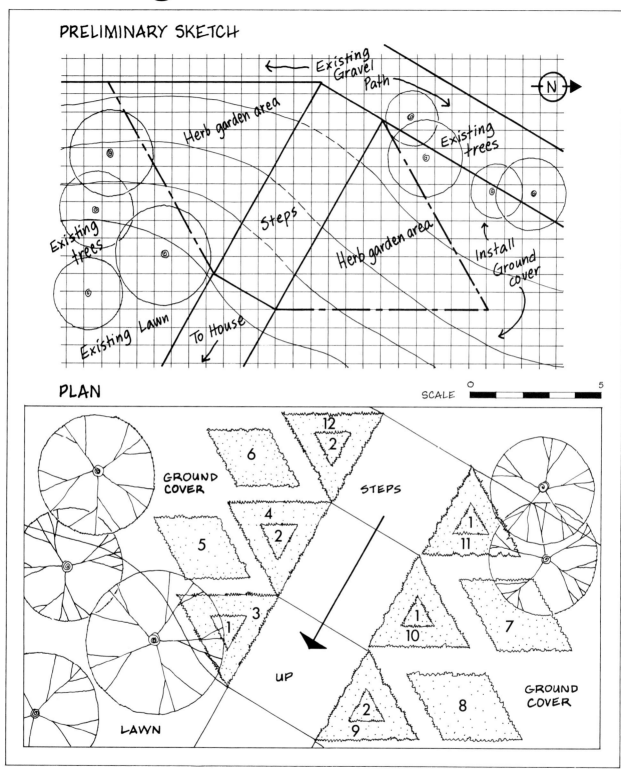

PRELIMINARY SKETCH

Existing Gravel Path

Herb garden area

Existing trees

Steps

Herb garden area

Install Ground cover

Existing trees

Existing Lawn

To House

N

PLAN

SCALE 0 — 5

GROUND COVER

STEPS

UP

LAWN

GROUND COVER

1. *Mentha spicata*
   Spearmint

2. *Artemisia dracunculus*
   Tarragon

3. *Salvia officinalis*
   Garden Sage

4. *Rosmarinus officinalis*
   Rosemary

5. *Marjorana hortensis*
   Marjorum

6. *Levisticum officinalis*
   Lovage

7. *Allium schoenoprasum*
   Chives

8. *Anethum graveolens*
   Dill

9. *Origanum vulgare*
   Oregano

10. *Ocimum basilicum*
    Sweet Basil

11. *Thymus vulgaris*
    Thyme

12. *Borago officinalis*
    Common Borage

Today, more herbs are grown in small plots as part of a landscape plan or simply in a corner or perhaps in pots on a porch. There are herbs for shady places, for sunny spots, for dry locations, and some that are almost too invasive, such as lemon balm and the mints.

You can start herbs from seed in spring or fall or buy prestarted plants ready for planting and so save time. Herbs are annuals that live one season or perennials that return year after year. When you select herbs, be aware of each category. (The list at the end of this chapter will guide you.)

TYPES OF HERBS/PLANTING

The most common herbs are those used in cooking or for fragrance: marjoram, oregano, parsley, sage, summer or winter savory, tarragon, and thyme. Basil, chervil, dill, fennel, and lemon verbena are other possibilities.

When danger of frost is past, you can sow the seeds. The soil should be at the crumbly, not wet stage. Prepare it for herbs as for garden flowers, making it porous, with good nutrition. If the soil has been used for years it is best to spade it up, rake it, and add top soil or humus to it. This will get the herbs off to a vigorous start.

Practically all herbs need a very well-drained soil and will not prosper if roots are constantly wet. So turn the soil to at least 12 to 16 inches and break up clods—add some organic matter as mentioned. You might want to check the soil's pH to determine whether it is alkaline or acidic. Most herbs like a neutral soil. Small test kits are available at suppliers or you can have your County Agricultural Extension Service agent do the testing.

In the author's cutting garden, herbs of many kinds are grown along with cutting flowers. Parsley grows along the brick wall. (M. Barr)

An extensive herb garden, each variety carefully labelled. (M. Barr)

After the bed is prepared, scratch some lines with a rake and press the seeds in lightly. Scatter a little soil over them—not a lot. Firm the soil with your hand so the seeds will be in contact with it. Now mist the area, taking care not to dislodge the seed.

The germination time for the seeds varies from 12 to 14 days for the annuals; the perennials take a little longer to sprout. In any case, keep the seed bed evenly moist, not too dry, not soggy. When two pairs of leaves have developed, thin out the plants by removing the smallest weakest ones.

Another type of seed sowing is broadcasting the seed, which only means scattering the seed from your hand. This is fine if you want a large planting of a single herb rather than a small row.

STARTING SEED

The advantage of starting seeds indoors in flats or containers is that it gives you a head start on spring. Also, indoors you have more control over soil conditions and climate. Started in late winter, annuals and perennials that take a long time to germinate will be tiny plants ready for the ground by spring.

Use any kind of a shallow container that has drainage holes—I like shallow clay pots. Get a starting mix that is loose and drains well; vermiculite is fine. Fill trays or containers with the starting mix to within ½ inch of the top and firm down soil with your hands. Mark tiny rows with a ruler edge and insert seeds. Don't bury them too deep. Firm the soil down so seeds are in contact with soil.

As with outdoor watering, moisten the seed bed with a light mist of water, being careful not to dislodge seeds.

Now you want a fairly warm location for seeds, about 65 to 75F until germination starts. Seeds do not need bright light until they have sprouted but will need a good circulation of air so mold and fungus do not start.

When seedlings start to sprout, move the container to a somewhat cooler place, about 60F, and give them more light but no direct sun, please. When the seedlings have two sets of leaves they are ready to be thinned. Now is the time for larger containers so plants have space to grow. For this planting use a soil mix—two parts garden loam and one part sand is good. Space seedlings about two inches apart in new containers. When the plants touch each other, it is time to move them to their permanent outdoor locations or into large tubs for indoor growing. Never transplant seedlings directly to the outdoors—rather condition them first: Put them in a shady place outside for a day or so and then into bright sun.

HARVESTING TIPS

Herbs are both beautiful and functional and provide a beautiful source of culinary delights and fragrance. Or, you may be growing herbs for medicinal teas as well. To use the herbs you must first harvest them.

Leaves such as basil, marjoram, parsley, rosemary, sage, and thyme can be picked at almost any time during the growing season and used fresh. Be careful, however, not to take too many leaves so that it is injurious to the plant. Most purchased herbs are of course dried, and you can dry your own, too, for winter use. The best time to do this is during the blooming period when the flowers first open. It is then the essential oils are at their best. Exceptions are rosemary, thyme, and lavender. Cut these when the blooms are fullest, and sage should be harvested when buds first open.

Try to pick herbs in the morning after the dew has dried from the foliage and before the sun gets too hot. You can dry herbs by several methods and all are relatively easy. The most important thing is that there is a good circulation in the drying area so oils are not destroyed. Choose a place that is shady and has a warm even temperature. Generally, herbs are tied at the ends and suspended upside down in an attic or pantry. If you dry them outside, dew can hinder the drying process. In about two weeks herbs should be crackly dry and you can remove the leaves.

Store herbs in airtight containers and label them. It is best to store whole leaves and break them up when you use them—more flavor this way. Keep containers sealed and out of light. Moisture should not accumulate inside the glass containers. If it does, start over again.

If you want to freeze herbs, simply blanch them in unsalted water, boiling for about one minute. Then cool them by dipping them in ice water or tap water for a few minutes. Then remove the leaves from stems

Herbs

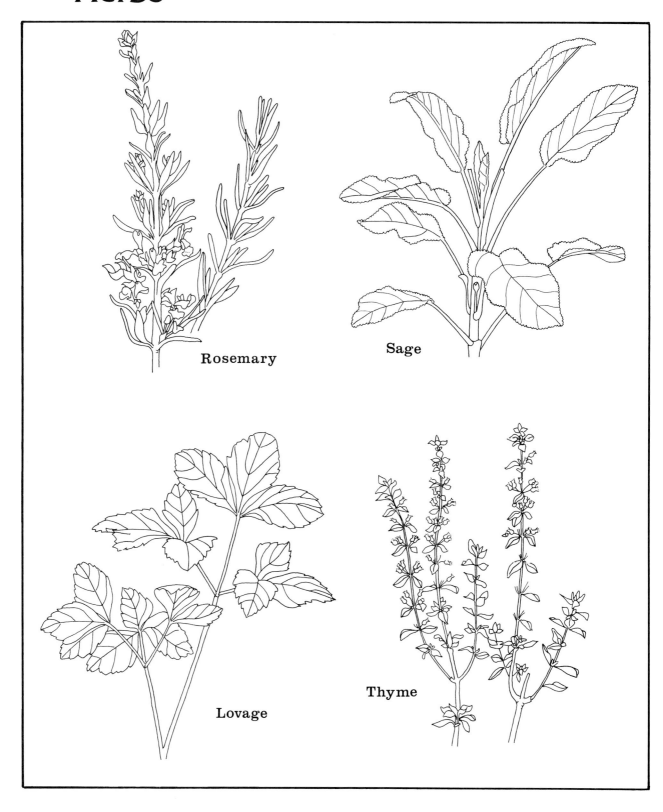

Rosemary

Sage

Lovage

Thyme

Herbs

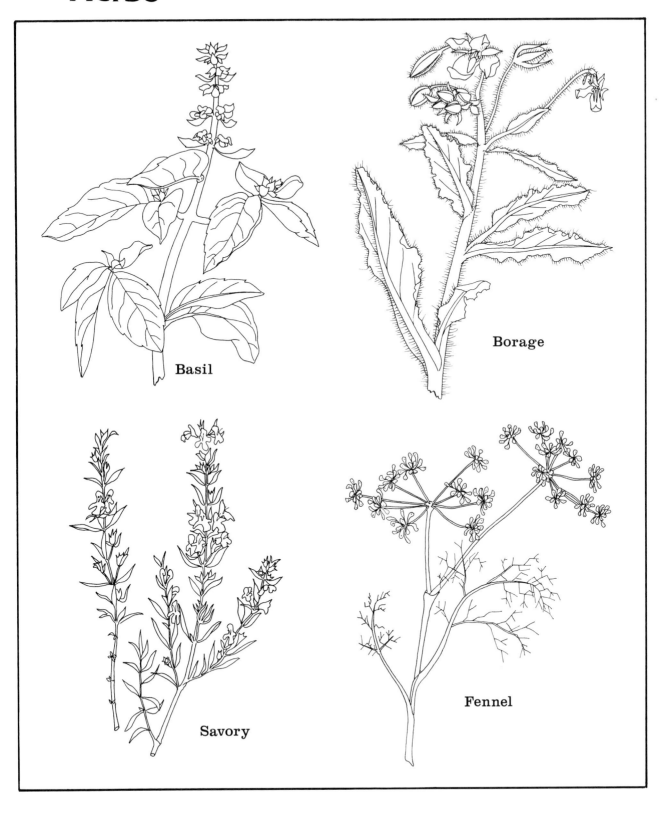

Basil

Borage

Savory

Fennel

and place in freezer bags and label. If you want, chop the leaves first before putting them in storage.

HERBS TO GROW AND KNOW

Basil: This annual plant is almost a basic ingredient in Italian cooking. There are many types of basil, from the wide-leaved kinds to the coppery ones, but basically most people grow sweet basil. Sweet basil grows to about 24 inches and needs really good sun. Plants in the garden will set seed, so you will have more plants the following summer.

Dill: You can do more with this annual herb than you think. For instance, use dill dried on boiled artichokes for a pleasant taste treat. Dill is feathery and ferny in appearance, and its only drawback in the garden is that it grows tall, to about six feet. The small yellow flowers are borne in clusters. Whenever the weather is warm you can sow seeds of dill in the garden; dill will tolerate some shade if necessary. Plants seed themselves.

Marjoram: This is a good herb for salads, fish dishes, and some meats. Marjoram is a perennial plant that generally lives over, but I find it just as easy to seed new plants each year. In spring, when the weather is safely warm, seed marjoram in a sunny place; plants grow to about 20 inches and are rather attractive in the garden.

Parsley: Try to get the plain-leaved parsley rather than the curly-leaved; the curly-leaved parsley looks prettier in the garden, but the plain-leaved type has more flavor. Parsley is a biennial that comes back the second year after seeding. This is the one herb that needs attention: a constantly moist bed for germination. Start plants indoors under controlled conditions. Plants will grow in bright light without too much sun if they have to, but the more sun the better.

Rosemary: If you have space, grow some rosemary because it is good in fish dishes and as a medicinal herb. Cuttings root easily, or plant seed. Plants grow to about 36 inches. There are both upright and creeping varieties of rosemary.

Sage: This perennial has gray-green leaves and pretty purple and white flowers. Plants will grow in a sunny place, even in poor soil. Although sage is not as popular as most herbs, it does have its uses in poultry stuffing.

Savory: There are both summer savory and winter savory; summer savory is a delicate-looking plant with a few leaves, and winter savory is big, with dark green leaves and pretty white flowers. Both winter and summer savory need a sunny spot, and both are good for vegetable dishes and poultry stuffing.

Tarragon: This is a favorite culinary herb, but get the right kind of tarragon: *Artemisia dracunculus*. My best tarragon grows in a somewhat shady place, although most herb experts say it does better in full sun. Tarragon is especially good for vinegars and as a sauce with white wine and butter for liver or fish.

Thyme: This perennial plant adds a nice taste to dishes with eggs, or use thyme as a tea. There are several varieties. Give plants sun.

Herbs and Their Uses

FOR COOKING, SALADS	FOR TEAS	FOR FRA- GRANCES
Chervil	Bergamot	Marjoram
Chives	Catnip	Rosemary
Dill	Chamomile	Thyme
Marjoram	Costmary	
Oregano	Feverfew	
Parsley	Lemon Balm	
Rosemary	Lovage	
Sage	Mint (many kinds)	
Summer savory	Pennyroyal	
Sweet basil	Sweet mar- joram	
Tarragon	Sweet woodruff	
Thyme	Thyme	
Winter Savory	Verbena	
	Yarrow	

16 🍃

Lawns and Ground Covers–The Setting

A RICH GREEN lawn is the ideal setting for a house, and a pleasing complement to a colorful garden. But a rich green lawn, commonly referred to as "velvet turf," is not easily come by in this country. In England with its beneficial conditions, lawns are not difficult to establish; some are claimed to be centuries old. Here it is the part of wisdom to restrict the lawn area not only because of the original expense but the continuous upkeep. This involves watering, mowing, weeding, crabgrass control, reseeding, fertilizing, and maybe pest (cinch bug) and disease (fungus) controls. Wherever possible plant areas of undemanding ground covers. Judiciously placed, they do more for a property than an extensive lawn whose eternal requirements may have been overlooked.

How much work is involved in lawns? How much time? Initially, a lot. However, once established, and this may take anywhere from three to twelve months—a good lawn takes care of itself. The maintenance of a lawn may not be exorbitant. Costly, yes. But there are ways of keeping costs down and still maintaining a healthy lawn.

The dandelion, a common lawn weed. (USDA)

GETTING READY FOR THE LAWN

Some lawns are best for show, some grasses better for walking on, and there are grasses for all situations and all regions. The type known as bent grass has a finely textured appearance and is excellent for golf greens but impossible to maintain for the average home. You must stay with the type of grass that will do best in your region. Basically there are cool-climate grasses and hot-climate grasses. (These are discussed later in detail.)

Another consideration is whether your site is sunny or shady. Some grasses can grow in semishade but most need sun. If the area is completely shaded select a ground cover (there are many that succeed in shade). (See end of chapter.)

Prepare the soil bed for the lawn with great care—no hit or miss here. Use fertile topsoil—not old soil that has been in the same spot for decades and without renewal of nutrients. You can recondition the soil—a mighty word for turning and mixing in humus—but in addition to a revitalized soil, a good lawn bed needs at least two to four inches of fresh topsoil.

When you select your lawn seed, read the package—the percentage of stated germination is important. It should not be lower than 80 percent and 90 percent is better. Buy the best seed you can afford; inferior seed only leads to disappointment.

Start your lawns in spring or early fall. In spring the good weather is on the way; in fall there is still little temperature fluctuation so lawns have an easier time getting established.

Preparing the Site

A good lawn also depends on preparation of the site itself—for example, leveling any area with mounds or depressions. There must be good surface drainage so excess water can run off readily. While it is true that lawns need good moisture, too much of it causes disease.

First, decide where the lawn will be— scout the area on foot; large shade trees nearby will hinder the grass, rocky or hilly places will hold water. And lawns in shade seldom are what you want them to be so a sunny area is necessary.

When you have laid out the site with stakes (small pieces of wood stuck in the ground) and string to define the lawn area, it is time to dig. And dig you must at least eight to 12 inches to eliminate compacted soil. You can do this with a spade or have the ground rototilled. Lawns have a porous soil and a site with compacted soil will not take water.

After the digging and leveling, recondition the subsoil; work organic matter into it; you can buy humus in sacks at nurseries or, if you are composting, add compost to the soil and level the site by raking it. You want the soil bed loose and with some tilth so don't rake too much. You can of course grow grass directly on this reconditioned soil but, if it is possible, add some topsoil now. A layer of at least four inches is good. This may seem like extra work and money but in the long run it pays because topsoil invariably assures a good stand of grass.

If you are establishing a lawn where trees are, provide "wells" for the trees so as to keep the soil from piling up over the root area. Or, easier still, slope the surface soil up

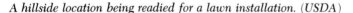

A hillside location being readied for a lawn installation. (USDA)

to the trees. In other words, grade away from the trees, and again remember that grass may not grow under surface-rooting shade trees.

Sowing the Seed

You can sow seed by hand or be more sophisticated and rent a spreader. If you do it by hand, mix a little soil or sand with the seed to spread it evenly. In any event, select a calm day; wind can scatter seed where you don't want it.

Before you sow seed, water the soil somewhat and then let it dry out before doing the sowing. Try to sow seed evenly (this is important) so the lawn will have uniform growth. Too much in one place will produce thick growth; too little, sparse growth, and the effect will be spotty. Once the seed is spread rake it with a light hand. You can roll the seed after it is spread with a rented roller or simply leave it be. The latter way is how it is generally done on home lawns. Rolling can compact the seed into the soil which is not advisable.

Water the seed now—but do it with a light misting; a strong spray of water will wash away the seed. And then keep misting. The idea is to keep the soil evenly moist so seed can germinate. Too dry and seed will die, and if the soil is too moist seed will succumb to disease. Apply water slowly— again, no harsh hosings.

In one to three weeks germination takes place and the grass starts growing. Keep watering but as the grass gets higher you can water less. But again, never allow the lawn to get bone dry.

If birds are a problem in your area and they eat the grass seed, you can put a mulch over the area after you sow seed. You can use a light covering of hay, grass clippings,

or peat moss. Peat moss is generally fine and works well to protect the seed from the birds. And peat will naturally decay to add nutrients to the soil.

Instant Lawns

Other methods of establishing the green are sodding, stripping, and plugging. In essence, this is buying the lawn already established and of course saves time and labor but it does not save money. All of these instant lawns are expensive and if you have any large area to cover they are exorbitant. However, for reasonable sized areas—spot gardens and so forth—the instant lawns may be for you. Of course you must still prepare a good soil bed.

Sod is grass that is mature and ready to be put on the site. It comes in sheets 12 x 12 inches and is generally about one inch thick. The bed is prepared and the sod is laid close together, flush with each other to create a green carpet. You then tamp down or roll the sod evenly after it is placed and water it thoroughly. For the first few weeks water carefully—a gentle sprinkling every other day if the weather is dry and warm. After that time and once the sod has taken hold, routine watering care is fine.

Stripping is another quick means to a good lawn. The process is similar to sodding except that the pieces of sod, four to six inches wide, are spaced three to six inches apart. The idea here is for the grass to spread and create an even lawn. There is a problem with stripping because the soil exposed between the strips usually becomes a meeting ground for all the weeds in the neighborhood and thus weeding is necessary. This takes time and toil and is a nuisance.

A third method is called plugging. The plugs are usually two to four inches square

Sowing Grass Seed

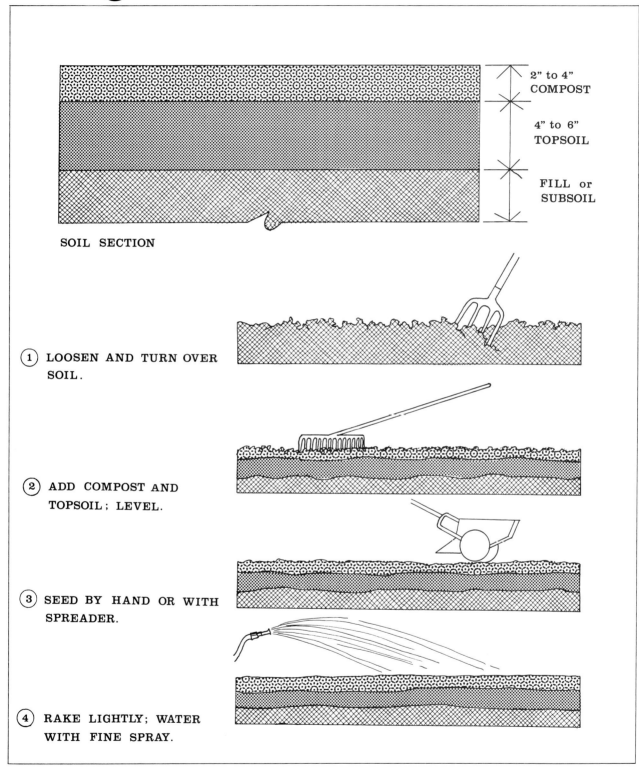

2" to 4"
COMPOST

4" to 6"
TOPSOIL

FILL or
SUBSOIL

SOIL SECTION

1. LOOSEN AND TURN OVER SOIL.

2. ADD COMPOST AND TOPSOIL; LEVEL.

3. SEED BY HAND OR WITH SPREADER.

4. RAKE LIGHTLY; WATER WITH FINE SPRAY.

and are set into predug holes about 12 to 16 inches apart. Again, in this method constant weeding is necessary so while some of the work is done for you there is still other work to be done. Like a sown lawn the area must be constantly moistened so there is even distribution of water and grass spreads to eventually create the green carpet—it takes about six to nine months to fully establish the lawn.

LAWN CARE

Much has been written about velvety green lawns and much money and time is spent trying to establish such a lawn. It is better to forget costly apparatus and settle for what you can do; generally, that means creating a nice lawn if not a superb one, because it is true that a good established lawn will, after a time, care for itself. So this means watering, mowing, and feeding to get the fledgling plants going and growing so they can fend for themselves.

Once the lawn is established, when you water it really water it—a gentle sprinkling of water often is better than thorough soakings every week or ten days. But thorough sprinkling requires time. It takes at least four hours for water to penetrate 20 inches. Certainly you cannot water a lawn with a hose—forget it. You will need a sprinkler to do the job whether it is automatic or manual. The idea is to keep the lawn moist but never soggy and never really dry.

In addition to moisture, grass needs plenty of nitrogen (about 20 percent) to prosper. Bermuda and bent grasses need more feeding than other grasses. Select a packaged lawn food at your nursery. A mechanical spreader will get it down evenly; otherwise there may be dark green streaks where the lawn has been fertilized, and yellow areas

where it has not been fed. The time to feed lawns is in spring and summer—early summer in the North and continual feeding through the summer in the South. A lawn exhausts the supply of food quickly so twice a month feedings are not too much for established lawns; for lawns just getting started feed somewhat less—say, twice a month.

Once the lawn is growing you can start mowing it; don't let it get too tall because cutting high grass shocks the grass and hinders growth. A good mower is essential—it must have sharp blades and be in tiptop condition. Whether you use a power mower or the old-fashioned hand mower, keep it in good condition—dull blades can injure grass.

Some gardeners leave short lawn clippings on the grass because they say it improves the soil while others believe that the clippings left on the turf may help encourage disease. Cut the grass even, but never cut away too much of the vital green leaves. Low-cut grass has a tendency to look shaggy.

Here are some guide lines on cutting heights:

1. Cut Kentucky bluegrass 1½ to 2 inches.
2. Cut Merion Kentucky blue 1 to 1¼ inches.
3. Cut bent grass ½ to ¾ inches.
4. Do not allow grass to grow more than 1 inch before cutting it again.
5. Start mowing grass in spring and continue to fall or until growth stops.
6. Do not let the lawn go into winter with a thick mat—disease may start.

LAWN CALENDAR

January-March: Keep foot traffic off the turf to avoid holes and gulleys. Wait until the ground is firm before walking on it.

March–April: Fertilize while grass is dormant and as soon as the snow thaws. Lightly rake the area, fill in low spots, and eliminate high spots. Mow the lawn as soon as the ground is free of frost.

April–June: Aerate the lawn; feed with a complete fertilizer.

June–August: Feed with complete fertilizer.

September: Feed the lawn and reseed bare spots in established turf.

October–December: Apply fungicide to combat snow and mold before the first snow. Smooth out hollows and valleys.

TYPES OF GRASSES

Cool-Climate Grasses

Cool-climate grasses are sold either singly or in blends. Lawns of a single grass type, although handsome, could be destroyed if attacked by pests or by disease or by environmental conditions. A blend of grasses is safer; even if the grass eventually dwindles to two kinds, it will still give a green carpet.

Bent grass

A fine-leaved grass that spreads by stolons. It needs close mowing, feeding, and watering but it does produce a lovely carpet of green. Takes sun or shade. Best of the Colonial bents are Astoria and Highland, which are somewhat tougher than Colonial. The creeping bent grasses include several strains—Penncross, Seaside, Toronto—with fine, flat, narrow blue-green leaves; they need meticulous care. Suggested areas for bent grass: Northeast, East Coast, Northwest Coast.

Bluegrasses

Generally considered the best of cool-climate grasses. Kentucky blue is fine-bladed, blue-green, long-lived, and produces a good stand of grass. It needs ample sun. Merion bluegrass is deeper rooted, more intense in color, and more resistant to heat. The Windsor strain is a dark vibrant green; it does well in sun or shade. Flyking Kentucky bluegrass is tough and somewhat more resistant to severe cold and standing water than others mentioned here. Rough bluegrass does well in damp, shady places; it is fine textured and apple-green in color. Suggested areas for blue-grass are Northeast, North Central, East Coast, Midwest, South Central, and parts of Southeast and Northwest coasts.

Fescues

Fescues can endure sun or shade, moist or dry soil, and generally take rough treatment and still thrive, although they cannot tolerate the summer heat of the Deep South. Red fescue, or one of its improved strains Chewing, Pennlawn, Rainer—is good for cool climates. Tall fescue and its strains are best for play areas, producing dense leaf systems and heavy roots. Suggested areas: Northeast, North Central, Northwest Coast.

Rye Grass

A perennial inexpensive part of grass mixes. It has a medium-coarse texture; it is easy to grow in a wide variety of climates, but it does not provide a lush carpet of green. Rye grass is often used as a temporary cover. It takes light shade.

Zoysia

A popular grass for the South. Some species are used in the North. Zoysia produces a low-growing, dark-green cover. It takes about two years for Zoysia to crowd out weeds and really become established, but then it is easy to care for. This grass browns off somewhat in cold weather. *Zoysia matrella*, or Manila grass, is fine-leaved, medium dark-green. Emerald zoysia grows faster than matrella; it has a richer color and is more frost resistant. *Zoysia japonica* and its improved varieties, Meyer Zoysia, are suggested for northern lawns; they prefer full sun. Suggested areas for Zoysia: Northeast, North Central, East Coast, South Central, West Coast, Southeast, and Gulf Coast.

St. Augustine Grass

St. Augustine grass is effective only in frost-free areas. The variety Bitter Blue makes a coarse deep-green carpet in the shade or the sun. It is available in sod or sprig. Suggested areas: Southeast, Gulf Coast.

Bermuda Grass

Most satisfactory grass for the South. It needs sun, slightly acid soil, and frequent watering in dry weather. This grass is fine-bladed and spreads well, is upright growing, and is a pale- to dark-green color. It browns out somewhat in winter, but some strains stay green longer than others. Suggested areas: Southeast, South Central, Southwest Coast.

Carpet Grass

A tall, coarse, broad-leaved species; light-green color. It needs a low-moist acid situation, and grows in the sun or in part shade. Carpet grass is tough to mow. Suggested areas: Southeast, South Central, Southwest Coast.

Dichondra

A tough, ground-hugging plant that spreads by surface runners. It has small bright-green, round leaves and grows best in areas with a minimum winter temperature of 25F. The number of plants determines how quickly it will cover an area. Plant dichondra early to avoid problems with midsummer heat.

ABOUT WEEDS

Broad-leaved weeds include chickweed, carpetweed, dandelion, dock, cress, purslane, pennywort, plantain, and others. Most of these can be controlled by hoeing or removing them with a hand weeder; the plants are generally recognizable as weeds and come out of the soil without too much of a struggle. The grassy weeds—crabgrass, foxtail, barnyard grass, goosegrass, and quackgrass—are more persistent because several of them spread quickly by runners that go deep underground, making it impossible to pull them out completely.

Weeds are perennial or annual; crabgrass starts from seed anew each spring (generally in April) and is at its weakest stage when it first starts to grow. With the difficult weeds, it is important to recognize them when they first appear and to undertake immediate measures to control them. Once established, they take the upper hand.

A good, dense stand of grass is the best protection against weeds developing. The next best control is to prevent annual lawn weeds from seeding; this means removing them at just the right time. Other precautions include the following:

1. Use a lawn sweeper after midsummer mowings to pick up weed seeds.
2. Aerate the soil as much as possible so that air and moisture get to the bottom of the soil to encourage good grass to grow. Aerate with a hand aerator or one that attaches to the tiller.

Dock is ever-invasive once it gets a foothold in a lawn. (USDA)

3. Pull weeds by hand; this is easy to do when soil is damp. Use a trowel or a hand weeder. Hoe weeds; this is easy to do when soil is somewhat dry. Cut through the crowns rather than try to dig up weeds.
4. On small areas of weeds, cover them with a heavy impervious mulch. Building paper, aluminum foil, can be used; after several weeks, roots and tops of weeds will die.

Of course, the most important precaution against weeds is to create a good soil structure with plenty of compost, humus, and leaf mold so there will be a quick and vigorous growth of grass. Consider that a clay or a sandy soil will not provide good growing conditions for grass, but it can support weeds that thrive in inferior situations.

Care with Chemicals

Keep chemicals out of children's reach.
Store in original container.
Avoid spilling.
Set aside a special set of mixing tools.
Avoid spray or drift.
Never smoke or eat while spraying.
Throw away, but do not burn, empty containers.
After spraying, wash all equipment.
After spraying, wash hands and face with soap.
Before mixing chemicals, read all labels carefully.

Other Grass Problems

Yellowish Grass: generally happens when there is not enough nitrogen in the soil, or if the soil has too much acidity or alkalinity.

Brown Patch: a fungus disease that attacks all kinds of turf. It produces irregularly shaped brown patches. Brown patch appears during times of high humidity. Control: Fungicide.

Dollar Spot: a fungus disease that mostly attacks Kentucky bluegrass, bent, and St. Augustine grass. It causes spots, forming irregular areas of damage. Prevalent in spring and in fall, with cool nights and warm humid days. Control: Fungicide.

Burrowing Animals: moles and gophers can cause havoc in a lawn. The ideal solution is to eliminate the grubs and other insects they are looking for. This is not always possible, so traps are occasionally used as are various old-fashioned remedies like mothballs inserted in the runs.

THE INDISPENSABLE GROUND COVERS

Where climate or a rough terrain make it difficult to establish a lawn, ground covers are invaluable substitutes. Such plants offer a great deal for little cost and low maintenance. In fact, once these plants are established, they bind sandy soil, check erosion on hillsides, and quickly cover an unsightly area. Many of them grow in shade; others tolerate full sun and even drought. Ground covers are tough plants. Evergreen types are attractive all year. For mild climates there are many. For severe climates, there are several handsome types.

In cold-weather areas, start plants in spring. Where winters are moderate, start them in the spring or fall. In temperate, all-year climates, plant them in fall or winter.

Plants are available in flats of 80 to 100 to a container. The majority need a rich soil; only a few, such as liriope and hosta, will thrive in poor soil. Most nurseries advise setting plants—in groups of two is recommended—12 to 16 inches apart. This is a matter of choice rather than rule. The closer the plants are set, the more rapidly they will cover an area. With 12- to 16-inch spacing, it may take some two years for complete coverage.

Shrubby ground covers, like junipers, continue to grow for years. In time, they may get out of bounds and grow too high. When this happens, thin out rampant growth; it will not harm the plants.

Many ground covers become a mass of branches—a solid bed of green—and will not tolerate foot traffic. Others—the flat-growers—do take foot traffic, but generally it is best to put in stepping stones if the area is to be walked on frequently.

Every region has its own "best" ground covers depending upon climate and soil. The plants offered at local nurseries will usually be those suitable for your area.

Some Excellent Ground Covers

Ajuga reptans (bugelweed). 6 inches; hardy perennial with rosettes of dark-green leaves and spikes of blue spring flowers. Sun or shade, ample moisture.

Anthemis nobilis (camomile). 3 to 5 inches. An overlooked but lovely cover with light-green fern-like leaves. Sandy soil, full sun, even moisture.

Arctostaphylos uva-ursi (manzanita). To 12 inches; evergreen with small, nodding leaves.

Asarum caudatum (wild ginger). Handsome woodlike plant for shady moist

Ground Covers

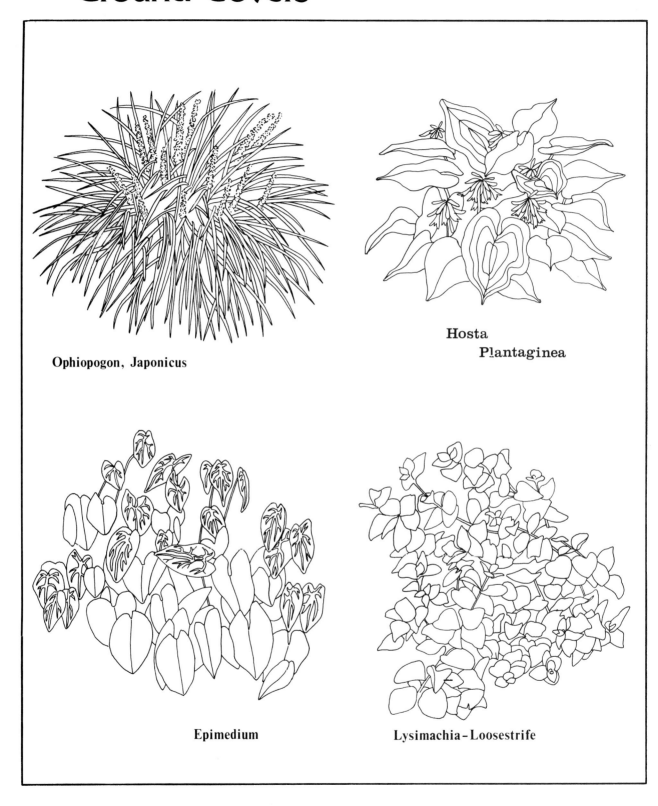

Ophiopogon, Japonicus

Hosta
Plantaginea

Epimedium

Lysimachia-Loosestrife

areas. Attractive heart-shaped leaves. One of the best.

Cotoneaster (many). Shrubby, with small leaves and decorative berries. Several good ones.

Duchesnea indica (mock-strawberry). Coarsely toothed leaves; good creeper.

Dichondra carolinensis. Small dark-green leaves form dense mats. Well-drained soil and plenty of water. Tender.

Epimedium (barrenwort). Semievergreen; to 9 inches, glossy leaves and dainty flowers. Moist, slightly acid soil, somewhat shaded conditions.

Erica vagans (heath). To 12 inches, pointed needle-like leaves.

Fragaria chiloensis (strawberry). Small semievergreen, to 6 inches, white flowers. Grows rapidly. Sun or shade.

Hedera helix (English ivy). One of the most popular; several handsome varieties. Some have tiny leaves; others, large foliage. Some grow quickly, whereas others take many months to become established. Sun or shade.

Hosta or Funkia (plantain lily). Many varieties. Some with large leaves, others with small leaves. Likes moisture but will survive a dry situation too. Prefers shade.

Hypercicum calcyinum (Aaron's beard). 12 inches. Sun or shade. Tolerates a sandy soil.

Iberis sempervirens (candytuft). Grows to 6 inches; dense little evergreens with white spring flowers. Sun and rich soil.

Juniperus (See Shrubs)

Liriope muscari. Grows to 12 inches, grassy foliage forming a dense mat. Sun or shade, any soil.

Lonicera japonica (honeysuckle Halliana). Tough rampant vine to 6 inches. Sun or shade. Evergreen in the South; semievergreen in the North. Can become a pest unless kept within bounds.

Mesembryanthemum (ice plant). Large group of succulent plants; annual and perennial. Recently renamed but still are available at nurseries under old name. Some have 1- to 2-inch stiff leaves; others grow to 8 inches. All have bright daisylike flowers. Needs sun.

Pachysandra terminalis (Japanese spurge). To 5 to 12 inches. Evergreen, whorls of dark-green leaves. For shady areas; slow growing. Does not do well in sun.

Rosmarinus officinalis (rosemary Prostratus). Evergreen; to 12 inches, narrow leaves, blue flowers in spring. Needs sun; tolerates poor soil.

Sedum amecamecanum (stonecrop). Low-growing succulent. Spreads rapidly.

Thyme (thymus). Low carpet plant. Tolerates hot, dry, sunny places and poor soil.

Vinca minor (periwinkle). Excellent shade-loving evergreen creeper. Dark glossy leaves, showy white or blue spring flowers.

A handsome rock garden scene, featuring iberis, artemaria, and alyssum. (M. Adams)

17 ✍

Special Gardens

A SPECIAL garden gives you a chance to indulge yourself, to concentrate on one type of flower or setting. If your extravagance is ferns or wildflowers, by all means, consider the wild or natural garden. If you are intrigued with rock gardens, make a tucked-away retreat where you can grow alpine plants. The special garden can become the feature of your landscape. It will give you hours of pleasure. If flower beds and borders are not for you, indulge in a specific interest.

ROCK GARDENS

A rock garden is not the easiest landscape to simulate on your property unless it is naturally rocky, but it can be a worthwhile undertaking. This garden requires labor, patience, and careful construction, but when finished it is a picturesque, highly desirable feature. The secret is to reflect nature as you imitate it; to build it slowly and with care so it can become a permanent landscape asset.

The rock garden takes you into the world of alpine plants, which are extremely attractive, often blazing with color in their season. The rock garden can take various forms; it can be a many-pocketed structure in a small area—a few rocks and plants—or it can be a large landscape scene where the plants are placed at intervals.

Whatever form it is, the garden must be a true representation of natural rock scenery. Find just the right place for it; in the wrong location it becomes an eyesore rather than an attractive picture. A woodland setting is, of course, the most convincing background for the garden, but many times the perfect setting is simply not available so the rock garden should be omitted. In general, keep rock gardens away from walls and buildings and avoid constructing them on a level site; a natural slope is ideal.

An important part of assembling the garden and how it will eventually look depends on the shapes of the stones used. Plan different levels to increase interest. It is easier to work with a slope or a bank that naturally lends itself to rock treatment than with a flat piece of ground.

The placement of rocks is hard work even if the new lightweight stone, such as featherock and lavarock, is used. The rocks should be used like a retaining wall—each one set in place with a slight tilt backwards. This gives stability to the structure and allows rain to run into the rock bed behind. Set the stones firmly in place. Most of them should be buried one-third their height and placed in a natural design of ledges and abutments.

Rocks must be firmly in place without air pockets behind them; those would cause the soil to dry out and the plants to die.

Bluets are the main flowers of this handsome rock garden, used as an accent next to a lawn.

Designing the Rock Garden

The site for a rock garden should preferably face south or southeast on an irregular slope with natural outcroppings of rocks. This is the ideal location. But ideal conditions are rarely found, and often we must settle for second-best—perhaps a corner where there are some big trees, or even a bare slope that will require rock placement to show the scene to its advantage.

Now, while the garden is an arrangement of rocks, it is essentially a place to grow alpine plants, those species that grow at high altitudes in cool conditions with lots of sun and with an active but short period of growth. These plants are colorful and infinitely charming; to grow well they need some approximation of their natural conditions—light, coolness, moisture. The emphasis in rock gardening is not so much in soil as location, and a place where water continually runs off rather than settles. There must be plenty of moisture in the soil, but it must be moisture in motion that constantly drains through. The soil can be dry on the surface but must be damp below.

A rock garden is three dimensional, and elevations and depressions are vital to the total design. This should be a study in heights with appropriate paths and steps to give adequate access to the plants. The paths can be stepping-stones or gravel. The finished appearance of the garden depends on the kinds of stones available and the way they are placed to create masses and slopes. Many rock plants are small and require little space; others grow rampant and should be placed within rock barriers.

New England areas and the cooler regions of the Great Lakes have favorable conditions for rock gardens. In warmer climates, this special landscape is difficult to create and usually best omitted.

In the first year, grow only a few plants rather than dozens. Rock gardening requires patience and skill that comes from experience. You are growing alpine plants from high altitudes quite unlike other flowers.

However, the flower bed and the rock garden do have one thing in common—good composition. The rock garden should have harmony, unity, and balance.

Rocks

When climate is conducive to rock gardening and there is a suitable location, obtaining rocks and placing them become the main concern of the gardener. All kinds of rocks and stones are available at local building suppliers who will deliver to your home; but moving and putting rocks in place is your project. And indeed it can be a project because rocks are heavy; and even for a small garden some very large ones will be needed. A conglomeration of small stones set into the landscape does not make a garden, only a mess of stones. Large and formidable boulders are needed to pattern the garden successfully.

There are several ways of lifting and placing rocks. Old-fashioned muscle power is the most inexpensive means, but a laborious business. You will need at least four people to lift a heavy rock. Another way to position a rock is to place a pipe under it, push the rock the length of the pipe, then move the pipe ahead on the ground, and so on. Setting planks of wood under the stones is another method whereby the rocks are pushed along the length of the planks to their location. And, of course, there are derricks and other equipment usually supplied by landscape contractors.

Select flat stones or irregular shapes with rough surfaces rather than rounded stones with smooth planes. Absorbent rock is preferred: Limestone and tufarock are suitable; granite is not a good choice. Porous sandstone and split and cracked rocks are good, too. Check in your area and see what kind of native stone is available. This would be the most suitable for your place.

Soil for the Rock Garden

Soil for the garden should be porous so that excess water will drain away fairly quickly and yet, at the same time, hold moisture long enough to keep plants growing. I use a mixture of three parts loam, two parts crushed stone, one part sand, and two parts humus. You can deviate from this soil mix somewhat, but you cannot deviate from the principle of perfect drainage for these small plants. Without it they will not survive. Provisions must be made to carry excess water away from plant roots. A four-inch layer of cinders under the soil works well in keeping water running below the plants. Or you can use small stones or broken pieces of clay pots as a drainage bed.

After the drainage material is in place, three-quarters of the soil is spread over the excavated site, the remainder left for filling in and between rocks as they are put in place. In the planting area, use soil to a depth of 18 inches. Start at the lowest point and place each rock on its broadest side. Sometimes it will be necessary for you to dig out soil to make space for a stone, or you can leave a free-standing stone and fill in around it with soil. Soil ranging from pH 6 to pH 8 is suitable for most rock plants.

Maintenance of a Rock Garden

Most alpine plants need bright light or partial sun, and during the hot months frequent waterings, for moisture is the key to success. In long hot summers, keep alpine plants as cool as possible. Exposed to wind and sun, they dry out quickly. While they can stand drought if necessary, there will be a better harvest of flowers if ample moisture is supplied.

Because most rock plants are small, they can get lost in weeds, so keep the rock garden free of them; cover bare places with stones to discourage weeds. Nothing destroys the appearance of this garden more than a crop of weeds.

Plants are set in place in fall or very early in spring. In winter, many alpines can go without protection, but others require protection against dampness (not cold) and the ill effects of freezing and thawing. Mulching the plants conserves moisture and keeps the soil cool. Plants that form heavy mats of foliage need no protection, and species that are deciduous can withstand winter, but plants that have rosettes of leaves need some mulch down under the foliage. Select a mulch that affords some air circulation. You do not want a wet decaying mat around the plant. Evergreen boughs, salt hay, and oak leaves make satisfactory mulches. Remove them gradually rather than all at once in spring when danger of frost is over.

Plants for Rock Gardens

Achillea tomentosa (yarrow)
Ajuga repens (bugleseed)
Alyssum saxatile (goldentuft)
Aquilegia vulgaris (columbine)
Campanula carpatica (bellflower)
Dianthus deltoides (maiden pink)
Geranium grandiflorum (cranesbill geranium)
Gypsophila repens (creeping gypsophila)
Iberis sempervirens (candytuft)
Iris pumila (dwarf bearded iris)
Myosotis scorpiodes (forget-me-not)
Phlox sublata (moss pink)
Primula polyantha (primrose)
Sedum album (stonecrop)

Sempervivum (many)
Veronica incana (speedwell)
Viola cornuta (viola)

Shrubs for Rock Gardens

Berberis thunbergi minor (barberry)
Cotoneaster microphylla (rock spray)
Cytisus kewensis (broom)
Potentilla fruitcosa (cinquefoil)
Spiraea bullata (spirea)

Dwarf Evergreens for Rock Gardens

Calluna vulgaris (heather)
Chamaecyparis obtusa nana (Hinoki cypress)
Erica carnea (heather)
Euonymus fortunei minimus (dwarf wintercreeper)
Juniperus horizontalis (creeping juniper)
J. procumbens nana (creeping juniper)
Pinus mugo compacta (Swiss mountain pine)
Rhododendron facenosum (rhododendron)
R. impeditum (rhododendron)

Rock Garden Plants for Shade

Ajuga repens (carpet bugle)
Allium moly (lilyleek)
Anemone canadensis (anemone)
Aquilegia caerulea (columbine)
Asarum canadense (wild ginger)
Asplenium trichomanes (maidenhair spleenwort)
Camassia esculenta (camass)
Dicentra eximia (fringed bleeding heart)
Epimedium macranthum (epimedium)
Hepatica triloba (hepatica)
Iris cristata (crested iris)
Mentha requieni (Corsican mint)

Mertensia virginica (Virginia bluebell)
Mitchella repens (partridgeberry)
Phlox divaricata (blue phlox)
Polypodium vulgar (common polypody)
Sanguinaria canadensis (bloodroot)
Sedum pulchellum (stonecrop)
S. ternatum (stonecrop)
Trillium grandiflora (trillium)
Viola (violet)

Bulbs for Rock Gardens

Camassia esculente (camass)
Chionodoxa lucilia (glory-of-the-snow)
Colchicum autumnale (autumn crocus)
Crocus, various (crocus)
Fritillaria meleagris (guinea-hen-flower)
Galanthus nivalis (snowdrop)
Muscari botryoides (grape hyacinth)
Narcissus species (narcissus, daffodil)
Puschkinia scilloides (puschkinia)
Scilla hispanica (Spanish bluebell)
S. nonscripta (English bluebell)
Tulipa kaufmanniana (tulip)

THE WILD GARDEN

The wild garden or natural setting may have ferns or wildflowers—a special place for each—or may be part of a native shrub and tree landscape. This is a garden where nature does the work with only a little help from you. It is the type of setting you would find if you strolled through meadows or woodlands—a patch of wildflowers, a shady place green with ferns. It is a lovely garden, appealing in many respects and not that difficult to accomplish.

Let us look at each type of plant first—ferns, wildflowers—and see what might fit into the location you have.

Ferns in the right location are amenable plants that will grow in poor or rich soil, dry or moist places, but almost always in a shady situation. Group ferns of the same size together rather than a small one with a large one (that creates a spotty effect). Consider texture; some ferns like the maidenhairs are lacy while ferns like blechnum and the leather fern are stiff and brittle. Use contrasting textures together—this is fine but again be sure plants are of similar size. The fern garden is also a natural place for wildflowers such as trilliums and mayapples because most ferns do not attain full growth for six to eight weeks after spring, so the wildflowers can live harmoniously with them, one taking over when the other finishes blooming. Many ferns last until frost and then hardy ones remain throughout winter.

Plan your fern garden under trees where there is natural shade. The plants should appear as if they have always been there, rather than just planted, and once established they will attain that natural look. To start the fernery dig down about twelve inches or more to break up the soil and then add some leaf mold and compost. While it is true that many ferns will grow in less than

A lush fern garden accents the entrance to a home. (*K. Molino*)

the best soil, a rich humusy soil will ensure good growth. For ferns such as the chain fern and lady fern work a little oak leaves or wood chips into the soil to provide that little bit of acid they like. For ferns like maidenhair spleenworts, add limestone to provide the soil with alkali. Put a few pebbles in place to anchor the roots and try to put plants in place in early fall. Space medium growers one to two feet apart and larger ferns about three feet apart. The soil should always be loose and porous, never tightly packed.

And if you really want that fern garden to prosper use a good leaf mulch on plants and of course be sure they get plenty of water. Ferns like moisture. Here is a list of ferns to grow in your wild garden.

Ferns to Grow

Adiantum pendatum (American maidenhair fern): soft, light to medium green. Forked and diverging. Rich humus constantly moist. Medium shade.

Asplenium platyneuron (ebony spleenwort): deep green, slender, double tapering. Loose, woodland soil. Medium shade to alternate sunlight.

A. trichomanes (maidenhair spleenwort): deep green, slender. Humus with small pieces of limestone. Requires good drainage. Medium shade to alternate sunlight.

Botrychium virginianum (rattlesnake fern): yellow-green to rich green. Rich, moist, woodland soil, neutral to slightly acid. Medium to deep shade.

Camptosorus rhizophyllus (walking fern): medium green, elongate, tapering. Grows best between limestone rocks. Avoid overwatering. Shade to alternate sunlight.

Cystopteris fragilis (fragile bladder fern): medium or green. Loose neutral soil. Shade to alternate sunlight.

Ferns have taken over this garden—wild but still beautiful. (M. Barr)

Dryopteris cristata: dark green, leathery, erect. Slightly acid, constantly damp, loose woodland mulch. Open to deep shade.

D. goldieana (Goldie's fern): deep green, leathery. Rich humus, constantly moist. Cool, open to medium shade.

D. intermedia: deep green. Deep, rocky soil rich in humus. Neutral or slightly acid. Open to medium shade.

Onoclea sensibilis (sensitive fern): yellow-green to green. Neutral or subacid, moist. Open shade. Tolerates full sunlight if in marshy area.

Osmunda cinnamomea (cinnamon fern): yellow-green to deep waxy green. Acid, constantly damp. Open shade.

O. claytoniana (interrupted fern): yellow-green to waxy green. Acid, constantly moist. Open shade to alternate sunlight in damper soil.

O. regalis v. spectabilis: deep green. Highly acid, constantly moist. Shade to alternate sunlight when growing in bogs.

Pellaea atropurpurea (purple cliff-brake): gray-green. Slightly alkaline. Open shade to alternate sunlight.

Polypodium virginianum (common polypody): yellow-green to medium green. Moist to slightly acid. Tolerates short dry periods. Open shade to alternate sunlight.

Polystichum acrostichoides (Christmas fern): various shades of green, darkening with age. Moist, stony woodland, mulch. Open shade. Tolerates some direct sunlight where moisture is sufficient.

Thelypteris noveboracensis (New York fern): yellow-green to medium green. Humusy acid. Will tolerate sun, but shade best. Deciduous.

Woodwardia areolata: glossy, medium to dark green. Acid soil. Open shade. Tolerates considerable sunlight when in moist soil.

W. virginica: deep green to yellow-green, depending on light. Acid soil. Open shade. Tolerates considerable sunlight when in moist soil.

WILDFLOWER GARDENS

There are few garden scenes that can beat the wildflower landscape in bloom. Here is vibrant color and beauty for everyone. The wildflower garden requires the same conditions as the fernery and here you can grow all the wonderful old-time plants you have heard about and read about. Indeed, there are so many wildflowers, it would be difficult to cover even half of them in the space allotted here but we can look at some of the more popular and generally grown ones that are most adaptable to soil and climate over a wide area of the United States.

Aquilegia canadensis (American columbine). Red-yellow bells on one- to two-foot stems signal the opening of the spring to summer columbine in your garden. There are species for almost every state. Most of them need a rather dry, sandy soil

Natural garden

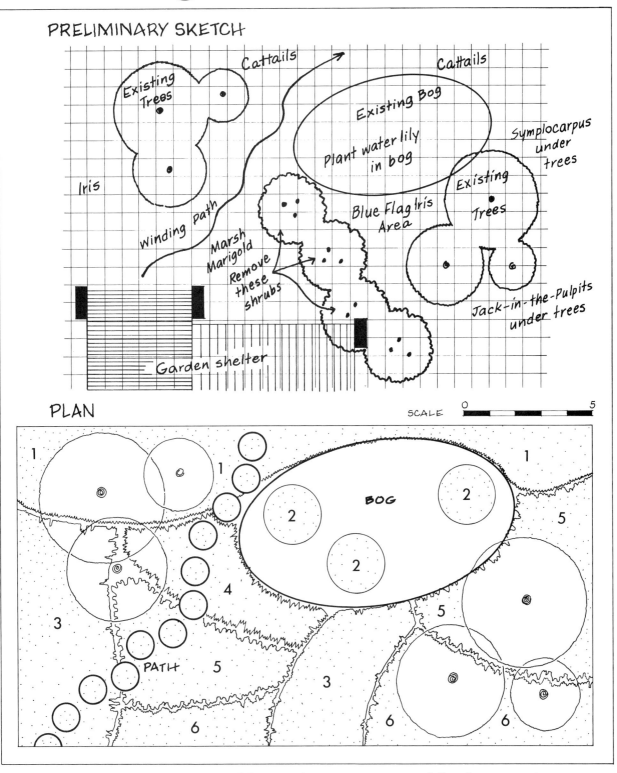

PRELIMINARY SKETCH

Cattails

Cattails

Existing Trees

Existing Bog

Plant water lily in bog

Symplocarpus under trees

Iris

Blue Flag Iris Area

Existing Trees

Winding Path

Marsh Marigold

Remove these shrubs

Jack-in-the-Pulpits under trees

Garden shelter

PLAN

SCALE 0 5

1

1

2

BOG

2

5

3

2

4

5

PATH

5

3

6

6

6

1. *Typha latifolia*
Cattail

2. *Nymphaea odorata*
Fragrant Water Lily

3. *Iris versicolor*
Blue Flag

4. *Caltha palustris*
Marsh Marigold

5. *Symplocarpus americanus*
Skunk Cabbage

6. *Arisaema triphyllum*
Jack-in-the-Pulpit

with full to semishade sun. Plants can be easily propagated by seed with some bloom the first year after sowing. Species include the blue *A. caerulea* (Colorado columbine), *A. chrysantha* (golden columbine), and *A. flavescens*.

Arisaema triphyllum (Jack-in-the-pulpit). Spathe-like pulpit type flowers striped maroon to pale green with white lining. (Colors vary somewhat in different plants.) Needs a rich woodsy soil. Unusual and very popular for shady places.

Asarum europaeum (European wild ginger). An excellent ground cover, lush, shining, and evergreen, very easy to grow. Give plants moist soil in shade and propagate by division of rootstocks at any time.

Claytonia virginica (spring beauty). In April, delicate pink flowers open in woodland on one-foot grassy plants. This is native to the East, but there are also species for the West. Plants need moist woodsy soil in shade. Propagate from offsets or seed. *C. caroliniana* (broad-leaved spring beauty) is also lovely.

Dicentra cucullaria (Dutchman's breeches). Nodding white-to-pink flowers have two spurs that suggest a pair of white breeches hanging upside down. Grows to one foot mainly in Eastern woods, and foliage dies as flowers fade. *D. eximia* (fringed bleeding-heart) and *D. formosa* (Pacific bleeding heart) are also good species. Plants like partial shade and well-drained soil. Divide large clumps after flowering.

Dodecatheon meadia (shooting star). Twenty species, 6 to 20 inches high, are

widely distributed throughout the Central and Western states. The deep rose petals point back to make the flower seem to shoot forward. Plants need partial shade and rich woodsy soil. Basal leaves disappear in summer. Divide dormant crowns for new plants.

Erythronium americanum (trout-lily). In the Northeast, tiny yellow flowers appear in April on one-foot plants. Easy to grow. This often volunteers—reseeds itself—beside a brook. It needs deep moist soil and prefers shade, although it will tolerate sun. For new plants, take offshoots. Seeds require almost seven years before blooming.

Geranium maculatum (wild geranium). These easy-to-grow 12- to 20-inch plants are found in the East and North Central states in a range of species. Pink-lavender flowers above finely cut leaves offer pretty April–May color. In large colonies, these geraniums make a fine display. They prefer a rich humusy soil in sun or partial shade. For new plants, divide old ones.

Hepatica americana (round-lobed hepatica). In the East this is one of the first wild flowers to open on 6-inch plants in early spring. Flowers are pale lavender to pink-white and are a lovely addition to a garden. *H. acutiloba* (sharp-lobed hepatica) holds its leaves through winter. Both species grow well in a somewhat gravelly soil, neutral or slightly acid and well drained. Divide clumps for new plants or let them self-sow.

Iris cristata (crested iris). This gem of an iris, 3 to 4 inches high, native in many states, bears lovely crested lavender or white flowers on 3- to 4-inch plants. It spreads rapidly; it is not choosy about soil, but requires part shade. It is a good ground cover. In the Central states, *I. missouriensis* is popular. In the East, the blue flag *I. versicolor* is especially handsome. *I. verna* is also desirable. Some iris need dry hillside conditions, but others like rich and shady woodsy places. For new plants, divide rhizomes in spring.

Lobelia cardinalis (cardinal flower). Brilliant red flowers make this 2- to 3-foot native outstanding in summer. Plants like moist rich soil in light to deep shade, decorative for the edge of a pool. They do not always winter over easily; for new ones, divide the fibrous roots of mature plants.

Mertensia virginica (Virginia bluebells). An easy and adaptable plant with clusters of pink-blue flowers on 15-inch stems, April to May. After flowering, plants die down completely. Provide a rather dry, acid soil and light to deep shade. Divide rootstocks after blooming for new plants, or sow seed.

Phlox divaricata (blue phlox). A large group of garden flowers—some low growers, others, tall. Spread rapidly. Blue phlox can be grown in twenty states, other species suitable depending upon your region. *P. stolonifera* has lavender flowers, *P. drummondi*, an annual from Texas, has red flowers.

Sanguinaria canadensis (bloodroot). White flowers with yellow stamens grow late March to May. It likes a woodsy soil, and even though it appreciates early spring sun, it thrives in light to deep shade

in summer. Obtain new plants from old ones by dividing the rootstock and planting one inch deep in fall. Or sow seed, press in, and cover with soil.

Solidago canadensis (goldenrod). Don't get this one mixed up with the plant that produces hay fever, ragweed. Goldenrod is a fine late summer plant that grows one to four feet high; there are more than one hundred species. Plants need a sandy soil and revel in sun. This self-sows so vigorously it is difficult to control in a wild garden.

Trillium grandiflorum (snow trillium). This fine 12- to 14-inch native gives a grand spring display; it is majestic in any garden, with large pink, red, purple, or white flowers. Trilliums are easy to grow, and there are species for almost every state. In the East, this *T. grandiflorum* is prized. *T. luteum*, from North Carolina, is yellow, and *T. erectum* is found in North and South Carolina; it has greenish-brown flowers. Other good trilliums include *T. cernuum*, with white flowers, and *T. sessile*, with red flowers. Grow the plants in shade with moist soil. To increase your stock, divide rootstocks in fall and plant them four inches deep. Plants bloom in the fourth or fifth year.

Viola (violet). There are seventy-five species, some in almost every state. Flowers range from yellow to violet to white to red-purple. Generally, violets prefer a moist shady spot, but they will also accept other conditions if necessary. Yellow species include *V. eriocarpa*, *V. pubescens*, and *V. rotundifolia*. Among the blue violets are *V. culcullata*, *V. pedata* (bird's-foot violet) that likes sun, *V. pedatifida,* and *V. sagittata.* Among good white violets are the fragrant *V. blanda, V. canadensis,* and *V. primulifolia.*

Other Native Plants

Now that you have the fern or wildflower garden growing and going you will need native trees and shrubs to provide a background. With these plants nature does all the work once they are installed. Here is a compendium of native plants for the wild garden:

Trees

Abies balsamea° (balsam fir): needlelike leaves to 1 inch, horizontal branches, and purple, oblong cones to 2½ inches long. Hardiness: −35 to 20°F.

A. concolor° (white fir): grows to 120 feet. Stiffly pyramidal and narrow, with horizontal branches and needlelike leaves to 2 inches long. Hardiness: −20 to −10°F.

Acer rubrum (red maple): grows to 120 feet. Round head when mature. Dense foliage, with three to five lobes on 4-inch leaves. Leaves turn bright red in autumn. Hardiness: −35 to −20°F.

A. saccharum (sugar maple): grows to 120 feet. Round head when mature. Dense foliage; leaves are lobed to 6 inches across and turn yellow or orange and red in autumn. Hardiness: −35 to −20°F.

Aesculus glabra (Ohio buckeye): grows to 30 feet. Rounded head. Coarse foliage, with five leaflets. Small, greenish-yellow panicles 6 inches high in mid-May; turn

° Evergreens

brilliant orange in autumn. Hardiness: −35 to −20°F.

Amelanchier canadensis (shadblow serviceberry): grows to 60 feet. Open foliage (grayish when young) that is upright and often narrow with small, white, nodding racemes in late April. Yellow to red berry-like fruit in autumn, turning maroon-purple in early summer. Hardiness: −20 to −10°F.

A. grandiflora (apple serviceberry): grows to 25 feet. Dense foliage with wide spreading branches. Flowers, tinged with pink when first open and pure white in early May, are 1¼ inches in diameter. Red to black edible berries in early summer. Hardiness: −20 to −10°F.

Betula papyrifera (white birch): grows to 100 feet. Open foliage, with ovate leaves to 4 inches long. Cones are cylindrical, to 2 inches long. White bark peels off in paperthin sheets. Yellow in autumn. Hardiness: −50 to −35°F.

Carya glabra (pignut): grows to 40 feet. Slow-growing tree. Usually five serrated leaflets. Close but not shaggy bark. Hardiness: −20 to −10°F.

C. ovata (shagbark hickory): grows to 120 feet. Compound leaves to 6 inches long with five to seven leaflets. Narrow and upright, with bark flaking off in loose plates. Golden brown in autumn. Hardiness: −20 to −10°F.

Cercis canadensis (Eastern redbud): grows to 40 feet. Flat top, irregular shape. Roundish, abruptly acute leaves. Pealike flowers in clusters, rosy-pink color, and about ½ inch long. Open foliage that turns yellow in autumn. Hardiness: −20 to −10°F.

Chamaecyparis lawsoniana * (Lawson false cypress): grows to 120 feet. Slender to broadly pyramidal in shape, with evergreen, scalelike foliage. Branches are usually drooping, and the branchlets are frondlike. Has shredding bark. Hardiness: −20 to −5°F.

Chionanthus virginica (fringetree): grows to 30 feet. Oblong leaves to 8 inches long and panicles to 8 inches in length. White and feathery in May–June, dark grapelike clusters of fruit in fall, and bright yellow in autumn. A deciduous tree. Hardiness: −20 to −10°F.

Cladrastis lutea (yellowwood): grows to 50 feet. Rounded, dense foliage, leaves have seven to nine ovate leaflets. Pendulous clusters of fragrant white flowers that turn orange to yellow in autumn. Hardiness: −35 to 20°F.

Cornus florida (flowering dogwood): grows to 40 feet. Definite horizontal branching. Dense, lustrous foliage; ovate leaves to 6 inches long. Flowers are in dense heads, subtended by four large white petal-like bracts. True flowers in mid-May; inconspicuous bright red berries in tight clusters in fall. Scarlet in autumn. Hardiness: −20 to −10°F.

Crataegus nitida (gloss hawthorn): grows to 30 feet. Round-headed. Thorny and dense branching. Coarsely toothed, lustrous leaves. White flowers in May. Dull red fruit, ⅜ inch in diameter, ½ inch long, all winter. Orange to red in autumn. Hardiness: −20 to −10°F.

C. phaenopyrum (Washington thorn): grows to 30 feet. Broadly columnar, with round head. Thorny and dense branching. Lustrous and dense leaves have three to five lobes. White flowers ½ inch in diameter in many clusters in mid-June. Bright red fruit, ¼ inch in diameter, in winter. Scarlet to orange in autumn. Hardiness: −20 to −10°F.

C. viridis (green hawthorn): grows to 40 feet. Rounded and thorny. Spreading, dense, branching and dense foliage, with oblong, ovate, or ellipticlanceolate leaves to 2½ inches long. White flowers ¾ inch in diameter borne in flat clusters 2 inches across in late May. Bright red fruit, ¼ inch in diameter in fall and winter. Hardiness: −20 to −10°F.

Diospyros virginiana (common persimmon): grows to 75 feet. Round-headed. Often has pendulous branches. Bark deeply cut into small blocks. Dense foliage with ovate leaves to 6 inches long. Yellow to orange fruit 1½ inches in diameter, edible after frost. Yellow in autumn. Hardiness: −20 to −10°F.

Fagus grandifolia (American beech): grows to 90 feet. Densely pyramidal. Dense foliage, with ovate or oblong leaves to 5 inches long. Leaves are dark bluish-green above. Light gray bark. Golden bronze in autumn. Hardiness: −35 to −20°F.

Franklinia alatamaha (franklinia): grows to 30 feet. Upright. Loose and open foliage, with leaves to 6 inches long. Brilliant orange to red in autumn. Hardiness: −20 to −5°F.

Fraxinus pennsylvanica (red ash): grows to 60 feet. Dense and rounded tree with lovely yellow autumn color. Vigorous, good. Hardiness: −50 to −35°F.

Gleditsia triacanthus (honey locust): grows to 140 feet. Broad, open, and fine-textured foliage, with single and double compound leaves 7 to 12 inches long. Hardiness: −20 to −10°F.

Gymnocladus dioicus (Kentucky coffee tree): a good winter tree with picturesque branching habit. Seldom seen, but robust. Hardiness: −20 to −10°F.

Halesia carolina (Carolina silverbell): grows to 40 feet. Pyramidal to round-topped. Coarse, open foliage, with oval or ovate leaves to 5 inches long. White bell-shaped flowers ¾ inch long in mid-May. Dry, three- to four-winged pod fruit, 2 inches long in fall. Yellow in autumn. Hardiness: −10 to −5°F.

H. monticola (mountain silverbell): grows to 100 feet. Pyramidal to round-topped. Coarse, open foliage, with oval or oblong leaves to 11 inches in length. White bell-shaped flowers to one inch long in mid-May. Two-inch long fruit on a two- to four-winged pod. Yellow in autumn. Hardiness: −10 to −5°F.

Ilex opaca * (American holly): grows to 50 feet. Pyramidal. Densely branching. Evergreen foliage, with spiny, dense, unlustrous leaves. Smooth light gray bark. Bright red berries ¼ inch in diameter on female plants of current year's growth in fall and early winter. Hardiness: −10 to −5°F.

Juniperus virginiana * (red cedar): grows to 100 feet. Densely pyramidal and often columnar. Evergreen, scalelike; foliage varies greatly. Bark shreds in long strips. Female plants have berries ¼ inch in diameter, ripening the first season in fall and winter. Hardiness: −50 to −35°F.

Libocedrus decurrens * (California incense cedar): grows over 100 feet. Fine columnar habit; evergreen, scalelike leaves. Good ornamental tree. Hardiness: −10 to −5°F.

Liquidambar styraciflua (sweetgum): grows to 140 feet. Broadly pyramidal and star-shaped. Dense foliage, with leaves of five to seven lobes. Branches often have corky twigs. Deeply furrowed bark. Fruit and round horned balls one inch in diameter in fall. Scarlet in autumn. Hardiness: −10 to −5°F.

Liriodendron tulipifera (tulip tree): grows to 200 feet. Broadly pyramidal. Massive branches. Eventually has a columnar, unbranched trunk. Dense foliage with square-shaped leaves. Greenish-yellow flowers marked with orange, tulip-shaped, in mid-June. Dry pods 2 to 3 inches long. Yellow in autumn. Hardiness: −20 to −10°F.

Magnolia acuminata (cucumber tree): grows to 100 feet. Pyramidal and upright while young; massive, with wide-reaching branches at maturity. Dense leaves 5 to 10 inches long. The rather inconspicuous flowers are greenish-yellow and 3 inches high in early June, fruit pink to red in peculiar cucumber-shaped shells in early fall. Hardiness: −20 to −10 °F.

M. grandiflora (Southern magnolia): grows to 100 feet. Pyramidal. Usually dense and evergreen. Leaves 5 to 8 inches long and dropping at end of second year. White, fragrant flowers 8 inches in diameter, with usually six petals in late May; peculiar cucumberlike pods split open to disclose red seeds in early fall. Hardiness: −5 to −10 °F.

M. macrophylla (large-leaved cucumber tree): grows to 50 feet. Round-headed and open. Leaves are often 20 to 30 inches long and 10 inches wide and very coarse. Fragrant, creamy white flowers are 10 to 12 inches in diameter with six petals in early July. Fruit in peculiar cucumberlike pods split open to reveal red seeds in early fall. Hardiness: −10 to −5 °F.

M. virginiana (sweet bay): grows to 60 feet. Tree in the South; shrub in the North. Half evergreen in the South, green above and white below. Oblong leaves are 2½ to 4½ inches long. Fragrant white flowers with leaves 2 to 3 inches in diameter in June. Cucumber pods split open in early fall to disclose red seeds. Hardiness: −10 to −5 °F.

Oxydendrum arboreum (sorrel tree): grows to 75 feet. Pyramidal. Lustrous, dense, and leathery foliage. Small white flowers in slightly pendulous racemes in mid-July. Fruit in dried capsules far into the winter. Brilliant scarlet in autumn. Hardiness: −20 to −10 °F.

Picea glauca ° (white spruce): grows to 90 feet. Pyramidal evergreen with light bluish-green needles. Hardiness: −50 to −35 °F.

P. g. conica ° (dwarf white spruce): grows to 10 feet. Pyramidal and compact evergreen, with needles light bluish-green. Hardiness: −35 to −20 °F.

Pinus ponderosa ° (Western yellow pine): grows to 150 feet. Upright, open, and evergreen with two or three needles 5 to 11 inches long in a bundle. Ovoid-oblong cones are to 6 inches long. Hardiness: −10 to −5 °F.

P. strobus (white pine): grows to 150 feet. Rounded or pyramidal. Evergreen with five soft and flexible needles 2½ to 5½ inches long in a bundle. Cylindric cones are to 4 inches long. Hardiness: −35 to −20 °F.

Prunus americana (American plum): grows to 30 feet. Ovate, dull, and sharply serrated leaves. Flowers are about one inch across with calyx-lobes (not glandular). Fruit, which is about ¾ inch in diameter but in some strains larger, is yellow or red. Hardiness: −35 to −20 °F.

Pseudotsuga menziesii ° (Douglas fir): grows to 300 feet. Pyramidal. Branching and horizontal evergreen, with needlelike and dense foliage. Fruit and pendulous cones 2 to 4½ inches long in fall and winter. Hardiness: −10 to −5 °F.

Quercus alba (white oak): grows to 100 feet. Broad round head. Wide spreading branches. Dense foliage that is purplish-red to violet purple in autumn. Deciduous, ovate leaves to 9 inches long, with five to nine entirely obtruse lobes. Hardiness: −20 to −10 °F.

Q. coccinea (scarlet oak): grows to 80 feet. Open and round-topped head. Rather lustrous but open foliage that is brilliant scarlet in autumn. Bright green deciduous, oblong, or elliptic leaves to 6 inches in length, seven to nine very deep lobes. Hardiness: −20 to −10 °F.

Robinia pseudoacacia (black acacia): grows to 80 feet. Upright. Few branches. Open foliage with seven to nine oval leaflets. Fragrant white flowers in pendulous clusters in May–June. Reddish-brown, pods to 4 inches long. Hardiness: −35 to −20 °F.

Salix nigra (black willow): grows to 35 feet. Lance-shaped leaves to 5 inches long, pale green underneath. Hardiness: −20 to −10 °F.

Sorbus americana (American mountain ash): grows to 30 feet. Leaves have eleven to seventeen leaflets and are to 4 inches long. Flowers are about 1/5 inch across. Hardiness: −50 to −35 °F.

Stewartia ovata (mountain stewartia): grows to 15 feet. Shrub. Flowers are to 3 inches across, with white stamens and orange anthers. Hardiness: −10 to −5 °F.

Taxus brevifolia° (Western yew): grows to 45 feet. Dark yellowish-green leaves are one inch or less in length and are abruptly pointed. Fruit in August–September. Hardiness: −50 to −35 °F.

T. canadensis° (ground hemlock): grows to 6 feet. Dark yellowish-green, sharply pointed leaves are one inch long. Fruit in August. Hardiness: −50 to −35 °F.

Thuja occidentalis (American arborvitae): grows to 60 feet. Almost columnar. Evergreen with scalelike and flat foliage. Glandular leaves are yellowish-green beneath. Cones are ½ inch long. Hardiness: −50 to −35 °F.

Tilia americana (American linden): grows to 120 feet. Narrowly pyramidal. Broad-ovate leaves to 6 inches or more in length. Leaves are acuminate, with long-pointed teeth and glabrous beneath. Turn yellow in autumn. Hardiness: −50 to −35 °F.

Tsuga canadensis° (Northern hemlock): grows to 90 feet. Long, slender, and horizontal to sometimes drooping branches from a pyramidal head. Evergreen, dense, needlelike foliage. Stalked cones are to ¾ inch long. Hardiness: −35 to −20 °F.

T. caroliniana° (Southern hemlock): grows to 75 feet. Compact, pyramidal. Often with somewhat pendulous branches. Evergreen, needlelike, and dense foliage. Leaves entire, obtuse, or slightly notched at apex, glossy dark green above. Cones to 1½ inch long. Hardiness: −30 to −10 °F.

Ulmus americana (American elm): grows to 100 feet. Vase-shaped with arching branches. Leaves lobed and toothed. Hardiness: −50 to −35 °F.

Shrubs

Azalea arborescens (Rhododendron sweet azalea): grows to 10 feet. Bright green foliage that turns dark glossy red in autumn. Leaves to 3 inches long. White, very fragrant flowers in mid-June. Hardiness: −20 to −10 °F.

A. R. calendulaceum (flame azalea): grows to 10, rarely 15 feet. Deciduous. Leaves to 3 inches long, pubescent when young. Orange-yellow to scarlet, funnel-shaped flowers 2 inches across in May–June. Hardiness: −20 to −10 °F.

A. R. canadense (rhodora): grows to 3 feet. Dull bluish-green foliage. Leaves are about 2 inches long. Rose-purple, two-lipped flowers to ¾ inch long in mid-May. Hardiness: −50 to −35 °F.

A. R. catawbiense (catawba rhododendron): great clusters of rose-purple flowers and shiny green leaves. Magnificent native and well-liked. Grows well in partial shade and moist soil. Hardiness: −20 to −10 °F.

A. R. macrophyllum: handsome western native that grows to 10 feet; pink or almost purple flowers. Hardiness: −20 to −10 °F.

A. R. maximum: spreading shrub that grows to 10 feet. Pale rose flowers in July (which is rather late for rhododendrons). Hardiness: −30 to −20 °F.

A. R. nudiflorum (pinxter flower): grows to 6 feet. Deciduous; leaves to 3 inches long, glabrous and green underneath or hairy on the midrib. Flowers, pink to nearly white, are funnel-shaped, 1½ inches across, and bloom April to May. Hardiness: −35 to −20 °F.

A. R. occidentale (Western azalea): grows to 10 feet. Deciduous. Leaves to 4 inches long. White or pinkish flowers, with a yellow blotch, 1½ to 2 inches in diameter in late May. Scarlet and yellow in autumn. Hardiness: −10 to −5 °F.

A. R. roseum (rosehall azalea): grows to 9 feet. Dull bluish-green foliage. Fragrant bright pink flowers are 2 inches in diameter and bloom in late May. At one time considered a form of *R. nudiflorum*. Hardiness: −35 to −20 °F.

A. R. vasey (pinkshell azalea): grows to 15 feet. Deciduous. Five-inch leaves. Rose spotted with brown, two-lipped flowers are 1½ inches across and bloom in mid-May. Light red in autumn. Hardiness: −20 to −10 °F.

A. R. viscosum (white swamp honeysuckle): grows to 9, rarely 15 feet. Deciduous. Leaves to 2½ inches long. White or suffused with pink, very fragrant flowers in early July. Orange to bronze in autumn. Hardiness: −35 to −20 °F.

Other Shrubs to Try

Aesculus parviflora (bottle brush buckeye): grows to 12 feet. Five to seven, nearly sessile, leaflets. Small white or pinkish flowers in panicles to one inch long in mid-July. Hardiness: −10 to −5 °F.

*Andromeda polifolia** (bog-rosemary): grows 1 to 2 feet. Creeping rootstocks. Oblong to linear leaves to 1½ inches long, with revolute margins. Flowers are white to pinkish, in small terminal clusters, and to ¼ inch in length. Hardiness: −50 to −35°F.

Aronia arbutifolia (red chokeberry): grows to 10 feet. Gray leaves; white or reddish flowers less than ½ inch in diameter bloom in late May. Bright red berries, less than ½ inch in diameter in fall. Red leaves in the autumn. Hardiness: −20 to −10°F.

Calycanthus floridus (Carolina allspice): grows to 10 feet. Ovate or elliptic leaves to 5 inches long, densely pubescent, and pale beneath; 2-inch flowers are dark reddish-brown. Yellowish in autumn. Hardiness: −20 to −10°F.

Ceanothus americanus (New Jersey tea): grows to 3 feet. Alternate ovate and finely toothed leaves. Small white flowers in upright oblong clusters in mid-June. Hardiness: −20 to −10°F.

*C. velutinus** (snow bush): grows to 15 feet. Alternate, elliptic, and finely toothed leaves, shining above and somewhat hairy beneath. White flowers. Hardiness: −5 to −10°F.

Cephalanthus occidentalis (buttonball bush): grows to 20 feet. Ovate to oval-lanceolate leaves to 6 inches long, shining above. Creamy white flowers in round heads about one inch in diameter in late July. Hardiness: −20 to −10°F.

Clethra alnifolia (summersweet clethra): grows to 10 feet. Ovate, obtuse, or acute leaves 4 inches long. Erect, usually panicled racemes. Yellow to orange in autumn. Hardiness: −35 to −20°F.

Cornus amomum (silky dogwood): grows to 8 feet. Elliptical leaves. Creamy white flowers. Grows in wet places along streams. Hardiness: −30 to −20°F.

C. stolonifera (red osier dogwood): grows to 10 feet. Dark red branches that spread by underground stems. Ovate or ovate-lanceolate leaves to 5 inches long. White or bluish flowers. Hardiness: −50 to −35°F.

Corylus americana (American hazelnut): grows to 10 feet. Leaves to 5 inches long, pubescent beneath. Two to six fruits; the involucre is about twice the length of the nut, with deep irregular lobes. Hardiness: −20 to −10°F.

Dirca palustris (leatherwood): grows to 8 feet in rich moist woods. Very early yellow bloom in May–June. Good for shady spots, woods, or gardens along paths. Hardiness: −10 to −5°F.

Elaeagnus commutata (silverberry): grows to 12 feet. Deciduous. Silvery leaves. One to three fragrant flowers in axils in May–June. Silvery fruit on very short stalks. Hardiness: Below −50°F.

Euonymus americanus (strawberry bush): grows to 6 feet, in woods along stream banks. Leaves egg-shaped and bright green. Flowers greenish-purple in May or June. Hardiness: −5 to 5°F.

Fothergilla gardeni (dwarf fothergilla): grows to 3 feet. Ovate to oblong leaves with rounded or broadly cuneate base to 2 inches long; pale beneath. White flowers over one inch long in terminal spikes in mid-May. Brilliant yellow to scarlet in autumn. Hardiness: −10 to −5 °F.

F. major (large fothergilla): grows to 10 feet. Leaves to 4 inches long, pubescent beneath. White flowers with leaves in terminal flower spikes often 2 inches long in mid-May. Brilliant yellow to scarlet in autumn. Hardiness: −10 to −5 °F.

F. monticola: fragrant white flowers like bottlebrushes; good yellow fall color and for foundation plantings. Needs moisture. Hardiness: −5 to 5 °F.

Gaylussacia brachycera * (box huckleberry): grows to 1½ feet. Evergreen foliage. Leaves to one inch long. White or pink, small, bell-shaped flowers in mid-May. Fruit is blue berry. Hardiness: −10 to −5 °F.

Hamamelis vernalis (spring witch-hazel): grows to 10 feet. Leaves to 5 inches long are nearly glabrous beneath. Yellow to reddish, ribbonlike, fragrant flowers to ½ inch long in January–March. Yellow in autumn. Hardiness: −10 to −5 °F.

H. virginiana (common witch-hazel): grows to 15 feet. Leaves to 6 feet long, pubescent only on veins beneath. Yellow flowers with ribbonlike petals to ¾ inch long in early October. Yellow in autumn. Hardiness: −10 to −5 °F.

Hydrangea arborescens (wild hydrangea): grows to 10 feet. Ovate leaves, to 8 inches long, are glabrous or slightly pubescent beneath. White flowers in rounded or globular clusters to 6 inches across in June–July. Hardiness: −20 to −10 °F.

H. arborescens grandiflora (hills of snow): grows to 3 feet. White flowers in large rounded clusters about 6 inches in diameter in early July. Hardiness: −20 to −10 °F.

H. quercifolia (oakleaf hydrangea): white summer flowers turn purplish with age. Dark red fall foliage. Needs shade. Good for house corners, and northern exposures. Hardiness: −5 to 5 °F.

Hypericum kalmianum (shrubby St. John's wort): bright yellow summer bloom even if tops winter-kill. Good for low informal hedge or fronting higher shrubs. Tolerates partial shade. Hardiness: −10 to −5 °F.

Ilex glabra * (inkberry): grows to 9 feet. Lustrous foliage. Dark leaves to 2 inches. Inconspicuous, often solitary flowers (sexes separate) in mid-June. Fruit is small black berries ¼ inch in diameter in fall. Hardiness: −35 to −20 °F.

I. verticillata (winterberry): grows to 10 feet. Deciduous. Oval to lanceolate, toothed leaves, pubescent beneath, at least on nerves. Inconspicuous flowers (sexes separate) in June–July. Fruit is bright red berries, ¼ inch in diameter in fall and winter. Hardiness: −35 to −20 °F.

I. vomitoria * (yaupon): can grow to 20 feet. Prefers sandy dunes. Leaves lustrous green. Flowers greenish-white in spring. Fruit is bright red in fall. Hardiness: 0 to 10 °F.

Itea virginica (sweet spire): grows to 10 feet. Deciduous. Finely toothed leaves to 4 inches long. White, fragrant flowers in upright dense racemes 2 to 6 inches long in June–July. Brilliant red in autumn. Hardiness: −10 to −5°F.

Kalmia latifolia° (mountain laurel): grows to 30 feet. Evergreen foliage. Leaves to 5 inches long. Pink and white flowers in large clusters in mid-June. Hardiness: −35 to −20°F.

Leucothoe catesbaei° (fetterbush): grows to 6 feet. Shining ovate-lanceolate to lance-ovate leaves to 7 inches long. White flowers in racemes to 3 inches long in April–May. Hardiness: −20 to −10°F.

Lindera benzoin (spice bush): grows to 15 feet. Deciduous. Oblong-ovate leaves to 5 inches long, turn yellow in autumn. Petiole usually less than ¾ inch long. Greenish-yellow, dense flowers in mid-April. Fruit is scarlet berries in early fall. Hardiness: −20 to −10°F.

Mahonia aquifolium° (holly mahonia): grows to 3, rarely 6 feet. Bronze to purplish in autumn. Semi- to evergreen. Lustrous dark green foliage. Five to nine ovate leaflets to 3 inches long. Petioles to 2 inches long. Bright yellow flowers in spikes or pyramidal clusters in early May. Bluish-black fruitlike small grapes. *M. nervosa* (cascades mahonia), somewhat similar but smaller. Hardiness: −20 to −10°F.

Myrica caroliniensis° (Northern bayberry): grows to 9 feet. Ovate, deciduous or sometimes evergreen leaves, to 4 inches long.

Does well in poor soil. Hardiness: Hardy to −50°F.

M. pennsylvanica° (bayberry): grows to 9 feet. Deciduous or sometimes evergreen. Ovate, acute, or obtuse leaves to 4 inches long. Fruit is small gray berries (sexes separate) in fall and winter. Hardiness: Hardy to −50°F.

Philadelphus inodorus (mock orange): grows to 10 feet growing on rocky slopes and along streams. Egg-shaped leaves pointed at tip. White flowers in May or June. Many garden varieties. Hardiness: −30 to −20°F.

Pieris floribunda° (andromeda): grows to 6 feet. Hairy branches. Cilate leaves. White flowers in nodding pyramidal clusters to 4 inches high. Small fruitlike blueberries in late April. Hardiness: −20 to −10°F.

Potentilla fruticosa (shrubby cinquefoil): growing in rocky or moist places, this 3-foot shrub has bright yellow flowers in June to September. Hardiness: −50 to −35°F.

Salix discolor (pussy willow): grows to 20 feet. Oblong, wavy-toothed, or nearly entire leaves to 4 inches long, glaucous beneath. Catkins appear before the leaves. Hardiness: −35 to −20°F.

Sambucus canadensis (American elder): grows to 12 feet. Oval or lanceolate leaves. Leaflets to 6 inches long. Small white flowers in large flat clusters 6 to 8 inches in diameter in late June. Fruit is blue to black small berries in large clusters in late summer. Hardiness: −35 to −20 °F.

Symphoricarpos albus (snowberry): grows to 5 feet, on dog-wooded slopes and banks. Green, somewhat wavy leaves. Pink flowers May to July. Round white berries in fall. Hardiness: −20 to −10 °F.

S. orbiculatus (Indian currant): grows to 6 feet. Oval or ovate leaves to 2½ inches long, glaucous and usually pubescent beneath. Small, dense, yellowish white, and bell-shaped flowers, 1/6 inch long in May–June. Fruit is purplish-red, corallike berries in fall. Hardiness: −50 to −35 °F.

Vaccinium corymbosum (swamp blueberry): grows to 15 feet. Deciduous. Long, ovate-lanceolate leaves to 3 inches, glabrous to pubescent. White or pinkish flowers to ⅓ inch long in clusters in May. Fruit is blue-black berries. Scarlet in autumn, red twigs in winter. Hardiness: −35 to −20 °F.

Viburnum acerifolium (maple-leaf viburnum): grows to 6 feet. Three-lobed, maplelike, coarsely toothed leaves to 5 inches long. Yellowish to white small flowers in flat clusters in mid-June. Fruit is black berries in fall. Purplish in autumn. Hardiness: −35 to −20 °F.

V. dentatum (arrowwood viburnum): grows to 15 feet. Toothed glossy green foliage; creamy white flowers in clusters. Blue berries in fall. Hardiness: −50 to −35 °F.

V. lantana (hobble bush): grows to 15 feet. Ovate, finely toothed leaves to 5 inches long. White flowers to 4 inches across in May–June. Red fruit turns black. Hardiness: −30 to −20 °F.

V. lentago (nanny berry): grows to 30 feet. Ovate, finely toothed leaves to 4 inches long. White flowers in flat clusters to 5 inches across in late May. Fruit is black berries in fall and winter. Purplish red in autumn. Hardiness: −20 to −20 °F.

V. prunifolium (black haw): grows to 15 feet. Ovate or broad-oval, finely toothed leaves to 3 inches long. White flowers in flat clusters to 4 inches across in mid-May. Fruit is blue-black berries in fall. Shining red in autumn. Hardiness: −30 to −20 °F.

V. trilobum (American cranberry bush): grows to 12 feet. Broad, ovate, three-lobed, and coarsely toothed leaves to 5 inches long. White flowers in flat clusters to 4 inches across in May–June. (Flowers are sterile.) Fruit is scarlet, berries in fall and winter. Hardiness: −30 to −20 °F.

18 🌿

The Rose Garden
BY CHARLES MORDEN FITCH

ROSES are America's favorite flower according to a recent nationwide survey. Fragrance, color, adaptability, and a long season of bloom are well appreciated features in modern roses. Even old-fashioned roses are being grown by an increasing number of gardeners although the older roses usually have a short season of bloom. Miniature roses are now the largest category seen in rose shows, a testimony to the charm and adaptability of these hardy yet diminutive roses, now available in so many colors.

Modern hybridizers, working with all classes of roses, have succeeded in creating an outstanding array of rose forms, usually coupled with improved texture, substance, color, and increased cold hardiness. The breeder may manage to retain or even intensify fragrance in new hybrids, but the trend has been to put more emphasis on disease resistance, color, form, floriferousness, and winter hardiness.

Fortunately you will find at least three or four very fragrant hybrids in each color group, so all of your roses can be pleasantly perfumed if you desire. Read the catalogs carefully to identify which new offerings are fragrant.

The Seashell, a hybrid tea rose.

GROWTH HABITS

"Si," my smallest rose, is only four inches tall. Miniature Si has pink buds the size of a rice grain which open to light pink ¼ to ½ inch flowers. My largest rose bush is a huge rambler with 15 to 20 foot canes gracefully arching over a waterside embankment. Every spring the rambler is covered with fragrant single white flowers followed by fat orange fruit (hips) which persist into the winter, looking festive against the snow, and providing food for the birds.

The four-inch bush and 20-foot rambler are rose extremes. Most floribunda and hybrid tea types grow two to four feet tall. You are sure to find a rose suited to your garden plans. Officially the American Rose Society divides roses into seven broad groups: Hybrid Teas (single to double flowers with long high buds produced singly or several together, often with long stems suited to cut flower use), Floribundas (wide range of growth styles but all featuring floriferous habit, bushy branching, and a long season of bloom), Grandifloras (free-flowering habit of the floribundas combined with classic bud shape of hybrid teas, but usually taller than hybrid tea bushes), Miniatures (small bushes with ¼ to two-inch flowers which come in many different forms and colors, representative of larger roses but always dwarf growth

Rose gardens are always a welcome addition to any setting.

Even a few roses can add that necessary color in a small garden. (M. Barr)

habit), Climbers and Rambler (noted for long stems, abundant display of flowers, often rambling versions of popular hybrid tea or miniature clones), Shrub and Old-Fashioned types (wide range of bushy growth styles, usually with seasonal bloom rather than all-season flowering, many types very adaptable and disease resistant), and Polyanthas (cluster-flowered, bushy habit).

NATIONAL TESTS

For many years the American Rose Society has conducted growing tests in all regions of the United States to determine which roses are most suitable for various uses. An excellent guide, the *Handbook for Selecting Roses* is published by the A. R. S. each year. You may obtain a copy of this helpful booklet by sending a self-addressed stamped envelope and 25 cents to the American Rose Society at P.O. Box 30,000 in Shreveport, Louisiana 71130.

The booklet lists hundreds of roses under a detailed system of classification which notes color, growth habit, and a rating number based on the national test reports. A special section features the highest rated commercially available roses, a useful guide in selecting roses suitable for any given situation.

RECOMMENDATIONS

After many years of growing roses in my New York garden, and studying other rose plantings around the world, I have found a few roses that are especially adaptable. These sturdy yet beautiful varieties are the most likely to survive and produce an abundance of color with minimum care.

The Fairy: a light pink double-flowered Polyantha hybrid which blooms from early season into late fall. Very resistant to disease, lightly perfumed, excellent for cut flowers, beautiful as rambling bush or as grafted tree rose, tough and winter hardy. Flower color deepens with cool fall weather.

Seafoam: a white-flowered shrub with spreading habit, low, suited to ground cover applications but also good for cut flowers or as an easy to grow long-season show in the garden.

Sparrieshoop: a light pink single flowered shrub rose from Germany. The habit is upright, with long gracefully arching stems, flowers all season long, attractive fruits, and very disease resistant.

Within the most popular classes the cultivars that have proven themselves over a period of years include:

Hybrid Teas Garden Party (creamy-white with pink blush, fragrant, very large double blooms)
Peace (outstanding blend of yellow, pink, creamy white, large fragrant, an international favorite)
Floribundas Europeana (brilliant red double-flowered hybrid with great vigor, slightly fragrant)
Fashion (fragrant coral-peach, good as beautifully shaped cut flower)
Grandifloras Montezuma (slightly perfumed double flower in salmon-rose color)
Queen Elizabeth (lightly fragrant rich pink double, good as cut flower or garden show)
Climbers Blaze (brilliant red double, slightly fragrant)

The Yankee Doodle hybrid tea rose.

America (relatively new but proven adaptable, salmon-pink double-flowered hybrid with spicy perfume, good as cut flower too)
Miniatures Cinderella (double white with pink blush, bushy)
Golden Angel (fragrant, floriferous)
Magic Carrousel (white with red edges, very double, fragrant, disease-resistant, outstanding as Patio Tree rose graft)

In special situations along the coast choose *Rosa rugosa* hybrids which are adapted to coastal conditions, produce thick leathery leaves, bright white, pink, or purple-red flowers followed by long-lasting fruit.

TREE ROSES

Roses are grafted on stiff upright stems of sturdy hybrids (often Dr. Huey or a *Rosa multi flora* hybrid cultivar) to form a rose tree. The root stock is different from the select hybrid on top but only the top is permitted to leaf out and grow. You can obtain these trees in several different sizes.

Miniature rose specialists offer a dwarf tree about eight inches tall with tops of popular miniatures such as fragrant Lavender Lace or bright golden Rise n' Shine. A slightly taller 18-inch stem is occasionally offered, too. Garden centers and a few mail-order nurseries offer Patio Tree roses, sturdy winter-hardy grafts on 36-inch stems. I like the Patio Tree roses as accents in the garden. Excellent types to have on Patio Trees are Polyantha's The Fairy and the modern miniatures such as Red Cascade or Magic Carrousel. Tree roses are also suitable for terrace decoration but the pots should be sunk below the frost line during cold months where winters are severe.

Planting Sites

Plant roses where they will receive at least four hours of direct sun each day. A few of the miniatures and old-fashioned shrub hybrids may produce flowers with less light but the popular showy modern hybrids need strong sun to do their best. Roses will thrive in raised beds, lawn borders, big outdoor containers, formal beds, shrub borders, in mixed plantings with annuals, just about anywhere they receive bright sun and adequate water.

Season to Plant

The spring is a good time to plant roses, just before the stems begin to sprout. During the growing season container-grown roses can be planted without setback if you avoid breaking the rootball.

Fall planting is practical where winters are not severe. When receiving bare-root roses, soak the roots in a warm water transplanting solution at least six hours and up to 24 hours before planting them. Make a transplanting solution by mixing ¼ teaspoon of balanced water soluble fertilizer per gallon of water with a commercially available root stimulant such as Transplantone.

Prepare the Soil

Give your roses the opportunity to produce a maximum show for many years by carefully preparing the soil at planting time. Dig each hole several inches larger than the root system or about 15 to 18 inches wide and deep for hybrid teas or eight to 12 inches for miniatures. I like to put all the soil from the hole into a wheel barrow or big mixing bin, then thoroughly stir in ⅓ rough sphagnum peatmoss.

To this ⅔ soil plus ⅓ sphagnum peat moss I add a sprinkling of gypsum powder and a

Formal Rose Garden

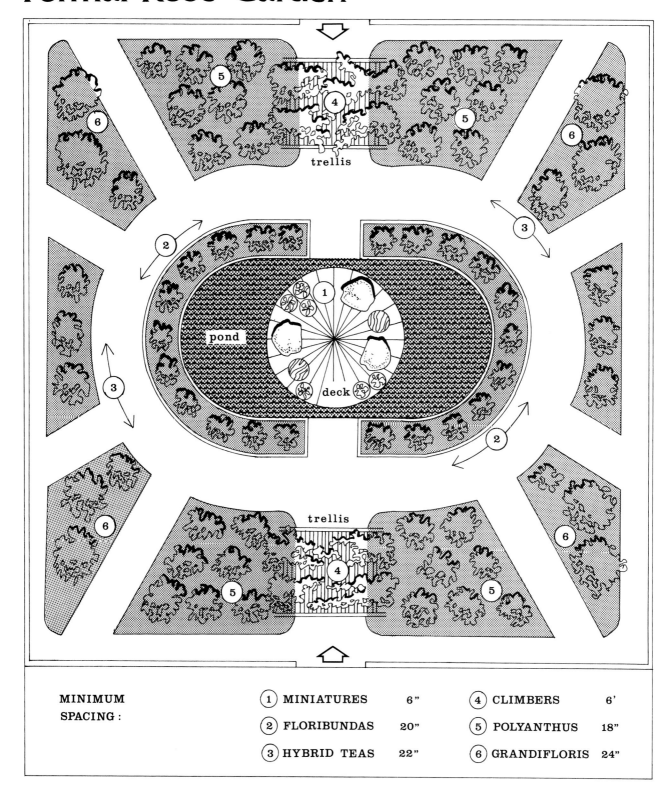

MINIMUM SPACING :					
(1) MINIATURES	6"	(4) CLIMBERS	6'
(2) FLORIBUNDAS	20"	(5) POLYANTHUS	18"
(3) HYBRID TEAS	22"	(6) GRANDIFLORIS	24"

three-gallon bucket of perlite/vermiculite (50–50) in each wheel barrow mix. The perlite loosens soil structure (soil in my garden is clay-loam) and the vermiculite will hold extra moisture. How much perlite and vermiculite you use will depend on the structure of your garden loam. Heavy soils will require more perlite while sandy soils can be improved with more vermiculite and peatmoss.

Roses do best in soil that is slightly acid (pH 5.6 to 6.5). If your soil is too acid add dolomite limestone; if soil is too alkaline dig in extra sphagnum peatmoss, then fertilize with an acid fertilizer. If your garden soil now supports healthy iris, peonies, and other perennials it will support healthy roses without major applications to change the pH.

Planting Techniques

Form a slight mound of prepared soil mix in the center of each hole. Spread the roots over this mound, carefully spreading the roots around the sides, then cover the roots with your prepared soil mixture about ¾ full. Water thoroughly with a transplanting solution to settle the soil. Now add more soil until the hole is full. Water again to settle the soil around all roots to eliminate air pockets. Tamp the soil around each bush once water is absorbed.

The transplanting solution recommended as a pre-planting soak is the same type to use for planting and transplanting at any time of the year. A stimulant such as Transplantone or Dexol Plant Starter with Vitamin B_1 mixed with ⅓ strength water soluble fertilizer helps get roses off to an excellent start. Ortho Up-Start is another commercial product that stimulates roots but the Ortho solution already contains a fertilizer so use it as

supplied, without added fertilizer at transplanting time.

After watering-in the bushes, mound soil around each stem to protect them from drying out during dry sunny and windy weather. Prune back canes to about eight to 12 inches tall.

Container-grown roses already leafed out need not be mounded but the mound is important for spring or fall planted bare-root bushes, especially in cold or dry climates. Once bushes start growth, the mounded soil can gradually be leveled over a period of weeks using a strong stream of water from your garden hose.

Mulch

Mulch protects the soil from drying out too fast, stops soil from splattering on leaves, and, if it is an organic mulch, enriches the soil as it decomposes.

I use salt hay or bark chips (fir and pine) around roses in garden beds, oak leaf compost around large roses in borders or on slopes. Other suitable materials for mulch include hay, buckwheat hulls, ground sugar cane, and partially rotted compost. Inorganic mulches practical for roses are pebbles or gravel, and the various plastic sheets sold in garden stores as mulch, although I feel these plastics are not attractive. In very dry climates you might elect to use a plastic mulch which is efficient and cheap, then make it more attractive by covering the plastic with bark or hay.

Watering and Fertilizing

Roses need an abundant supply of water to produce a maximum display. Lack of water means smaller flowers and debilitating leaf loss. An inch or two of water every week during the growing season, to produce an

Planting Bare Root Roses

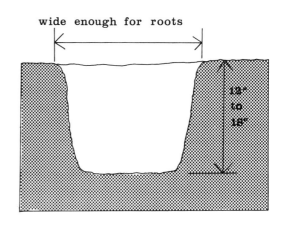

wide enough for roots

12" to 18"

(1) PRUNE & TRIM BROKEN ROOTS & BRANCHES.

(2) SOAK ROOTS FOR A FEW HOURS; DIG HOLE.

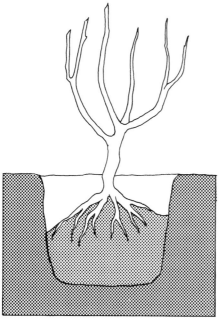

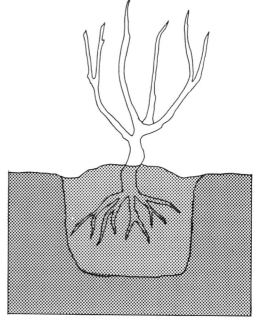

(3) MOUND SOIL; SPREAD ROOTS OVER.

(4) COMPLETE FILLING; WATER.

evenly moist but not soggy soil, results in healthy foliage and an abundance of top sized flowers. Apply water with soakers, sprinklers, or hand-held hose; which you choose often depends on the size of your collection and local climate. In areas where black spot fungus is a problem it is wise to avoid wetting the leaves, especially just before sunset, so ground watering soakers are best.

During the growing season apply a balanced water soluble rose fertilizer according to package directions, but only when bushes have moist soil. Spraying fertilizer solution on the foliage encourages good color and size in leaves. For an easy way to fertilize roses apply the timed release pellets which release nutrients gradually, according to water and temperature, over a period of many weeks.

Suitable formulas are offered by several national companies and the packages show complete directions. One handy product from Ortho combines a balanced timed release rose fertilizer with a relatively safe systemic insecticide to protect roses from sucking pests.

Fertilizers are aids to bushes being grown under suitable conditions but do not rely on fertilizers to make up for lack of sun or water. When water and sun are abundant then fertilizers can be fully utilized by the roses for sturdy floriferous growths.

In cold climates stop fertilizing roses by the end of August, to avoid encouraging new growth that will be killed by frosts. In the spring apply fertilizer just as leaf buds start to swell.

Pruning and Training

Pruning roses is much easier than you may imagine. The basic idea is to encourage new growth for flowers, and to remove dead or damaged canes, all while keeping the bush to a size you desire. Hybrid teas, floribundas, grandifloras, polyanthas, and most shrub hybrids are best pruned lightly in the fall, only enough to stop extra long canes from blowing around during winter storms.

In the spring, just as leaf buds begin to swell, use a sharp pair of top quality pruners to cut back canes ½ to ¾, depending on the size you wish to maintain in the bush. Actually, one can cut a healthy rose back to within a few inches of the ground and it will sprout again, but there is no need for such extreme pruning.

Cut away any canes that are causing congestion in the center of each bush. With large canes make the cuts just above an outward facing bud. This technique encourages new stems to grow outward, creating an attractive habit with adequate air circulation and room for the display of flowers. Such precision is not necessary in extra bushy shrub roses and indeed some miniature roses as well. Some miniature rose specialists prune their plants with hedge clippers every spring.

Pruning roses for show competition is more time consuming since one usually removes all but the strongest canes to produce the largest flowers possible in hybrid teas, grandifloras, and floribundas. Personal advice from a neighbor is offered free through the consulting rosarian plan of the American Rose Society. Experienced members of the A. R. S. volunteer to assist gardeners in their regions. To locate consulting rosarians in your area write to the local rose society or direct to the American Rose Society national headquarters in Shreveport, LA 71130. Local botanical gardens and rose test gardens often offer rose pruning demonstrations where you can actually see experts prune roses branch by branch.

Remember that some of the ground cover and shrub roses will thrive without any special pruning at all, short of removing the occasional cane that dies. Ramblers (climbers) of the hybrid tea type such as Climbing Peace need little pruning but will benefit from being trained along a fence. Train the long stems in a horizontal direction to encourage short upright stems all along the branch. These short new stems will produce the flowers. Climbing cultivars which have seasonal bloom are best cut back up to half their length after blooms fade. On cultivars which tend to repeat, as most modern hybrids do, cut off all flowers as they fade.

Winter Protection

If winters are severe in your region protect garden roses with the system recommended by your local rose society or botanical garden. The most popular method of protecting roses is hilling soil or compost around the stems. Loose soil and humus mixed together is placed over the bottom six to eight inches of each bush. The mound is then covered with salt hay, leaf mold, or straw. Apply protection in the late fall or early winter, just before hard frosts start.

Some old-fashioned shrub roses and new hybrids bred in the Plains states for extra winter hardiness (i.e., Griffith Buck hybrids) will not require protection to survive hard winters but hilling them will help to protect the bushes against heaving during spring thaws. In very severe climates tree roses will have to be buried below the frost line to protect the graft union. However, in regions where the temperature seldom stays below oF for more than a few days, tree roses will

survive with an above-the-ground wrap of burlap and straw, mainly to protect the graft from winter winds and drying sun.

Miniature roses are just as hardy as hybrid teas and much easier to protect for the winter. In my New York garden a loose oak leaf mulch covering the bushes is all that is needed to bring each tiny bush through the most severe winters.

Potted roses should be buried up to the pot rim, then covered with burlap or loose mulch of straw as protection from heaving, frozen roots, and drying winter winds. In the spring, just as buds begin to swell, start to remove protection, doing so gradually over a period of two to three weeks.

Preventing Disease

Roses are subject to fungus problems, especially mildew and black spot. In some parts of the country one disease may be no problem while in another region it must be constantly battled. General climate and day-to-day weather influence the fungus. Cool damp days encourage powdery mildew, although the spores do not grow directly in drops of water.

Black spot fungus, in contrast, spreads mainly in splashing water. Dry foliage seldom succumbs to black spot fungus. If you are not concerned with growing roses for show competition you can avoid having to spray with fungicides by selecting hybrids that are resistant to disease. Consult local rosarians and botanical gardens to determine adaptable cultivars that are most free from disease in your state.

If black spot is a problem on your roses then avoid wetting leaves when you water the bushes. Irrigate with on-ground soakers or hoses with water-breakers running on the

THE ROSE GARDEN · 281

soil directly. When black spot persists begin a spray program using benomyl or one of the general fungicides offered specifically for rose diseases. You will find these products at garden centers and in the catalogs of rose growers. Use them according to directions, never stronger or weaker.

Powdery mildew is a problem in my garden, because the climate is humid. Some cultivars always get powdery mildew while others hardly ever suffer, even when grown in the same bed. If you grow susceptible cultivars begin a spray program using folpet (Phaltan) or one of the brand name products recommended for powdery mildew in your part of the country. Here again the recommendations of local rose growers and county agents are available.

The effectiveness of various sprays differs from region to region. In my garden I use Phaltan and Benlate together as a control for black spot and powdery mildew. A few drops of fish emulsion in the spray solution helps active ingredients to stick on leaf surfaces. Powdery mildew is also discouraged if you wash away the mildew with a strong stream of water, although this technique will not stop the disease.

Controlling Pests

The two worst pests of roses are red spider mites, which suck sap from foliage, and beetles, which chew buds. A third troublesome pest is the thrip, an almost microscopic creature that disfigures flower buds. Aphids will also attack new growth and flower buds but these soft-bodied sucking insects can be washed away with a strong stream of water.

Control red spider mites by misting the bottom surface of leaves every few mornings during the growing season. Spider mites thrive under warm dry conditions. If mites are still a problem spray bushes with a specific miticide such as Kelthane or Malathion every seven to ten days, according to bottle directions. The mite spray must be repeated for three cycles with seven to ten days between each application for complete control. Since mites thrive when summers are dry you may find them a problem some years and not others. Chewing caterpillars can be safely controlled by spraying with Thuricide or a similar product containing *Bacillus thuringiensis*. This biocontrol spray causes paralysis of the pest's digestive tract. Japanese beetles can be controlled biologically by dusting the garden beds with a powder containing the milky-disease bacterium spore which attacks the beetle grubs. Doom is one such product.

I prefer to use biological controls that do not harm useful insects, humans, or wildlife. The bacillus products are useful and safe but will not control spider mites.

The next safest way to control sucking pests or chewing insects is with a systemic poison which is absorbed by plant roots. For example Ortho Systemic Rose and Flower Care is a dry granular product with 8-12-4 balanced fertilizer and a systemic insecticide, Di-Syston, which will feed and protect roses for six weeks.

Roots absorb the toxic substance, then pests that attack the rose are killed while harmless creatures are not bothered. A specific liquid spray applied to control pests is biologically preferable to general weekly spraying as a prevention against pests. I prefer sharing my roses with a few "pests" to a constant insecticide spray program which may also kill useful creatures and endanger humans.

Dust products are offered for rose protection but they cause a mess which looks unsightly for weeks. I see no advantage of dust over liquid or granular pesticides so I do not recommend dusts.

Propagation

You can grow roses from cuttings but modern hybrid offerings are sold as grafted bushes, except for miniatures. Species roses are fun to grow from seed and you will see flowers the first season. The most practical roses to grow from seed are miniature strains of *Rosa rouletii* which have very fragrant flowers in shades from white into deep pink, usually followed by small red fruit clusters.

Seed of miniature roses is available from several national mail order nursery catalogs. The flowers on roses grown from *Rosa rouletii* or *R. multiflora nana* seed are charming but not of classic hybrid tea form which you will find in cutting-propagated miniature rose hybrids.

19 🖎

The Miracle of Plant Increase

THE WORD propagation sounds technical, and some of the processes—air layering, grafting, division, and seed sowing—can be complex. But propagation is simply a means of increasing plants. Some methods are so simple even a child can manage it, and does, when he sprinkles radish seed in a garden bed or sticks a piece of a geranium plant in a pot of soil. What complicates propagation is the number of methods. Propagation from seed is termed sexual, from the vegetative parts of a plant, asexual.

SEXUAL PROPAGATION

Flowers are lovely and a joy to look at but their purpose in nature is the production of seed that will perpetuate the species. Propagation by seed, the most common means, is also the quickest and least expensive. This sexual method produces seedlings that may vary somewhat in their characteristics since seeds do not always exactly reproduce their parents. But the variable seedlings may adapt better.

Seeds are actually fertilized embryos that, when mature, include rudimentary plants or embryos, protected seed coats, and nutrients to nourish growth. In flowers, two organs produce a seed: the stamen, which has pollen grains that will become the male cells, and the pistil, or female organ, which is generally in the center of the flower.

The word miracle aptly describes a seed. A seed is a veritable powerhouse of stored food that can, in many cases, even survive freezing and drought. When we sow seeds, we imitate nature and thus have her same problems. We must provide the proper conditions of temperature and moisture that will result in germination and growth.

Seeds come in various sizes, from the fine dust of some begonias to the pea-sized seeds of morning glories. Some seeds can catch the air and ride with the wind or, as with spruces, develop a catapult device that propels them for a hundred feet or more. Dandelion and milkweed seeds develop flimsy parasols of silky hairs; you have no doubt seen these tufts floating on the wind on breezy summer days. And some seeds, like those of the lotus, have a watertight coating that enables them to float for miles until they find a suitable place to germinate. Birds and animals also transport seeds.

What makes seeds grow? Different degrees of viability, water, air, temperature, age, and stage of maturity produce the proper life-starting combination. Heat may cook seeds, and cold, along with frost, may injure some of them. Thus, special conditions are necessary for germination: Proper humidity, ventilation, light, and moisture. The stages of germination involve absorption of moisture by the seed, favorable temperatures to transform stored food into sugars by enzymes or natural ferments, and the bursting of the seed coat.

A seed needs water because the plant foods it holds must be in solution if they are to be available to the embryo. Too little moisture or not enough will fail to do the trick, but an evenly moist soil that provides moderate moisture usually initiates the germination process. Light also has an effect; some seeds are indifferent to light exposure, others need light to start growth.

COMMERCIAL SEEDS—YOUR OWN SEEDS

Most gardeners buy processed and packaged seeds from suppliers. Of course you can gather seeds from your own plants, but unless they are taken from true species they will not produce replicas. Seeds from hybrids, the usual kinds in your garden, have been developed by crossing best with best. They will not produce plants exactly like their parents. They may even revert to some unsatisfactory characteristic of one of the parents used in their breeding, such as smaller flowers or poor color. As a rule, collect your own seeds when they are ripe; then clean and store them in a cool place until you are ready to sow. Some types, however, have to be gathered before they are fully ripe to prevent dispersal. With pines, for example, fully matured seed cones can open rapidly in warm spring weather and then the seeds are lost.

No special processing is needed with commercial seeds. They are ready for use when you get them, and commercial growers constantly seek new ways to bring the best strains to you. The commercial breeder knows exactly the proper stage of maturity for harvesting, the proper seed-collection methods, the proper means of cleaning and processing, and, most important, the proper way to store seeds so they will remain viable until you are ready to sow them.

ASEXUAL PROPAGATION

You have probably often practiced the method of asexual propagation. Have you ever cut a runner from a house plant like *chlorophytum* (Spider plant) or *Saxifraga sarmentosa* (strawberry geranium) and potted it in soil? Have you ever, when repotting a plant too large for its container, taken a chunk to grow separately? These are asexual methods of propagation, that is, the use of such vegetative parts as roots, stems, or leaves to produce new plants. The characteristics of the parent are thus passed on to the new plant because an exact duplication of chromosomes has occurred during cell division.

Taking cuttings of stem, leaf, or root is a most convenient way of getting new plants. A cutting can be taken in a few minutes, it does not harm the parent plant, and is ridiculously simple. But not all plants can be satisfactorily increased by cuttings; most stone fruits must be grafted or budded because cuttings do not strike root. The advantages of cuttings over seeds is that you often get stronger plants in less time and the new plants are assured duplicates of the parent.

For the indoor gardener, leaf propagation, that is, taking a leaf or piece of leaf from the parent and inserting it in a propagating mix, is another good method. African violets and begonias are frequently started in this way.

Outline of Methods

1. **Sexual**
   - Seed Sowing
   - Germination
   - Thinning
   - Transplanting
2. **Asexual Division**
   - Offsets
   - Crowns
   - Tubers
   - Rhizomes
   - Runners
3. **Cuttings**
   - Stem
   - Hardwood
   - Semihardwood
   - Softwood
   - Herbaceous
   - Root
   - Leaf
4. **Grafting**
   - Root
   - Crown
   - Top
5. **Layering**
   - Simple
   - Tip
   - Mound
   - Trench
   - Air

CUTTINGS

Getting new plants from cuttings is indeed easy if the cuttings are taken at a propitious time and then given proper care. A cutting is a section of a plant, a small portion of stem, root, or leaf. Different species are propagated in different ways. As a rule cuttings produce new plants identical to the parents. Shrubs and many evergreens are best propagated by cuttings; it's easier and faster. And many new plants can be started in a small space from just a few parent plants.

Types of Cuttings

Depending upon the part of the plant from which they are taken, cuttings can be classified as root, hardwood, softwood, semi-hardwood, and leaf. Because some plants can be propagated by several different methods, the type you select usually depends on what is easiest and least expensive. Some plants cannot root from soft cuttings; these must be hardened first, when the first flush of soft growth is over.

Cuttings of some plants can be rooted in water, but most need a rooting medium. There are various kinds, but a well-aerated sandy loam is usually preferred. Be sure the soil mix is sterile. Plain sand can also be used with good results, as can vermiculite, peat, shredded sphagnum moss, or a combination of these materials. Apply hormone- or growth-producing substances, powder or liquid, such as rootone. These preparations speed rooting and can be found at suppliers.

Cuttings can be started in a flower pot, a shallow box, or even a discarded aquarium. Make sure your container is at least four inches deep. To provide humidity, which most cuttings need, invert a jar over a flower pot (or put a Baggie in place). If you use a shallow box (flat) or an aquarium, place on top a pane of glass that is two inches shorter than the size of the container. Plastic wrap may also be used.

A hotbed or cold frame may also be used for cuttings during mild seasons of the year if they are shaded and protected from drafts.

Root

Plants that have thick and fleshy roots— wind-flower, butterfly weed, plumbago, bleeding-heart, summer phlox, and poppy— can be started from root cuttings. In fall, take the thick end of the fleshy root attached to the plant and remove the lower portion. Cut the first end square and the last end at a $45°$ angle about two inches down. Place the cuttings in soil in flats or in beds outdoors.

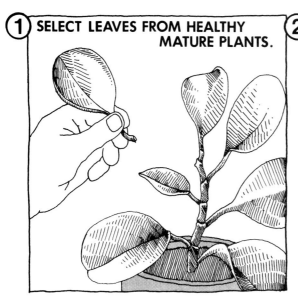

① SELECT LEAVES FROM HEALTHY MATURE PLANTS.

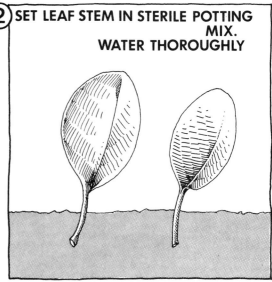

② SET LEAF STEM IN STERILE POTTING MIX. WATER THOROUGHLY

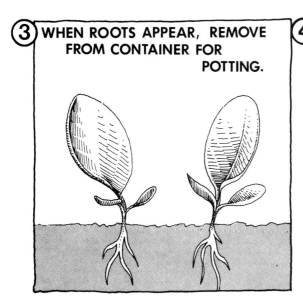

③ WHEN ROOTS APPEAR, REMOVE FROM CONTAINER FOR POTTING.

④ POT NEW PLANT IN POROUS SOIL.

STARTING PLANTS FROM LEAVES

Cover with half an inch of soil. Then it's a good idea to spread a light layer of leaves or hay (a mulch) over the soil to protect the cuttings from the cold or heavy rain. When leaves appear in spring, the newly rooted plants can be set permanently in the garden.

1. choose fresh, robust stems for cuttings—use sharp knife

2. trim bottom leaves

3. dip ends into root hormone powder

4. set cuttings in flats of sterile potting mix, then water

5. plant sticks alongside cuttings, then drape clear plastic over it

Starting Plants from Cuttings

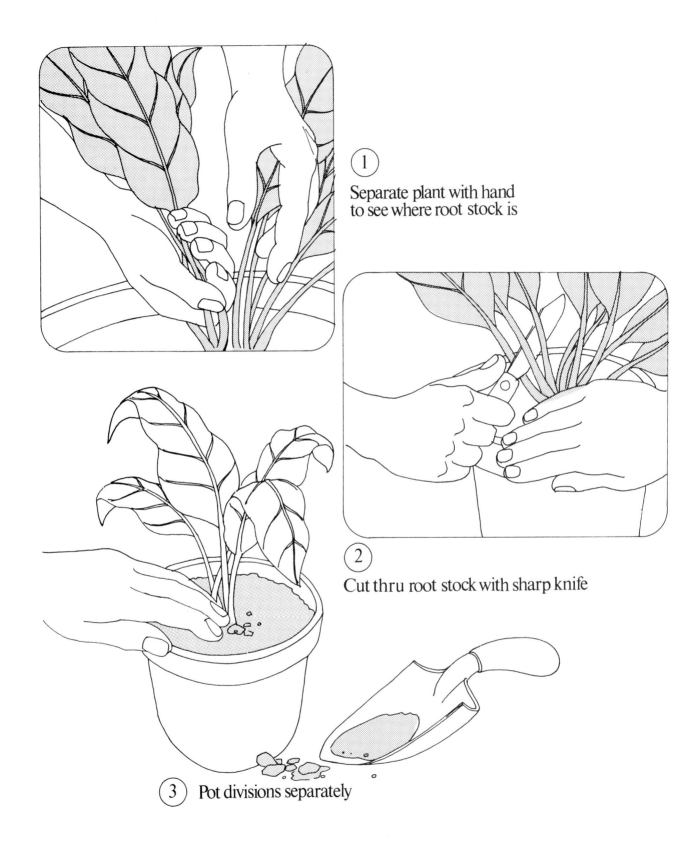

1. Separate plant with hand to see where root stock is

2. Cut thru root stock with sharp knife

3. Pot divisions separately

Dividing Plants

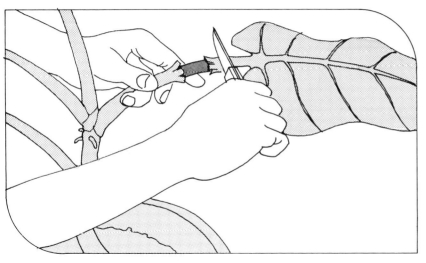

① Notch one inch
band around stem.
Do not cut thru stem.
Discard bark.

②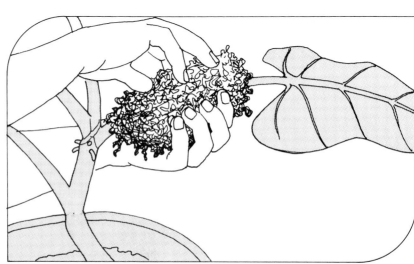
Cover entire notch
with sphagnum moss

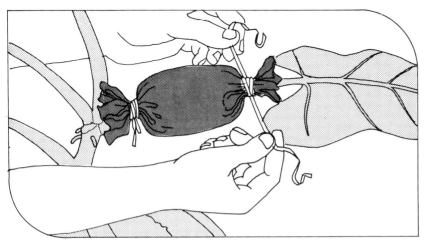

③ Cover sphagnum moss
with plastic sheet
and tie both ends.

Air Layering

Hardwood

Deciduous ornamental shrubs, such as forsythia, honeysuckle, and spirea, can be readily started from hardwood cuttings. Three different kinds of cutting are possible: mallet, heel, or straight cutting. Take a hardwood cutting from a mature woody stem of the previous season's growth, branch, or twig; this is an easy and inexpensive way of vegetative propagation. Take cuttings when a plant is dormant in winter or very early spring. Select firm, stiff, and unbendable growth. Take cuttings four to 12 inches long with at least two nodes; make the basal cut just below a node (the point where a leaf is attached to a stem) and the top cut about one inch above a node.

The easiest way to handle hardwood cuttings is to start by tying them in bundles with wire or string, the tops placed in one direction. Bury the bundles outside in sandy soil in a well-drained place or in sand in large boxes under cool and moist (40 to 50F) conditions. Place the bundles horizontally. In spring, after calluses have formed at the ends of the cuttings, insert them individually and vertically in the ground, the callused end of each cutting several inches below the ground.

A somewhat easier method is to take cuttings during the dormant season, bundle and wrap them in sphagnum moss or peat (damp), and store them at 35 to 40F until spring, when they can be put in the ground. Don't let them dry out or get wet in storage. Check them occasionally; if you see buds developing, lower the storage temperatures. At planting time, cuttings with developed buds will form leaves before roots appear.

You can also take cuttings in fall; you should plant these. However, with this method winter freezes and thaws may cause heaving and plants will be harmed.

Softwood

Take softwood cuttings (also called greenwood cuttings) from active growth of the current season before it hardens, generally in spring or early summer. Stems should be soft and succulent, never hard. Deciduous or evergreen species may be used; these include forsythia, spirea, and weigela, for example. Take softwood cuttings with leaves attached.

Select material that is flexible but strong enough to break when bent. Avoid weak or heavy shoots. Make the cuttings about five inches long with at least two nodes. Remove leaves from the lower part of the cuttings but retain those on the upper part so they can manufacture food while the cuttings root. Insert them in a moistened rooting medium with two or three nodes below the ground. Get them planted as soon as possible. Even a few hours in sun may kill them. Softwood cuttings require high humidity and warmth, 72 to 80F. Keep the cuttings moist in flats or in a cold frame. Shade until roots form and growth starts; then give plenty of light. Transplant the cuttings as soon as they are well rooted and show growth.

Many herbaceous plants—begonia, candytuft, chrysanthemum, impatiens, lantana, verbena—can be propagated by softwood cuttings, sometimes referred to as herbaceous cuttings, but the process is the same.

Semihardwood

Take semihardwood cuttings from broadleaved evergreens or from partially mature wood of deciduous plants as abelia, camellia, cotoneaster, pyracantha, mahonia, pittosporum, holly, and evergreen azaleas. The best time is summer just after peak growth and when wood is almost completely mature. Select material that feels pliable but is brittle when bent. Make the cuttings three to six inches long and remove leaves from the lower part, but keep them on the upper part. House them in a box or cold frame where they have ample humidity and light, but no sun. Keep the soil moist. As with softwood cuttings, once leaves show, they are ready for transplanting.

Propagation of Trees

BOTANICAL AND COMMON NAME	PROPAGATION METHOD	HINTS
Abies balsamea° (balsam fir)	Seed	Use fresh seed or stratify for 60–90 days (See Chapter 2)
Acacia baileyana° (Bailey acadia)	Seed	Soak in boiling water for 20 hours
Acer (Japanese maple)	Seed	Stratify 60–120 days; sow in spring
	Hardwood cuttings	Some species respond
Aesculus carnea (red horse-chestnut)	Seed	Stratify 120 days
	Layering	Low-growing types respond
Ailanthus altissima (tree of heaven)	Root cuttings	Choose female trees only; male trees smell bad
	Suckers	Take readily in spring
Albizzia julibrissin (silk tree)	Seed	Sow soon as ripe; soak in boiling water for 24 hours
	Root cuttings	Plant in early spring
Alnus incana (speckled alder)	Seed	Sow in fall or spring
	Cuttings	From mature wood
Betula papyrifera (canoe birch)	Seed	Sow in fall or in spring after stratifying 4–8 weeks
	Leaf cuttings	In summer
Catalpa speciosa (western catalpa)	Seed	Germinate readily; sow in late spring
	Softwood cuttings	In summer
Cedrus atlantica° (atlas cedar)	Seed	Soak in water
	Hardwood cuttings	Take in late summer or fall
Celtis occidentalis (hackberry)	Seed	Sow in fall or stratify 60–90 days for spring sowing
	Cuttings	Works sometimes

° Evergreens

Propagation of Trees (continued)

BOTANICAL AND COMMON NAME	PROPAGATION METHOD	HINTS
Cercis canadensis (eastern redbud)	Seed	Stratify 60 days
	Softwood cuttings	In spring or summer
Chamaecyparis obtusa° (Hinoki false cypress)	Seed	Stratify 60 days
	Cuttings	Sometimes respond
Chionanthus virginica	Seed	Stratify 90–120 days
Cornus florida (flowering dogwood)	Ripe wood cuttings	Take in fall or spring
Cryptomeria japonica° (Japanese cedar)	Seed	Sow soon as ripe; germinates in 4 months
	Cuttings	In sand in fall; takes 1 year to root
Elaeagnus angustifolia (Russian olive)	Seed	Stratify 90 days and sow in spring
	Root cuttings	Sometimes responds
	Layering	Often responds
Eucalyptus globulus° (blue gum)	Seed	In spring as soon as ripe
Fagus sylvatica (European beech)	Seed	Stratify 90 days
Fraxinus americana (white ash)	Seed	Stratify 60–90 days
Ginkgo biloba (maidenhair tree)	Softwood cuttings	In spring
Gleditsia tiacanthos (sweet locust)	Seed	Scald in water; sow in spring
	Hardwood cuttings	In spring
Koelreuteria paniculata (goldenrain tree)	Softwood cuttings	In spring
	Root cuttings	In spring
Laburnum watereri (golden chain tree)	Seed	In spring; germinates easily
Liquidambar styraciflua (sweet gum)	Seed	Stratify 30–60 days in summer
	Softwood cuttings	In summer
Liriodendron tulipifera (tulip tree)	Seed	Stratify 60 days
Magnolia soulangeana (saucer magnolia)	Seed	Stratify 120–180 days
Malus baccata (Silberian crab apple)	Seed	Stratify 30–90 days

° Evergreens

Propagation of Trees (continued)

BOTANICAL AND COMMON NAME	PROPAGATION METHOD	HINTS
Phellodendron amurense (cork tree)	Seed	Germinates readily; fall
	Root cuttings	In spring
Picea abies (excelsa)° (Norway spruce)	Seed	Stratify 60–90 days
Pinus densiflora° (Japanese red pine)	Seed	Stratify 30–90 days
Platanus acerifolia (London plane tree)	Seed	Let seed overwinter on tree; collect in early spring and sow
Populus alba (white poplar)	Seed	Plant at once
	Hardwood cuttings	Some root readily; plant in spring
	Softwood cuttings	Some root when planted in summer
Quercus alba (white oak)	Seed	White-oak seed ready to germinate as soon as mature in fall; black oak needs stratification
Robinia pseudoacacia (black acacia)	Seed	Soak 20–120 minutes in hot water before sowing
	Root cuttings	Occasionally successful with some varieties
Salix alba (white willow)	Root cuttings	Easy
	Stem cuttings	Easy
Sorbus aucuparia (European mountain ash)	Seed	Stratify 60–120 days
Taxus baccata° (English yew)	Cuttings	Easy (seeds too difficult)
Thuja occidentalis° (American arborvitae)	Cuttings	Take in summer
Tilia americana (American linden; basswood)	Seed	Stratify for 90–120 days; difficult
Tsuga canadensis° (northern hemlock)	Seed	Stratify 69–90 days or plant in fall for spring germination
Ulmus americana (American elm)	Softwood cuttings	In spring

° Evergreens

Propagation of Shrubs

BOTANICAL AND COMMON NAME	PROPAGATION METHOD	HINTS
Abelia grandiflora (glossy abelia)	Leafy cuttings	Take from matured growth
	Hardwood cuttings	In spring or fall
Amelanchier canadensis (shadblow service berry)	Seed	Stratify 90–180 days
Andromeda polifolia (bog rosemary)	Seed	Germinates easily
Arbutus unedo (strawberry tree)	Seed	In early spring
	Cuttings	In autumn
Arctostaphylos uva-ursi (barberry)	Cuttings	In spring
Berberis koreana (Korean barberry)	Softwood cuttings	In spring
Buddleia davidi (summer lilac)	Softwood cuttings	In spring
Buxus sempervirens (common boxwood)	Softwood cuttings	In spring or fall
Callistemon citrinus (bottlebrush)	Leaf cuttings	Seedlings rarely satisfactory
Calluna vulgaris (heather)	Seed	In spring
	Leaf cuttings	Any time of year
Camellia	Seed, cuttings, layering	Cutting easy to root
Ceanothus americanus (New Jersey tea)	Seed, cuttings, layering	Soak in water overnight
Cotoneaster	Seed	Difficult
	Leaf cuttings	In spring
Daphne odora (fragrant daphne)	Leaf cuttings	Take in late spring
	Layering	In spring
Deutzia	Hardwood cuttings Softwood cuttings	Either method easy
Euonymus	Leaf cuttings	Take mature wood
Forsythia intermedia (border forsythia)	Hardwood and softwood cuttings	Easiest from hardwood cuttings
Gardenia jasminoides (Cape jasmine)	Leaf cuttings	Take from fall to spring
Hamamelis vernalis (spring witch hazel)	Seed	In spring

Propagation of Shrubs (continued)

BOTANICAL AND COMMON NAME	PROPAGATION METHOD	HINTS
Hibiscus syriacus (shrub althea)	Hardwood cuttings	Take in fall; store until spring
Hydrangea arborescens	Hardwood and softwood cuttings	Take in early spring
Ilex cornuta (Chinese holly)	Softwood cuttings	Spring, fall
Jasminum officinale (Poets' jasmine)	Hardwood cuttings	Easy
Kalmia latifolia (mountain laurel)	Seed	In spring
	Softwood cuttings	Works well with most
Kerria japonica	Hardwood cuttings	Generally easy
Lagerstroemia indica (crape myrtle)	Hardwood cuttings	In spring
	Seed	Occasionally successful
Laurus nobilis (sweet bay)	Seed	Sow immediately
Ligustrum amurense (amur privet)	Hardwood cuttings	Take in spring
Lonicera fragrantissima (winter honeysuckle)	Hardwood cuttings	Take in spring
Mahonia aquifolium (holly mahonia)	Seed	Stratify through winter
	Leaf cuttings	Generally successful
Nerium oleander (oleander)	Seed	Plant immediately
	Cuttings	Trim mature wood
Philadelphus	Hardwood cuttings	In spring
	Softwood cuttings	In summer
Photinia serrulata (Chinese photinia)	Seed	Stratify 30–60 days
Potentilla fruticosa (shrubby cinquefoil)	Seed, hardwood cuttings	Take in autumn
Pyracantha coccinea (scarlet firethorn)	Softwood cuttings	Spring, fall
Rhododendron	Seed, cuttings, grafting, layering	Cuttings difficult, grafting generally successful
Rosa	Softwood and hardwood cuttings, layering	All asexual methods generally easy
Spiraea prunifolia (bridal wreath spiraea)	Hardwood cuttings	Use root-promoting substances

Propagation of Shrubs (continued)

BOTANICAL AND COMMON NAME	PROPAGATION METHOD	HINTS
Syringa vulgaris (common lilac)	Hardwood cuttings	Difficult
Viburnum davidi	Seed	Complicated seed dormancy conditions
	Cuttings	Cuttings generally successful
	Grafting	
	Layering	
Weigela florida	Hardwood cuttings	In spring
	Softwood cuttings	From spring to fall
Wisteria	Softwood cuttings	In midsummer

Propagation of Perennials

BOTANICAL AND COMMON NAME	OPTIMUM TEMP. FOR SEED GERMINATION	WEEKS SEEDS NEED TO GERMINATE	HINTS
Achillea ptarmica (yarrow)	68° to 70°F	1 to 2	Division in spring or fall
Allium pulchellum	68° to 74°F	3 to 4	Division
Alyssum saxatile (golden tuft)	68° to 86°F	3 to 4	Division in spring or fall
Althaea rosea (hollyhock)	68° to 70°F	2 to 3	Division
Anchusa (bugloss)	68° to 86°F	3 to 4	Division in spring or fall; root cuttings
Anemone coronaria (poppy anemone)	68° to 70°F	5 to 6	Division
A. pulsatilla (pasqueflower)	68° to 70°F	5 to 6	Division
Aquilegia (columbine)	68° to 86°F	3 to 4	Division in spring
Arabis (rock-cress)	60° to 68°F	1 to 2	
Armeria (thrift)	68° to 70°F	3 to 4	Division
Artemisia (dusty miller)	50° to 55°F	1 to 2	Division
Ascelepias tuberosa (butterfly milkweed)	68° to 86°F	3 to 4	Division

Propagation of Perennials (continued)

BOTANICAL AND COMMON NAME	OPTIMUM TEMP. FOR SEED GERMINATION	WEEKS SEEDS NEED TO GERMINATE	HINTS
Aster (michaelmas daisy)	68° to 70°F	2 to 3	Division in fall or spring
Aubrieta deltoidea	50° to 55°F	2 to 3	Stem cuttings
Begonia (tuberous)	68° to 72°F	2 to 3	Leaf, stem cuttings; division of roots
Bellis perennis (English daisy)	68°F	1 to 2	Division
Campanula carpatica (Carpathian harebell)	68° to 86°F	2 to 3	Division in spring or fall
Canna			Division of rhizome
Cerastium tomentosum (snow-in-summer)	68° to 70°F	2 to 4	Division
Cheiranthus cheiri (wallflower)	50° to 56°F	2 to 3	
Chrysanthemum	68° to 70°F	2 to 4	Division; softwood cuttings
Coreopsis	68° to 70°F	2 to 3	
Cyclamen indicum	68° to 70°F	3 to 4	Division
Delphinium grandiflorum (delphinium)	54° to 56°F	3 to 4	Division
Dianthus (pinks)	68° to 70°F	2 to 3	Layering, division
Dicentra spectabilis (bleeding heart)	°	6	Division; stem cutting; root cuttings
Dictamnus albus (gasplant)	°	6	
Digitalis (foxglove)	68° to 86°F	2 to 3	Division in spring
Echinops (globe thistle)	68° to 86°F	1 to 4	Division; root cuttings
Erigeron (midsummer aster)	68° to 70°F	3 to 4	
Gerbera jamesoni (transvaal daisy)	68°F	2 to 3	Division
Geum (avens)	68° to 86°F	3 to 4	Division
Helenium autumnale (sneezeweed)	68°F	1 to 2	Division
Helianthemum nummularium (sunrose)	68° to 86°F	2 to 3	Division; summer cuttings

° Needs stratification

Propagation of Perennials (continued)

BOTANICAL AND COMMON NAME	OPTIMUM TEMP. FOR SEED GERMINATION	WEEKS SEEDS NEED TO GERMINATE	HINTS
Heliopsis	68° to 86°F	1 to 2	Division
Helleborus (Christmas rose)	°		Division
Hesperis matronalis (sweet rocket)	68° to 86°F	3 to 4	
Heuchera sanguinea (coral bells)	68° to 86°F	2 to 3	Division; leaf cuttings
Lathyrus latifolius (pen vine)	68° to 86°F	2 to 3	
Lavandula officinalis (lavender)	52° to 90°F	2 to 3	
Linum (flax)	54°F	3 to 4	Division
Lobelia cardinalis (cardinal flower)	68° to 86°F	3 to 4	Division
Myosotis (forget-me-not)	68°F	2 to 3	Division; cuttings
Nierembergia (cupflower)	68° to 86°F	2 to 3	Division; cuttings in fall
Oenothera (evening primrose)	68° to 86°F	1 to 3	Division
Ornithogalum thyrsoides (Star of Bethlehem)	68° to 78°F	2 to 6	Division
Papaver nudicaule (Iceland poppy)	54°F	1 to 2	
P. orientale (oriental poppy)	54°F	1 to 2	Root cuttings in late summer
Pelargonium (geraniums)	68° to 76°F	2 to 8	Cuttings
Penstemon (beard tongue)	68° to 86°F	Slow, un-even	Division
Phlox divaricata	°		Division; root cuttings
P. paniculata (garden phlox)	°		Division; root cuttings
Platycodon grandiflorum (balloon flower)	68° to 86°F	2 to 3	Division in spring
Primula (primrose)	68° to 74°F	3 to 6	Division; cuttings in spring

° Needs stratification

Propagation of Perennials (continued)

BOTANICAL AND COMMON NAME	OPTIMUM TEMP. FOR SEED GERMINATION	WEEKS SEEDS NEED TO GERMINATE	HINTS
Pyrethrum (painted daisy)	68° to 76°F	2 to 3	Division
Ranunculus	68° to 72°F	1 to 4	Division
Rudbeckia (coneflower)	69° to 86°F	2 to 3	Division
Sinningia speciosa (gloxinia)	68° to 72°F		Leaf cuttings
Tigridia (tiger flower)	68° to 74°F	2 to 4	Division
Trollius europaeus (globeflower)	°		Division
Verbena canadensis (clump verbena)	54° to 90°F	2 to 4	Cuttings
Veronica (speedwell)	54° to 90°F	2 to 3	Division
Vinca minor (periwinkle)	68°F	2 to 3	Cuttings
Viola cornuta (violet)	54° to 90°F	2 to 3	Division; runners; cuttings in spring

° Needs stratification

Propagation of Annuals

BOTANICAL AND COMMON NAME	OPTIMUM TEMP. FOR SEED GERMINATION	WEEKS SEEDS NEED TO GERMINATE	HINTS
Agathea (felicia) (blue daisy)	68° to 70°F	2 to 3	Start indoors
Ageratum houstonianum	68° to 86°F	3	Seedlings fragile
Alyssum maritimum (alyssum)	68°F	2 to 3	Start indoors
Amaranthus	68° to 86°F	3 to 4	Plant directly in garden
Anchusa capensis (forget-me-not)	68° to 70°F	1 to 2	Self-sows

Propagation of Annuals (continued)

BOTANICAL AND COMMON NAME	OPTIMUM TEMP. FOR SEED GERMINATION	WEEKS SEEDS NEED TO GERMINATE	HINTS
Antirrhinum majus (snapdragons)	60° to 65°F	1 to 2	Pinch plants
Arctotis stoechadifolia (African daisy)	68° to 70°F	2 to 3	Plant directly in garden
Begonia semperflorens (wax begonia)	68° to 86°F	1 to 3	Fine bedding plant
Browallia	70° to 75°F	2 to 3	Hanging plant
Calendula officinalis (pot marigold)	68° to 70°F	2 to 3	Likes coolness
Callistephus chinensis (China aster)	68°F	2 to 3	Sow indoors
Celosia argentea cristata (cockscomb)	68° to 86°F	1 to 2	Resents transplanting
Centaurea (dusty miller)	68° to 86°F	3 to 4	Start indoors
Chrysanthemum (annual)	68° to 70°F	2 to 4	Good cool-region plant
Clarkia elegans	54° to 70°F	1 to 2	Good cool-region plant
Cleome spinosa (spiderflower)	54° to 90°F	1 to 2	F1 hybrids excellent
Cosmos bipinnatus (cosmos)	68° to 86°F	1 to 2	Easy annual
Cynoglossum (Chinese forget-me-not)	68° to 80°F	1 to 2	Lovely annual
Delphinium ajacis (larkspur)	60° to 68°F	2 to 3	Plant directly in garden
Dianthus	68° to 70°F	2 to 3	Easy; start indoors
Dimorphotheca (Cape marigold)	68° to 70°F	2 to 3	Cool-region plant
Eschscholzia (California poppy)	54° to 70°F	2 to 3	Plant directly in garden
Euphorbia variegata (snow-on-mountain)	68° to 74°F	1 to 2	Handsome
Gaillardia (blanketflower)	68° to 72°F	2 to 3	Easy; start in garden
Gazania	68° to 72°F	2 to 3	Robust
Godetia	68° to 70°F	2 to 3	Takes some shade
Gypsophila (baby's breath)	68° to 70°F	2 to 3	Best started in garden

Propagation of Annuals (continued)

BOTANICAL AND COMMON NAME	OPTIMUM TEMP. FOR SEED GERMINATION	WEEKS SEEDS NEED TO GERMINATE	HINTS
Helianthus annuus (sunflower)	68° to 86°F	2 to 3	Grows quickly; start outdoors
Helichrysum (strawflower)	68° to 78°F	1 to 2	Needs long season; start indoors
Heliotropium (heliotrope)	68° to 86°F	3 to 4	Start in garden
Impatiens balsamina (snapsweet)	68° to 70°F	2 to 4	Many new varieties
I. Sultana (impatiens)	68° to 70°F	2 to 3	Start indoors
Ipomoea purpurea (morning glory)	68° to 86°F	1 to 3	Crack seed coat
Linaria (toadflap)	54° to 60°F	2 to 3	Easy
Lobelia erinus	68° to 86°F	2 to 3	Difficult to transplant
Mathiola incana (stock)	54° to 90°F	2	Sow indoors
Matricaria (feverfew)	74° to 86°F	1 to 2	Easy
Mirabilis (four-o'clock)	68° to 86°F	1 to 2	Easy
Molucella laevis (bells of Ireland)	86° to 90°F	2 to 3	Self-sows
Nemesia	60° to 74°F	2 to 3	Good edge plant
Nicotiana (flowering tobacco)	76° to 80°F	2 to 3	Do not cover seed
Nigella (love-in-a-mist)	86° to 90°F	2 to 3	Plant directly in garden
Papaver (Shirley poppy)	55°F	1 to 2	Short bloom season
Petunia	68° to 70°F	2 to 3	Bountiful flowers; some varieties need higher temperatures
Phlox drummondi (annual phlox)	58° to 60°F	2 to 3	Needs coolness for germination
Portulaca grandiflora (moss rose)	68° to 86°F	2 to 3	Needs warmth for germination
Reseda odorata (mignonette)	54°F	2 to 3	Not easy

Propagation of Annuals (continued)

BOTANICAL AND COMMON NAME	OPTIMUM TEMP. FOR SEED GERMINATION	WEEKS SEEDS NEED TO GERMINATE	HINTS
Salpiglossis sinuata (painted tongue)	68° to 86°F	2	Needs warmth for germination
Salvia splendens	68° to 86°F	2 to 4	Good red color
Scabiosa (pincushion flower)	68° to 86°F	2 to 3	Needs warmth for germination
Schizanthus (butterfly flower)	54°F	1 to 2	Start in ground
Tagetes (marigold)	68° to 86°F	1 to 2	Self-sows
Thunbergia (clockvine)	68° to 86°F	2 to 3	Start indoors
Thymophylla (Dahlborg daisy)	68° to 84°F	2 to 3	Popular
Tithonia (Mexican sunflower)	68° to 86°F	2 to 3	Start in garden
Tropaeolum majus (nasturtium)	68°F	1 to 3	Easy; start in garden
Verbena hortensis (verbena)	68° to 86°F	3 to 4	Start indoors; needs long growing season
Viola (pansy)	60° to 74°F	1 to 2	Self-sows
Zinnia elegans (zinnia)	68° to 86°F	1 to 2	Start in garden

20

Pests and Diseases–Ways to Cope

IF YOU are going to have a garden, you will have to deal with insects—good ones and bad ones. It is the nature of things that you cannot garden completely pest free. However, for the most part insects are not a problem if you take precautions, and today you can eliminate pests without having to resort to poisons. Natural preventatives exist to help you fight the battle of the bugs. But first be sure that it is insects that are harming your plants and not just poor culture. Indeed, few problems in the small garden are the result of either insects or disease.

When you see something going wrong, consider whether the plants are getting enough water, whether drainage is adequate, light or sunshine is sufficient, the soil suitable for the specific plants you are growing. If the answers check out yes (you are giving reasonably good care to your plants), then look for insects or disease as the cause of the trouble.

CULTURAL SYMPTOMS

Plants exhibit telltale signs when you are not caring for them properly, and some of these signs, in fact a great many, are often blamed on insects. For example, plants that develop brown or crisp leaf edges may be getting too much heat or the temperature of the soil may be fluctuating too much. If possible, install a device—a screen, a tree—to help shade the plants and thus reduce heat. To remedy the soil condition try to keep it evenly moist. If neither of these procedures helps, then look for insects or disease as the cause of the trouble.

A common complaint is that the leaves are turning yellow and dropping off. This could be a natural condition and have nothing to do with pests.

When foliage seems lifeless and wan, don't just assume aphids are at work—you may not be watering enough. If your perennials or annuals are not blooming properly, the problem could be a lack of sun—no disease or insect at work at all.

When buds drop, and this is a common problem, it could be that temperatures are fluctuating too much. You have to live with this situation—there is no remedy here.

It is a fact and repeated many times that a healthy plant is less prone to pests and disease than a sickly plant, and this is very, very true. A strong plant wards off the predator.

When you buy plants, do inspect them for insects—most are visible to the naked eye. Also, it is vitally important to keep your garden clean. Trash or faded flowers strewn on the ground are a natural hiding place for bacteria and insects.

INSECTS

There are insects and there are insects—but for simplicity, they can be divided into sucking and chewing pests. The sucking pests, such as aphids, pierce stems or leaves and sap the juices; the chewers, such as thrips, bite and eat out tiny pieces of plants. Some insects attack almost any plant, others have a preference, for instance, for an azalea. Most insects, such as aphids or mealybugs, are easily seen but such pests as root lice, mites, nematodes, to mention a few, are hardly visible.

Many insects lay eggs to provide food for their hatching young, but some (and aphids are a good example) produce living young. In their immature stages, insects grow by a process called molting—the periodic shedding of the outer skin. The insects change gradually as repeated moltings occur and in this stage are called nymphs until they mature.

Nymphs have a different coloring from adults, but they retain the same habits and auxiliary parts. Nymphs may be wingless or winged when mature, depending on their species. Sometimes the insects may be represented by both winged and wingless adults. However, once the wings have developed, the insect stops growing, and is considered mature. All sucking insects and some chewing ones go through this gradual transformation. If you can destroy the eggs or the nymphal stages of these insects, so much the better.

Some insects upon maturation hardly look as they did when young. There is a complete transformation, and their eggs hatch into wormlike forms called larvae. (In many groups even the plants they feed on differ between the larval and adult stages.) Mature beetles are known as grubs in the larval stage. Caterpillars are the young stage of moths, butterflies, and sawflies; wireworms are the larvae of click beetles.

Larvae are heavy feeders; they grow by molting. When they reach their full size, they go into an inactive nonfeeding period called a pupa; in this stage they are often protected by a cocoon or chrysalis. (You have probably seen pupae in the woods or in your garden.) This is the time when they undergo amazing transformation, finally emerging as full-fledged adults.

You can find larvae on trees or the plants on which they feed, although they often go into the soil. All larvae have a chewing-type mouth that makes it easy for them to eat quickly and voraciously.

Chewers

Chewing insects are fast feeders equipped with powerful mandibles and maxillae that allow them to rip and tear edges of leaves, make holes, or skeletonize foliage. These insects range from many forms of caterpillars to numerous kinds of beetles and their grublike larvae. Cabbage worms eat large holes in leaves. The elm leaf beetle and Japanese beetle skeletonize the leaf, and many caterpillars, sawflies, and other insects feed at the edge of the leaf. Some larvae have a protective coloration that makes it difficult to see them.

Sap Feeders

Sap-sucking insects are devastating because they can attack a plant from the stem to the growing tips to the roots. They have a needlelike proboscis that they insert into a plant and use to suck out juices. Even the insertion of the proboscis can weaken a plant severely enough so that it becomes prone to other pests that feed on sickly plants. Furthermore, some sap-sucking insects often transmit viruses to the plants they attack.

Like the chewing insects whose damage is seen in scalloped leaves and holes in foliage, the sap-sucking insects can be recognized by the harm they do. Leaves become yellowed or stippled, brown or wilted. Dieback of twigs and branches is often seen, and frequently sticky honeydew and sooty mold cover leaves and branches. The most common sap-sucking insects are aphids, leafhoppers, lace bugs, scale insects, mealybugs, whiteflies, thrips, and plant bugs.

Aphids

Aphids, sometimes called plant lice, can work havoc in a garden. They do their damage by piercing stems, leaves, buds, practically all parts of a plant, with sharp stylets; then they extract vital plant juices. The result is curled leaves and stunted or checked growth. Where there is a heavy aphid infestation, the plant usually dies. In addition, aphids can also introduce virus diseases into the garden, and these diseases in some cases can be more damaging than the aphids.

Aphids breed incredibly fast and in large numbers; in warm climates they reproduce continuously. Some aphids have no wings, others do, but all migrate to other plants, starting new colonies. There are many kinds, but generally most are black or green, occasionally red. There are pea aphids, melon aphids, plant aphids, bean aphids, and so forth.

The aphid is really a triple threat in the garden; it is destructive itself, it introduces bacterial diseases; furthermore, it gives off a

sort of honeydew from the tip of its abdomen that is a favorite food of some ants. These ants move the aphids about to productive plants and protect them at night or when the weather is bad in their own nests. Generally where there are ants there will soon be aphids, so take precautionary steps to eliminate ants as soon as you see them. (Ladybugs and the praying mantis are excellent aphid predators.) You can use a soapy solution of half water and half detergent to thwart the pests.

Leafhoppers

Leafhoppers are small active insects that suck sap from leaves. Some also contribute to virus diseases. When disturbed, leafhoppers, as their name implies, hop away or sometimes fly. The nymphs are wingless and move quickly out of sight if touched. Like aphids, leafhoppers also excrete a sweet honeydew that will attract ants. Use botanical sprays for control.

Thrips

Thrips are slender, needlelike winged insects that scrape stems or leaves and then suck out the sap. Nymphs are wingless. Thrips hibernate in winter, but when warm weather comes, they start feeding on young plants. They can produce a new generation every two weeks in hot weather, so don't let them get established. Use insect predators for control or spray plants with a blast of water.

Scale

Scale, a common damaging insect of shrubs and flowers, is less well known than aphids or mealybugs, and yet it does considerable damage. It is soft shelled or, in most cases, has an armored hull. Scale is difficult

Harmful Insects

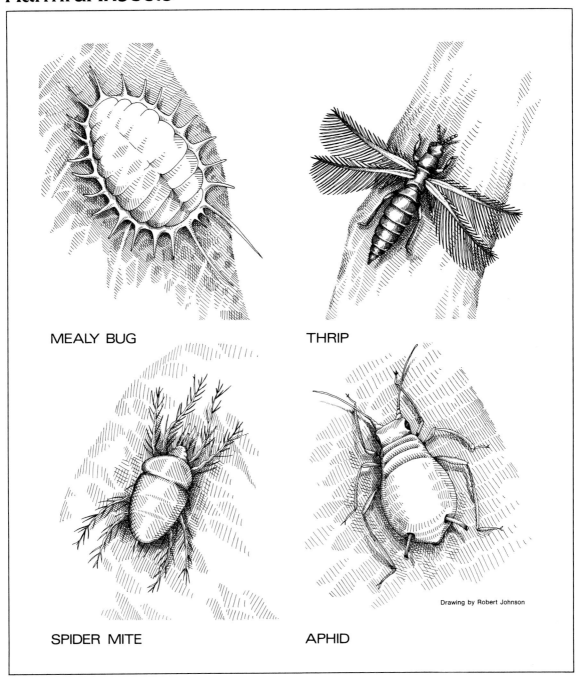

MEALY BUG

THRIP

SPIDER MITE

APHID

Drawing by Robert Johnson

to eliminate because it sticks stubbornly to leaves and stems. It sucks sap and can kill a healthy specimen in short order unless checked. Further, like the other notorious garden pests, aphids and thrips, scale produces honeydew that attracts ants. Use dormant oil sprays at proper intervals for control.

Mealybugs

Mealybugs are tiny white, cottony insects that hide in leaf axils. They form colonies and can rapidly ruin a plant if they are not eliminated quickly. The male of the species can fly; females are wingless. For mild infestations, use cotton swabs dipped in alcohol; in severe cases, let insect predators do the job.

Lace Bug

Lace bugs may be handsome insects, but both they and their nymphs suck juices from leaves and stems and can do considerable damage in the garden. If you see dark, shiny excrement on plants, look for lace bugs as culprits. They overwinter as eggs attached to leaves and in warm weather produce their broods. Control them with botanical sprays. (Do not confuse these harmful insects with the beneficial lacewings.)

Japanese Beetle

The Japanese beetle is a colorful and extremely harmful insect. It feeds on the foliage of many shade and fruit trees, and the grubs are major pests of lawns. The milky spore disease sold commercially as Doom has been highly effective as a control.

Leaf Miner

The larva of the leaf miner feeds and lives for a part of or for all its life on a leaf. The miner, feeding on the surface of the foliage, causes defoliation. Evidence of leaf miners is easily seen, for they imprint designs on leaves; the designs may be long and narrow or blotchy. An agricultural station in your area will be able to help you identify the miner you are fighting. The best protection is to kill the adults before they begin laying or thwart the larvae as soon as they begin feeding. Keeping the area free of debris will also help. The adults of leaf miners may be sawflies, moths, or flies, and many of these can be controlled with light traps.

Borers

Borers feed somewhat like leaf miners, but they dig deeper into the leaf; generally they are the larval stage of such insects as beetles; moths, and sawflies. Borers are devastating because, unlike leaf miners which generally stay in one place, they can attack the hard woody parts of a tree or shrub, the softer tissue beneath the bark, or even soft-stemmed herbaceous plants. Also, they are difficult to see, so injury occurs suddenly and control methods are difficult. The sun helps to aggravate the damage they do and hastens the wilting of plants. Control of the borer depends on proper timing; the newly hatched larvae must be destroyed before they have a chance to enter the plant. Once they are beneath the surface, it is virtually impossible to kill them.

Gall-Causing Insects

The plant deformities produced by gall-causing insects are generally familiar, but the organisms that produce them are frequently small and hard to identify. The galls are home for the pests in their immature stage and sometimes in their adult stage. When the insects are mature, they either bore their way out or escape when the gall cracks. The galls may be on leaves, twigs, stems, or flower parts and may take the form of blisters, bladders, or projections on leaves. Generally, leaf galls are not too serious; the insects responsible for them may be wasp-like insects, aphids, or midges. Pruning out the galls is one form of control. Using botanical sprays before adults form is a preventative.

Plant Mites

Plant mites are not insects; they belong to the group known as Arachnids (spiders and ticks). They are variously called spider mite, red spider mite, red mite, and so forth. When young, they have six legs, just as insects do; but when mature, they have eight legs. Plant mites have sharp and piercing mouth parts and can penetrate plant tissues in a second, sucking up vital juices and desiccating a plant. There are many kinds of mites, and their eggs, spherical and colorless, yellowish, or reddish, can be detected on the bark of twigs and branches or, more commonly, on the undersides of leaves. In heat, the eggs hatch within a few days, and in a few weeks the adults are ready to start a new generation; they build up tremendous numbers in a short time. Generally, signs of their work are grayish striped foliage, which later turns yellow or brown and drops off. If you look closely, you will see a fine webbing and a white dusty residue on the leaves. There is no reason to allow mites in the garden; a dormant oil spray will kill over-wintering eggs in spring or early fall.

Gall Mites

There are several types of gall mites, and they look nothing like plant mites. These are almost impossible to see without a magnifying glass; they have wedge-shaped bodies and two pairs of legs well forward on the blunt end. Some destroy leaves by producing puckered or bronzy areas on the foliage; others form cotton growths. Most gall mites as adults overwinter under scales of buds or on twigs. To eliminate gall mites, apply dormant sprays when the buds begin to swell.

Nematodes

Nematodes have been classified as eel-like or threadlike worms that are too small to be seen by the unaided eye. There are hundreds of kinds. Some attack only one type of plant; others feed on different species indiscriminately. The majority seem to attack roots and underground plant parts; nematodes are particularly insidious. It seems no garden is free of them.

Nematodes have spearlike mouths that puncture roots and suck out cell contents. They leave open wounds through which rot- and wilt-causing fungi can enter and get a foothold. Nematodes cannot move very far on their own, but they can be carried in water, in plant roots, and, of course, in soil. As they increase they cause a decline of the plant. Yellow or bronzed foliage is a symptom. Below ground it is difficult to determine their work, but roots become stunted, malformed, or decayed. Root-knot nematodes attack almost two thousand species of plants; they are more likely prone to attack during drought. Good soil conditions and proper feeding will frequently keep a plant growing in spite of nematodes.

NATURAL PREVENTATIVES

Predatory insects and birds offer two ways of keeping the garden generally insect free, but there are other ways, too. Companion planting—putting in plants certain insects don't like with plants they do like—deters some insects. This is a simple, easy method of no-poison gardening; nature works for you.

Dormant oil sprays are valuable for thwarting many insects, and they are not harmful to soil or animal life. However, they destroy good bugs as well as bad ones, so should be used with discretion. Some of the newer botanical garden sprays such as pyrethrum, derived from plant substances, are also perfectly safe to use against insects. And, of course, you can always hand pick pests, but this is not pleasant.

Companion Plantings

Combining plants in flower or vegetable gardens is an easy way to keep away pests. Nasturtiums repel aphids, and tansy, a pretty herb, deters cutworms and cabbageworms. Rue, a hardy, shrubby evergreen, is another insect repellent; the leaves have a disagreeable odor and a bitter taste, and insects just won't touch them or plants growing nearby. Mixed with more insect-prone plants, such as dahlias or lupine, rue provides a splendid defense against pests. Marigolds and asters deter insects, too. Cosmos and coreopsis are other plants that insects seldom trouble.

The most popular plants that repel are garlic and chives; amateur gardeners report that a few of these in the flower bed or vegetable garden *do* keep insects away, including aphids and certain kinds of beetles. Some of the culinary herbs, like savory and thyme, generally ward off insects, too, and can be scattered throughout the garden.

Botanical Repellents

Although the true organic gardener will not use any sprays in his yard, I find the botanical insecticides perfectly safe. These sprays are not persistent or harmful to man

or land. They include pyrethrum, rotenone, quassia, and ryania and are now being sold in conventional chemical spray form. However, check labels to be sure the botanicals are not being used in combination with persistent poisons.

Pyrethrum is derived from a chrysanthemum species, sometimes called *C. cinerariaefolium* or *C. roseum;* it was formerly called insect flower or insect plant. It is a handsome daisylike flower, pink or white. The pulverized flowers are toxic to insects, and, even if accidentally swallowed by man, pyrethrum does not accumulate in live tissue. Pyrethrum kills on contact aphids, whitefly, leafhoppers, and thrips.

Rotenone comes from the derris root—a woody climber with purple and white flowers. The root is ground into an effective powder that wards off spittle bug, aphid, spider mite, chinch bug, harlequin bug, pea weevil, and the common housefly.

Appearing recently as an insecticide is ryania, a shrub from Latin America. The dusty or spray solution made from the roots and woody stems, although not lethal, incapacitates (perhaps by paralysis) many pests: squash bug, Japanese beetle, elm-leaf beetle, and cabbage looper.

Quassia, a tree native to South America, has an intensely bitter root and bark that repels several insects. The spray, mixed with water, is made from the crushed root and bark.

Hellebore, a common garden flower in Roman times, is also used as an insect repellent. Hellebore is of the lily family, and its pulverized roots and rhizomes contain helleborin, which has a burning acrid taste. The generic name of the plant is derived from the Greek, *elein* (to injure) and *bora* (food). The specific name refers to the dark rootstock.

More and more, the chemical companies that formerly manufactured deadly poisons for garden protection are now seeking plants like hellebore and rotenone for their products. No doubt these packaged conveniences will soon be available to the public (some are already). However, you can grow most of these plants in your garden and brew your own remedies.

Chrysanthemum flowers can be dried easily on newspaper sheets in a well-ventilated place and pulverized into a powder to be mixed with water for spraying. Soak rotenone and hellebore roots overnight in a little water. Crush them the next day and boil in water; the extract is the insecticide.

Before leaving the botanical repellents, we should look at a very old one—nicotine, which is derived from the tobacco plant. Nicotine, which has been used as an insecticide since the late seventeenth century, is a very poisonous alkaloid for insects, but it is also highly toxic to mammals. However, it dissipates rapidly and is useful against aphids, whitefly, leafhopper, and dozens of other pests. The product most commonly used is called nicotine sulfate, somewhat less toxic than nicotine. It is mixed with soap and water and is an effective insecticide.

Several years ago, when I realized the dangers of the persistent chemicals, I resorted to nicotine sulfate. I occasionally use it in the garden now but some gardeners still consider it a highly toxic product with possible deleterious effects.

Old-Fashioned Remedies

Hand picking insects is a primitive means of control; if you can bring yourself to do this, it is one of the best ways to keep a small garden pest free. I don't use snail bait because my dog thinks the pellets are food. After one emergency visit to the hospital with him, I decided to pick up snails. Now I close my eyes, collect them, and dispatch them immediately. A recent remedy suggested by the United States Department of Agriculture suggests beer in small bottle caps, placed strategically on the property. Sometimes I find this works, but most times I am sorry to say it does not; I don't know why.

Oil Sprays

When used properly, dormant oil sprays are effective against such chewing and sucking insects as aphids, mealybugs, scale, and red spiders. Oil sprays are used on orchard trees before the leaf buds open, and some gardeners also use them on shrubs and other plants. The mixture of oil and water is nontoxic, of course, and cleans up insect eggs that are overwintering in trees. The spray makes a very tight film over the eggs and literally suffocates them. Thus, it should be applied only over leafless trees.

Commercial oil sprays, with instructions for their use and dilution, are sold at garden suppliers. You can also make your own spray with a gallon of light-grade oil and a pound of fish-oil soap, as an emulsifier, and a half-gallon of water. Combine the ingredients and then boil and mix thoroughly until well blended. Because oil emulsions tend to separate after a while, apply the spray as soon as possible. It is generally mixed with twenty or more times its volume of water.

If the right amounts are used, oil sprays do not harm plants or soil; some insects develop a resistance to certain insecticides, but not to oil sprays.

If you use an oil spray on shrubs, apply

only a light mixture, and always remember that it will kill the good bugs along with the bad ones, so it is prudent to apply it only in specific cases.

Other Protective Measures (Plant Rotation, Tilling)

The rotation of plants is another wise garden practice. Not only does it improve fertility but it has a basic intelligent premise: when you mix plants, no one insect gets the upper hand. This method may not prevent all pests from entering the flower garden, but it will make it easier to control them without resort to unacceptable chemical sprays. (After all, a few pests in the garden are better than a sterile poison-free garden without any plants.)

Monoculture (growing the same plant in the same place year after year) has revealed a buildup of certain insects. Rotation and diversity of plants will reduce this hazard; this is a simple and inexpensive way to protect your garden, as is plowing at the right time or simply disking the soil. In early spring or fall, disking exposes the eggs of some insects that cannot survive in the open. Disking in summer can destroy grubs of the Japanese beetle and European chafer.

Insects and How to Control Them

INSECT	DESCRIPTION	VICTIMS	DAMAGE	CONTROL
Aphids	Green or black, pink or yellow, or red, soft-bodied insects	Almost all plants	Stunted and deformed plants	Malathion, rotenone
Beetles (many kinds)	Usually brown or black, wingless	Flowers and vegetables	Eaten leaves	Hand pick if possible, or use Sevin
Borers (many kinds)	Caterpillars, grugs	Woody and herbaceous plants	Wilting; holes in stems and branches	Diazinon
Caterpillars (including bagworms, cutworms, cankerworms)	Familiar insect	All kinds of plants	Defoliated plants	Rotenone, diazinon, Malathion
Chinch bugs	Small black-and-white insects	Mainly lawns	Brown patches	Sevin
Cutworms (generally in soil)	Hairless moth caterpillars	Many plants	Eaten leaves	Sevin, dibrom

Insects and How to Control Them (continued)

INSECT	DESCRIPTION	VICTIMS	DAMAGE	CONTROL
Grasshoppers	Familiar insect	Plants, trees	Eaten leaves	Sevin
Lacebugs	Small bugs with lacy wings	Azaleas, oaks, birches, haw-thorns; others	Mottled leaves	Malathion
Leafhoppers	Wedge-shaped insects that hop	Many plants	Pale or brown leaves; stunted plants	Malathion
Leaf miners (many kinds; hollyleaf miner, boxwood miner)	Larvae of vari-ous insects	Many plants	Spotted or blotched leaves	Systemics, diaz-inon
Leaf rollers	Small caterpil-lars	Deciduous plants; other plants	Leaves roll up	Sevin
Mealybugs	White cottony insects	Many plants	Plants stunted, don't grow	Sevin, diazinon
Mites	Minute sucking insects	Almost all plants	Discolored leaves	Systemics
Nematodes	Microscopic worms	Many plants	Plants stunted, die back	Sterilize soil
Scale	Tiny, hard, oval insects	Many plants	Yellowing or loss of leaves	Diazinon
Snails, slugs (not insects but com-mon pests)	Easily recog-nized	Many plants	Eaten foliage	Metaldehyde
Spittle bugs	Brown, gray, or black insects wrapped in froth	Many plants	Stunted plants and fruits	Malathion
Springtails	Tiny black jumping bugs	Some plants	Pitted leaves	Malathion
Squash bugs	Dark-brown in-sects	Few plants	Plants turn black and die	Malathion, Sevin
Thrips	Tiny winged in-sects	Few plants	Leaves become silvery	Malathion
Wireworms	Hard, shiny, coiled worms	Flowers, vegeta-bles	Kill seedlings; work under-ground	Diazinon

SOURCE: Much of this data was derived from "The Thoughtful Gardener's Guide," *Cry California, the Journal of California Tomorrow*, Vol. 4, No. 3 (Summer 1969).

Notes on Insecticides

Malathion safest to humans and pets.

Sevin—a carbonate, should be avoided if pregnant.

Dibrom—quite toxic

Diazinon—very toxic

Systemics—highly toxic (cumulative and persistent effects not yet proven)

Do not use metaldehyde which contains arsenicals.

Check with your local Agricultural Station (listed in the Appendix) for further information on insects in your area and suggestions for how to eliminate them.

PLANT DISEASES

Many destructive plant diseases are caused by bacteria, fungi, and viruses. Diseases are generally named for their dominant symptoms—blight, canker, leaf spot—or for the organism causing disease—rust, powdery mildew. Many times unfavorable conditions and poor culture open the way for these agents to cause trouble. A poorly grown plant, like a human being in poor health, is more susceptible to bacteria and viruses. Insects, too, add to the problem because many of them spread diseases from one plant to another.

Environment also plays a part in the development of bacterial and fungus attacks, since they are responsive to moisture and temperature. Moisture is particularly important because it is necessary for the germination of spores of the organisms of disease. Excessive moisture in the soil can lead to root rot. Frequently, plants in shade are more prone to develop disease than those in sun.

Here is a simple explanation of the organisms that cause plant disease.

Fungi: This is familiar to us because we have seen old bread and fruits and mushrooms on which fungi have developed. There are thousands of different kinds of fungi, some of which can cause serious plant damage. Rot, wilt, rust, and powdery mildew are basically due to specific fungi.

Bacteria: Microscopic organisms that survive in soil or plant parts and cause blights, rot, galls, or wilting. Human diseases are caused by bacteria, and so are some plant ailments. Bacteria is the causative agent of fire blight and iris rhizome rot.

Virus: Many of the most serious diseases of ornamental plants are caused by a virus. We are still trying to decipher viruses in humans, and they are as much of a mystery when they attack plants.

Listed here are some of the diseases that can occur in plants and the remedies for them. However, to be quite frank, once plants are infected, it is difficult to save them. Further, generally highly poisonous controls are necessary and, while we list some here, we do not sanction using them unless as a last resort. Often it is better to get rid of badly diseased plants.

Rust: Leaves and stems are affected with reddish spores in powdery pustules or gelatinous lumps. Foliage turns yellow. Several kinds of rust affect hollyhocks, snapdragons. Control: Spray with Actidione or Ferbam.

Powdery mildew: White or gray growth usually on the surface of leaves or branches or fruit. Leaves are powdery with blotches and sometimes curled. Plants are often stunted. Control: Hosing or heavy rain will naturally control it.

Leaf Spot: Can do extensive damage to ornamental plants, resulting in defoliation. Leaves have distinct spots with brownish or white centers and dark edges. Rarely fatal, but cut off and destroy affected foliage. Control: Spray with Zineb or Ferbam.

Rot: Many kinds of rot occur on plants. The disease can attack irises, calla lilies, and other plants—crown rot on delphiniums, for instance. Affected spots appear watery and turn yellow or brown. (The iris borer helps to spread this disease.) Control: Destroy infected plant parts. Sterilize soil before planting again.

Blight: Many blights caused by several kinds of organisms. Azalea petal blight, camellia flower blight, botrytis blight. Gray mold appears on plant parts. Control: For botrytis, spray with Zineb or Ferbam. For other blights, spray with Zineb or treat soil with Terraclor.

Wilt: Due to various causal organisms, and can affect mature plants and seedlings. Usually wilt organisms live in soil. Cut away infected parts. Control: No known chemical control.

Mosaic: Virus affected leaves show a yellow and green mottling; sometimes deformed. Plants are stunted. Many viruses distributed by aphids and leafhoppers. Control: Destroy infected plants.

Cankers: Lesions on woody stems, with fungi entering through unbroken tissue. Control: Cut away infected parts.

Dodder: A parasitic plant; a leafless vine that suckers to the stem of the host plant. Control: Cut away dodder.

Galls: Enlargements of plant tissue due to fungi, bacteria, or insect attack. Control: Destroy plant.

21 🌿

Regional Gardening

THE FOLLOWING section contains information on gardening in specific regions: Northeast, Midwest, and so forth, written by gardeners in each area. While the information is not comprehensive, it does contain enough advice to get you started growing in your own region.

GARDENING IN THE NORTHEAST
Elinore B. Trowbridge

The New England area consists of six states of which five actually touch the Atlantic Ocean. Although the nearness of the sea tempers the climate, we are in zones 4 and 5 of the U.S. Department of Agriculture climatic zone map. Thus winter temperatures may be (rarely) 30 degrees below zero. High summer temperatures reach into the 100s. Most New Englanders can expect from 120 to 200 growing days (i.e. frost free) although this is dependent upon microclimates. In other words, there is enormous local variation in temperatures. For example, in my former home one mile away, killing frost came regularly about September 9, sweeping down the garden behind the house. This was a low area where at one time (when we were double-digging for an English type rosebed) the water table was so close to the soil surface that neighbors thought we were

putting in a pool. Where I now garden I count on picking some chrysanthemums for the Thanksgiving table, and gentians flower until November.

Other factors may also produce unexpected hardiness in plants. Hardiness, or the ability to withstand certain amounts of cold, is not an absolute trait in plants. There are hardy plants which succumb to a very sudden temperature drop in November—from 70F to night temperatures in the low 30s. These same plants, adjusting gradually to cold, will survive a winter of gradual onset with a low of 25F below zero. The survival of "borderline hardy" plants in the area often depends on the skillful use of an insulating layer of mulch. This is to stabilize the reduced soil temperature of winter and prevent the expansion and contraction of soil produced by cycles of freeze/thaw/freeze that tear and uproot the plants.

Rainfall in New England averages about 40 inches annually although we have our cycles of several years of drought in summer or prolonged rainy periods in spring which necessitate replanting. Much of our precipitation is snow. Accumulated snow in northern Vermont enables gardeners there to grow plants under the insulation of the snow which would perish in a typical Massachusetts "open winter"—one with little snow or only briefly-lasting snow. In 1978 New England had one exceptionally heavy snow-fall—50 inches. This snow lasted a full month. In late spring some plants bloomed which had never before had a blossom. For example, a clematis Elsa Spaeth I planted over twenty years ago.

Soil

New England is glacial country. This means plenty of boulders, sand, and gravel, and very thin soil in some places, but deep and fertile in others. The landscape contours are hilly. The Appalachian Chain does not consist of mountains in the true geological sense. The boulder detritus is particularly evident in New Hampshire and Vermont where the rocks were used for freestanding (unmortared) boundary stone walls genera-tions ago.

The soil of New England is on the acid side of neutrality. This is good and means that if other conditions are suitable, a wide variety of species can be grown. Where the soil is markedly acid, as in wooded areas or where there has been a great deal of plant decomposition, some of our regional special-ties include dogwoods, kalmias (mountain laurel), pieris, bearberry, *Cypripedium acaule* (pink ladyslipper), *Arbutus cana-densis* (Mayflower, the Massachusetts state flower), and cranberries.

Beneath New England topsoil are deposits of heavy red/brown clay. If the particles are broken up and mixed with organic material like compost or peat moss, or even sand, an excellent, fertile soil is had. However, a tough layer of clay under the topsoil ac-counts for many of the problems of New England gardeners since such clay does not drain. Plant roots reach the clay and smother for lack of oxygen or perish from rot. Some-times deep digging reveals sand and gravel

and perhaps another commercial sand-and-gravel enterprise is born. Compared with the difficulties of gumbo clay in Texas or adobe in California, or hungry sandy soil in parts of the south, the New Englander is happy with his soil—it definitely "has the makings"!

Many parts of New England that have been long settled produce a special problem. This is the ruin of the soil by liming. Tam-pering with the natural acidity of the soil by the compulsive spreading of lime is a sad New England reality. No gardener should lime without a soil test and a far-reaching decision that he always wants lime in that area—for that is what he will have. You can put lime in but you can't get it out again! Soil tests are available throughout New England at state agricultural field sta-tions.

Wooded New England

An airplane flight over New England on a clear day, flying low, would lead a stranger to think the area was primeval woodland. Actually, the woodlands are all secondary growths but the effect is certainly wooded. This is quite unlike the views of Oklahoma, for instance—a checkerboard of open fields, or even California.

New England has many trees and garden-ers intend to keep it that way. My own half-acre lot has a sixty-foot beech, two larches, a silk tree, a sourwood tree, a pepperidge, a huge magnolia, and probably a dozen hem-locks, pines, firs, etc., in addition to small flowering trees like crab apples, dogwoods, and cherries. This abundance of trees leads to a problem—shade. The enjoyment of trees is logical in this area where we are par-ticularly fortunate in our fall color. In au-tumn around Columbus Day, New England is the goal of many visitors who come to enjoy the fall foliage show.

Design

Not only does our common cultural heritage decree plenty of trees; it also influences our garden design. George Washington and Thomas Jefferson, not to speak of various DuPonts, left plot plans, plant import orders and bills, and the cumulative horticultural realities to be seen at Mt. Vernon, Monticello, Longwood Gardens, and Winterthur, to mention a few fine gardens.

In New England we had the period of the great estates. This lasted until about the Great Depression. The annual spring flower show of the Massachusetts Horticultural Society for 75 years offered shows to the general public displaying literally acres of acacias, hundreds of feet of orchids, clematis blooms the size of dinner plates, and simulations of outdoor gardens under roofs planted with literally thousands of Dutch hardy bulbs in full bloom. This kind of exposure to the products of taste and wealth caused many householders to aspire to horticultural achievements which were impossible in terms of acreage, labor available, and cost. Happily nowadays the Massachusetts Horticultural Society is displaying smaller exhibits, suited to adaptation by the average gardener.

Dooryard Garden

Today we have come a long way from our colonial past. Some small-scale relics of colonialism still are seen. On Cape Cod in Massachusetts we often see replicas of the English cottage garden. A low, weathered shingled wooden house typically has a picket fence enclosing the house about midway along the front of the property, with a pathway in the center, and with a latching gate. Within the fence and surrounding the little house is a lovely confusion of bloom—roses, delphinium, Oriental poppies, Madonna lilies, gas plants—followed later by zinnias, marigolds, petunias, and ultimately by dahlias, asters, day lilies in variety.

Rock Garden

Another type of garden is the rock garden. Unlike the English rock garden, which is almost always constructed of expensive rock brought in and arranged according to strict rules, the New England rock garden is often the acceptance of reality. A rocky ledge which would cost a fortune to dynamite is developed as a garden. The rocks are often part of a front sloping lot and may be planted with junipers and Kurume azaleas if climate permits (the New England northwest winds are often lethal to such plants). If the area is sunny, true alpine plants may be grown in the fissures of the rocks or just a tumble of cerastium and Johnny-Jump-Ups, unimproved violas. Some rock gardens are a rather static affair with a garish display of azaleas and masses of evergreens the rest of the year.

Foundation Planting

Probably the most abundant style of planting in New England is the "foundation planting." Because of the rigorous winters, the front door of the dwelling is likely to be flanked on both sides by evergreens. Cone-bearing evergreens are preferred to broadleafed. Rhododendrons especially roll their leaves into cigars at freezing weather. This forlorn appearance is protective to the economy of the plant and prevents excessive transpiration. I often look out the window at the *Rhododendron catawbiensis* instead of peering at the thermometer when I decide how warmly to dress in winter. Favorite choices for front door planting are Arborvitae, which contractors just love but house buyers hate because most of them (the plants) turn brown during cold weather. Another usual choice is hemlocks which look lovely in the tenderness of their youth but less attractive when in six years they have mounted to the eaves and darkened rooms in passing. More durable material like yews can be bought dwarf or pruned annually to specifications and require no artificial protection. These front door plantings are often "faced down" with shrubs, probably forsythia, lilac, or mock orange.

When the front is treated rather formally and symmetrically as has just been described, the rear of the property becomes the true garden. It will be fenced for the safety of children. Here will be flowers, the vegetable plot, and some attempt at a mixed border of decorative flowering shrubs, perennials, and bulbs. If the fence is suitable, there will be climbing roses—Paul's Everblooming Blaze is highly esteemed although lacking in fragrance. Incidentally, in New England no everblooming roses are everblooming! If cleverly managed we *may rarely* have a bit of recurrent bloom here and there, but "ever"—NEVER!

Wild Garden

Perhaps the most important contemporary trend in New England garden design is the "wild garden." This is a naturalistic planting of native materials. I write "naturalistic" because genuine natural gardening would allow vegetation to compete with the result unpredictable—depending on the terrain and the species it might be woodland, meadow, or swamp.

What the naturalistic gardener seeks is the emotional experience of viewing selected species in informal settings. By obscuring adjacent structures by trees like the oak, tupelo, dogwood, pine, larch, and hemlock, he attains a feeling of isolation from the noisy world. Early hepatica, trillium, or some other "wild" plant, meaning unimproved, nonhybridized species, are planted. All the revelations of spring after a harsh New England winter will be enjoyed. The needles of the larch, showing misty green along the branches; an underplanting of *Cercis canadensis* (redbud tree), possibly in its rare white form instead of the common magenta, later a *Cladrastis lutea* (yellowwood), with ferny foliage and dangling wisteria-like white bloom which is delightfully fragrant, and extremely attractive to honeybees. The wild gardener tends to be a plant connoisseur—he has traveled full circle horticulturally. He returns to native plants whose charms go unappreciated by the average gardener. Even his pachysandra will be choice, either the native Appalachian spurge seen mainly in arboreta or variegated Japanese pachysandra. The super wild plant gardener eschews plants which in no way are native to his region. He will avoid primroses, for example, since they are not an Appalachian mountain plant. He will take to his heart *Lilium canadensis* (provided he can grow it). The New England wild gardener is perhaps the closest thing we have in the Northeast to the "plantsman" venerated in contemporary England. He culminates the design skills of individual gardeners.

The Gardening Seasons

The gardening year starts in New England in March, although some gardeners start raking leaves from beds in a sunny interlude in February. Whatever time one picks in New England to start, it is always too early or too late. It's never just right. In March the enthusiast is on his knees, brushing away maple and oak leaves and looking for the first crocus (or winter aconite, if he is a "wild" gardener). He is thatching his lawn to scratch out dead fungus-inviting grass. He is often spreading fertilizer and crabweed preventatives from a single bag as crabgrass is the scourge of the East. He may even, if he prepared the soil last fall, get in a planting of peas on the traditional date, March 17.

The premature operations of March are often ineffectual. The *real* beginning for the New England gardener is April. Now he can plant bare root trees, shrubs, and perennials as our area fares best with spring planting. He also starts seed. An exception to this is starting a lawn. Although most lawns *are* started in spring the *recommended* season is late August. In April almost anything can be planted, especially if it is balled and burlapped, which it usually is. The great burst of April activity spills over into May—probably *the* best time to enjoy a New England garden. June may offer roses, delphinium, bridal wreath, viburnums, peonies, Oriental poppies, and madonna lilies. By July the average New England garden has shot its bolt—the mountain laurel, magnolias, azaleas, flowering dogwoods, forsythia, the beloved lilac, the fragrant mock orange, the bearded iris are all past. The trees are leafy green. There may be day lilies, butterfly bushes, large flowered climbing roses carrying the brunt of the color effect. August is very difficult indeed. The hardy silk tree, the varnish tree, the pagoda tree offer blossoms. The shrubs that bloom in August are often bluish, oddly enough: caryopteris, buddleias, certain Rose of Sharon, escholtzia, and vitex

among them. Only a few perennials appear with any frequency—late-season day lilies, many of the hostas, rose mallows, and asters are seen. Sometimes there will be a fine stand of rubrum lilies although in New England contemporary gardeners are rather afraid of failure with lilies.

By September we are admiring the hardy albizzia still (silk tree); the famous eastern Franklinia (a member of the camellia family), and the fruits of many woody plants like mountain ash, cotoneaster, and pyracantha, those dogwood-fruits the birds have spared, rose hips, bittersweet berries. *The* perennials are asters in profusion and chrysanthemums. Most of the chrysanthemums are bought during the summer or early fall from nurseries, dropped into the garden bed, and discarded with the severe killing frosts which will occur by Thanksgiving Day, as a rule. October is the month of turning leaves. In New England the Christmas rose does not bloom until March. It would be only truthful to say that virtually *nothing* blooms—for that we must await nature's reawakening. The test of the quality of our garden design will become apparent during the long winter months. Then the "bones" of the garden stand revealed in the shapes and textures of the woody trunks and branches, the beauty of cones on evergreens, and furry buds on pussywillows and magnolias. When snow decorates the branches it is the ultimate tribute to nature and to the gardener if the scene be appreciated as beautiful.

In this survey of seasonal aspects of New England gardens, we know that each season has its special responsibilities for the gardener. Spring is the time of planting and transplanting. Midsummer is a maintenance period with fertilization and watering primary cares. Late summer is the opportunity for correcting past mistakes and moving things around. Autumn is the time for corrective pruning, and pruning which is prophylactic—protecting woody material from heavy snow loads and catastrophic winds. Another protective activity is the mulch which must be applied in the New England area—*after* the ground is frozen for several inches. Such a mulch keeps the ground frozen and by achieving constant temperature at the root level protects plants from "heaving and hauling" or soil movement from frost which tears roots.

New England Gardening Enemies

Certain plants here are the gardener's enemies. Among them are the ubiquitous crab grass of lawns and the even more evil witch grass of vegetable gardens. I myself am still coping with the witch grass *set out in rows* by a well-intentioned helper who mistook the stolons (horizontally creeping root-like stems) for iris rhizomes. In the Victorian period ground ivy was a substitute for lawns in shady places. This pretty little scalloped "runner" with violet flowers (to give the devil his due) has a certain charm. This plant is the ruin of any lawn and few chemical substances deal with it. Fortunately dodder and bindweed are seldom troubling here.

Animal enemies include various caterpillars (the gypsy moth is back after a long absence). The Japanese beetle succumbed many places to the milky spore disease. That was 20 years ago—it is about time for another attack. The chestnut blight is still with us. More than 50 years ago it wiped out all the marvelous American chestnuts which were native to this region—fine nuts and wonder timber. Rail fences still stand all over the country made from American chestnut. Chlorosis or a metabolic iron-deficiency disease is seen in New England, particularly where plants are grown in limey soil which are native to acid soil. Virus diseases have about eradicated the American elm here (and elsewhere). New England was particularly noted for elm-lined main streets in country towns. At the Arnold Arboretum the ornamental Japanese cherries are virtually doomed. Some are being grown in another area to develop virus-free stock but the outlook is poor (as it is in the Washington D.C. basin display). Fundamentally New England is healthy plant-wise.

Despite these few enemies of the gardener, the New England gardener has many friends. He has the resources of an area very hospitable to instruction in gardening. It runs the gamut from horticultural slide-talks at local garden clubs to Open House to the public by agricultural stations of the government, public gardens, and private ones. The Massachusetts Horticultural Society has a huge membership and sends mobile bookmobiles around, and mails from its well-stocked library. The Arnold Arboretum welcomes the general public, and publishes a popular level journal of wide distribution. It maintains 265 acres of display, labeled living specimens in Boston, and 125 acres of suburban grounds type display in its Weston area.

Although I've travelled a good deal, to me New England is the most interesting gardening area of the entire country. It is our seasonal diversity which I so enjoy.

GARDENING IN THE MIDWEST
Peggy Macneale

Mid-America covers a lot of territory. A temperature zone map will show variations from Zone 3 to Zone 6, although the greatest area is a broad band through the states of Ohio, Indiana, Illinois, Missouri, and Kansas that is largely in Zone 5. Transition zones, micro-climates, and record-breaking variations, such as occurred in the winters of 1976–77 and 1977–78, play hob, however, with plantings that are done strictly according to the maps. Lists given at the end of this chapter should all be considered in the light of what is growing in local nurseries, and what the county extension service in any particular area advises.

A winter with a long spell of below-zero temperatures is not hard on plants as long as there is a good snow blanket to insulate the roots. The greatest danger to plants in this area is a delightful long warm fall. Dormancy is delayed, growth continues, and then suddenly the thermometer plunges into the 20's. Similarly, a heat wave in March will break dormancy of such trees as *Magnolia soulangeana,* only to be overcome by an April freeze that browns the flowers. Probably every region in this vast country produces such horror stories, but the Midwest gardener seems to face a continual challenge.

The broad-leaf evergreens are particularly vulnerable to climatic vacillations. Recommended as protection measures: thorough watering in the fall and an anti-desiccant spray applied in November and again in January. The problem is not so much the cold as it is the burning from sun and thawing winds when the ground is still frozen. The general practice is to plant materials such as Ilex, Cherry laurel, and rhododendron on the north or east sides of the house for greater protection from prevailing winds.

Soils, too, have a lot to do with what will grow where. In the Midwest the underlying structure varies from sandstone and shale in eastern Ohio to heavy-bedded limestone in Indiana, and deep, deep loam farther to the west in the prairie states. The cycles of glaciation, ending with the Wisconsin ice sheet, dumped sand, gravel, and boulders in moraines and out-wash terraces over large sections of the Midwest, and also carved out numerous lakes which moderate the climate in local areas. A study of geology explains all of this, but the average gardener knows only his own yard, and most of the time he cares only if he can dig a hole without needing a pickaxe, or plant a garden that will grow vegetables and flowers without a lot of insect and disease problems.

As bedrock weathers and breaks down we find that the great complaint of the Midwest gardener is the heavy clay he must contend with. Actually, the mineral content of the clay soils found throughout the area east of the Mississippi is fairly high. Historically, these hills and valleys supported huge forests of mixed hardwoods. It is said that a squirrel could travel from east Ohio to the western edge of Indiana without coming down to ground level. When these lands were cleared they supported farms that were—and are— equally productive. It is when the modern developers come in with earth-moving machinery to reshape the land that the subsoil of clay is laid bare. The owners of all those new homes in subdivisions are left with the problem of gardening in yards that have been stripped of topsoil.

Lime has been the recommended ingredient for breaking up clods of clay, but when the soil is already on the neutral-to-alkaline side, it is better to use gypsum, which does not lift the pH. Another aid to soil improvement is Old Man Winter. If the plot is turned over in the fall, sod and all, and left in heavy clumps for the freezing and thawing action of the cold months, by the time the weather warms up enough to inspire spring planting the garden site will be considerably easier to work. Then, a liberal (six inches plus) layer of peat moss, well-rotted manure, or compost should be spaded in. These organic materials soon break down, and the acids of decomposition react with the minerals in the clay. The result is that soluble salts—mineral compounds—are formed that plant roots can ultilize for nutrition. The compounds can be put directly on as fertilizers, of course, but, without going overboard on organic gardening, it must be emphasized that the organic materials do much more than just help produce plant foods. They also lighten the soil physically, allowing oxygen and water to penetrate, and they provide food for earthworms that further enrich and aerate the earth. Then, too, when organic material is added to a garden, it warms up sooner in the spring. After a few years of this kind of care the soil will suddenly become wonderfully friable, and the gardener will have something to be proud of: a rich, easily-worked loam that will grow prize-winning flowers and vegetables.

The areas that received glacial deposits have sandy soils that also need organic additions to help retain water and provide nutrients. Thus, the first thing a home owner should do is figure out a place for a compost pile. There are now bins on the market that advertise quick composting, but most old-time gardeners are perfectly satisfied with an informal heap of accumulated leaves, grass clippings, green kitchen wastes, and weeds, layered with soil if possible, and moistened every so often. Forking this over once or twice a year is good exercise on a

cool morning. The bottom layers, ready to use, are revealed. Heavy stems not completely broken down can be tossed back on the pile. Shrubs planted strategically around the area will screen it from the neighbors and from the terrace, but one should never be apologetic about a compost pile. Recycling is the "in" thing!

The most important factor for gardening success in the Midwest, as everywhere, is rainfall. Fortunately, there is rarely a water shortage in this part of the country so sprinklers can be used if summers are very dry. Usually Midwest summers are steamy hot with frequent, though scattered, thunderstorms. Mulches of grass clippings, bark, or compost are advised to retain soil moisture, keep the soil cool, and discourage weeds. Black plastic, newspapers, and even old braided rugs have been utilized for these same purposes! An aluminum foil mulch has the added virtue of repelling aphids, and can be recycled at the end of summer.

Before becoming involved with these details, however, the Midwest gardener is usually most concerned with the establishment of a good lawn. Many fine new products have been tested and put on the market in the past decade or so, and the lawn picture is getting greener all the time. Heretofore it was a yearly cycle of spring growth, summer burning, and winter mud. Now, with the advice of numerous experts guiding us, the result can be all that we dream of (though the expense can be considerable!). Thus, a heavy application of fertilizer in September, followed by the sowing of a good mixture of several bluegrasses and a quick-germinating perennial ryegrass, is the up-to-date approach for a new lawn. A couple of mowings and leaf rakings during the fall should get the lawn through the winter. In the spring grass rarely needs fertilizing, but granules of a pre-emergent material to inhibit crabgrass germination can be applied in early May. Come June, an application of "hot weather" slow-release lawn food should be spread on and watered in for at least four hours. Avoid "sprinkling" at any time, which just encourages grass roots to grow near the surface rather than seeking moisture down deep. Set the lawn mower as high as it will go, never removing more than one-third of the blade of grass at a time.

A good turf discourages weeds but if dandelions, plantain, etc., become a threat, apply a herbicide. Work only on a windless day, and never overdo this because of the danger to nearby shrubbery and herbaceous plants. It is better to keep up a good fertilizer program than to sow grass seed too thick. Blue-grass spreads by creeping roots and will fill in bare spots with a little patience and adequate food. It is important to remember that the *timing* of the application of all lawn care products must be observed to achieve good turf.

In developing a garden the planting of trees ranks high, along with the lawn. No one in the whole Midwest region could go wrong if the red oak were first choice as a shade tree. The red oak is native over most of the area. It grows reasonably fast, especially when young. It is not a problem in the maintenance of a lawn, and it provides fine shade and autumn color. Other oaks are also good choices, especially the willow oak and the pin oak. A problem may occur with these two if the soil is deficient in available iron: yellowing (chlorosis) of the leaves warns of this but a good tree man can remedy the condition with foliar feeding and treatment of the soil. The sugar maple is also a popular tree, but with a surface root system. Any maple may heave a sidewalk and may inhibit grass because of root competition. The glorious fall color of maples, however, can compensate for the faults.

Numerous ornamental trees are available. Native all over the Midwest is the redbud, an understory tree at the edge of woods. So is the flowering dogwood. Both of these provide blossoms during April, and the dogwood also has magnificent fall color. Problems with these: the redbud grows with a taproot, so is difficult to move. Dogwoods are liable to suffer shock, too, when transplanted, so these two should be moved only in the spring. This advice also holds for magnolias, which have fleshy roots, easily rotted by cold soil in fall planting.

Flowering crabapples are perhaps the favorite ornamental in the Midwest. They seem to thrive in any soil and are easily moved. Their only fault is a scab disease that disfigures the leaves and causes early defoliation. However, disease-resistant varieties are on the market and should be sought. Red Jade, White Angel, Van Esteltine, Snowdrift, Sargenti, *Zumi calocarpa*, and *Comus floribunda* are all highly rated. They vary in size, form, and flower and fruit color so can satisfy any need. Get acquainted with these and many other choice ornamentals.

Every garden is enhanced by fine shrubs. Does the gardener want colorful fruits as well as flowers? Look into the many varieties of viburnums. Is summer bloom important? Check out the new *Althaea* Diana (white Rose of Sharon). Is shade a problem? *Deutzia gracilis* has much to offer, and grows to only three feet or so. How about winter twig interest? There is no greater conversation piece than the Harry Lauder walking stick (*Corylus avellana contorta*). Remember the climate zones, however. Though forsythia is a joy in April in the southern part of Zone 5, the buds may freeze out even there in a very bad winter, and it never blooms in Zone 4. On the other hand, the colder the winter, the better the lilacs bloom.

Another factor in the proper choice of ornamental shrubs is the available space. Such plants as beauty bush (*Kolkwitzia*), *Weigela*, and *Philadelphus* need an indefinite amount of room so they may send out long sprays of bloom. This is the way they really should grow, so it is tragic when they are crowded and chopped, and even forced to become clipped hedges. Some pruning, however, is required to keep them healthy. New growth must be encouraged by annual removal of one-third of the old wood to the ground right after the blooming period. Judicious shaping of upper branches may also be done at this time. If pruning is done too late in the season, the flower buds already formed for the following year will be cut off. A good way to prune forsythia is to cut branches in January or February to force into bloom indoors.

Often, long before the woody plants are completely established in the yard, the gardener has laid out a flower border and dug up a bed for vegetables. The bedding plant industry sells thousands of begonias and potted geraniums, but there are still untold numbers of home owners who like to plant seeds. Zinnias and marigolds are the big favorites in the Midwest. Petunia seeds are so tiny that few gardeners start their own, but almost every other popular annual can be seeded right in place by mid-May in Zone 5. The rule most often ignored in growing plants from seed is "Thin seedlings as required." No matter how painful, thinning is an absolute necessity for healthy foliage and good bloom. With the advent of fluorescent tubes and reflector units, providing light but little heat, many enthusiasts are tackling the growing of annuals that need an early start, biennials, and perennials that are difficult to maintain in Midwest gardens. Delphinium, for instance, does not flourish for more than about three years in this region, but delphinium seed costs a fraction of the money required to buy a few plants from a local supplier—if one can even be found.

Perennials, on the whole, are favored in the Midwest as the backbone of the May–June garden. One sees columbines, Shasta daisies, iris, peonies, and Oriental poppies everywhere. Less common, but very good, are *Dictamnus* (gasplant), *Baptisia*, and *Veronica*. The Midwest climate and soils are not very kind to true lilies but in July and August the magnificent daylilies (*Hemerocallis*) thrive at the back of the border. Hardy phlox is a good companion, blooming all summer. At the front of the border the color is provided by annuals that can be seeded between disappearing spring bulbs. By September chrysanthemums are beginning to bloom, but seldom are these permanent residents of the border. They are hardy enough, but may be fatally desiccated by late winter freeze-and-thaw action that heaves the shallow-rooted chrysanthemums right out of the ground. For safety sake, one plant of each cherished variety may be lifted in late November and set in a cold frame. When new growth starts in April the clumps can be divided. Sturdy stolons with roots can be re-set in the border, or cuttings can be rooted in the cold frames. In either case the growing tips are pinched out every few weeks until mid-July. By that time the plants are bushy, and ready to set buds. It is customary to move plants even in full bloom to a place in the border—if watered in well there is no evident setback.

The cold frame is a handy horticultural asset for other plants, too. The protection of the covered box is all that is necessary to hold over the rosemary plants from the herb bed and the variegated vinca vines from the hanging baskets. A fall planting of lettuce in the cold frame can be harvested until really bitter weather, which usually comes after Christmas. Pansies seeded in the cold frame in September will be ready to move, often in full bloom, into the garden in April.

The Midwest gardener's vegetable patch is about the same as any in other regions. Unless the soil has been improved to a good depth, however, the growing of carrots isn't too successful. Any root crop must receive plenty of water during even short dry spells to ensure a tender crop. Beans, tomatoes, and corn all do very well in the Midwest heat and humidity, but lettuce is an early crop that bolts in July sunshine and peas are a failure unless planted no later than early April.

Aside from these types of plants already discussed there are numerous specialty gardens that appeal to hobbyists. Spring bulbs, roses, wild flowers, and rockeries all come to mind.

Daffodils demand good drainage, so if the clay soil holds too much water, it is advisable to build raised beds for prize bulbs. Foliage should be allowed to ripen off naturally, and moisture at the level of the dormant bulb should be avoided during the hot summer. A cover crop of annuals or leafy vegetables such as squash will shade the daffodils plantings and will drink up normal rainfall so that the bulbs may stay dry. If a

fall drought threatens, however, bulbs must be watered to start root growth, and lack of spring rains calls for supplementary watering during the blooming period.

Roses demand constant care during the summer to prevent blackspot and mildew from defoliating the plants. It is better to make every effort to keep the foliage healthy, and send roses into the winter with clean leaves and strong canes than to worry about damage from cold. There are many ways to cover roses, but the great question is: when should they be uncovered? Some experts are coming to the conclusion that roses bought from a northern source, fed and tended carefully, and cut back in the fall only to the point that canes do not whip in the wind, will survive as well or better than roses that have been covered with protectors.

Wildflower gardens are a delight in April and May. The native hepatica, rose Anemone, Bloodroot, Celandine poppy, blue-eyed Mary, and a host of other woodland beauties can still be found growing in patches of oak-hickory and maple-beech forests. Home owners lucky enough to have even a smidgeon of native woods can enlarge upon this by purchasing plants from nurseries dealing in wildflowers and ferns. Other gardeners who are unhappy with a yard that is all shade can take advantage of this and begin a wildflower garden from scratch simply by letting the leaves fall and refusing to rake them up. After several years a nice mulch will build up, ready to receive the planting of a few easy-to-grow wildflowers such as *Phlox divaricata* and Solomon-seal. It would not be amiss to plant compatible things such as hosta, epimedium, and an azalea or two. The greatest problem in such a venture is keeping the seedling trees from taking over.

Rockeries, in contrast, are usually built in sunny areas where bed rock is exposed, or even constructed on a slope to imitate a natural outcrop of stone. Arabis, dwarf phlox, various sedums and houseleeks, *Veronica* Crate Lake, *Alyssum saxatile* are all easy to grow, tucked in between the rocks. The serious rock gardener will go further into growing true alpine plants and dwarf evergreens, making a vision out of what had been a barren hillside.

All of these types of gardens, and more, may be discovered by those interested in gardening in the Midwest.

Choice Plants for the Midwest

Shade trees

Red oak
Willow oak
Pin oak
Swamp white oak
Sugar maple
Red maple (selected cultivars)
Norway maple (also varieties)
Ginkgo (grafted male)
Tulip tree
Sweet gum
Eucomia (hardy rubber tree)
Cork tree (*Phellondendron*)

Good for patio

River birch
Zelkova (elm substitute)
Moraine honey locust
Yellowwood (*Cladrastis*)
Chinese elm (*Ulmus parvifolia*)
Pagoda tree (*Sophora japonica*)

Street trees

Little leaf linden
London plane
Marshall seedless ash

Evergreen

Scotch pine
White pine
Austrian pine
Douglas fir
Norway spruce
Colorado spruce
Metasequoia (deciduous conifer)
American holly
Magnolia grandiflora (Zone 6)

Spring-flowering shrubs

Witch hazel (American and Chinese)
Forsythia Spring Glory
Japanese quince
Deutzia (especially gracilis)
Weigela
Kolkwitzia
Philadelphus
Azalea
Lilac (many named varieties)
Rosa hugonis
Viburnum tomentosum
V. carlesi
V. burkwoodi
V. sieboldi

Flowering and fruiting trees

Flowering crabapple (many varieties)
Redbud (including white-flower variety)
Flowering dogwood
Cornelian cherry dogwood
Washington hawthorn

Lavalle hawthorn
Blackhaw viburnum
Magnolia soulangeana
M. virginiana (sweet bay)
Golden raintree (*koelreuteria*)
Callery pear (bradford, aristocrat)
Halesia (silverbell)
Flowering cherry
Purple-leaf plum
Amelanchier (serviceberry, shadblow)
Fringe tree (*Chionanthus*)
Mountain ash (Zone 4)

Trees of distinctive landscape value

Corkscrew willow
Fastigiate English oak
Upright European hornbeam
Cercidiphyllum (katsura tree)
Sourwood
"Brioti" red horse-chestnut
Paperbark maple (*Acer griseum*)
Russian olive
White birch (Zone 4)

Native trees to be cherished
(Most hard to transplant; should be preserved)

American beach
Sour gum
White oak
Black walnut
Hickory varieties
White ash
Sycamore
Sassafras

Summer-flowering shrubs

Althaea (hibiscus, named varieties of Rose of Sharon)
Potentilla (many varieties)

Hypericum (St. John's wort)
Bottle-brush buckeye
Hydrangea "Pee Gee"
Clethra (sweet pepperbush)
Spiraea froebeli
S. billardi
Butterfly bush (Zone 6)
Abelia

Fall-fruiting shrubs

Aronia (chokeberry)
Cornus alba (dogwood)
C. amonum
C. racemosa
C. stolonifera
Cotoneaster apiculata
C. divaricata
Ilex verticillata (deciduous holly)
Honeysuckle (*Lonicera*)
Pyracantha (firethorn)
Viburnum dentatum
V. cassinoides
V. opulus
V. sargenti
V. setigerum
V. wrighti

Shrubs of distinctive landscape value

Aralia spinosa (hercules club)
Bayberry
Cornus alba siberica (coral twig dogwood)
Corylus avellana contorta
Cotinus (smoke bush)
Euonymus alatus (wingbark burning bush)
Spicebush (*Lindera benzoin*)
Staghorn sumac

Shrubs for hedges

Alpine currant
Mentor barberry

Privet
Rhamnus "Tallhedge"
Rosa rugosa
Viburnum opulus "compactum"
Winter honeysuckle (*Lonicera fragrantissima*)

Perennials

Amsonia
Baptisia
Bergenia
Bocconia
Chrysanthemum
Columbine
Coreopsis
Daylily
Dictamnus
Echinops (globe thistle)
Epimedium
Gypsophila (baby's breath)
Hardy aster (New England, frikarti)
Heuchera (coral bells)
Hosta (many varieties)
Iberis
Iris (German, Siberian)
Lythrum
Oenothera
Oriental poppy
Peony
Phlox paniculata
Platycodon
Shasta daisy
Thermopsis
Veronica

Broad leaf evergreen

Cherry laurel (Zone 6)
Euonymus kiautschovicus
E. vegetus
Japanese holly (*Ilex convexa*)

Korean boxwood
Mahonia
Rhododendron

Needed evergreens

Arborvitae
Chamaecyparis (many forms)
Juniper andorra
J. "Blue Rug"
J. canarti (upright)
J. pfitzer
Taxus (yews) (upright and spreading)

Biennials

Canterbury bells
Foxglove
Gloriosa daisy
Lunaria (moneyplant, honesty)

Bulbs, etc.

Minor spring bulbs
Allium (various species)
Chionodoxa
Crocus
Daffodil
Fritillaria
Grape hyacinth
Hyacinth
Leucojum
Scilla
Snowdrop
Tulip

Hardy summer bulbs
Lycoris
Regal lily

Tender summer bulbs
Dahlia
Gladiola
Ismene

Annuals that re-seed
(or sow in fall)

Alyssum
Larkspur
Poppy

GARDENING IN THE PLAINS

Chuck Marson

The Mid-Plains

The Mid-Plains area does have some problems for the average gardener but none is insurmountable. Most garden books show areas of the Plains in various plant zones that run from coast to coast. It is true that certain plants can be grown in each of them but, for instance, a plant adapted to Zone 6 in Indiana or the East Coast will have problems in Kansas or Oklahoma that are unknown in the East. We have a great divergence of soils and altitudes that make a considerable difference. Most experts divide the Mid-Plains at the 100th meridian but it would be better divided at the 98th meridian. This is a line running from about Niobrara, Nebraska, down through Hastings to Beloit and Hutchison in Kansas and then through Enid to Lawton, Oklahoma. The elevation varies from 800 to 1000 feet in the east to above 4000 feet in the west. The eastern section gets from 30 to 40 inches of rainfall per year while the western section gets only 16 to 20 inches in good years. Generally speaking, the eastern section has clay-loam type soils that are fairly neutral while the western section is quite alkaline and with more sandy and prairie-type soils.

The most important factor to consider is the wind. Prevailing winds in summer are southwest and are strong and dry. There is not much improvement in winter as the winds are northwest and usually very dry also. We do have to take this into consideration when we garden. Many plants that would die if exposed directly to the wind will do fine if given shelter. It is important in all the Mid-Plains to provide windbreaks or to take advantage of natural wind barriers. Form your own mini-climates with hardy shrubs or trees for a windbreak or plant on the lee side of a building. If you provide protection from the wind and give plants plenty of water, they will do quite well in their proper plant zone.

Drainage is another factor that must be taken into account. In the eastern half, the soil is quite heavy and often does not drain well. Not many plants like wet feet. If you have heavy clay or gumbo, here is a good way to check on drainage. Dig a hole 12 to 24 inches deep and fill it with water. If the water has not drained away in about two hours, make provision for extra drainage. Either dig a planting hole twice as deep as seems necessary and then fill the lower half with coarse rock, or make a dry well by drilling a hole with a post auger in the bottom and fill it with coarse rock. Both methods work well. In some sandy or silty soils, the water drains away too fast. The best remedy for this is to add lots of organic material and mix it in.

The use of mulch is one of the very best ways to retain moisture, keep down weeds, hold down temperatures, and, when incorporated into the soil, add tilth. This is one of the most important factors in Mid-Plains gardening. Nature makes natural mulches through the dying of the foliage so you can't go wrong patterning after nature. Walk into any prairie or wood lot and see what a fine job mulches do. There are many good mulches and throughout the Plains straw and prairie hay are readily available. The only drawback is that they may contain some weed seeds and you must be careful of fire when they are dry. Weeds are not a great problem and can be controlled. Making a compost pile with all the organic debris from the garden and lawn is a good source of mulch and material for soil incorporation. We have had good results with grass clippings as a mulch but they must be applied in thin successive layers. If spread too thick, grass tends to mold and heat up. We have found that newspapers work well. Spread them four or five sheets thick and put a little soil on them to keep them from blowing. They work well in vegetable gardens and can be tilled into the soil easily. Keep in mind that newspaper is slightly alkaline. There are other mulches such as peat moss, stone mulch, plastics, shredded bark, and wood chips. One of the best we have used is ground up corn cobs but they are sometimes hard to find. If you have a farmer friend you may be able to prevail on him to run some through his feed grinder. We are stressing the mulch angle as it is important in the Plains area.

A healthy lawn is one of the basics of good landscaping. For the eastern section we still feel that Kentucky bluegrass makes the best lawn but it does require more maintenance. Kentucky 31 fescue is fine for bright sunny areas. It is coarser than bluegrass but, if sown at a high rate of 10 pounds per 1000 square feet and mowed at three inches, it makes a good lawn with drought resistance and excellent wearing qualities. In the western sections, bluegrass and K31 fescue are fine in irrigated areas, but in non-irrigated areas buffalo grass, crested wheat grass, and blue grama will do better. Zoysia and Bermuda grass are very satisfactory for the southern sections of the

Plains. From the middle of Kansas on south they do well. The only drawback is their rather short season but they are great for hot weather. Some of the new perennial rye grasses have done a good job and should be looked into. A light mulch will help get a new lawn started faster. It must be kept moist. Bermuda and zoysia are started from plugs or sprigs in spring, but other grasses are best started in early fall.

Mowing heights must be high for cool-season grasses in the Plains. Minimum height for bluegrass and K31 fescue is 2½ to 3 inches. The taller growth will keep the soil cooler, conserve moisture, and inhibit weeds. Zoysia, Bermuda, and buffalo grass can be mowed as low as 1 to 1½ inches. For cool season grasses, three fertilizations per year are considered best. Zoysia and Bermuda need a high nitrogen feeding early and again at midsummer. Buffalo grass and blue grama should not be fertilized at all. A crabgrass inhibitor in the spring will benefit cool-season grasses. A well-fed and well-watered lawn, mowed at the proper height, will give a minimum of trouble and a good base for your yard.

There are some alternative ground covers that can be used in difficult places to enhance appearance and prevent soil erosion. Once established they do not require much maintenance and should be considered for tough areas. For sunny areas, crown vetch, low-growing junipers, memorial rose, wintercreeper, honeysuckle vines, and even day lilies are good. Shady areas can grow ajuga, English ivy, *Vinca minor*, lily-of-the-valley, and plantain lily. Try some of these for hard-to-cover areas.

Vegetable and flower gardens in the plains may include almost any of the common varieties if there is proper soil preparation and adequate watering during dry periods. Annual flowers, such as petunias, ageratum, salvia, zinnias, marigolds, and geraniums do well. We have successfully raised almost any vegetable we wanted. Some cool-season plants like lettuce, radishes, and the cabbage-family plants have to be planted early to mature before hot weather. Some of them can be very successful in a fall garden. Hot-weather plants such as tomatoes, peppers, squash, and cucumbers must not be planted until after the last frost date. In the western section this can be as late as mid-May; in the southeastern section it can be as early as mid-April.

The planting of most tender annuals is governed by the frost dates. For your flower bed, consider some of the native wildflowers. There is a great interest in them and for good reason. They have grown in the area for ages and have become adapted to local conditions. There are many very beautiful ones that will enhance your flower beds. Seeds and plants are available from many of the seedhouses. Most of them thrive on neglect so don't be too good to them. We have used some and found that under the good soil conditions of our beds and with water and fertilizer, they become rampant and get out of hand. Talk to some of the wildflower enthusiasts in your neighborhood about the possibilities. Kansas has a Wildflower Society that can give you good information.

Shade trees are essential for Mid-Plains landscapes. Plant the deciduous plants to the south and west for the shade protection they afford in hot summers. In winter when the leaves are gone the sun can penetrate and help warm up the house. Large evergreens are better on the north or east as they will help break the force of the cold winter winds. Select the shade and ornamental trees to frame your home, screen out undesirable views, or set off a desirable one. Count on them for privacy for your outdoor living areas. Try to use trees that you know will do well in your area. The lists that follow will give you some ideas.

Try working some of your ornamentals into the windbreaks. Flowering shrubs are excellent for small windbreaks and for privacy, with the berry-producers very attractive to birds. All shrubs and ornamental plants that are adapted to our region will benefit from extra water. You must give intense care to all newly-set woody plants until they are well established. Protection from wind and thorough watering will ensure their success. Most transplanting of dormant woody and herbaceous ornamentals is best done in late winter or early spring to give them time to get established before cold weather. Here are some of the native trees and shrubs best adapted and many are very attractive. Among large native trees are some oaks, some maples, cottonwood, walnut, ash, honey locust, and Kentucky coffee tree. Smaller trees include osage orange, redbud, some hawthorns, and crabapples. Shrubs include coralberry, rough dogwood, wahoo, and sumac.

Among evergreens the junipers are best adapted for the area. Both Rocky Mountain and Eastern varieties do well. There are upright, shrub, and procumbent forms that can add a lot to the landscape scene. Red cedar or Rocky Mountain junipers are great for windbreaks. Scotch pine stands up the best of the pines although in the western area the ponderosa pine seems to do well. Colorado spruce also does well in the west as it does in the east. A windbreak made up of junipers, Russian olive, and native shrubs in a stag-

---

gered planting is effective and longlasting. An occasional tree adds interest and also increases protection.

Some fruit trees also do very well with protection. Apples, pears, and plums will grow almost anywhere in the Plains. Peaches and apricots do better in the southern parts. Strawberries thrive almost all over the area and seem to be very adaptable. Get the right varieties for the best production. Your local nurseryman can advise you. We have seen dwarf fruit trees used as facers for windbreaks. They not only look good but also produce.

Insect and disease problems in the Plains do not vary much from the rest of the country. Fungus diseases are usually not much of a problem due to the drier climate. Borers can be bad at times as well as grasshoppers. A close watch for coming problems allows you to head off trouble before it starts. We do feel that we may have fewer problems with insects and disease than many other areas.

In spite of the problems that face us, many people in the Plains have well-landscaped homes, beautiful flower beds, and bountiful vegetable gardens. This is true in the towns and on the farms and ranches. It does take some planning and thought and some hard work but it is all well worth it.

Choice Plants for the Mid-Plains

Small deciduous trees (to 30 feet)

Flowering crabapples
Washington hawthorn
Redbud
Golden raintree
Bradford pear
Russian olive

Medium deciduous trees (to 60 feet)

Black walnut
Box elder
Green ash
Hackberry
Honeylocust
Kentucky coffee tree
Northern Catalpa

Tall deciduous trees (to 100 feet)

Cottonwood
Pecan
Silver maple
Sycamore

Evergreens

Black Hills spruce
Colorado spruce
Junipers (most varieties)
Mugho pine
Ponderosa pine
Scotch pine

Shrubs

Buckthorn
Cistena plum
Common lilac
Coralberry
Pea shrub
Pekin cotoneaster
Rough dogwood
Spirea
Sumac
Wahoo

Vines

Climbing rose
Grape

Honeysuckle
Silverlace vine
Virginia creeper

The Plains

Here are some of the more reliable plants to grow in the Plains. This list is by no means complete as there are many others that can be used with special consideration.

Deciduous Trees (to 100 feet)

Cottonwood: A native that does very well. There are seedless varieties that remove the cotton undesirability. Keep in mind when planting: trees grow large.

Sycamore: Large leaves—the London plane is an excellent choice. Does well in either dry or damp locations.

Silver maple: Fast-growing and tolerant to all conditions. Some fine selections on the market do better than the native ones.

Pecan: Especially good in the southern sections but new selections are now on the market that do well as far north as Nebraska.

Deciduous Trees (to 60 feet)

Northern Catalpa: Leaves are large and flowers showy. Somewhat messy so give them plenty of room.

Green ash: This is a native and does well, but the seedless varieties on the market today are even better than the natives.

Honey locust: Another native that is very desirable especially in the thornless, seedless selections. Good light shade for a lawn tree.

Box elder: This member of the maple family is not the most desirable tree but in some difficult areas it will succeed where others fail. Good pruning helps keep it in better shape.

Hackberry: More like an elm in habit but disease resistant and very hardy and tough. It is native to most of the area and makes a fine shade tree. Pruning when young helps shape it up.

Kentucky coffee tree: A native that is not used as much as it should be. Not very attractive when small but soon develops into a fine shade tree. The black seed pods are attractive in winter and large enough to be easy to clean up.

Black walnut: Plant away from garden areas as most plants do not do well close to the walnut. A hardy tree with the extra advantage of the nuts. Some new varieties are available now that grow faster and produce nuts sooner—check with your county agent.

Small Deciduous Trees (to 30 feet)

Flowering crabapple: There are many selections with blooms from white to dark pink. Many sizes and shapes are sold from columnar to broad spreaders—some with large and others with very small fruits. If there are junipers close by, it is better to get crabs of Japanese origin as they are more resistant to cedar-apple rust.

Washington hawthorn: A very showy small tree—good bloom in spring, bright red haws in summer, and excellent fall color. Attractive to many birds and tough and easy to grow.

Redbud: A native that is not used as much as it should be. Good as a multiple stem plant; no disease or insect problems.

Goldenrain tree: Used as highway plantings. A hardy, showy small tree. The odd-shaped seed pods add interest in winter.

Bradford pear: A columnar tree from China that does well in the Plains. Showy white blooms but no fruit. Outstanding fall color.

Russian olive: An irregular tree with silvery foliage that is attractive. Very hardy; the fruits are attractive to birds. One of the best windbreaks.

Evergreens

Junipers: Both the Rocky Mountain and Virginia types do well. Their range overlaps in the mid-Plains and many crosses are found. The natives or red cedars as they are called can be a nuisance in pastures but they do have many uses. Colors range from blue to dark green, silver and inbetween. Procumbent types are available from pfitzers that will get 8 to 10 feet tall to low growers, such as Andorra, that stays less than one foot. There are many color and size selections so see your local nurseryman for the best choices for your area.

Mugho pine: Makes a good low evergreen for foundation use. Does better with some protection from the southwest wind.

Scotch and Ponderosa pines: The hardiest of the large pines for the mid-Plains. The Ponderosa seems to do better in the western parts but the Scotch does well almost everywhere. Both do well in poor soil. Use as specimens or in a windbreak.

Black Hills spruce: A dense spruce that makes a good ornamental.

Colorado spruce: Both the blue selections and the dark greens make excellent specimens. Give them plenty of room as they will get big.

Shrubs

Buckthorn: A good hedge or screening plant.

Rough dogwood: A native that can be a nuisance in a pasture but if kept in bounds makes a good border plant.

Pea shrub: A tough tall hedge shrub that seems to do better in the northern part of the Plains.

Sumac: A native that is irregular in growth. Makes a good accent plant; beautiful fall color.

Coralberry: A shrub that will grow anywhere. Tolerates shade. Called buckbrush by farmers finding it flourishing in pastures. Keep under control.

Wahoo: A native of the euonymus family with colorful berries and fall foliage, glossy green leaves; excellent border shrub.

Cisteana plum: A bush-type plum; attractive shrub plus good fruit.

Pekin cotoneaster: A tall glossy green foliage shrub for the border; birds like the berries.

Common lilac: Adaptable everywhere; likes alkaline soil. Always dependable.

Spirea: An old standby that always performs well; dwarf types are available that make it more useful.

Vines

Honeysuckle: A rampant grower that is good for problem slopes; some are semi-evergreen.

Silver lace vine: Does well on a trellis or a fence. Hardy and blooms late when it is more appreciated.

Virginia creeper: A native that is a relative of Boston ivy but hardier; good in shade or on problem slopes.

Memorial or Wichuraiana rose: A colorful cover for bad slopes.

There are other plants besides these that can be grown. If you have a favorite, try it. The ones listed will grow well in the mid-Plains and you may find some that will please you.

GARDENING IN THE SOUTH

The climate in the southern part of the United States—Zones 7 through 10—is more variable than you might think. It is not always moderate but it can be freezing in winter in Mississippi and even in southern Florida. Of all regions, perhaps the South is the most perplexing as to plants and temperatures. And as variable as the climate is, so is the rainfall. Although it is true that the rainfall is heavy, it is frequently unevenly distributed through the seasons—some years may be very dry while others are wet.

In the South, June to October is usually the season of heavy rainfall while October to about June is comparatively dry. Perhaps the period from March to June should be considered the driest. With such erratic rainfall it is wise to avoid Mediterranean species as we do in certain California regions. Many woody plants, such as broom and tamarix, for example, hardly ever do well.

In most of the South the light is good—bright and sunny, and the average sunny days far exceed, say, those in the Midwest. So while broadleaf evergreen shrubs grow well in light shade, they may not be suitable for the southern garden that has excessive sun.

In many regions wind has a bearing on the growth of plants, and its strength and direction have a definite relationship to what may be grown in gardens. Along the coast of the lower South hardy native shrubs will become beautiful sculptures and, close to the ocean, salt spray can affect many plants so only suitable species should be grown there. (See the plant list at the end of this chapter.)

In windy areas we find the coconut palm and banana plant whose leaves can withstand gales, but inland in still-air regions of moisture and heat, plants like caladiums and colocasias thrive.

From southeastern Virginia, southward to the tip of Florida, and including the coastal sections of South Carolina, Georgia, and Florida, we find a level plain. On the western side it is bounded by rolling uplands. As a rule, the soils of the lower South along the Atlantic have been washed down from the West and Northwest; along the Gulf, they come from higher ground where streams and rivers carry sand, silt, and clay to the ocean. Marshland is common, too, in Florida—in the Everglades, for example—so it is that different kinds of soil occur throughout the southern states. The central interior and western part of Florida northland to Georgia, and much of southern Alabama, have sandy or sandy-loamy soils, while in southern Mississippi and Louisiana the soil is alluvial.

Soil acidity affects the choice of plants. Azaleas, kalmias, and vaccinum like a high degree of acidity; other plants, such as holly and fringe trees, will not tolerate much. Most plants respond best to a neutral soil. It is wise to examine your soil with a soil test kit to determine its acidity and alkalinity. Then, if necessary, you can remedy the situation as explained in Chapter 3.

Spring is usually the best time to start planting in many parts of the United States, but in the South, spring is not always good. The better season may be late autumn into winter. It is hard to realize in temperate climates that there is a "best" time for planting.

The Upper South

This region, comprising Tennessee, Georgia, South Carolina, North Carolina, Virginia, and West Virginia—Zones 6, 7, and 8—offers a wealth of opportunity for lovely gardens. Here you can almost have the best of both worlds—northern plants and southern ones. Live oaks and majestic magnolias abound, and, of course, the rhododendrons and azaleas of this area are world famous.

Rainfall of the Upper South is usually abundant, over 50 inches, and well distributed with the driest periods in midsummer. However, in parts of the Alabama coast there can be too much rain, as much as 80 inches.

On the western edge of this belt, soil is usually quite neutral so there is a variety of plants that will thrive beautifully. However, the whole region is likely to have acid soil with a few spots of alkalinity. The soil can run from sandy loam to almost heavy clay. Most important, these soils are likely to be low in nutrients and humus because of so much summer heat and high rainfall. Special conditioning is therefore usually necessary.

A wealth of plants can be enjoyed in the Upper South with the long growing season of more than 200 frost-free days. In the coastal plains and sandhills beautiful azaleas are prolific, gardenias and camellias as well. Favorite trees are magnolia, dogwood, willow, and live oak, but such bulbs as tulips and daffodils are hardly worthwhile because there is no cold dormant season for these. Roses only do well in early spring; in summer, heat and humidity are too much for them. Broadleaf evergreens, such as hollies and aucuba, do very well and many flowering shrubs, such as lilacs, give a stellar performance.

Because of excellent climatic conditions—heat and rainfall—plants grow lushly and quickly use up nutrients in the soil so a regular feeding program is necessary. Humus must be replaced periodically. High humidity and heat also make for great visits from pests: preventatives are necessary, as in most other parts of the country.

Annuals do fairly well in the Upper South—better than in the Lower, but only those perennials that can tolerate high heat and humidity should be planted. Dahlias and chrysanthemums of all kinds grow well but delphiniums and peonies are not likely candidates unless you are in a mountainous area.

Choice Plants for the South

Flowering Trees

Albizzia julibrissin (mimosa)
Bauhinia
Cercis canadensis (Judas tree)
Cornus florida (flowering dogwood)
Gordonia lasianethus (loblolly bay)
Grevillea robusta (silk oak)
Halesia carolina (silver bell)
Koelreutrea formosana
Lagerstraemia indica (crape myrtle)
Magnolia grandiflora
M. virginiana (sweet bay)
Prunus americana (wild plum)
P. caroliniana (cherry laurel)
Pyrus angustifolia (southern crab)
Vitex agnus-castus (chaste tree)

Shrubs

Aronia arbutifolia
Azaleas
Buddleia officinalis
Camellia japonica
Cestrum elegans

C. nocturnum
Chaenomeles lagenaria
Clethra alnifolia
Hibiscus rosa-sinensis
Hamamelis virginiana
Ilex glabra
Jasminum
Kalmia latifolia
Lonicera fragrantissima
Myrica pumila
Philadelphus
Spiraea prunifolia
S. thunbergeri
S. vanhouttei

GARDENING IN THE PACIFIC NORTHWEST AND CALIFORNIA

In the Pacific Northwest you have a unique climate. This region of Oregon and the state of Washington as well as northern California has a far milder climate than the eastern coast of the country which is the same latitude. The nearness of the Pacific Ocean and the Japan Current are responsible. There are natural divisions along the upper Pacific Coast running in a north-south direction: The seacoast, the east and west slopes of coastal mountain ranges, and an interior lowland.

Most people think of the Pacific Northwest as a wet area, yet most of the rainfall occurs there from October to March. From April to early June there is a drying out time when little rain normally falls. This is the season when most trees are starting to grow and broad-leafed evergreens require a lot of moisture. So watering is essential—nature alone won't do enough during this period.

The amount of rain varies considerably.

An average of 40 inches for Seattle may be considered normal. However, this can vary tremendously by moving inland or south on the coast. Five or ten miles may show a striking difference in climate and rainfall.

While rainfall is vastly important, as to what you grow and how, winter temperatures are even more restrictive on your choice of plant material. The Pacific Northwest includes Zones 7, 8, and 9—a range of hardiness temperatures from 20 to 50 degrees. Hardiness refers to the resistance of plants to winter cold—the degree of cold they can tolerate. However, a plant listed as hardy for Zone 7 may survive in Zone 8, depending on microclimates and adaptability of the particular plant.

Wind can also be a hazard in Northwest gardening—west, southwest, and southerly winds prevail throughout this region a great part of the year. Winds are felt particularly on the seacost; they lessen as the land extends into the inland valleys. Winds generally rise in midsummer and midwinter and can be damaging to gardens then because a bitter cold spell accompanied by strong January winds can dry out plants severely. Summer drying winds can also affect plants adversely. These are the times of year when it is essential to protect your plants against wind.

Broad-leaf evergreen shrubs and flowering trees are perhaps the backbone of the Northwest garden for these plants are magnificent in foliage size, color, and texture, as well as beauty of flower and fruit. Shrubs, such as *Mahonia aquifolium, Vaccinum ovatum,* and *Gaultheria shallon* are highly valued in the Northwest and can do much to beautify gardens there—so can some of the finer flowering trees. Fast-growing trees and shrubs rarely work well in Northwest gar-

dens—or anywhere, really, except in isolated cases. The range of beautiful plant material for the region is vast and we include below a list from which you might make selections.

Here as elsewhere proper soil preparation is vital. Of course, some plants will grow in any type of soil—English holly and the privets come to mind—but most shrubs need a soil that is well-drained and supplied with adequate nutrients. Soil varies throughout the region and different treatments are necessary for different soils. Gravelly soil, which is found through the southern end of Puget Sound, will need more preparation than the sandy loam found in inland valleys.

To determine what kind of soil you have, dig up a deep spadeful and run it through your fingers. It should be mealy and porous but probably will not be rich enough without some preparation. It would be impossible to suggest preparation of all types of soil within the region so let me concentrate on the sandy loam prevalent here. Beds should be excavated to two to three feet and about two inches of seasoned manure laid in place before the planting of trees or shrubs. Another two inches of manure should be mixed in with topsoil; an inch of peat moss would also do wonders for your plants. Some of the old subsoil may be mixed in as well. Holes for shrubs should be wide as well as deep—at least three feet across and six feet for trees.

While the physical properties of the soil are important, the chemical content is also. Plants here as everywhere need nitrogen, phosphorus, and potash—each of which contributes to the well-being of a plant. If you are in a fertile region, there will be a sufficient quantity of nitrogen, but the soil may still lack phosphate and potash. Sandy or gravelly soils are sure to need potash. Peat and mucky soils, rich in nitrogen, usually are deficient in phosphorus.

Lime is also important, for this determines acidity. East of the Cascade Mountains the soil is quite alkaline, while west of the Cascades it is usually more or less acid, except in some areas along the seacoast. However, the majority of shrubs grown in this region do not want lime. To be sure have your soil analyzed by your local agricultural station or do it yourself with an inexpensive soil test kit.

In general, broad-leaved evergreen shrubs should be kept free of lime while lilacs, roses, and vegetables will need it. For plants liking acidity, such as rhododendrons, a formula of cottonseed meal, acid superphosphate, sulfate of potash, and sulfate of ammonia with granulated charcoal makes a healthy mix. Use equal parts of each.

As for all planting in all regions, adequate humus is necessary to assure a good soil. Manure, well-seasoned, can also be used but judiciously. Too much can burn plants.

Planting times vary but generally deciduous materials can be moved at any time when they are dormant, usually from November until the end of February. Broadleaf and coniferous evergreens are usually transplanted just after they start active growth in early spring. The next best time would be early fall when the ground is still somewhat warm.

Most trees and shrubs suffer in this region from too much water at the wrong times of the year. In spring it is almost impossible to give too much water (provided drainage is excellent). But frequent watering at any season may be detrimental. In general, water heavily in spring, not so much in summer, but do give thorough soakings when you water, never light sprinklings.

Also, keep in mind that overhead sprinkling can ruin conifers if the sun is on them. In most areas the need for water from midsummer on is much less than it is in spring. Lawns and flowers require less water than shrubs and trees but they should be thoroughly soaked at least once a week or, in very hot weather, at least twice a week.

Southern California

Gardening in southern California is unlike gardening in other parts of the United States. The range of plants is limited to those that will grow in Zone 9 (a few from Zone 8). Zone 10, a practically frost-free area, also supports plants of a very tender nature that cannot be grown elsewhere (with the exception of southern Florida). So, if you were to pick up a book on tropical gardening, you could follow it for southern California where the growing season is long and there is a high number of sunny days. Humidity is generally low. Periods of little rain reduce the problems of insects and fungus disease. Most of the soil is fertile and loamy with isolated sections of sandy loam.

Plants prosper in cool evenings and warm days—they can make food quickly and this is exactly what happens in the region. Adverse conditions can be the duration of hot summer days, but usually cooling occurs in the evening. Soils are generally alkaline and lacking in organic matter. Adding humus and nutrients is a universal practice.

Annuals, such as petunias and snapdragons, are well suited to the climate, and perennials, such as Shasta daisies and other chrysanthemums, are successful. Roses do extremely well producing heavy spring bloom and a similar fall blossoming.

But many of the favorite annuals and perennials of Midwestern gardens simply do not tolerate the heat and dryness of the Southwest area. In realistic terms, the summer annuals of the East are the winter annuals here, planted in fall. Heat-tolerant plants put in the ground in spring for summer and fall bloom include zinnias, marigolds, and cosmos, all of which do exceptionally well. Flowering bulbs are not a good choice, for you will get only one season of bloom. Lacking a cold dormant period, they must be discarded.

The Southern California coast and the Imperial Valley are practically frost-free. In central California, the low desert of Arizona, the coast ranges of California, and the foothill regions of the Sierras, plants suitable for Zone 9 are grown but with some exceptions—those from Zone 8 where a few cold nights may not hinder tender plants if they are grown in protected areas. In various areas of the frost-free zones, desert plants are abundant and many gardens are based on a desert theme.

The Southern California coast abounds in geraniums and hydrangeas. Lily-of-the-Nile is a popular plant seen almost everywhere through Zone 9. Delphiniums and dahlias do well and tuberous begonias are more likely to reach perfection here than anywhere else in the United States. Mesembryanthemums, those fleshy-leaved desert herbs, hold the sandy hills and banks and seem indestructible, watered mostly by dew. The rainfall here is generally low—about 15 inches a year.

Many shrubs are suited for the Zone 9 area throughout the California southern section and these include the ever popular pyracantha and pittosporum, which are widely grown. Photinias and viburnums are often seen and oleander practically grows wild.

Choice Plants for All California Zones

BOTANICAL AND COMMON NAME	HARDINESS	REMARKS
Albizia julibrissin (silk tree)	to −20F	Ferny foliage; tree to 25 feet; deciduous
Alnus rhombifolia (white alder)	to −20F	Fast growing tree to 50 feet; deciduous
Berberis julianae (wintergreen barberry)	to −20F	Dark green upright shrub; red fall colors
Berberis thunbergi Crimson Pygmy (Dwarf red-leaf Barberry)	to −20F	Beautiful red foliage. Deciduous shrub
Berberis thunbergil (Japanese barberry)	to −20F	Green, fall colors; red berried shrub. Deciduous
Betula verrucosa (white birch)	to −20F	Tree prized for lacy foliage. White trunk
Buxus microphylla japonica (Japanese boxwood)	to −20F	Nice yellow-green leaves; pretty small shrub

Choice Plants for All California Zones (continued)

BOTANICAL AND COMMON NAME	HARDINESS	REMARKS
Callistemon citrinus (lemon bottlebrush)	25F	Good small tree; bright red flowers
Cedrus deodara (deodar cedar)	to −20F	Gray-green evergreen to 50 feet. Pyramid shape
Cotoneaster dammeri (barberry cotoneaster)	to −20F	Creeping shrub with light green leaves
Cupressus glabra (smooth Arizona cypress)	to −20F	Blue-gray foliage tree to 40 feet
Cupressus sempervirens Glauca (blue Italian cypress)	to −20F	Dark-blue-green evergreen tree to 40 feet
Elaeagnus pungens (silverberry)	to −20F	Large shrub with grayish-green leaves
Eriobotrya japonica (bronze loquat)	25F	Large leaves; good small tree
Eucalyptus camaldulensis (red gum)	15F	Slender-leaved tree to 80 feet
Euonymus japonicus (evergreen euonymus)	to −20F	Many varieties; popular shrub
Fraxinus uhdei (evergreen ash)	25F	Dark green foliage. Fast-growing tree to 30 feet
Fraxinus velutina (Modesto ash)	to −20F	Leaves turn yellow in fall. Large tree. Deciduous
Ginkgo biloba (maindenhair tree)	to −20F	Favorite shade tree to 60 feet. Yellow fall color. Deciduous
Ilex altaclarensis Wilsoni (Wilson holly)	Hardy 10F	Favorite shrub with dark green leaves and red berries
Ilex cornuta Burfordi Nana (dwarf Burford holly)	10F	Glossy-leaved shrub, red berries
Ilex cornuta Rotunda (Dwarf Chinese holly)	10F	Slow-growing shrub but pretty
Juniperus chinensis Gold Coast (Gold Coast juniper)	to −20F	Golden-tipped foliage, good compact shrub
Juniperus chinensis Mint julep (Mint Julep juniper)	to −20F	Bright green shrub; good background

Choice Plants for All California Zones (continued)

BOTANICAL AND COMMON NAME	HARDINESS	REMARKS
Juniperus chinensis totulosa (twisted juniper)	to −20F	Grows for statuesque shape. Shrub or tree-like
Juniperus horizontalis (prostrate juniper)	to −20F	Favorite small shrub; gray green foliage
Juniperus chinensis pfitzeriana glauca (blue Pfitzer juniper)	to −20F	Blue gray foliage—good
Juniperus procumbens Nana (Japanese garden juniper)	to −20F	Blue-green low-growing shrub
Lagerstroemia indica (crape myrtle)	15F	Small tree grows for lovely pink flowers. Deciduous
Lantana montevidensis (lavender lantana)	20F	Good low shrub with dark green leaves
Ligustrum japonicum Texanum (Wax-leaf privet)	10F	Excellent hedge plant, dark green foliage
Ligustrum lucidum (glossy privet)	to −20F	Large dark green leaves; tree-like
Liquidambar styraciflua (American sweet gum)	to −20F	Maple-like leaves; beautiful fall foliage tree
Magnolia grandiflora (dwarf Southern magnolia)	15F	Slow-growing but beautiful small tree
Mahonia lomarifolia (holly-leaf mahonia)	20F	Shiny leaves; yellow flowers
Morus alba Stribling (fruitless mulberry)	to −20F	Tree to 25 feet; fast grower. Dark green leaves
Myrtus communis Boetica (desert myrtle)	10F	Feather-leaved shrub; needs good drainage
Nandina domestica Compacta (compact heavenly bamboo)	10F	Fern-like shrub; needs lots of water
Nandina domestica (heavenly bamboo)	10F	Great fern-like shrub; excellent

Choice Plants for All California Zones (continued)

BOTANICAL AND COMMON NAME	HARDINESS	REMARKS
Olea europaea (olive)	15F	Olive-green foliage; graceful tree
Platanus acerifolia (London plane tree)	to −20F	Lobed leaves, large trees, fast growing. Deciduous
Platanus racemosa (California sycamore)	to −20F	Large leaves, white bark. Fast growing tree.
Podocarpus macrophyllus (yew pine)	10F	Dark green narrow-leaved shrub
Populus nigra Italica (Lombardy poplar)	to −20F	Pyramidal tree to 40 feet—Yellow fall foliage
Prunus Atropurpurea (purple-leaf plum)	to −20F	Lovely purple flowers; show tree. Deciduous
Prunus caroliniana (Carolina laurel cherry)	Hardy 15F	Dense shrub on tree; good background
Pyracantha (dwarf pyracantha)	to −20F	Many varieties. Seem to grow in any situation. Red- or orange-berried shrub
Pyracantha coccinea (pyracantha)	to −20F	Most popular coast shrub; orange or red berries
Pyrus kawakami (evergreen pear)	20F	Good flowering tree; nice form
Photinia fraseri (Fraser photinia)	10F	Large shrub; fine red foliage
Phyllostachys aurea (golden bamboo)	10F	Another good bamboo shrub
Pinus canariensis (Canary Island pine)	20F	Needle-like leaves; pyramidal form to 40 feet
Pinus halepensis (Aleppo pine)	to −20F	Large tree, evergreen
Pinus pinea (Italian stone pine)	to −20F	Pyramidal-shaped tree; nice accent
Pinus thunbergiana (Japanese black pine)	to −20F	Nice small tree; handsome
Pittosporum tobira Variegata (variegated tobira)	10F	Green and white foliage
Pittosporum tobira Wheeler's Dwarf (Wheeler's dwarf tobira)	10F	Small leaves. Slow-growing shrub

Choice Plants for All California Zones (continued)

BOTANICAL AND COMMON NAME	HARDINESS	REMARKS
Rhamnus alaternus (Italian buckthorn)	to −20F	Fast growing small tree; shiny green leaves
Rosa (rose)	to −20F	Grandiflora and floribunda varieties by the hundreds
Rosmarinus officinalis Prostratus (prostrate rosemary)	to −20F	Narrow dark green leaves; nice low shrub
Salix babylonica (weeping willow)	to −20F	Graceful tree. Fast growing. Deciduous
Santolina chamaecyparissus (lavender cotton)	to −20F	White gray leaves; low shrub
Sequoia sempervirens (coast redwood)	10F	Pryamidal tree, dark green foliage. Fast growing to 50 feet
Ulmus parvifolia (evergreen elm)	20F	Shiny-leaved tree. Fast growing to 30 feet
Viburnum tinus (laurestinus)	5F	Dense shrub, pink flowers
Xylosma congestum (shiny xylosma)	15F	Light green shiny-leaved shrub; arching growth

Choice Plants for the San Francisco Bay Area and Northern Coast

BOTANICAL AND COMMON NAME	HARDINESS	REMARKS
Acacia longifolia (Sydney golden wattle)	20F	Good large shrub; pretty yellow flowers
Ajuga reptans (carpet bugle)	to −20F	Lovely dark green carpet plant
Aloe arborescens (tree aloe)	25F	Interesting succulent; grows easily
Azara microphylla (boxleaf azara)	20F	Good small tree, light golden leaves
Carpobrotus chilensis (ice plant)	20F	Drought-tolerant ground cover; good hill plant
Coprosma repens (mirror plant)	20F	
Crataegus phaenopyrum (Washington hawthorn)	to −20F	Small tree with good fall color. Deciduous

Choice Plants for the San Francisco Bay Area and Northern Coast (continued)

BOTANICAL AND COMMON NAME	HARDINESS	REMARKS
Cycas revoluta (sago palm)	15F	Handsome with stiff fronds. Grows slowly
Escallonia species (escallonia)	20F	Nice evergreen shrub with pretty white or rose red flowers
Fatsia japonica (aralia)	20F	Large leaves; can make nice background
Ficus pumila minima (creeping fig)	10F	Small-leaved; grows fast on any surface
Hedera helix (English ivy)	to −20F	Small-leaved and large-leaved varieties. Grows like weed when established
Hydrangea macrophylla (bigleaf hydrangea)	to −20F	Hard to grow shrub but bears handsome flowers
Hypericum calycinum (Aaron's beard)	to −20F	Rampant ground cover but holds soil
Juniperus conferta (shore juniper)	to −20F	Tight green shrub to about 12 inches high. Good in sandy soil
Lagunaria patersoni (primrose tree)	25F	Medium tree, gray-green foliage. Pink flowers
Liriope gigantea (giant lirope)	15F	Strap-like leaves; small violet flowers. Nice small accent
Malus species (flowering crabapple)	to −20F	Many varieties; small tree with handsome flowers. Deciduous
Ophiopogon japonicus (mondo grass)	10F	Good ground cover; graceful
Parthenocissus tricuspidata (Boston ivy)	−20F	Turns beautiful red in fall. Deciduous
Pieris japonica (Japanese pieris)	to −20F	Nice shrub, white flowers in early spring; grows to 10 feet
Pittosporum eugenioides P. crassifolium (pittosporums)	20F	Nice leafy shrubs; good in garden
Podocarpus gracilior (fern pine)	20F	Fine-textured medium size tree. Graceful
Raphiolepis indica (Indian hawthorn)	15F	Dark green foliage; lovely pink flowers
Rhododendron species	to −20F	Many varieties; excellent evergreen background shrubs
Skimmia japonica (skimmia)	Tender	An evergreen shrub with yellowish fine flowers
Viburnum daviddi (David viburnum)	to −20F	Handsome shrub, always good for background planting

Choice Plants for the California Coast and Low Desert

BOTANICAL AND COMMON NAME	HARDINESS	REMARKS
Agave attenuata (soft agave)	30F	Rosettes of gray-green leaves. Handsome
Archontophoenix cunninghamiana (king palm)	30F	Averaging feather-like fronds. Fast grower
Asparagus sprengeri (sprenger asparagus)	25F	Ferny foliage shrub; does well as background cover
Bougainvillea in variety	40F	Dazzling colors; beautiful vine. Needs support
Carissa grandiflora Tuttle (Tuttle Natal Palm)	30F	Shiny dark green leaves, white flowers. Nice shrub
Dizygotheca elegantissima (threadleaf aralia)	30F	Nice upright shrub; graceful
Erythrina caffra (Kaffirboom coral tree)	30F	Lovely large tree with red-orange flowers
Eucalyptus citriodora (lemon-scented gum)	30F	Long scale-shaped fragrant leaves; narrow upright tree
Ficus retusa (Indian laurel fig)	30F	Medium size tree with drooping branches
Howeia forsteriana (Kentia palm, Paradise palm)	30F	Green, feather fronds
Limonium perezi (sea lavender)	25F to −4F	Nice small accent, large leaves and purple flowers
Phoenix roebelini (pigmy date palm)	30F	Can take abuse; stiff fronds
Soleirolia soleirolii (baby's tears)	30F	Ground cover; no hot sun or frost
Syzgium panicalatum (common Eugenia)	20F	Upright shrub with red foliage. Can grow into tree

Low Desert Ground Cover

BOTANICAL AND COMMON NAME	HARDINESS	REMARKS
Delosperma alba (white ice plant)	20F	Best for holding hills, pretty flowers
Euonymus fortunei radicans (common winter creeper)	to −20F	Ground cover with dark green leaves

Low Desert Ground Cover (continued)

BOTANICAL AND COMMON NAME	HARDINESS	REMARKS
Gazinia spledens (gazinia)	20F	Daisy-like ground cover
Hedera canariensis (Algerian ivy)	20F	Favorite for covering hills
Osteospermum fruiticosum (trailing African daisy)	20F	Brilliant white to purple flowers, ground cover. Rapid growers
Potentilla verna (spring cinquefoil)	to −20F	Bright-green-leaved ground cover
Vinca major (periwinkle)	to −20F	Dark green ground cover, blue flowers
Zoysia tenuifolia (Korean grass)	10F	Moss olive dark green ground cover

Low Desert Vines

BOTANICAL AND COMMON NAME	HARDINESS	REMARKS
Clytostoma callistegioides (violet trumpet vine)	15F	Large orange flowers. Excellent one
Gelsemium sempervirens (Carolina jasmine)	10F	Green leaves, fragrant yellow flowering vine
Lonicera japonica halliana (Hall's honeysuckle)	Hardy	Can have drought. Sprawling vine
Rosa (climbing rose)	Hardy	Deciduous vines; need pruning and support but beautiful
Vitis (grape)	Hardy	Excellent for leafy color
Wisteria sinensis (Chinese wisteria)	Hardy	Popular vine with white or purple pendent trusses of flowers

Low Desert Palms

BOTANICAL AND COMMON NAME	HARDINESS	REMARKS
Chamaerops hulilis (Mediterranean fan palm)	10F	Blue gray green leaves. Nice low palms for gardens
Livistona chinensis (Chinese fountain palm)	25F	Dark green fan-shaped leaves. Low growing

Low Desert Palms (continued)

BOTANICAL AND COMMON NAME	HARDINESS	REMARKS
Phoenix canariensis (Canary Island date palm)	20F	Similar to date palm; greener, more receiving fronds
Phoenix dactylifera (date palm)	15F	Feather-like fronds. Grows to 30 feet
Trachycarpus fortunei (fortune windmill palm)	10F	Green fan-shaped leaves; grows to about 20 feet
Washingtonia filifera (California fan palm)	15F	Large fan-shaped palm
Washingtonia robusta (Mexican fan palm)	20F	Fan-shaped leaves; grows to 50 feet

Appendix

Glossary

Annual: Plant that completes its life cycle in one season.

Biennial: Plant that requires two seasons to complete its life cycle; sometimes grown as an annual.

Broadcast: To scatter seeds rather than to sow them in rows.

Cambium: Layer of cells between bark and wood of some trees.

Chlorophyll: Green coloring matter of plants.

Coniferous: A tree that bears woody cones containing naked seeds.

Cutting: A piece—leaf, stem, or root—cut from a living plant for propagation use.

Damping-off: Decaying of stems of seedlings caused by fungi.

Deciduous: Plants that drop their leaves annually.

Dormant: The period when a plant makes no active visible growth.

Ecology: The study of the relationship between living organisms and their total environment.

Epiphyte: A plant growing on an elevated support, such as a tree.

Erosion: Washing away of sand or rock.

Flats: Shallow boxes used for young plants.

Forcing: A process of hastening the development of plants with heat.

Germination: The start of growth.

Grafting: A process by which one part of a plant is made to unite with another.

Habitat: The area where a plant is found growing wild.

Hardening-off: The process of reducing the amount of water and lowering temperature in order to toughen plants to withstand colder conditions.

Hardy: Frost-tolerant plant that can live over winter without protection.

Inorganic: Matter other than that of vegetable or animal origin.

Leaching: The loss of soluble fertilizers from the soil.

Mulch: A material spread on ground that covers soil to keep it moist or cool.

Organic: Relating to or derived from living organisms.

pH: A term that represents the hydrogen content by which scientists measure soil acidity and alkalinity.

Perennial: A plant that lives from year to year.

Pinching back: Taking off or plucking away the ends of shoots to encourage flower production.

Propagation: The process of increasing or multiplying plants.

Species: Plants possessing one or more distinctive characteristics common to all of them.

Stolon: A runner used to propagate a plant.

Subsoil: A stratum of earth lying directly beneath topsoil.

Succulent: Having leathery or watery tissue.

Sucker: Vegetative growth from the base of a plant.

Top-dressing: A process where soil or compost or fertilizer is used on the surface of the ground and cultivated in the top few inches.

Transplanting: The act of moving seedlings or mature plants from one place to another.

Shrubs

Deciduous Shrubs for Hedges (to 5 feet)

Berberis koreana (Korean barberry)
B. mentorensis (mentor barberry)
B. thunbergii "Erecta" (Japanese barberry)
Cotoneaster lucida (hedge cotoneaster)
Euonymus alata "Compacta" (winged euonymus)
Ligustrum vulgare "Lodense" (privet)
Rosa species (rose)
Salix purpurea gracilis (dwarf purple osier)

Evergreen Shrubs for Hedges (to 5 feet)

Berberis julianae (wintergreen barberry)
B. sempervirens suffruticosa (dwarf box)
B. verruculosa (warty barberry)
Euonymus kiautschovica
E. fortunei
Ilex crenata (Japanese holly)
I. crenata "Microphylla"
Picea glauca "Conica" (white spruce)°
Pinus mugo (Swiss mugo pine)°
Taxus canadensis (Canada yew)°
T. cuspidata (Japanese yew)°
Thuja occidentalis varieties (American arborvitae)

° Tree-like

Deciduous Shrubs for Hedges (to 30 feet)

Acer ginnala (Amur maple)
Crataegus species (hawthorn)
Hibiscus syriacus (shrub althea)
Lonicera maacki (Amur honeysuckle)
L. tatarica (Tatarian honeysuckle)
Philadelphus coronarius (sweet mock orange)
Spiraea prunifolia (bridal wreath spiraea)
S. thunbergi
Syringa persica (Persian lilac)
S. vulgaris (common lilac)
Viburnum lantana (wayfaring tree)
V. sieboldi (Siebold viburnum)

Evergreen Shrubs for Hedges (to 30 feet)

Abelia grandiflora (glossy abelia)
Buxus sempervirens (common box)
Photinia serrulata (Chinese photinia)
Pittosporum tobira (Japanese pittosporum)
Podocarpus macrophyllus
Pyracantha coccinea (firethorn)
Tsuga canadensis (Canada hemlock)°
T. caroliniana (Carolina hemlock)°

° Tree-like

Shrubs with Fragrant Flowers

Abelia grandiflora (glossy abelia)
Ceanothus americanus (New Jersey tea)
Clethra alnifolia (summer sweet)
Daphne odora (winter daphne)
Deutzia gracilis (slender deutzia)

Fothergilla, several (fothergilla)
Gardenia jasminoides (gardenia)
Jasminum officinale (common white jasmine)
Lonicera, several (honeysuckle)
Osmanthus heterophyllus (holly olive)
Philadelphus coronarius (sweet mock orange) *umbellata* (yeddo hawthorn)
Raphialepis
Rosa (rose)
Skimmia japonica

Shrubs for Screens and Windbreaks

Ealaeagnus angustifolia (Russian olive)
Hamamelis vernalis (vernal witch hazel)
Lagerstroemia indica (crape myrtle)
Laurus nobilis (sweet bay)
Lonicera tatarica (Tatarian honeysuckle)
Philadelphus coronarius (mock orange)
Spiraea veitchi (Veitch spiraea)
Syringa henri "Lutece" (lilac)
S. villosa (late lilac)
S. vulgaris (common lilac)
Viburnum arboreum
V. dentatum (arrowwood)
V. opulus (European cranberry bush)
Viburnum prunifolium (black haw)

Shrubs for Wet Soil

Andromeda species (andromeda)
Calluna vulgaris (common heather)
Clethra alnifolia (summer sweet)
Cornus alba (dogwood)
Cornus sanguinea (bloodtwig dogwood)
Ilex glabra (inkberry)
I. verticillata (winterberry)
Kalmia angustifolia (sheep laurel)
Rhododendron
Sabal minor (dwarf palmetto)
Salix caprea (goat willow)
S. repens (creeping willow)
Spiraea menziesi (spiraea)
S. tomentosa (hardhack)
Viburnum alnifolium (hobblebush)

Shrubs for Dry Soil

Arctostaphylos uva-ursi (barberry)
Berberis, several (barberry)
Buddleia alternifolia (fountain buddleia)
Callistemon citrinus (lemon bottlebrush)
Canothus americanus (New Jersey tea)

Chaenomeles speciosa (flowering quince)
Cotoneaster
Cytisus (broom)
Elaeagnus angustifolia (Russian olive)
Euonymus japonica (evergreen euonymus)
Hamamelis virginiana (common witch hazel)
Juniperus communis (juniper)
Kolkwitzia amabilis (beauty bush)
Nerium oleander (oleander)
Pittosporum tobira (Japanese pittosporum)
Pyracantha coccinea (scarlet firethorn)
Raphiolepis umbellata (yeddo hawthorn)
Rosa rugosa (rose)
Tamarix species (tamarix)
Viburnum lentago (nannyberry)

Shrubs with Colorful Fruit

Arctostaphylos uva-ursi (barberry)
Ardisia crenata (ardisia)
Berberis koreana (Korean barberry)
B. thunbergi (Japanese barberry)
Ceanothus ovatus (ceanothus)
Cornus mas (cornelian cherry)
Cotoneaster divaricata
C. horizontalis (rock-spray cotoneaster)
C. microphylla (small-leaved cotoneaster)
Elaeagnus multiflorus (cherry elaeagnus)
Euonymus alata (winged euonymus)
E. japonica (evergreen euonymus)
E. latifolius (broadleaf euonymus)
E. sanguineus
Ilex cornuta (Chinese holly)
I. verticillata (winterberry)
Lonicera fragrantissima (winter honeysuckle)
L. maacki (Amur honeysuckle)
L. tatarica (Tatarian honeysuckle)
Magnolia stellata (star magnolia)
Malus sargenti (Sargent crab apple)
Photinia serrulata (Chinese photinia)
Pyracantha coccinea (scarlet firethorn)
Rosa, many (rose)
Sarcococca ruscifolia (fragrant sarcococca)
Skimmia japonica (Japanese skimmia)
Viburnum dilatatum (linden viburnum)
V. japonicum (Japanese viburnum)
V. trilobum (cranberry bush)

BLUE FRUIT
Fatsia japonica
Gaultheria veitchiana (Veitch wintergreen)
Ligustrum obtusifolium (border privet)
Mahonia aquifolium (holly grape)
Viburnum davidi
V. dentatum (arrowwood)

BLACK FRUIT
Mahonia repens (creeping mahonia)
Viburnum lantana (wayfaring tree)
V. prunifolium (black haw)
V. sieboldi

Flowering Calendar for Shrubs

EARLY SPRING

Daphne odora (fragrant daphne)
Hamamelis mollis (Chinese witch hazel)
H. vernalis (vernal witch hazel)

SPRING

Amelanchier canadensis (shadblow service berry)
A. grandiflora (service berry)
Andromeda polifolia (bog rosemary)
Chaenomeles japonica (Japanese quince)
C. speciosa (flowering quince)
Cornus mas (cornelian cherry)
Cytisus decumbens
Enkianthus perulatus
Epigaea repens (trailing arbutus)
Forsythia intermedia, many (forsythia)
F. ovata (early forsythia)
Jasminum nudiflorum (winter jasmine)
Lonicera fragrantissima (winter honeysuckle)
Mahonia species (holly grape)
Pieris floribunda (mountain andromeda)
P. japonica (Japanese andromeda)
Rhododendron

SUMMER

Abelia grandiflora (glossy abelia)
Kalmia latifolia (mountain laurel)
Kolkwitzia amabilis (beauty bush)
Philadelphus, various (mock orange)
Potentilla fruitcosa (bush cinquefoil)
Rosa (shrub type), (rose)
Spiraea, various (spiraea)

FALL

Clethra alnifolia (summer sweet)
Hamamelis virginiana (common witch hazel)
Hibiscus syriacus (althea, or hibiscus)
Hydrangea, various (hydrangea)
Prunus subhirtella
Spiraea billardi (billiard spiraea)
Tamarix, various (tamarix)

Shrubs for Background Planting

Arbutus unedo (strawberry tree)
Callistemon lanceolatus (bottlebrush)
Ceanothus thyrsiflorus (blue blossom)
Cornus mas (cornelian cherry)
C. officinalis
Cotoneaster frigida
Elaeagnus angustifolia (Russian olive)
Enkianthus campanulatus (bellflower)
Euonymus latifolius
E. sanguinea
E. yedoensis
Hamamelis mollis (Chinese witch hazel)
H. virginiana (common witch hazel)
Ilex cornuta (Chinese holly)
I. crenata
I. glabra (inkberry)
Jasminum officinale (common white jasmine)
Kalmia latifolia (mountain laurel)
Lagerstroemia indica (crape myrtle)
Ligustrum lucidum (privet)
Nerium oleander (oleander)
Osmanthus heterophyllus (holly osmanthus)
Photinia serrulata (Chinese photinia)
Poncirus trifoliata (hardy orange)
Pyracantha atlantioides
Rosa odorata
Syringa chinensis (Chinese lilac)
S. vulgaris (common lilac)

Shrubs by Common Name

Abelia (*Abelia grandiflora*)
American cranberry bush (*Viburnum trilobum*)
Amur honeysuckle (*Lonicera maacki*)
Amur privet (*Ligustrum amurense*)
Andromeda (*Pieris floribunda*)
Arrowwood (*Viburnum dentatum*)
Aucuba (*Aucuba japonica*)

Banks rose (*Rosa banksiae*)
Barberry (*Arctostaphylos uva-ursi*)
Barberry cotoneaster (*Cotoneaster dammeri*)
Beauth bush (*Kolwitzia amabilis*)
Bellflower (*Enkianthus campanulatus*)
Black barberry (*Berberis gagnepaini*)
Black haw (*Viburnum prunifolium*)
Blue blossom (*Ceanothus thyrisflorus*)
Bog rosemary (*Andromeda polifolia*)
Border forsythia (*Forsythia intermedia*)
Bottlebrush (*Callistemon citrinus*)
Box honeysuckle (*Lonicera nitida*)
Bridal wreath spirea (*Spiraea vulgaris*)

Broadleaf euonymus (*Euonymus latifolius*)
Buttercup shrub (*Potentilla fruitcosa*)
Butterfly bush (*Buddleia davidi*)
Cabbage rose (*Rosa centifolia*)
California mock orange (*Carpenteria californica*)
California privet (*Ligustrum ovalifolium*)
Cape jasmine (*Gardenia jasminoides*)
Carolina jasmine (*Gelsemium sempervirens*)
Chaste tree (*Vitex agnus-castus*)
Cherry elaegnus (*Elaeagnus multiflorus*)
China rose (*Rosa chinensis*)
Chinese hibiscus (*Hibiscus rosa-sinensis*)
Chinese holly (*Ilex cornuta*)
Chinese lilac (*Syringa chinensis*)
Chinese photinia (*Photinia serrulata*)
Chinese witch hazel (*Hamamelis mollis*)
Common boxwood (*Buxus sempervirens*)
Common camellia (*Camellia japonica*)
Common juniper (*Juniperus communis*)
Common lilac (*Syringa vulgaris*)
Common privet (*Ligustrum vulgare*)
Common white jasmine (*Jasminum officinale*)
Cornelian cherry (*Cornus mas*)
Cranberry bush (*Viburnum trilobum*)
Cranberry cotoneaster (*Cotoneaster apiculata*)
Crape myrtle (*Lagerstroemia indica*)
Creeping mahonia (*Mahonia repens*)
Creeping willow (*Salix repens*)
Cut-leaf lilac (*Syringa laciniata*)

Damask rose (*Rosa damascena*)

Early deutzia (*Deutzia grandiflora*)
Early forsythia (*Forsythia ovata*)
English holly (*Ilex aquifolium*)
European cranberry bush (*Viburnum opulus*)
Evergreen euonymus (*Euonymus japonica*)

Father Hugo rose (*Rose hugonis*)
Flowering currant (*Ribes sanguineum*)
Flowering quince (*Chaenomeles japonica*)
Fountain buddleia (*Buddleia alternifolia*)
Fragrant daphne (*Daphne odora*)
Fragrant snowball (*Viburnum carlcephalum*)
French pussy willow (*Salix caprea*)
French rose (*Rosa gallica*)

Glossy privet (*Ligustrum lucidum*)

Hardy orange (*Poncirus trifoliata*)
Heather (*Calluna vulgaris*)
Heavenly bamboo (*Nandina domestica*)
Hills-of-snow (*Hydrangea arborescens "Grandiflora"*)
Holly osmanthus (*Osmanthus heterophyllus*)
Hungarian lilac (*Syringa josikaea*)

Indian hawthorn (*Raphiolepis indica*)
Inkberry (*Ilex glabra*)

Japanese andromeda (*Pieris japonica*)
Japanese aralia (*Fatsia japonica*)
Japanese barberry (*Berberis thunbergi*)
Japanese boxwood (*Buxus microphylla japonica*)
Japanese holly (*Ilex crenata*)
Japanese pittosporum (*Pittosporum tobira*)
Japanese rose (*Rosa multiflora*)
Japanese skimmia (*Skimmia japonica*)
Japanese snowball (*Viburnum plicatum*)
Japanese viburnum (*Viburnum japonicum*)

Korean barberry (*Berberis koreana*)
Korean boxwood (*Buxus microphylla koreana*)
Korean white forsythia (*Abeliophyllum distichum*)

Late lilac (*Syringa villosa*)
Littleleaf lilac (*Syringa microphylla*)

Magellan barberry (*Berberis busifolia*)
Magellan fuchsia (*Fuchsia magellanica*)
Mentor barberry (*Berberis mentorensis*)
Midwinter euonymus (*Euonymus bungeanus semipersistent*)
Mountain laurel (*Kalmia latifolia*)

Nannyberry (*Viburnum lentago*)
Natal plum (*Carissa grandiflora*)
New Jersey tea (*Ceanothus americanus*)

Oleander (*Nerium oleander*)
Oregon holly (*Mahonia aquifolium*)

Pfitzer juniper (*Juniperus chinensis pfitzeriana*)

Red box cotoneaster (*Cotoneaster rotundifolia*)
Rock spray (*Cotoneaster horizontalis*)
Rugosa rose (*Rosa rugosa*)
Russian olive (*Eaeagnus angustifolia*)

Salal (*Gaultheria shallon*)
Sasanqua camellia (*Camellia sasanqua*)
Scarlet firethorn (*Pyracantha coccinea*)
Scentless mock orange (*Philadelphus grandiflora*)
Shadblow service berry (*Amelanchier canadensis*)
Sheep laurel (*Kalmia angustifolia*)
Siberian dogwood (*Cornus alba "Sibirica"*)
Silverberry elaeagnus (*Elaeagnus pungens*)
Silverleaf cotoneaster (*Cotoneaster pannosa*)
Slender deutzia (*Deutzia gracilis*)
Small-leaf cotoneaster (*Cotoneaster microphylla*)
Spanish jasmine (*Jasminum grandiflorum*)
Spice viburnum (*Viburnum carlesi*)
Spreading cotoneaster (*Cotoneaster divaricata*)
Spring witch hazel (*Hamamelis vernalis*)
Strawberry tree (*Arbutus unedo*)
Surinam cherry (*Eugenia uniflora*)
Summer sweet (*Clethra alnifolia*)
Sweet bay (*Laurus nobilis*)
Sweet mock orange (*Philadelphus coronarius*)

Tatarian honeysuckle (*Lonicera tatarica*)
Tea rose (*Rosa odorata*)
Tender viburnum (*Viburnum dilatatum*)
Thunberg spiraea (*Spiraea thunbergi*)

Veitch wintergreen (*Gaultheria veitchiana*)

Warty barberry (*Berberis verruculosa*)
Wayfaring tree (*Viburnum lantana*)
Weeping forsythia (*Forsythia suspensa*)
Winged spindle tree (*Euonymus alata*)
Winterberry (*Ilex verticillata*)
Wintergreen cotoneaster (*Cotoneaster conspicua*)
Winter honeysuckle (*Lonicera fragrantissima*)
Winter jasmine (*Jasminum nudiflorum*)

Trees
Best Flowering Trees

Acacia baileyana (Bailey acacia)
Aesculus glabra (Ohio buckeye)
Albizzia julibrissin (silk tree)
Catalpa speciosa (catalpa)
Cercis canadensis (redbud)
Cornus florida (dogwood)
C. kousa chinensis
Franklinia alatamaha
Jacaranda acutifolia
Koelreuteria paniculata (goldenrain tree)
Magnolia grandiflora (southern magnolia)
M. stellata (star magnolia)
Malus species (crab apple)
Prunus species (fruit trees)
Sophora japonica (Japanese pagoda tree)

Trees for Windbreaks

Acer ginnala (Amur maple) D
Crataegus mollis (downy hawthorn) D
Eucalyptus species (eucalyptus) E
Fagus species (beech) D
Fraxinus americana (white ash) D
Pinus nigra (Austrian pine) E
P. thunbergiana (Japanese black pine) E
Populus alba (white poplar) D
Quercus imbricaria (shingle oak) D
Q. palustris (pin oak) D
Thuja occidentalis (American arborvitae) E
Tilia species (linden) E
Tsuga canadensis (hemlock) E

D = deciduous
E = evergreen

Trees for Wet Soil

Abies balsamea (balsam fir) E
Acer rubrum (red maple) D
Alnus glutinosa (black alder) D
Betula populifolia (gray birch) D
Gleditsia aquatica (water locust) D
Liquidambar styraciflua (sweet gum) D
Platanus occidentalis (buttonwood) D
Quercus palustris (pin oak) D
Salix alba (white willow) D
Thuja occidentalis (arborvitae) E
Tilia americana (American linden) D
Tsuga canadensis (hemlock) E

Trees for Dry Soil

Acer tataricum (Tatarian maple) D
Carya glabra (pignut) D
Juniperus chinensis (Chinese juniper) E
J. virginiana (red cedar) E
Picea alba (Canadian spruce) E
Pinus sylvestris (Scotch pine) E

Fast-Growing Trees

Acer platanoides (Norway maple) D
A. rubrum (red maple) D
Betula populifolia (gray birch) D
Catalpa speciosa (catalpa) D
Fraxinus americana (white ash) D
Ginkgo biloba (maidenhair tree) D
Gleditsia triacanthos (honey locust) D
Quercus palustris (pin oak) D
Salix alba (white willow) D
Sorbus aucuparia (European mountain ash) D
Tilia americana (American linden) D

Trees for Shade

Acer circinatum (vine maple)
A. ginnala (Amur maple)
A. palmatum (Japanese maple)
A. spicatum (mountain maple)
Albizzia julibrissin (silk tree)
Alnus species (alder)
Betula papyrifera (canoe birch)
Cercis canadensis (redbud)
Cornus alba
C. kousa (Chinese dogwood)
C. mas (cornelian cherry)

Crataegus oxyacantha "Paul's scarlet" (hawthorn)
Elaeagnus angustifolia (Russian olive)
Franklinia alatamaha (franklinia)
Fraxinus holotricha
Magnolia soulangiana (saucer magnolia)
M. stellata (star magnolia)
Malus species and hybrids (flowering crab apple)
Pinus bungeana (lacebark pine)
Prunus, various (flowering cherry and others)
Sorbus, various (mountain ash)
Taxus species (yew)
Thuja species (arborvitae)
Tsuga species (hemlock)

Trees by Common Names

Aleppo pine (*Pinus halepensis*)
American arborvitae (*Thuja occidentalis*)
American ash (*Fraxinus americana*)
American beech (*Fagus grandifolia*)
American elm (*Ulmus americana*)
American linden (*Tilia americana*)
Amur maple (*Acer ginnala*)
Anise magnolia (*Magnolia salicifolia*)
Arizona ash (*Fraxinus velutina*)
Arnold crab apple (*Malus arnoldiana*)
Arnold hawthorn (*Crataegus arnoldiana*)
Atlas cedar (*Cedrus atlantica*)
Austrian black pine (*Pinus nigra*)
Austrian pine (*Pinus nigra*)

Bailey acacia (*Acacia baileyana*)
Balsam fir (*Abies balsamea*)
Big-leaf magnolia (*Magnolia macrophylla*)
Big-leaf maple (*Acer macrophyllum*)
Black alder (*Alnus glutinosa*)
Black cherry (*Prunus serotina*)
Black locust (*Robinia pseudoacacia*)
Blue gum (*Eucalyptus globulus*)
Bristlecone pine (*Pinus aristata*)
Buttonwood (*Platanus occidentalis*)

California black oak (*Quercus kelloggii*)
California laurel (*Umbellularea californica*)
California live oak (*Quercus agrifolia*)
Camphor tree (*Cinnamomum camphora*)
Canary Island pine (*Pinus canariensis*)
Canoe birch (*Betula papyrifera*)
Carmine crab apple (*Malus atrosanguinea*)
Carolina poplar (*Populus canadensis* "Eugenei")
Carolina hemlock (*Tsuga caroliniana*)
Cedar of Lebanon (*Cedrus libani*)
Chinese chestnut (*Castanea mollissima*)
Chinese juniper (*Juniperus chinensis*)

Chinese paper birch (*Betula albo-sinensis*)
Cider gum (*Eucalyptus gunnii*)
Colorado spruce (*Picea pungens*)
Common alder (*Alnus incana*)
Cork oak (*Quercus suber*)
Cornelian cherry (*Cornus mas*)

Deodar cedar (*Cedrus deodara*)
Downy hawthorn (*Crataegus mollis*)

Eastern redbud (*Cercis canadensis*)
Eastern red cedar (*Juniperus virginiana*)
Eastern white pine (*Pinus strobus*)
English hawthorn (*Crataegus oxyacantha*)
English oak (*Quercus robur*)
English yew (*Taxus baccata*)
European ash (*Fraxinus excelsior*)
European beech (*Fagus sylvatica*)
European white birch (*Betula verrucosa* (pendula))

False cypress (*Chamaecyparis pisifera*)
Fern pine (*Podocarpus gracilior*)
Flowering ash (*Fraxinus ornus*)
French pussy willow (*Salix caprea*)
Fringe tree (*Chionanthus virginica*)
Full-moon maple (*Acer japonicum*)

Giant arborvitae (*Thuja plicata*)
Glossy hawthorn (*Crataegus nitida*)
Goldenchain tree (*Laburnum watereri*)
Goldenrain tree (*Koelreuteria paniculata*)
Gray birch (*Betula populifolia*)
Green ash (*Fraxinus pennsylvanica lanceolata*)
Green wattle (*Acacia decurrens*)

Hackberry (*Celtis occidentalis*)
Hankow willow (*Salix matsudana*)
Hinoki cypress (*Chamaecyparis obtusa*)
Holly oak (*Quercus ilex*)
Honey-locust (*Gleditsia triacanthos*)

Italian stone pine (*Pinus pinea*)

Jack pine (*Pinus banksiana*)
Japanese black pine (*Pinus thunbergi*)
Japanese dogwood (*Cornus kousa*)
Japanese flowering cherry (*Prunus serrulata*)
Japanese flowering crab apple (*Malus floribunda*)
Japanese hemlock (*Tsuga diversifolia*)
Japanese maple (*Acer palmatum*)
Japanese pagoda tree (*Sophora japonica*)
Japanese red pine (*Pinus densiflora*)
Japanese white pine (*Pinus parviflora*)
Japanese yew (*Taxus cuspidata*)
Judas tree (*Cercis siliquastrum*)

Kangaroo thorn (*Acacia armata*)
Kobus magnolia (*Magnolia kobus*)
Korean fir (*Abies koreana*)

Lacebark pine (*Pinus bungeana*)
Large Chinese hawthorn (*Crataegus pinnatifida major*)
Laurel oak (*Quercus laurifolia*)
Lavalle hawthorn (*Crataegus lavallei*)
Little-leaf linden (*Tilia cordata*)
Loquat (*Eriobotrya japonica*)

Maidenhair tree (*Ginkgo biloba*)
Mountain ash (*Sorbus aucuparia*)

Norway maple (*Acer platanoides*)
Norway spruce (*Picea abies*)

Ohio buckeye (*Aesculus glabra*)
Orchid tree (*Bauhinia blakeana*)

Pacific dogwood (*Cornus nuttalli*)
Pecan (*Carya illinoinensis*)
Persimmon (*Diospyros virginiana*)
Pignut (*Carya glabra*)
Pin oak (*Quercus palustris*)
Plane tree (*Plantanus acerifolia*)
Plume albizzia (*Albizzia distachya*)
Ponderosa pine (*Pinus ponderosa*)

Red cedar juniper (*Juniperus virginiana*)
Red fir (*Abies magnifica*)
Red gum (*Eucalyptus camaldulensis*)
Red horse-chestnut (*Aesculus carnea*)
Red maple (*Acer rubrum*)
Red oak (*Quercus rubra*)
Rocky Mountain juniper (*Juniperus scopulorum*)
Russian olive (*Elaeagnus angustifolia*)

Sargent crab apple (*Malus sargenti*)
Saucer magnolia (*Magnolia soulangeana*)
Scarlet oak (*Quercus coccinea*)
Scotch pine (*Pinus sylvestris*)
Shagbark hickory (*Carya ovata*)
Siberian crab apple (*Malus baccata*)
Silk tree (*Albizzia julibrissin*)
Silver dollar gum (*Eucalyptus polyanthemos*)
Silver linden (*Tilia tomentosa*)
Single seed hawthorn (*Crataegus monogyna*)
Sitka spruce (*Picea sitchensis*)
Smoke tree (*Cotinus americanus*)
Southern magnolia (*Magnolia grandiflora*)
Star magnolia (*Magnolia stellata*)
Sugar maple (*Acer saccharum*)
Sugar pine (*Pinus lambertiana*)
Sweet gum (*Liquidambar styraciflua*)
Swiss mountain pine (*Pinus mugo*)
Sydney golden wattle (*Acacia longifolia floribunda*)

Tatarian dogwood (*Cornus alba*)
Tree of heaven (*Ailanthus altissima*)
Trident maple (*Acer buergerianum*)
Tulip tree (*Liriodendron tulipifera*)

Veitch fir (*Abies veitchi*)
Vine maple (*Acer circinatum*)

Washington hawthorn (*Crataegus phaeonopyrum*)
Water locust (*Gleditsia aquatica*)
Weeping acacia (*Acacia pendula*)
Weeping willow (*Salix babylonica*)
Western catalpa (*Catalpa speciosa*)
Western hemlock (*Tsuga heterophylla*)
White fir (*Abies concolor*)
White oak (*Quercus alba*)
White poplar (*Populus alba*)
White spruce (*Picea glauca*)
White willow (*Salix alba*)

Yew pine (*Podocarpus macrophylla*)
Yulan magnolia (*Magnolia denudata*)

Perennials
Perennials for Wet Soil

Arundo "Donax" (giant reed)
Asclepias incarnata (swamp milkweed)
Caltha palustris (marsh marigold)
Equisetum hyemale (horsetail)
Gentiana asclepiadea (willow gentian)
Helenium (various) (Helen's flower)
Hibiscus moscheutos (swamp rose mallow)
Iris pseudacorus (yellowflag)
Iris versicolor (blue flag)
Lobelia cardinalis (cardinal flower)
Lythrum (various) (loosestrife)
Monarda didyma (bee balm)
Myosotis scorpioides (true forget-me-not)
Oenothera (various) (evening primrose)
Sarracenia purpurea (pitcher plant)
Saxifraga (saxifrage)
Vinca (periwinkle)

Perennials for Dry Soil

Achillea (various) (yarrow)
Ajuga reptans (carpet bugle)
Anthemis tinctoria (golden marguerite)
Artemisia pycnocephala
Asclepias tuberosa (butterfly weed)
Aster novae-angliae (New England aster)
Callirhoe involucrata (poppy mallow)
Cerastium tomentosum (snow-in-summer)
Coreopsis grandiflora (tickseed)
Dianthus (various) (pinks)
Echinops exaltatus (globe thistle)
Echium
Gazinia hybrids

Geranium grandiflorum (cranesbill)
Gypsophila paniculata (baby's breath)
Helianthus (various) (sunflower)
Limonium latifolium (statice, sea lavender)
Papaver nudicaule (Iceland poppy)
Phlox subulata (moss pink)
Potentilla atrosanguinea (cinquefoil)
Rudbeckia hirta (coneflower)
Veronica (various) (speedwell)
Yucca filamentosa (Adam's needle)

Perennials for Semishade

Aconitum anthora (monkshood)
Ajuga (bugle)
Althaea rosea (hollyhock)
Anemone hupehensis japonica (Japanese anemone)
Anemonella thalictroides (rue anemone)
Aquilegia hybrids (columbine)
Asperula (woodruff)
Campanula rotundifolia (harebell)
Convallaria majalis (lily-of-the-valley)
Cornus canadensis (bunchberry)
Dicentra spectabilis (bleeding heart)
Dictamus albus (gas plant)
Epimedium grandiflorum (bishop's hat)
Geranium grandiflorum (cranesbill)
Helleborus niger (Christmas rose)
Hemerocallis (various) (day lily)
Hepatica
Heuchera sanguinea (coral bells)
Hibiscus moscheutos (swamp rose mallow)
Hosta (various) (plantain lily)
Hypericum (Saint-John's-wort)
Iberis sempervirens (evergreen candytuft)
Lobelia cardinalis (cardinal flower)
Mertensia virginica (Virginia bluebell)
Monarda didyma (bee balm)
Phlox divaricata (sweet William phlox)
Platycodon grandiflorum (balloonflower)
Primula (various) (primrose)
Trollius europeaus (globeflower)

Perennials for Background Planting

Althaea rosea (hollyhock)
Aster (various)
Delphinium (various)
Echinops exalatus (globe thistle)
Helenium (various) (Helen's flower)
Helianthus (various) (sunflower)
Hemerocallis (various) (daylily)
Rudbeckia hirta (coneflower)

Solidago altissima (goldenrod)
Yucca filamentosa (Adam's needle)

Perennials for Best Ground Cover

Ajuga reptans (carpet bugle)
Anthemis nobilis (camomile)
Arabis alpina (mountain rock cress)
Campanula (bellflower)
Cerastium tomentosum (snow-in-summer)
Convallaria majalis (lily-of-the-valley)
Drosanthemum floribundum
Gazania splendens (gazania)
Iberis sempervirens (evergreen candytuft)
Lampranthus psectabilis (trailing ice plant)
Malephora croceum (ice plant)
Mentha requieni (mint)
Myosotis (forget-me-not)
Nepeta mussini
Pachysandra terminalis (Japanese pachysandra)
Phlox divaricata (sweet William phlox)
Phlox subulata (moss pink)
Sedum acre (stonecrop)
Vinca minor (common periwinkle)

Perennials for City Conditions

Astilbe japonica
Bergenia
Chrysanthemum
Coreopsis
Dianthus barbatus (sweet William)
Gaillardia
Hemerocallis (daylily)
Heuchera sanguinea (coral bells)
Hosta plantaginea (plantain lily)
Iris (bearded iris)
Paeonia (peony)
Phlox
Sedum (stonecrop)

Perennials for Edging

Achillea tomentosa (woolly yarrow)
Ajuga reptans (carpet bugle)
Alyssum saxatile (alyssum or basket of gold)
Arabis alpina (mountain rock cress)
Arabis caucasia (wall rock cress)
Armeria maritima (sea-pink or thrift)
Aubrietia deltoide (common aubrieta)
Bellis perennis (English daisy)
Campanula carpatica (bellflower)

Cerastium tomentosum (snow-in-summer)
Dianthus plumarius (grass pink)
Festuca ovina "Glauca" (blue fescue)
Heuchera sanguinea (coral bells)
Iberis sempervirens (evergreen candytuft)
Papaver nudicaule (Iceland poppy)
Phlox procumbens (hairy phlox)
Phlox subulata (moss pink)
Primula (various) (primrose)
Sedum (various) (stonecrop)
Veronica (various) (speedwell)
Viola (various)

Perennials for Cut Flowers

Achillea (various) (yarrow)
Anemone japonica (Japanese anemone)
Aster (various)
Chrysanthemum morifolium (florists' chrysanthemum)
Delphinium (various)
Dianthus barbatus (sweet William)
Gaillardia grandiflora (blanket flower)
Paeonia (various) (peony)
Rudbeckia hirta (coneflower)

Perrenials for Fragrance

Anthemis nobilis (camomile)
Arabis (various) (rock cress)
Artemisia abrotanum (southernwood)
Asperula odorata (sweet woodruff)
Convallaria majalis (lily-of-the-valley)
Dianthus (various) (pinks)
Dictamnus albus (gas plant)
Heliotropium arborescens (heliotrope)
Hemerocallis (various) (daylily)
Hesperis matronalis (sweet rocket)
Hosta plantaginea (plaintain lily)
Lathyrus grandiflorus (everlasting pea)
Monarda didyma (bee balm)
Oenothera (various) (evening primrose)
Paeonia (various) (peony)
Phlox (various)
Rosa species (roses)
Viola cornuta (tufted viola)
Viola odorata (sweet violet)

Perennials by Color

WHITE

Achillea ptarmica (yarrow)
Althaea rosea (hollyhock)

Anemone hupenhensis japonica (Japanese anemone)
Anemonella thalictroides (rue anemone)
Aquilegia (columbine)
Arabis alpina (mountain rock cress)
Arabis caucasica (wall rock cress)
Arctotis
Artemisia frigida (fringed wormwood)
Asperula odorata (sweet woodruff)
Aster
Astilbe
Bellis perennis (English daisy)
Bergenia cordiflora (heartleaf bergenia)
Campanula persicifolia (peach-leafed bellflower)
Cerastium tomentosum (snow-in-summer)
Chrysanthemum coccineum (painted daisy)
Chrysanthemum maximum (Shasta daisy)
Chrysanthemum morifolium (florists' chrysanthemum)
Convallaria majalis (lily-of-the-valley)
Cornus canadensis (bunch berry)
Delphinium hybrid (Connecticut Yankee and Pacific Giant)
Deltoides plumarius (grass pink)
Dianthus barbatus (sweet William)
Dianthus deltoides (maiden pink)
Dicentra spectabilis (bleeding heart)
Dictamnus albus (gas plant)
Gypsophila paniculata (baby's breath)
Helleborus niger (Christmas rose)
Heliotropium arborescens (heliotrope)
Hemerocallis (daylily)
Hesperis matronalis (sweet rocket)
Heuchera sanguinea (coral bells)
Hosta plantaginea (plantain lily)
Iberis sempervirens (evergreen candytuft)
Iris (bearded iris)
Iris kaempferi (Japanese iris)
Kniphofia uvaria (torch lily)
Lathyrus latifolius (perennial pea)
Limonium latifolium (statice, sea lavender)
Monarda didyma (bee balm)
Paeonia (various) (peony)
Papaver orientale (Oriental poppy)
Pelargonium domesticum (Lady Washington geranium)
Penstemon (various) (beard tongue)
Phlox divarticata (sweet William phlox)
Phlox paniculata (summer phlox)
Phlox subulata (moss pink)
Platycodon grandiflorum (balloonflower)
Primula malacoides (fairy primrose)
Polygonatum multiflorum (Solomon's seal)
Rudbeckia hirta (coneflower)
Scabiosa caucasica (pincushion flower)

Saxifraga (saxifrage)
Viola cornuta (tufted viola)
Viola odorata (sweet violet)
Yucca filamentosa (Adam's needle)

BLUE

Anchusa capensis (summer forget-me-not)
Aquilegia (columbine)
Aquilegia alpina (dwarf columbine)
Aster frikarti (aster)
Aster novae-angliae (New England aster)
Aubrieta deltoidea (common aubrieta)
Campanula carpatica (bellflower)
Campanula rotundifolia (harebell)
Delphinium hybrid (Connecticut Yankee and Pacific Giant)
Echinops exalatus (globe thistle)
Felicia amelloides (blue marguerite)
Gentiana asclepiadea (willow gentian)
Heliotropium arborescens (heliotrope)
Limonium latifolium (statice, sea lavender)
Linum perenne (blue flax)
Lithodora diffusa (gromwell)
Lupinus polyphyllus (lupine)
Mertensia virginica (Virginia bluebell)
Myosotis scorpiodes (true forget-me-not)
Penstemon (various) (beard tongue)
Phlox divaricata (sweet William phlox)
Phlox subulata (moss pink)
Platycodon grandiflorum (balloonflower)
Primula malacoides (fairy primrose)
Primula polyantha (polyanthus)
Salvia patens (blue salvia or meadow sage)
Veronica (speedwell)
Viola cornuta (tufted viola)

LAVENDER

Althaea rosea (hollyhock)
Anemone pulsatilla (prairie windflower, pasque flower)
Aquilegia (columbine)
Aster frikarti (aster)
Aster novae-angliae (New England aster)
Aubrieta deltoides (common aubrieta)
Bergenia crassifolia
Chrysanthemum morifolium (florists' chrysanthemum)
Dianthus (pink)
Digitalis purpurea (foxglove)
Hesperis matronalis (sweet rocket)
Hosta plantaginea (plantain lily)
Iris dochotoma (vesper iris)
Paeonia (peony)

Pelargonium domesticum (Lady Washington geranium)
Phlox subulata (moss pink)
Primula malacoides (fairy primrose)
Primula polyantha (polyanthus)
Tulbaghia fragrans
Valeriana officinalis (common valerian)
Vinca minor (common periwinkle)
Viola cornuta (tufted viola)

VIOLET

Anemone pulsatilla (prairie windflower, pasque flower)
Delphinium hybrid (Connecticut Yankee and Pacific Giant)
Epinedium grandiflorum (bishop's hat)
Gentiana asclepiadea (willow gentian)
Iris kaempferi (Japanese iris)

LILAC

Acanthus mollis (Grecian urn)
Althaea rosea (hollyhock)

PURPLE-LAVENDER

Bergenia crassifolia

PURPLE-VIOLET

Aquilegia (columbine)
Aster novae-angliae (New England aster)
Aubrieta deltoidea (common aubrieta)
Chrysanthemum morifolium (florists' chrysanthemum)
Dianthus (pink)
Digitalis purpurea (foxglove)
Heliotropium arborescens (heliotrope)
Helleborus niger (Christmas rose)
Pelargonium domesticum (Lady Washington geranium)
Platycodon grandiflorum (balloonflower)
Primula polyantha (polyanthus)
Viola cornuta (tufted viola)
Viola odorata (sweet violet)

PURPLE

Althaea rosea (hollyhock)
Armeria maritima (sea-pink or thrift)
Iris kaempferi (Japanese iris)
Liatris pycnostachya (gayfeather)
Lupinus polyphyllus (lupine)
Lythrum (loosestrife)
Phlox paniculata (summer phlox)
Scabiosa caucasica (pincushion flower)

RED-PURPLE

Callirhoe involucrata (poppy mallow)
Lathyrus grandiflorus (everlasting pea)
Lathyrus latifolius (perennial pea)

RED

Althaea rosea (hollyhock)
Anemone hupehensis japonica (Japanese anemone)
Aquilegia (columbine)
Aster
Astilbe (various) (meadowsweet)
Aubrieta deltoidea (common aubrieta)
Digitalis purpurea (foxglove)
Epimedium grandiflorum (bishop's hat)
Gaillardia grandiflora (blanket flower)
Geranium grandiflorum (cranesbill)
Hemerocallis (daylily)
Heuchera sanguinea (coral bells)
Iris kaempferi (Japanese iris)
Kniphofia (various) (torch lily)
Lobelia cardinalis (cardinal flower)
Lupinus polyphyllus (lupine)
Monarda didyma (bee balm)
Paeonia (peony)
Papaver nudicaule (Iceland poppy)
Papaver orientale (Oriental poppy)
Pelargonium domesticum (Lady Washington geranium)
Penstemon (various) (beard tongue)
Phlox paniculata (summer phlox)
Phlox subulata (moss pink)
Primula malacoides (fairy primrose)
Primula polyantha (polyanthus)
Saxifraga (saxifrage)
Sedum spectabile (stonecrop)
Senecio (cineraria)
Viola cornuta (tufted viola)

ROSE

Acanthus mollis (Grecian urn)
Althaea rosea (hollyhock)
Bellis perennis (English daisy)
Bergenia cordifolia (heartleaf bergenia)
Bergenia crassifolia
Dianthus deltoides (maiden pink)
Dianthus plumarius (grass pink)
Dicentra spectabilis (bleeding heart)
Hibiscus moscheutos (swamp rose mallow)
Iris kaempferi (Japanese iris)
Lythrum (various) (loosestrife)
Phlox paniculata (summer phlox)
Physostegia virginiana (false dragonhead)

PINK

Althaea rosea (hollyhock)
Anemone hupehensis japonica (Japanese anemone)
Anemonella thalictroides (rue anemone)
Aquilegia (columbine)
Armeria maritima (sea-pink or thrift)
Aster
Astilbe (various) (meadowsweet)
Aubrieta deltoidea (common aubrieta)
Bellis perennis (English daisy)
Campanula carpatica (bellflower)
Chrysanthemum coccineum (painted daisy)
Dianthus barbatus (sweet William)
Dianthus deltoides (maiden pink)
Dianthus plumarius (grass pink)
Dicentra spectabilis (bleeding heart)
Digitalis purpurea (foxglove)
Heleborus niger (Christmas rose)
Hemerocallis (daylily)
Heuchera sanguinea (coral bells)
Iris (bearded iris)
Iris kaempferi (Japanese iris)
Limonium latifolium (statice, sea lavender)
Lupinus polyphyllus (lupine)
Monarda didyma (bee balm)
Paeonia (peony)
Papaver nudicaule (Iceland poppy)
Papaver orientale (Oriental poppy)
Pelargonium domesticum (Lady Washington geranium)
Penstemon (various) (beard tongue)
Phlox divartica (sweet William phlox)
Phlox paniculata (summer phlox)
Phlox subulata (moss pink)
Platycodon grandiflorum (balloonflower)
Primula malacoides (fairy primrose)
Primula polyantha (polyanthus)
Rudbeckia hirta (coneflower)
Saxifraga (saxifrage)
Sedum spectabile
Senecio (cineraria)
Tulbaghia fragrans
Veronica (speedwell)
Viola odorata (sweet violet)

SALMON

Papaver orientale (Oriental poppy)

ORANGE

Althaea rosea (hollyhock)
Asclepias incarnata (swamp mildweed)
Asclepias tuberosa (butterfly weed)

Chrysanthemum morifolium (florists' chrysanthemum)
Dianthus (pink)
Erysimum asperum (Siberian wallflower)
Gazinia hybrids
Geum chiloense (coccineum) (geum)
Helenium (Helen's flower)
Heliopsis (various) (orange sunflower)
Hemerocallis (various) (daylily)
Kniphofia (torch lily)
Linaria vulgaris (toadflax)
Papaver nudicaule (Iceland poppy)
Papaver orientale (Oriental poppy)
Penstemon (various) (beard tongue)
Phlox paniculata (summer phlox)
Primula polyantha (polyanthus)
Rudbeckia hirta (coneflower)
Strelizia reginae (bird of paradise)
Viola cornuta (tufted viola)

YELLOW

Achillea tomentosa (woolly yarrow)
Aconitum anthora (monkshood)
Althaea rosea (hollyhock)
Alyssum saxatile (alyssum or basket of gold)
Anthemis nobilis (camomile)
Anthemis tinctoria (golden marguerite)
Aquilegia chrysantha (golden columbine)
Artemisia abrotanum (southernwood)
Caltha palustris (marsh marigold)
Centaurea gymnocarpa (dusty miller)
Chrysanthemum morifolium (florists' chrysanthemum)
Coreopis grandiflora (tickseed)
Dianthus (pink)
Digitalis purpurea (foxglove)
Gaillardia grandiflora (blanket flower)
Gazinia hybrids
Geum chiloense (coccineum) (geum)
Helenium (Helen's flower)
Helianthus decapetalus multiflorus (sunflower)
Heliosis (various) (orange sunflower)
Hemerocallis (various) (daylily)
Hypericum (Saint-John's-wort)
Kniphofia (torch lily)
Oenothera (various) (evening primrose)
Paeonia (various) (peony)
Papaver nudicaule (Iceland poppy)
Primula polyantha (polyanthus)
Rudbeckia hirta (coneflower)
Saxifraga (saxifrage)
Solidago (various) (goldenrod)
Viola cornuta (tufted viola)

Perennials by Common Name

Adam's needle (*Yucca filamentosa*)
Alyssum (*Alyssum saxatile*)
Astilbe (*Astilbe*)

Baby's breath (*Gypsophilia paniculata*)
Balloonflower (*Platycodon grandiflorum*)
Basket of gold (*Alyssum saxatile*)
Bearded iris (*Iris*)
Beard tongue (*Penstemon*)
Bee balm (*Monarda didyma*)
Bellflower (*Campanual carpatica*)
Bishop's hat (*Epimedium grandiflorum*)
Blanket flower (*Gaillardia grandiflora*)
Bleeding heart (*Dicentra spectabilis*)
Blue flag (*Iris versicolor*)
Blue flax (*Linum perenne*)
Blue marguerite (*Felicia amelloides*)
Blue salvia (*Salvia patens*)
Bugle (*Ajuga*)
Bunchberry (*Cornus canadensis*)
Butterfly weed (*Asclepias tuberosa*)

Carpet bugle (*Ajuga reptans*)
Camomile (*Anthemis nobilis*)
Chinese lantern (*Physalis alkekengi*)
Christmas rose (*Hilleborus niger*)
Cinquefoil (*Potentilla astrosanguinea*)
Common aubrieta (*Aubrieta deltoidea*)
Common periwinkle (*Vinca minor*)
Coneflower (*Rudbeckia hirta*)
Coral bells (*Heuchera sanguinea*)
Cranesbill (*Geranium grandiflorum*)
Creeping speedwell (*Veronica rupestris*)
Crested iris (*Iris cristata*)

Daylily (*Hemerocallis*)
Dusty miller (*Centaurea gymnocarpa*)
Dwarf basket of gold (*Alyssum saxatile compactum*)
Dwarf columbine (*Aquilegia alpina*)

English daisy (*Bellis perennis*)
Evening primrose (*Oenothera biennis*)
Evergreen candytuft (*Ibiris sempervirens*)
Everlasting pea (*Lathyrus grandiflorus*)

False dragonhead (*Physostegia virginiana*)
Florists' chrysanthemum (*Chrysanthemum morifolium*)
Forget-me-not (*Myosotis sylvatica*)
Four-o'clock (*Mirabilis jalapa*)
Foxglove (*Digitalis purpurea*)
Fringed wormwood (*Artemisia frigida*)

Gas plant (*Dictamnus albus*)

Gayfeather (*Liatris pycnostachya*)
Geneva bugle (*Ajuga genevensis*)
Geum (*Geum chiloense*)
Giant reed (*Arundo donax*)
Globe thistle (*Echinops exaltatus*)
Golden columbine (*Aquilegia chrysantha*)
Golden marguerite (*Anthemis tinctoria*)
Goldenrod (*Solidago*)
Gold moss (*Sedum acre*)
Grass pink (*Dianthus plumarius*)
Grecian urn (*Acanthus mollis*)

Harebell (*Campanula rotundifolia*)
Heartleaf bergenia (*Bergenia cordifolia*)
Helen's flower (*Helenium*)
Heliotrope (*Heliotropium arborescens*)
Hollyhock (*Althaea rosea*)
Horsetail (*Equisetum hyemale*)
Houseleek (*Sempervivum tectorum*)

Indian paintbrush (*Lobelia cardinalis*)

Japanese anemone (*Anemone japonica*)
Japanese iris (*Iris kaempferi*)

Lady Washington geranium (*Pelargonium domesticum*)
Lily-of-the-valley (*Convallaria majalis*)
Loosestrife (*Lythrum*)
Lupine (*Lupinus polyphyllus*)

Maiden pink (*Dianthus deltoides*)
Marsh marigold (*Caltha palustris*)
Meadow sage (*Salvia paterns*)
Meadowsweet (*Spiraea alba*)
Michaelmas daisy (*English aster*)
Monkshood (*Aconitum anthora*)
Moss pink (*Phlox subulata*)
Mountain rock cress (*Arabis alpina*)

New England aster (*Aster novae-angliae*)

Orange sunflower (*Heliopsis*)
Oriental poppy (*Papaver orientale*)

Painted daisy (*Chrysanthemum coccineum*)
Painted daisy (*Pyrethrum*)
Pansy (*Viola tricolor hortensis*)
Pasque flower (*Anemone pulsatilla*)
Peony (*Paeonia*)
Perennial pea (*Lathyrus latifolius*)
Pincushion flower (*Scabiosa caucasica*)
Pitcher plant (*Sarracenia purpurea*)
Plantain lily (*Hosta plantaginea grandiflora*)
Poppy-flowered anemone (*Anemone coronaria*)
Prairie windflower (*Anemone pulsatilla*)
Primrose (*Primula*)

Roof houseleek (*Sempervivum tectorum*)
Rue anemone (*Anemonella thalictroides*)
Running sedum (*Sedum stoloniferum*)

Sand pink (*Dianthus armarius*)
Saint-John's-wort (*Hypericum*)
Saxifrage (*Saxifraga*)
Sea lavender (*Limonium latifolium*)
Sea-pink (*Armeria maritima*)
Shasta daisy (*Chrysanthemum maximum*)
Siberian wallflower (*Erysimum asperum*)
Snow-in-summer (*Cerastium tomentosum*)
Solomon's seal (*Polygonatum multiflorum*)
Southernwood (*Artemisia abrotanum*)
Speedwell (*Veronica*)
Statice (*Limonium latifolium*)
Stock (*Mathiola incana*)
Stonecrop (*Sedum*)
Summer forget-me-not (*Anchusa capensis*)
Summer phlox (*Phlox paniculata*)
Sunflower (*Helianthus multiflorus*)
Swamp milkweed (*Asclepias incarnata*)
Swamp rose mallow (*Hibiscus moschentos*)
Sweet rocket (*Hesperis matronalis*)
Sweet violet (*Viola odorata*)
Sweet William (*Dianthus barbatus*)
Sweet William phlox (*Phlox divaricata*)
Sweet woodruff (*Asperula odorata*)

Thrift (*Armeria maritima*)
Tickseed (*Coreopsis grandiflora*)
Toadflax (*Limaria vulgaris*)
Torch lily (*Kniphofia*)
True forget-me-not (*Myosotis scorpiodes*)
Tufted viola (*Viola cornuta*)

Vesper iris (*Iris dichotoma*)
Virginia bluebell (*Mertensia virginica*)

Wall rock cress (*Arabis caucasica*)
Wax begonia (*Begonia semperflorens*)
Willow gentian (*Gentiana asclepiadea*)
Woodruff (*Asperula*)
Wooly yarrow (*Achillea tomentosa*)
Wormwood (*Artemesia albula*)

Yarrow (*Achillea ptarmica*)
Yellowflag (*Iris pseudacorus*)

Annuals

Annuals for Dry soil

Arctotis stoechadifolia grandis (African daisy)
Browallis americana (browallia)

Centaurea cyanus (bachelor's button or cornflower)
Convolvulus tricolor (dwarf morning glory)
Coreopsis tinctoria (calliopsis)
Cryophytum crystallinum (ice plant)
Delphinium ajacis (larkspur)
Dimorphoteca (various) (Cape marigold)
Eschscholzia californica (California poppy)
Euphorbia marginata (snow-on-the-mountain)
Gaillardia pulchella (rose-ring Gaillardia)
Gypsophila elegans (baby's breath)
Helianthus annuus (sunflower)
Impomoea purpurea (morning glory)
Mirabilis jalapa (four-o'clock)
Phlox drummondi (annual phlox)
Portulaca grandiflora (rose moss)
Salvia splendens (scarlet sage)
Zinnia elegans (giant-flowered zinnia)

Annuals for Light Shade

Ageratum houstonianum (floss flower)
Bellis perennis (English daisy)
Catharanthus roseus (Vinca rosea) (Madagascar periwinkle)
Celosia "Plumosa" (plume cockscomb)
Centaurea americana (basket flower)
Centaurea moschata (sweet sultan)
Clarkia elegans (Clarkia)
Cryophytum crystallinum (ice plant)
Delphinium ajacis (larkspur)
Euphorbia marginata (snow-on-the-mountain)
Gerbera jamesoni (Transvaal daisy)
Godetia amoena (farewell-to-spring)
Impatiens balsamina (balsam)
Lobelia erinus (lobelia)
Lobularia maritima (sweet alyssum)
Lupinus hartwegii (lupine, annual)
Myosotis sylvatica (forget-me-not)
Nicotiana sanderae (flowering tobacco)
Phlox drummondii (annual phlox)
Primula malacoides (fairy primrose)
Salpiglossis sinuata (painted tongue)
Viola tricolor hortensis (pansy)

Annuals for Background Planting

Amaranthus caudatus (love-lies-bleeding)
Celosia (various) (cockscomb)
Cosmos bipinnatus (cosmos)
Delphinium ajacis (larkspur)
Helianthus annuus (sunflower)
Nicotiana (various) (flowering tobacco)

Salvia splendens (scarlet sage)
Tagetes (various) (marigold)
Zinnia elegans (zinnia)

Annuals for City Conditions

Ageratum
Antirrhinum (snapdragon)
Cleome
Lobelia erinus (lobelia)
Lobularia
Mirabilis
Nicotiana
Petunia
Phlox
Salvia
Tagetes (marigold)
Verbena
Zinnia

Annuals for Edging

Ageratum (various)
Antirrhinum (dwarf kinds) (snapdragon)
Begonia semperflorens (wax begonia)
Brachycome iberidifolia (Swan River daisy)
Browallia americana (browallia)
Calendula officinalis (calendula or marigold)
Celosia (various) (cockscomb)
Centaurea cineraria (dusty miller)
Coreopsis tinctoria (calliopsis)
Cryophytum crystallinum (ice plant)
Dianthus chinensis (China pink)
Eschscholzia californica (California poppy)
Iberis umbellata (globe candytuft)
Linum grandiflorum "Rubrum" (scarlet flax)
Lobelia erinus (lobelia)
Petunia (various) (petunia)
Phlox drummondii (annual phlox)
Portulaca grandiflora (rose moss)
Tagetes (marigold)
Tropaeolum majus (nasturtium)
Verbena (various)

Annuals for Cut Flowers

Amaranthus caudatus (love-lies-bleeding)
Antirrhinum majus (snapdragon)
Artotis stoechadifolia grandis (African daisy)
Browallia speciosa (major) (browallia)
Calendula officinalis (calendula or pot marigold)

Callistephus chinensis (aster or China aster)
Centaurea moschata (sweet sultan)
Chrysanthemum
Clarkia elegans (Clarkia)
Coreopsis tinctoria (calliopsis)
Cosmos
Delphinium ajacis (larkspur)
Dianthus chinensis (China pink)
Dimorphoteca (various) (African daisy, Cape marigold)
Eschscholzia californica (California poppy)
Gaillardia
Comphrena globosa (globe-amaranth)
Gypsophila
Helianthus annuus (sunflower)
Helichrysum bractaetum (strawflower)
Lathyrus odoratus (sweet pea)
Lupinus (lupine)
Mathiola bicornis (night-scented stock)
Mathiola incana (stock)
Nicotiana sanderae (flowering tobacco)
Nigella damescena (love-in-a-mist)
Papaver glaucum (tulip poppy)
Papaver rhoeas (Shirley poppy)
Phlox drummondii (annual phlox)
Polygonum orientale (princess feather)
Reseda odorata (mignonette)
Salpiglossis sinuata (painted tongue)
Scabiosa atropurpurea (pincushion flower)
Senecio elegans (purple ragwort)
Tagetes (marigold)
Verbena hybrida (hortensis) (garden verbena)
Zinnia elegans (small-flowered zinnia)
Zinnia haageana (orange zinnia)

Annuals for Fragrance

Ageratum houstonianum (floss flower)
Antirrhinum majus (snapdragon)
Calendula officinalis (calendula or pot marigold)
Centaurea moschata (sweet sultan)
Delphinium ajacis (larkspur)
Iberis umbellata (globe candytuft)
Lathyrus odoratus (sweet pea)
Lobularia maritima (sweet alyssum)
Lupinus luteus (yellow lupine)
Mathiola bicornis (night-scented stock)
Matholia incana (stock)
Nicotiana sanderal (flowering tobacco)
Oenothera biennis (evening primrose)
Petunia
Phlox drummondii (annual phlox)
Reseda odorata (mignonette)

Scabiosa atropurpurea (pincushion flower)
Tagetes (marigold)
Tropaeolum majus (nasturtium)
Verbena (various)
Viola tricolor hortensis (pansy)

Annuals by Color

WHITE

Ageratum houstonianum (floss flower)
Antirrhinum majus (snapdragon)
Arctotis stoechadifolia grandis (African daisy)
Begonia semperflorens (wax begonia)
Brachycome iberidifolia (Swan River daisy)
Browallia americana (browallia)
Calendula officinalis (calendula or pot marigold)
Callistephus chinensis (aster or China aster)
Campanula medium (Canterbury bell)
Catharanthus roseus (Vinca rosea) (Madagascar periwinkle)
Centaurea cyanus (bachelor's button, or cornflower)
Centaurea imperialis (royal sweet sultan)
Chrysanthemum
Clarkia amoena (farewell-to-spring)
Clarkia elegans (Clarkia)
Clarkia unguiculata (mountain garland)
Cleome spinosa (spider flower)
Cosmos bipannatus (cosmos)
Delphinium ajacis (larkspur)
Dianthus species (pinks)
Dimorphoteca sinuata (Cape marigold or African daisy)
Echium
Euphorbia marginata (snow-on-the-mountain)
Gomphrena globosa (globe-amaranth)
Gypsophila elegans (baby's breath)
Helichrysum bracteatum (strawflower)
Iberis amara (rocket candytuft)
Iberis umbellata (globe candytuft)
Impatiens balsamina (balsam)
Ipomea purpurea (morning glory)
Lathyrus odoratus (sweet pea, summer)
Limonium bonduelli (statice, sea lavender)
Lobelia erinus (lobelia)
Lobularia maritima (sweet alyssum)
Lupinus mutabilis (lupine)
Mathiola incana (stock)
Mirabilis jalapa (four-o'clock)
Nemesia strumosa (nemesia)
Nicotiana alata
Nicotiana sanderae (flowering tobacco)
Nicotiana sylvestris

Nigella damascena (love-in-a-mist)
Oenothera biennis (evening primrose)
Papaver nudicaule (Iceland poppy)
Papaver rhoeas (Shirley poppy)
Petunia hybrids
Phlox drummondi (annual phlox)
Physalis alkekengi (Chinese lantern)
Portulaca grandiflora (moss rose)
Primula malacoides (fairy primrose)
Scabiosa atropurpurea (pincushion flower)
Schizanthus pinnatus (butterfly flower)
Senecio elegans (purple ragwort)
Tropaeolum majus (nasturtium)
Verbena hybrida (hortensis) (garden verbena)
Viola tricolor hortensis (pansy)
Zinnia angustifolia (Mexican zinnia)
Zinnia elegans (small-flowered zinnia)
Zinnia elegans (giant-flowered zinnia)

BLUE

Ageratum houstonianum (flossflower)
Browallia americana (browallia)
Callistephus chinensis (aster or China aster)
Campanula medium (Canterbury bell)
Centaurea cyanus (bachelor's button or cornflower)
Convolvulus tricolor (dwarf morning glory)
Cosmos
Delphinium ajacis (larkspur)
Echium
Ipomoea purpurea (morning glory)
Limonium bonduelli (statice, sea lavender)
Linaria maroccana (baby snapdragon)
Lobelia erinus (lobelia)
Mathiola incana (stock)
Muosotis sylvatica (forget-me-not)
Nemesia strumosa (nemesia)
Nierembergia caerulea (blue cupflower)
Nigella damascena (love-in-a-mist)
Papaver rhoeas (Shirley poppy)
Salvia (sage)
Scabiosa atropurpurea (pincushion flower)
Trachymene caerulea (blue lace flower)
Verbena hybrids
Viola tricolor hortensis (pansy)
Zinnia elegans (giant-flowered zinnia)

LAVENDER

Callistephus chinensis (aster or China aster)
Centaurea cyanus (bachelor's button or cornflower)
Clarkia elegans (Clarkia)
Delphinium ajacis (larkspur)
Dianthus chinensis (China pink)
Limonium bonduelli (statice, sea lavender)

Lobularia maritima (sweet alyssum)
Zinnia elegans (small-flowered zinnia)

VIOLET

Antirrhinum majus (snapdragon)
Gomphrena globosa (globe-amaranth)
Ipomoea purpurea (morning glory)
Lobelia erinus (lobelia)
Trachymene caerulea (blue lace flower)
Zinnia elegans (giant-flowered zinnia)

MAUVE

Impatiens
Schizanthus pinnatus (butterfly flower)

LILAC

Browallia speciosa major (browallia)
Cosmos
Iberis umbellata (globe candytuft)
Lathyrus odoratus (sweet pea, summer)
Lupinus (lupine)
Mathiola bicornus (night-scented stock)
Mathiola incana (stock)
Petunia hybrids
Phlox drummondi (annual phlox)

PURPLE

Antirrhinum majus (snapdragon)
Browallia americana (browallia)
Browallia speciosa major
Dianthus chinensis (China pink)
Echium
Impatiens
Ipomoea purpurea (morning glory)
Lathyrus odoratus (sweet pea, summer)
Linaria maroccana (baby snapdragon)
Lobularia maritima (sweet alyssum)
Lupinus (lupine)
Mathiola bicornus (night-scented stock)
Mathiola incana (stock)
Nemesia strumosa (nemesia)
Petunia hybrids
Phlox drummondii (annual phlox)
Salpiglossis sinuata (painted tongue)
Scabiosa atropurpurea (pincushion flower)
Schizanthus pinnatus (butterfly flower)
Senecio elegans (purple ragwort)
Verbena hybrids
Viola tricolor hortensis (pansy)
Zinnia elegans (giant-flowered zinnia)

MAGENTA

Impatiens

WINE

Centaurea cyanus (bachelor's button or cornflower)
Gaillardia pulchella (rose-ring Gaillardia)

MAROON

Coreopsis tinctoria (calliopsis)
Gaillardia pulchella (rose-ring Gaillardia)
Tropaeolum majus (nasturtium)
Zinnia angustifolia (Mexican zinnia)

CARMINE

Delphinium ajacis (larkspur)

SCARLET

Linum grandiflorum "Rubrum" (scarlet flax)
Salvia splendens (scarlet sage)
Verbena hybrida (hortensis) (garden verbena)
Zinnia elegans (small-flowered zinnia, giant-flowered zinnia)

CRIMSON

Amaranthus caudatus (love-lies-bleeding)
Gomphrenia globosa (globe-amaranth)
Linaria maroccana (baby snapdragon)
Mathiola incana (stock)
Nicotiana
Papaver rhoeas (Shirley poppy)
Portulaca grandiflora (rose moss)
Tropaeolum majus (nasturtium)

RED

Antirrhinum majus (snapdragon)
Brachycome iberidifolia (Swan River daisy)
Callistephus chinensis (aster or China aster)
Confolvulus
Helichrysum bracteatum (strawflower)
Impatiens balsamina (balsam)
Ipomoea purpurea (morning glory)
Mirabilis jalapa (four-o'clock)
Papaver glaucum (tulip poppy)
Primula malacoides (fairy primrose)
Salpiglossis sinuata (painted tongue)

ROSE

Begonia semperflorens (wax begonia)
Centaurea moschata (sweet sultan)
Clarkia amoena (farewell-to-spring)

Clarkia elegans (Clarkia)
Cosmos bipannatus (cosmos)
Delphinium ajacis (larkspur)
Dianthus barbatus (sweet William)
Eschscholzia californica (California poppy)
Gypsophila elegans (baby's breath)
Iberis umbellata (globe candytuft)
Impatiens balsamina (balsam)
Lathyrus odoratus (sweet pea, summer)
Limonium bonduelli (statice, sea lavender)
Linum grandiflorum "Rubrum" (scarlet flax)
Lobularia maritima (sweet alyssum)
Mathiola incana (stock)
Nemesia strumosa (nemesia)
Nigella damascena (love-in-a-mist)
Oenothera biennis (evening primrose)
Petunia hybrids
Phlox drummondi (annual phlox)
Polygonum orientale (princess feather)
Primula malacoides (fairy primrose)
Salvia splendens (scarlet sage)
Scabiosa atropurpurea (pincushion flower)
Schizanthus pinnatus (butterfly flower)
Senecio elegans (purple ragwort)
Viola tricolor hortensis (pansy)

PINK

Ageratum houstonianum (flossflower)
Antirrhinum majus (snapdragon)
Begonia semperflorens (wax begonia)
Callistephus chinensis (China aster)
Campanula (Canterbury bell)
Catharanthus roseus (Vinca rosea) (Madagascar periwinkle)
Celosia "Plumosa" (plume cockscomb)
Centaurea cyanus (bachelor's button or cornflower)
Clarkia elegans (Clarkia)
Cleome spinosa (spider flower)
Cosmos bipinnatus (cosmos)
Cryophytum crystallinum (ice plant)
Delphinium ajacis (larkspur)
Dianthus chinensis (China pink)
Eschscholzia californica (California poppy)
Gypsophilia elegans (baby's breath)
Helichrysum bracteatum (strawflower)
Iberis umbellata (globe candytuft)
Impatiens balsamina (balsam)
Ipomoea purpurea (morning glory)
Lathyrus odoratus (sweet pea, summer)
Linaria maroccana (baby snapdragon)
Lobelia erinus (lobelia)
Lupinus hartwegi (lupine, annual)
Mathiola incana (stock)
Mirabilis jalapa (four o'clock)

Myosotis sylvatica (forget-me-not)
Nemesia strumosa (nemesia)
Papaver rhoeas (Shirley poppy)
Petunia hybrids
Polygonum orientale (princess feather)
Primula malacoides (fairy primrose)
Salpiglossis sinuata (painted tongue)
Salvia splendens (scarlet sage)
Tropaeolum majus (nasturtium)
Verbena hybrida (hortensis) (garden verbena)

SALMON

Delphinium ajacis (larkspur)
Dimorphoteca sinuata (African daisy, Cape marigold)
Iberis umbellata (globe candytuft)
Papaver rhoeas (Shirley poppy)

ORANGE

Antirrhinum majus (snapdragon)
Calendula officinalis (calendula or pot marigold)
Chrysanthemum
Clarkia
Coreopsis tinctoria (calliopsis)
Dimorphoteca sinuata (African daisy, Cape marigold)
Eschscholzia californica (California poppy)
Gerbera jamesonii (Transvaal daisy)
Nemesia strumosa (nemesia)
Papaver rhoeas (Shirley poppy)
Portulaca grandiflora (rose moss)
Salpiglossis sinuata (painted tongue)
Tithonia rotundifolia (Mexican sunflower)
Viola tricolor hortensis (pansy)
Zinnia angustifolia (Mexican zinnia)
Zinnia elegans (small-flowered zinnia, giant-flowered zinnia)
Tagetes (marigold)

BRONZE

Chrysanthemum

GOLD

Calendula officinalis (calendula or pot marigold)
Celosia "Plumosa" (plume cockscomb)
Eschscholzia californica (California poppy)
Gomphrena globosa (globe-amaranth)
Helianthus annuus (sunflower)
Tagetes (marigold)

YELLOW

Antirrhinum majus (snapdragon)
Calendula officinalis (calendula or pot marigold)

Callistephus chinensis (aster or China aster)
Celosia "Plumosa" (plume cockscomb)
Centaurea moschata (sweet sultan)
Chrysanthemum
Clarkia
Coreopsis tinctoria (calliopsis)
Cosmos sulphureus (yellow cosmos)
Dimorphoteca sinuata (African daisy, Cape marigold)
Eschscholzia californica (California poppy)
Gaillardia pulchella (rose-ring Gaillardia)
Gerbera jamesonii (Transvaal daisy)
Limonium sinuatum (statice, sea lavender)
Linaria maroccana (baby snapdragon)
Lupinus mutabilis (lupine)
Lupinus luteus (yellow lupine)
Mathiola incana (stock)
Mirabalis jalapa (four-o'clock)
Nemesia strumosa (nemesia)
Oenothera biennis (evening primrose)
Portulaca grandiflora (rose moss)
Reseda odorata (mignonette)
Rudbeckia bicolor (coneflower)
Salpiglossis sinuata (painted tongue)
Tagetes (marigold)
Thunbergia alata (clockvine)
Tropaeolum majur (nasturtium)
Viola tricolor hortensis (pansy)
Zinnia angustifolia (Mexican zinnia)
Zinnia elegans (small-flowered zinnia)
Zinnia elegans (giant-flowered zinnia)

Annuals by Common Name

African daisy (*Arctotis stoechadifolia grandis*)
African daisy (*Dimorphoteca sinuata*)
African marigold (*Tagetes erecta*)
Annual lupine (*Lupinus hartwegi*)
Annual phlox (*Phlox drummondi*)
Aster (*Callistephus chinensis*)

Baby's breath (*Gypsophila elegans*)
Bachelor's button (*Centaurea cyanus*)
Balsam (*Impatiens balsamina*)
Basket flower (*Centaurea cyanus*)
Bells of Ireland (*Molucella laevis*)
Blue cup flower (*Nierembergia caerulea*)
Blue lace flower (*Trachymene caerulea*)
Browallia (*Browallis americana*)
Butterfly flower (*Schizanthus pinnatus*)

Calendula (*Calendula officinalis*)
California poppy (*Eschscholzia californica*)
Calliopsis (*Coreopsis tinctoria*)
Candytuft (*Iberis*)

Canterbury bell (*Campanula medium*)
Cape marigold (*Dimorphotheca sinuata*)
China aster (*Callistephus chinensis*)
China pink (*Dianthus chinensis*)
Chinese lantern (*Physalis alkekengi*)
Clarkia (*Clarkia elegans*)
Clockvine (*Thunbergia alata*)
Coleus (*Coleus blumei*)
Coneflower (*Rudbeckia bicolor*)
Cornflower (*Centaurea cyanus*)
Cosmos (*Cosmos bipinnatus*)

Evening primrose (*Oenothera biennis*)

Fairy primrose (*Primula malacoides*)
Farewell-to-spring (*Clarkia amoena*)
Floss flower (*Ageratum houstonianum*)
Flowering tobacco (*Nicotiana alata*)
Four-o'clock (*Mirabilis jalapa*)
Forget-me-not (*Myosotis sylvatica*)
French marigold (*Tagetes patula*)

Garden nasturtium (*Tropaeolum majus*)
Garden verbena (*Verbena hybrida* [*hortensis*])
Giant-flowered zinnia (*Zinnia elegans*)
Globe amaranth (*Gomphrena globosa*)
Globe candytuft (*Iberis umbellata*)

Ice plant (*Cryophytum crystallinum*)

Joseph's coat (*Amaranthus tricolor*)

Larkspur (*Delphinium ajacis*)
Lobelia (*Lobelia erinus*)
Love-in-a-mist (*Nigella damascena*)
Love-lies-bleeding (*Amaranthus caudatus*)

Madagascar periwinkle (*Catharanthus roseus*)
Mexican sunflower (*Tithonia rotundifolia*)
Mignonette (*Reseda odorata*)
Morning glory (*Ipomoea purpurea*)
Mountain garland (*Clarkia unguiculata*)

Nasturtium (*Tropaeolum majus*)
Nemesia (*Nemesia strumosa*)
Night-scented stock (*Mathiola bicornis*)

Painted tongue (*Salpiglossis sinuata*)
Pansy (*Viola tricolor hortensis*)
Petunia (*Petunia*)
Pincushion flower (*Scabiosa atropurpurea*)
Pink (*Dianthus*)
Plume cockscomb (*Celosia plumosa*)
Pot marigold (*Calendula officinalis*)
Princess feather (*Polygonum orientale*)
Purple ragwort (*Senecio elegans*)

Rocket candytuft (*Iberis amara*)
Rose moss (*Portulaca grandiflora*)

Rose-ring Gaillardia (*Gaillardia pulchella*)
Royal sweet sultan (*Centaurea imperialis*)

Scarlet flax (*Linum grandiflorum "Rubrum"*)
Scarlet sage (*Salvia splendens*)
Sea lavender (*Limonium bonduelli*)
Shirley poppy (*Papaver rhoeas*)
Small-flowered zinnia (*Zinnia elegans*)
Snapdragon (*Antirrhinum majus*)
Snow-on-the-mountain (*Euphorbia marginata*)
Statice (*Limonium bonduelli*)
Stock (*Mathiola incana*)
Strawflower (*Helichrysum bracteatum*)
Summer forget-me-not (*Anchusa capensis*)
Sunflower (*Helianthus annuus*)
Swan River daisy (*Brachycome iberidifolia*)
Sweet alyssum (*Lobularia maritima*)
Sweet pea, winter (*Lathyrus odoratus*)
Sweet pea, summer (*Lathyrus odoratus*)
Sweet sultan (*Centaurea moschata*)
Sweet William (*Dianthus barbatus*)

Touch-me-not (*Impatiens balsamina*)
Transvaal daisy (*Gerbera jamesonii*)
Tulip poppy (*Papaver glaucum*)

Wax begonia (*Begonia semperflorens*)

Vines
Vines for Shady Places

Akebia quinata (five-leaf akebia)
Ampelopsis breviped-unculata (porcelain ampe-
lopsis or blueberry climber)
Aristolochia durior (Dutchman's pipe)
Clytosoma (Bignonia capreolata) (cross vine or
trumpet vine)
Celastrus scandens (American bittersweet)
Euonymus fortunei (wintercreeper)
Fatshedera lizei
Ficus pumila (repens) (creeping fig)
Gelsemium sempervirens (Carolina jessamine)
Hedera helix (English ivy)
Hydrangea petiolaris (climbing hydrangea)
Jasminum nudiflorum (winter jasmine)
Lonicera hildebrandiana (Burmese honeysuckle)
Lonicera japonica "Halliana" (Hall's honeysuckle)
Parthenocissus quinquefolia (Virginia creeper)
Pueraria thunbergiana (Kudzo vine)
Smilax rotundifolia (horse brier)
Trachelospermum jasminoides (star jasmine)
Vitis coignetiae (glory grape)

Vines for City Conditions

Akebia quinta (five-leaf akebia)
Clematis paniculata
Cobaea scandens (cup and saucer vine)
Hedera helix (English ivy)
Lonicera japonica "Halliana" (Hall's honeysuckle)
Parthenocissus quinquefolia (Virginia creeper)
Parthenocissus tricuspidata (Boston ivy)
Phaseolus coccineus (scarlet runner bean)
Polygonum auberti (China fleece vine)

Vines for Flowers

Bignonia capreolata (cross vine)
Bougainvillaea
Clematis species
Clytosoma
Hydrangea petiolaris (climbing hydrangea)
Mandevilla suaveolens (Chilean jasmine)
Passiflora caerulea (passion flower)
Plumbago capensis (plumbago)
Rosa (rose)
Stephanotis floribunda (Madagascar jasmine)
Trachelospermum species (star jasmine)
Wisteria floribunda (Japanese wisteria)

Vines for Fragrance

Akebia quinata (five-leaf akebia)
Gelsemium sempervirens (Carolina yellow jessamine)

Vines for Rapid Growth

Akebia quinata (five-leaf akebia)
Ampelopsis acontifolia
Aristolochia durior (Dutchman's pipe)
Clytosoma (Bignonia capreolata) (cross vine, trum-
pet vine)
Clematis species
Doxantha unguis-cati (cat's claw)
Ficus pumila (repens) (creeping fig)
Hedera helix (English ivy)
Lonicera species (honeysuckle)
Trachelospermum jasminoides (star jasmine)
Vitis species (glory grape)
Wisteria floribunda (Japanese wisteria)
Wisteria sinensis (Chinese wisteria)

Twining Vines

Akebia quinata (five-leaf akebia)
Aristolochia durior (Dutchman's pipe)
Celastrus species (bittersweet)
Mandevilla suaveolens (Chilean jasmine)
Smilax species (horse brier)
Trachelospermum species (star jasmine)
Wisteria floribunda (Japanese wisteria)

Climbing Vines

Ampelopsis species
Clytosoma (Bignonia capreolata) (cross vine)
Clematis species
Doxantha unguis-cati (cat's claw)
Parthenocissus quinquefolia (Virginia creeper)
Passiflora species (passion flower)
Vitis species (glory grape)

Vines by Common Name

American bittersweet (*Celastrus scandens*)

Blueberry climber (*Ampelopsis breviped-unculata*)
Burmese honeysuckle (*Lonicera hildebrandiana*)

Carolina jessamine (*Gelsemium sempervirens*)
Cat's claw (*Doxantha unguis-cati*)
Chilean jasmine (*Mandevilla suaveolens*)
Climbing hydrangea (*Hydrangea petiolaris*)
Common allamanda (*Allamanda cathartica*)
Convolvulvus (*ipomoea purpurea*)

Coral vine (*Antigonon leptopus*)
Creeping fig (*Ficus pumila* [*repens*])
Cross vine (*Clystoma*) (*Bignonia capreolata*)

Dutchman's pipe (*Aristolochia durior*)

English ivy (*Hedera helix*)
Evergreen clematis (*Clematis armandi*)

Five-leaf akebia (*Akebia quinata*)

Glory grape (*Vitis coignetiae*)

Hall's honeysuckle (*Lonicera japonica* "Halliana")
Horse brier (*Smilax rotundifolia*)

Japanese wisteria (*Wisteria floribunda*)

Kudzo vine (*Pueraria thunbergiana*)

Morning glory (*Ipomoea purpurea*)

Passion flower (*Passiflora caerulea*)
Plumbago (*Plumbago capensis*)
Porcelain ampelopsis (*Ampelopsis breviped-unculata*)

Rambler rose (*Rosa*)

Scarlet kadsura (*Kadsura japonica*)
Scarlet runner bean (*Phaseolus coccineus*)
Star jasmine (*Trachelospermum jasminoides*)
Sweet honeysuckle (*Lonicera caprifolium*)

Trumpet vine (*Bignonia capreolata*)

Virginia creeper (*Parthenocissus quinquefolia*)

White jasmine (*Jasminum officinale*)
Wintercreeper (*Euonymus fortunei*)
Winter jasmine (*Jasminum nudiflorum*)

General Index

Index of Plant Names